Forbidden France

Robin Brinaert

JONGLEZ PUBLISHING

Table of contents

The decadence of a forgotten heritage

The scourge of time takes over abandoned places; humidity seeps through walls and an array of objects are sometimes scattered around. Such scenes make it hard not to imagine what the lives of those who passed by these places before us might have been like. Forgotten castles and manors, abandoned courthouses and theatres, factories, fire trucks, hovertrains and planes all still hide treasures and are, to me, playing fields and perfect settings to capture with my camera. Rays of light that pass through a crack or a chapel bathed in sunlight shed a magical light. The world is a theatre stage and I've chosen to look behind the curtains. Being the first person to tread upon unclaimed land is a unique and exhilarating feeling. This type of underground activity can lead to resorting to illegal practices, like infiltration, but explorers like me who have been practising the activity for many years all share the same strict rules: no touching, no destroying, just a few photographs and then we leave ...

Urban exploration is a uniquely emotional experience.

Robin Brinaert

A Civil War farm castle • *Hauts-de-France*

In a small village is an abandoned farm castle where time stands still.

The cannon in the corner of the room, the patriotic flags and the antiques from a bygone era take us back to a time of war we never knew.

The owner, a fencing enthusiast, displays his preferences above the fireplace on the red cloth that lines the walls of this sitting room, concealing the sketch of a knight's painting that was never completed.

The stunning details of this place, which remains in an incredible state, give it a very special atmosphere.

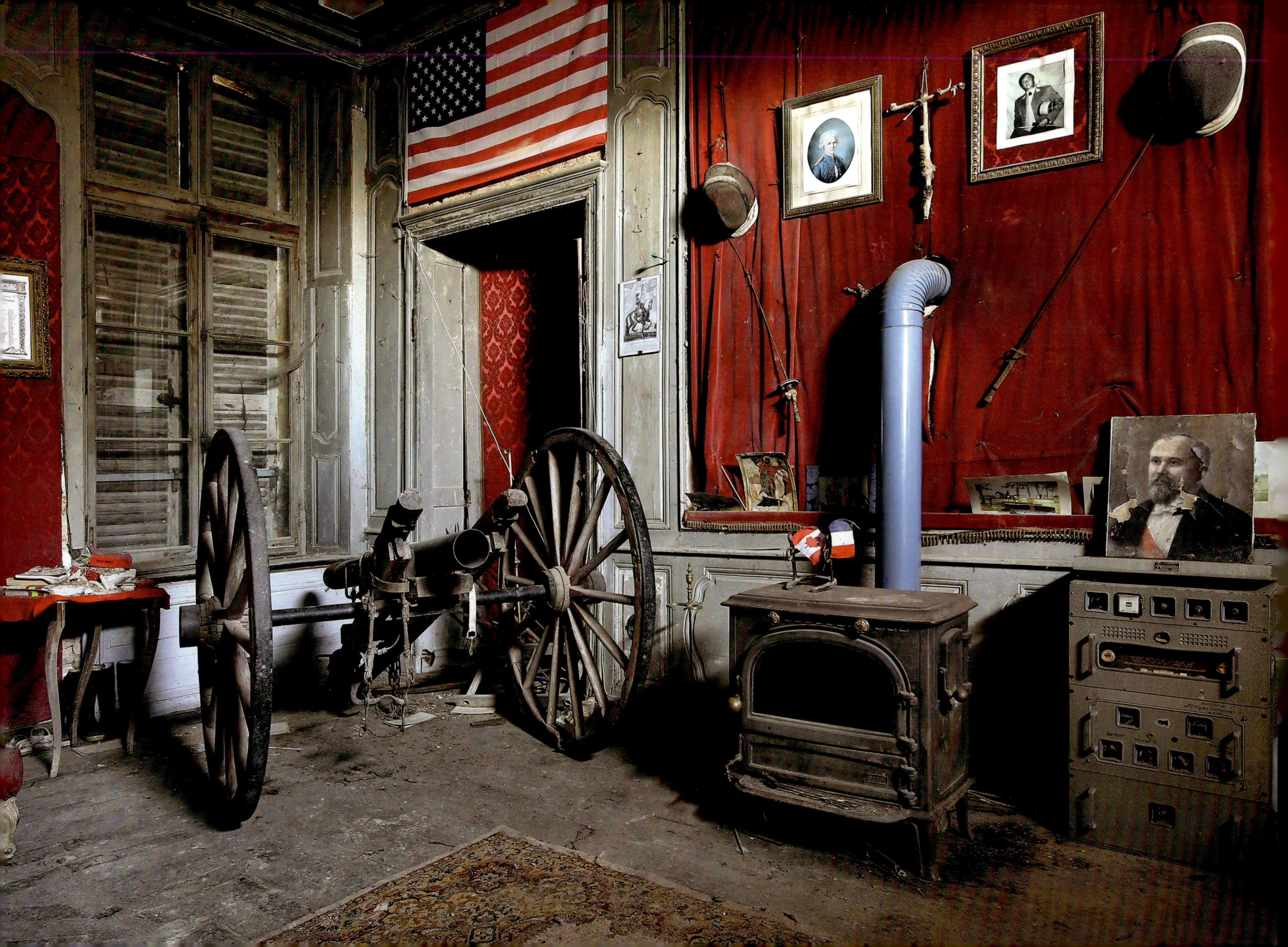

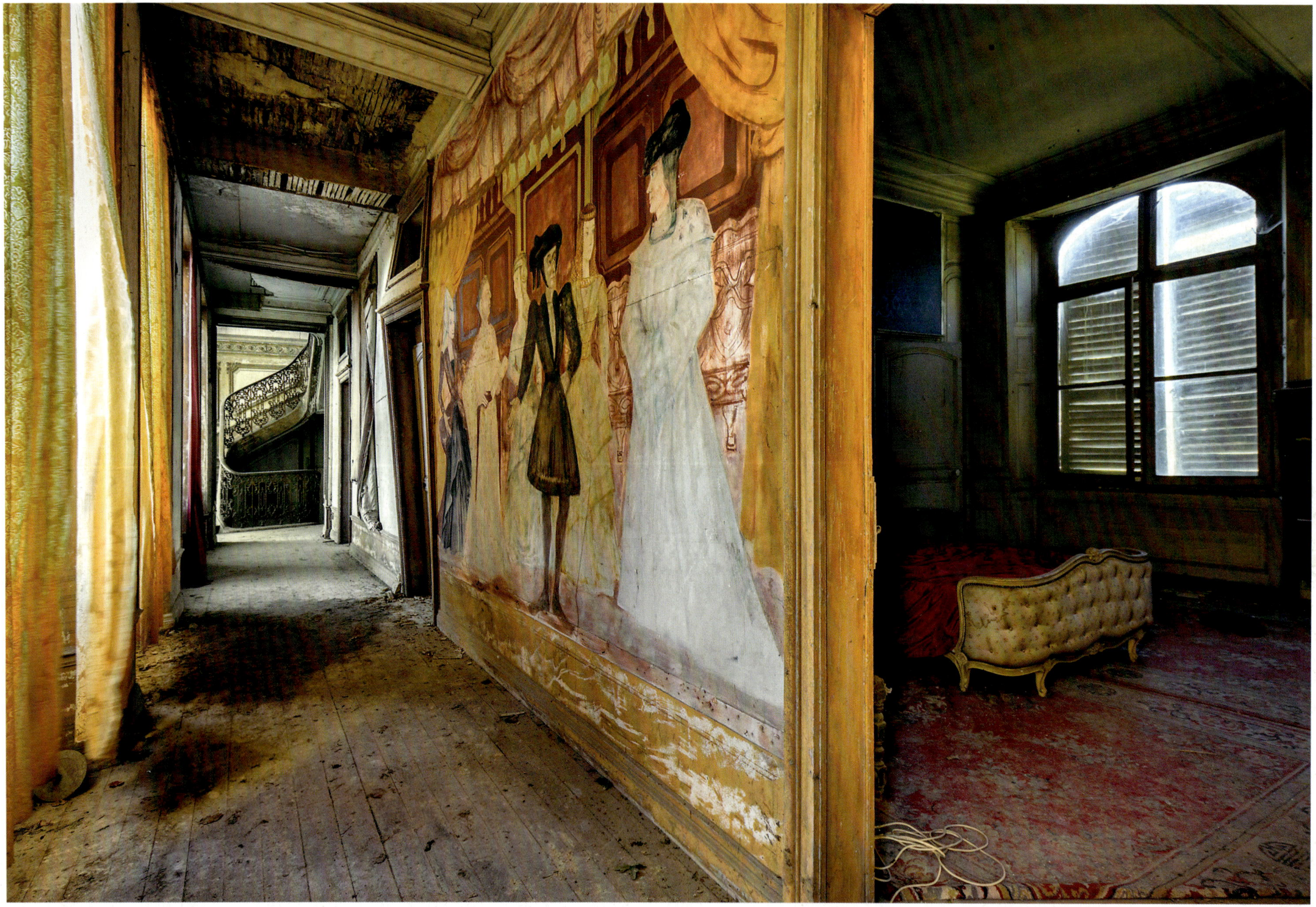

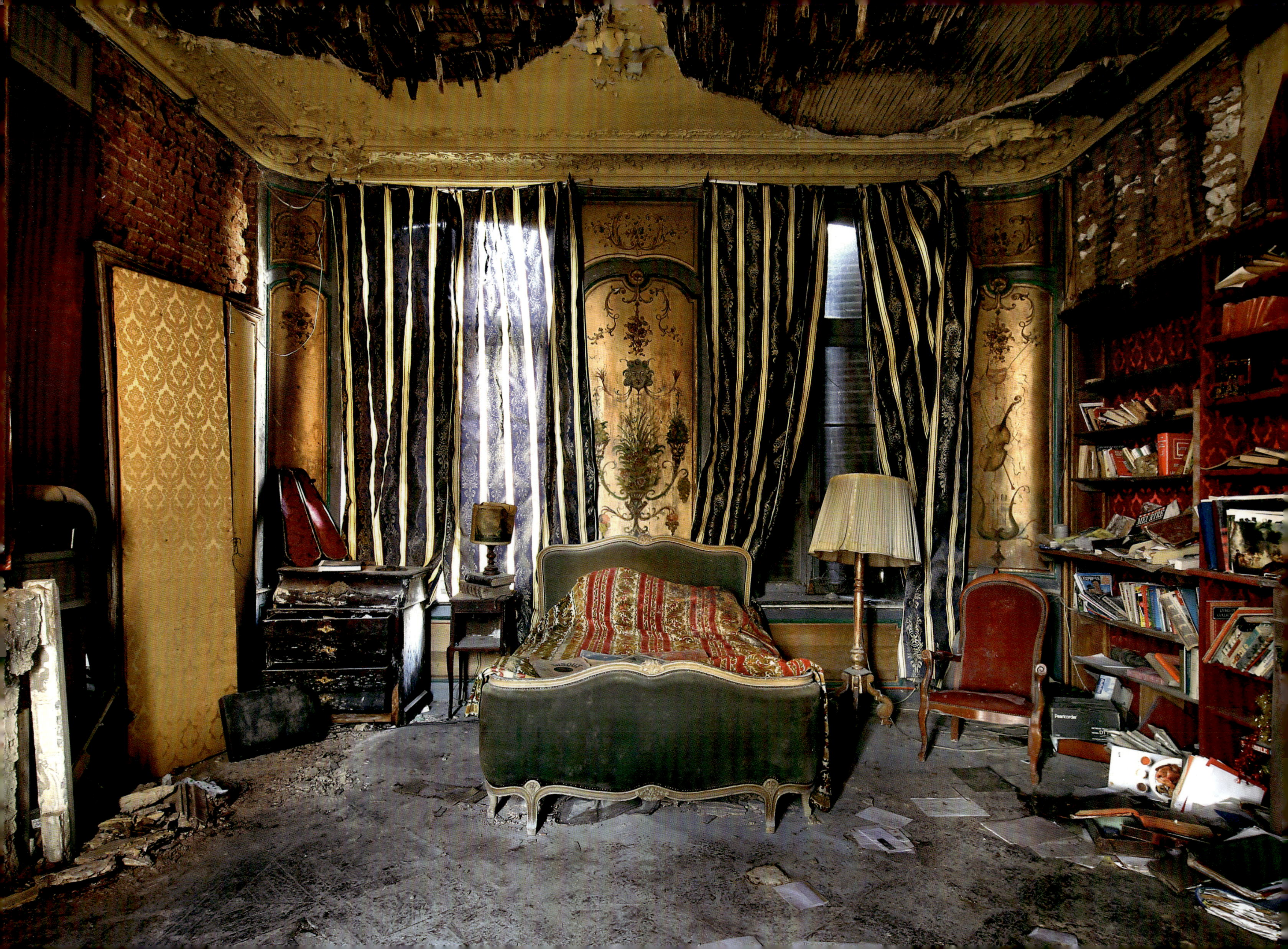

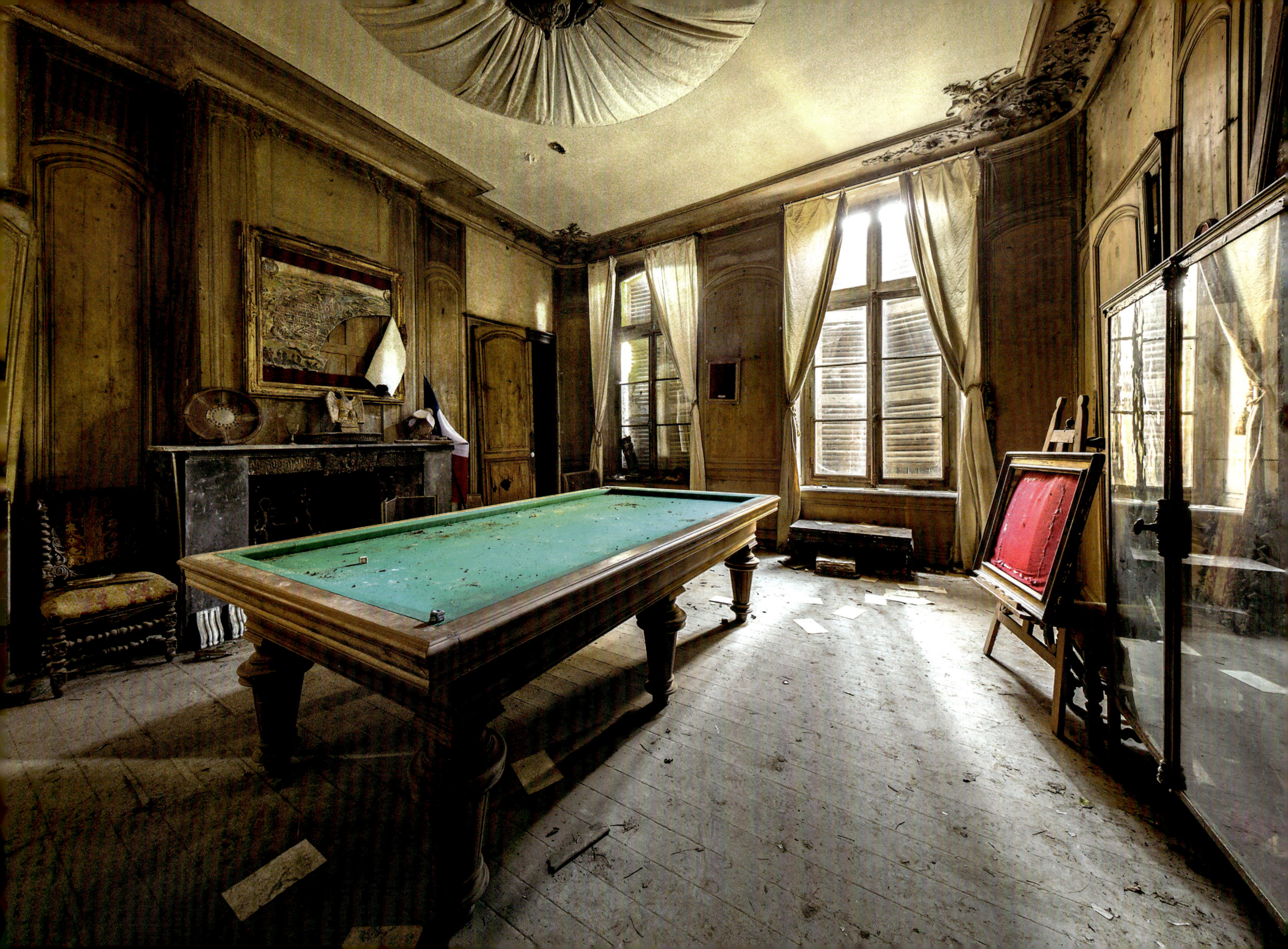

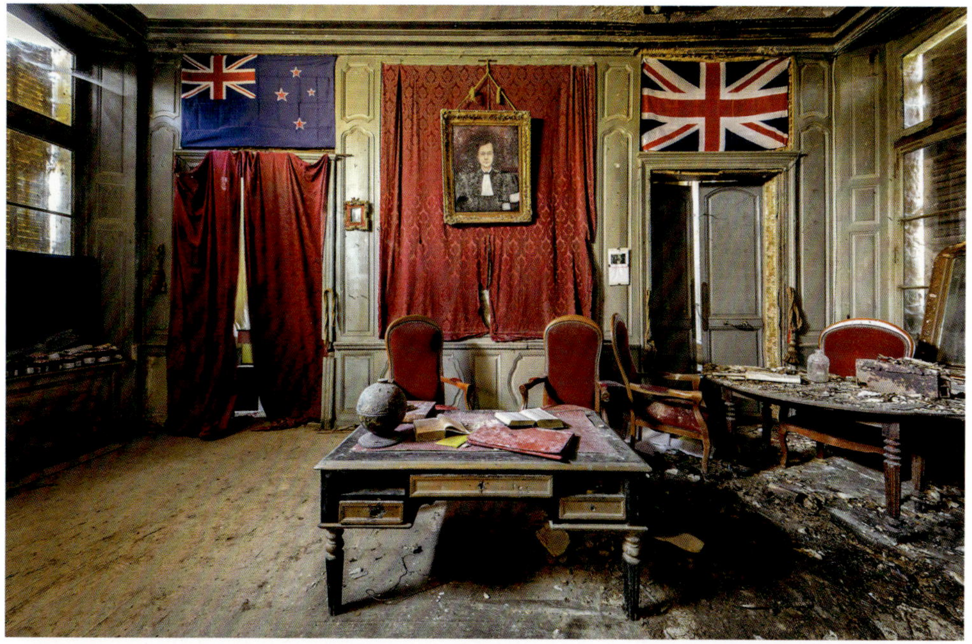

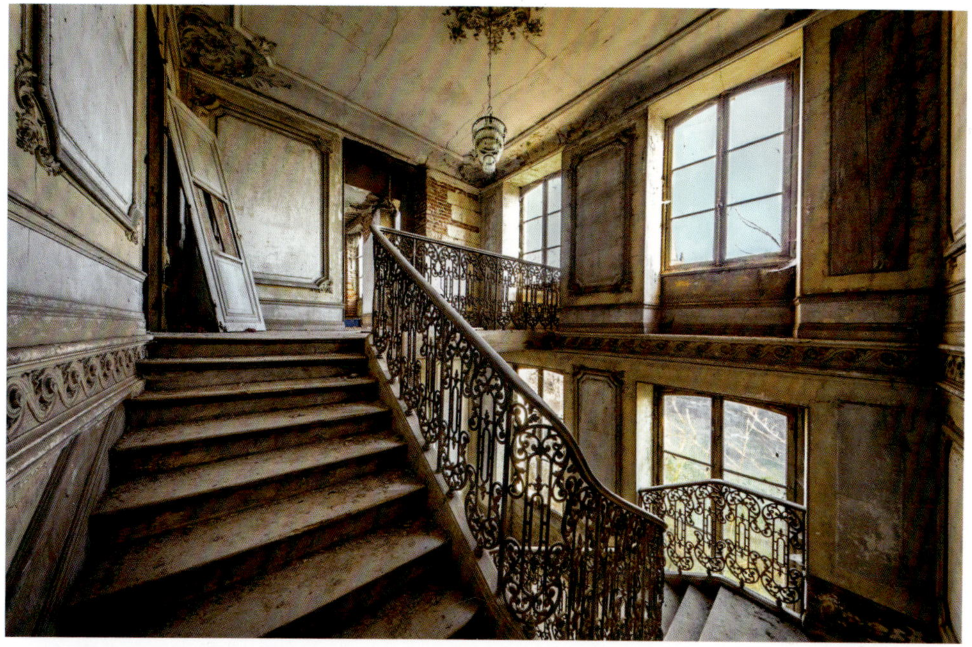

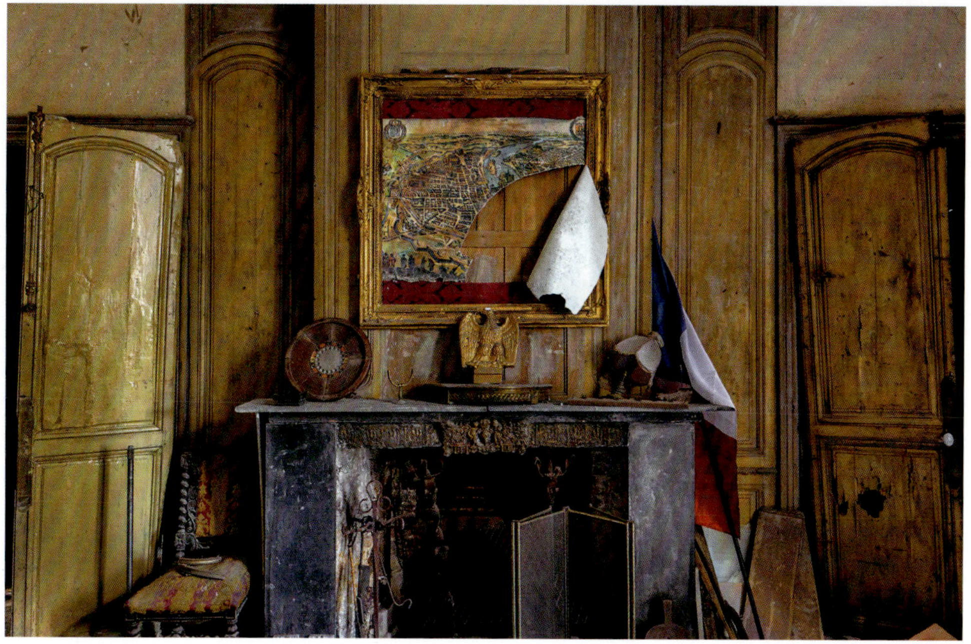

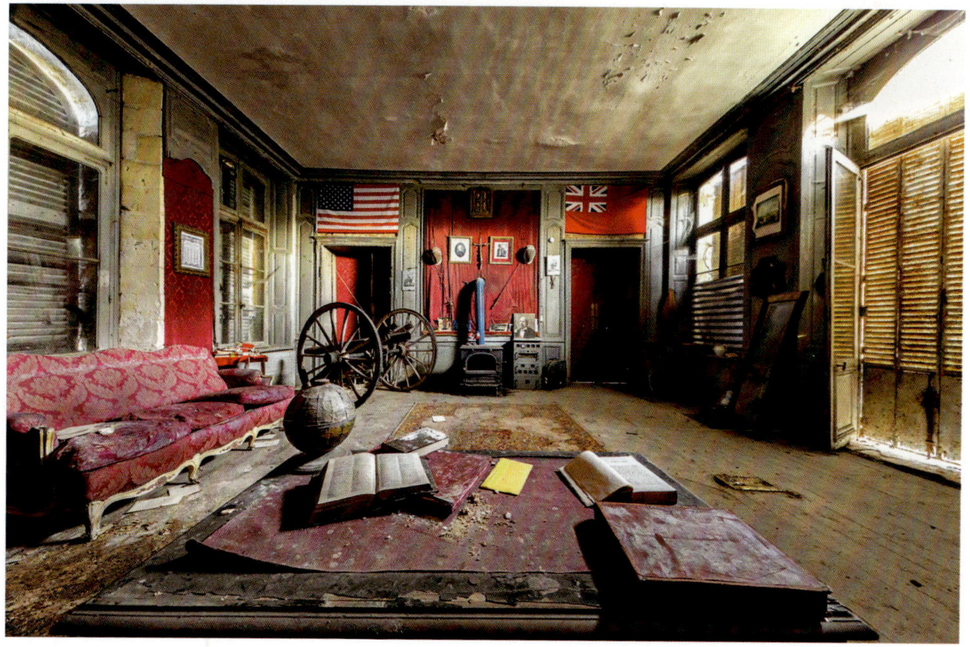

The chateau with the wild boar • *Hauts-de-France*

At the bottom of a meadow that must have once been a beautiful garden, reflecting the personality of its owner and attracting the eye of passers-by, stands a lovely, solitary building of red brick and light stone. An unusual clock adorns a tower on its roof.

This is an old, private bourgeois house. Life here must have been pleasant, with the sunshine coming in through the large windows. As soon as you enter, a boar's head – the guardian of the place – graces the entrance hall. The living room, the main room of the manor, is still fully furnished. Only the dust and leaks in the roof confirm the house's abandoned state.

The splendid chateau has recently been put up for sale, which probably explains why it has been placed under surveillance.

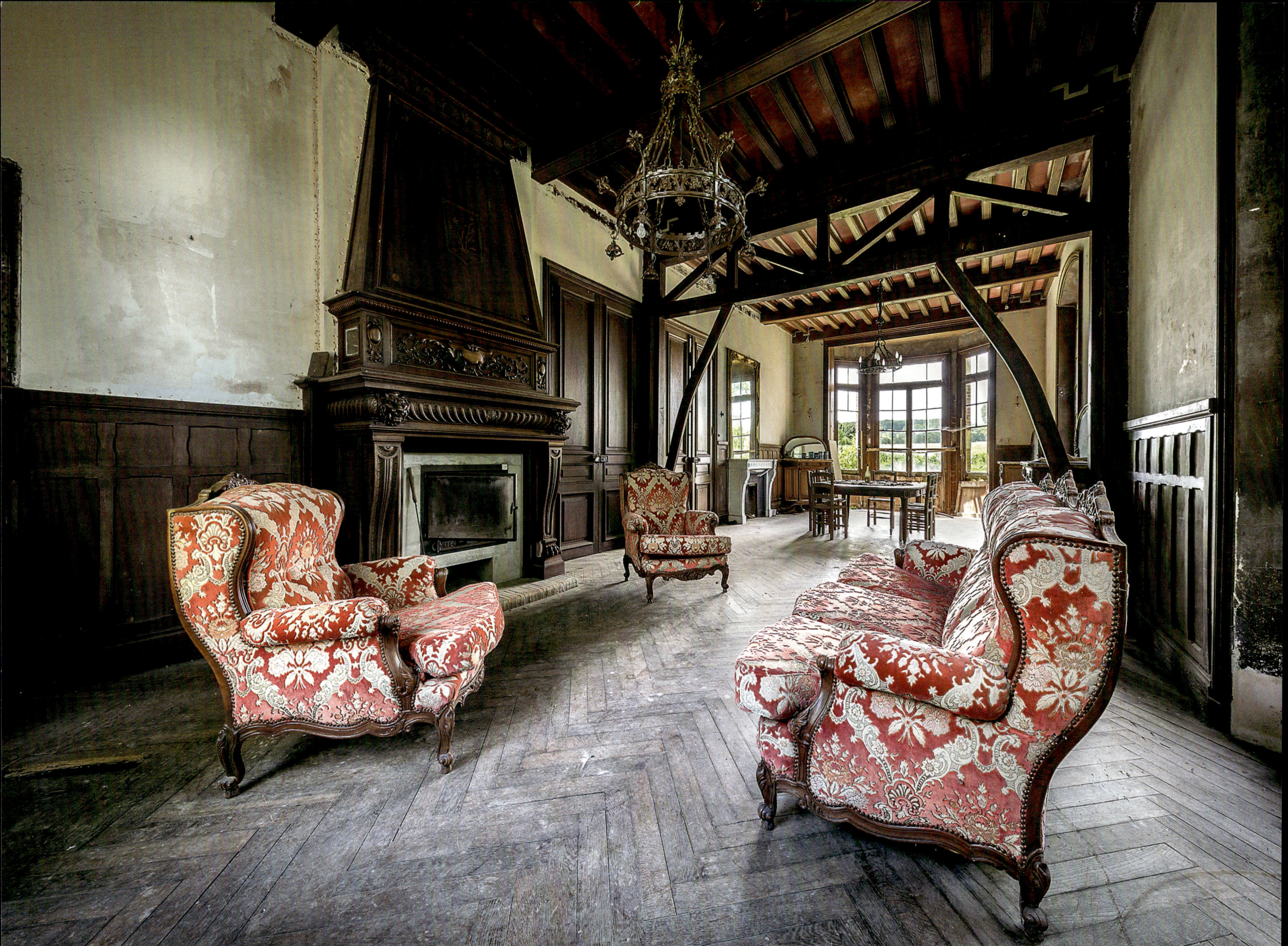

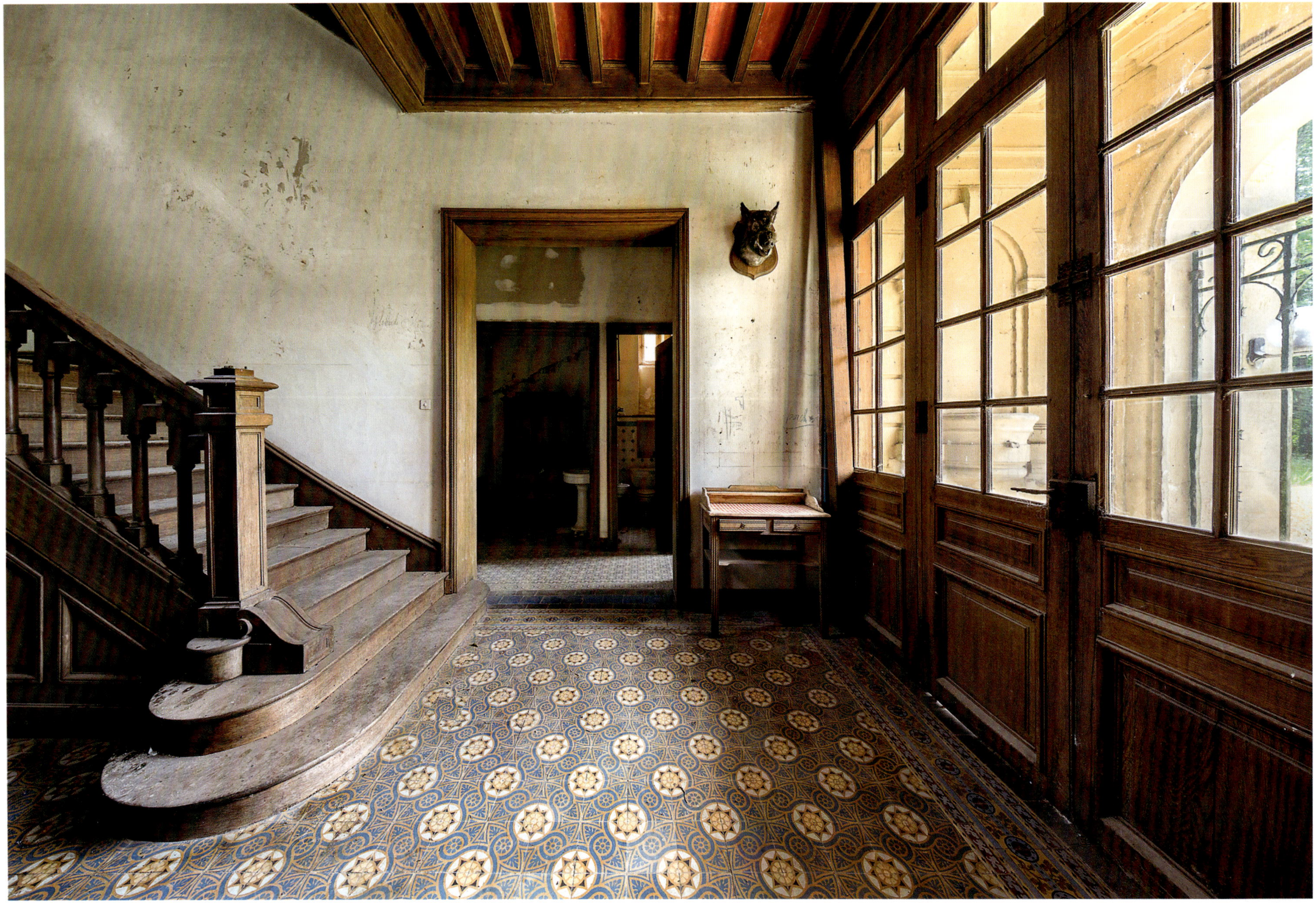

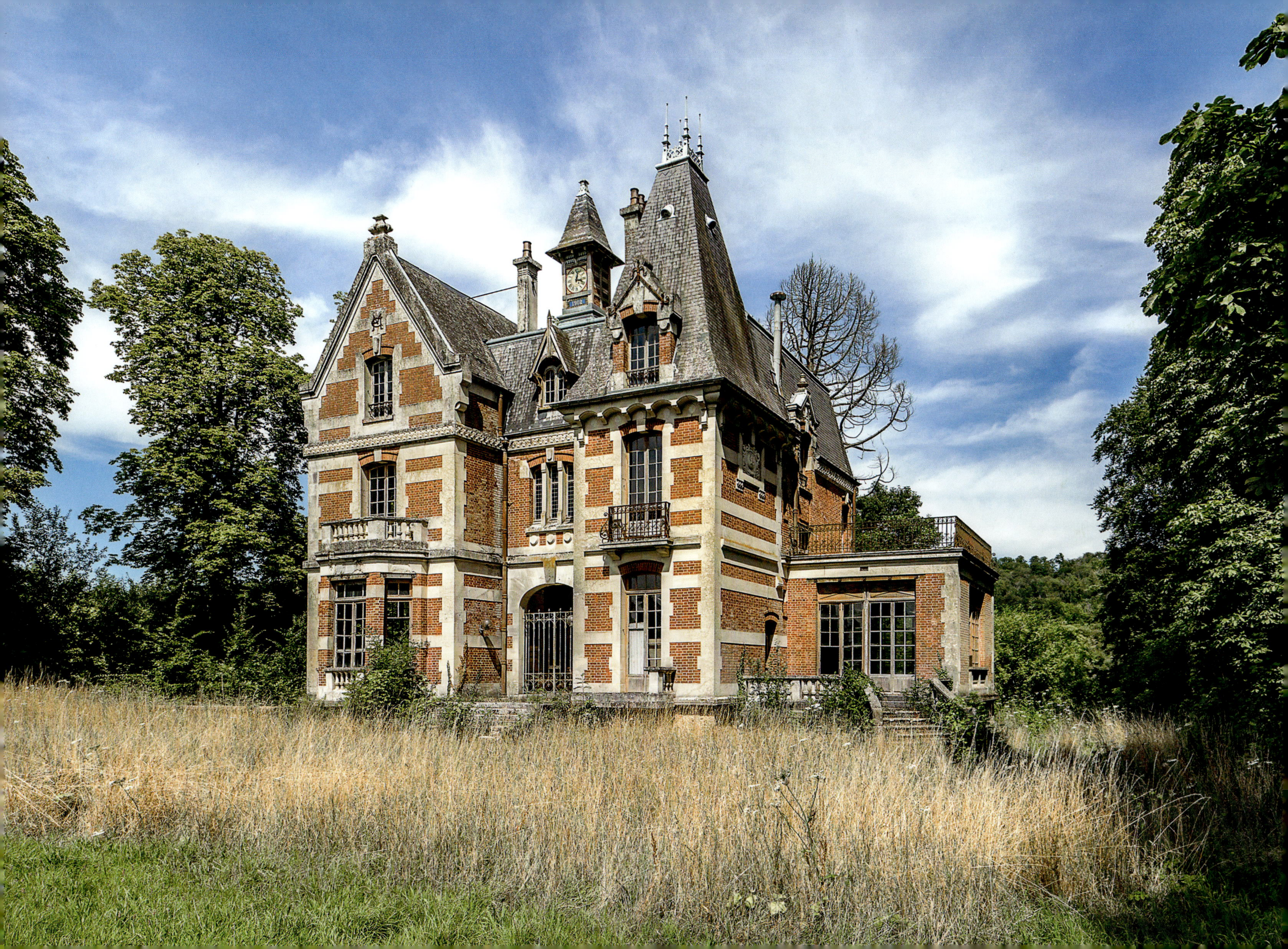

The castle of many interests • *Hauts-de-France*

Inside and out, the castle of this tiny rural village is in a superb state. It seems to be patiently waiting for its occupants to return. Everything, literally everything, is still there. Yet the house has been abandoned for 20 years. What a treasure among abandoned places!

The large blue room is bathed in a serene atmosphere, inviting you to settle down and take a moment. The place makes you want to soak it all up and learn more about its well-preserved history. In all the rooms, there are bookcases filled with books and albums. The colour scheme of the different rooms is varied, spanning the colour wheel from green and blue to red.

The many photos and clothes found in the cupboards suggest the house may have belonged to a naval family who travelled extensively around the world. There are at least 100 albums from the 1920s, 1950s and 1960s in the bookcases, suggesting the family who occupied the castle owned it for a very long time. Books ranging from psychology to medicine to world history attest to their varied interests.

The beautiful house continues to wait patiently.

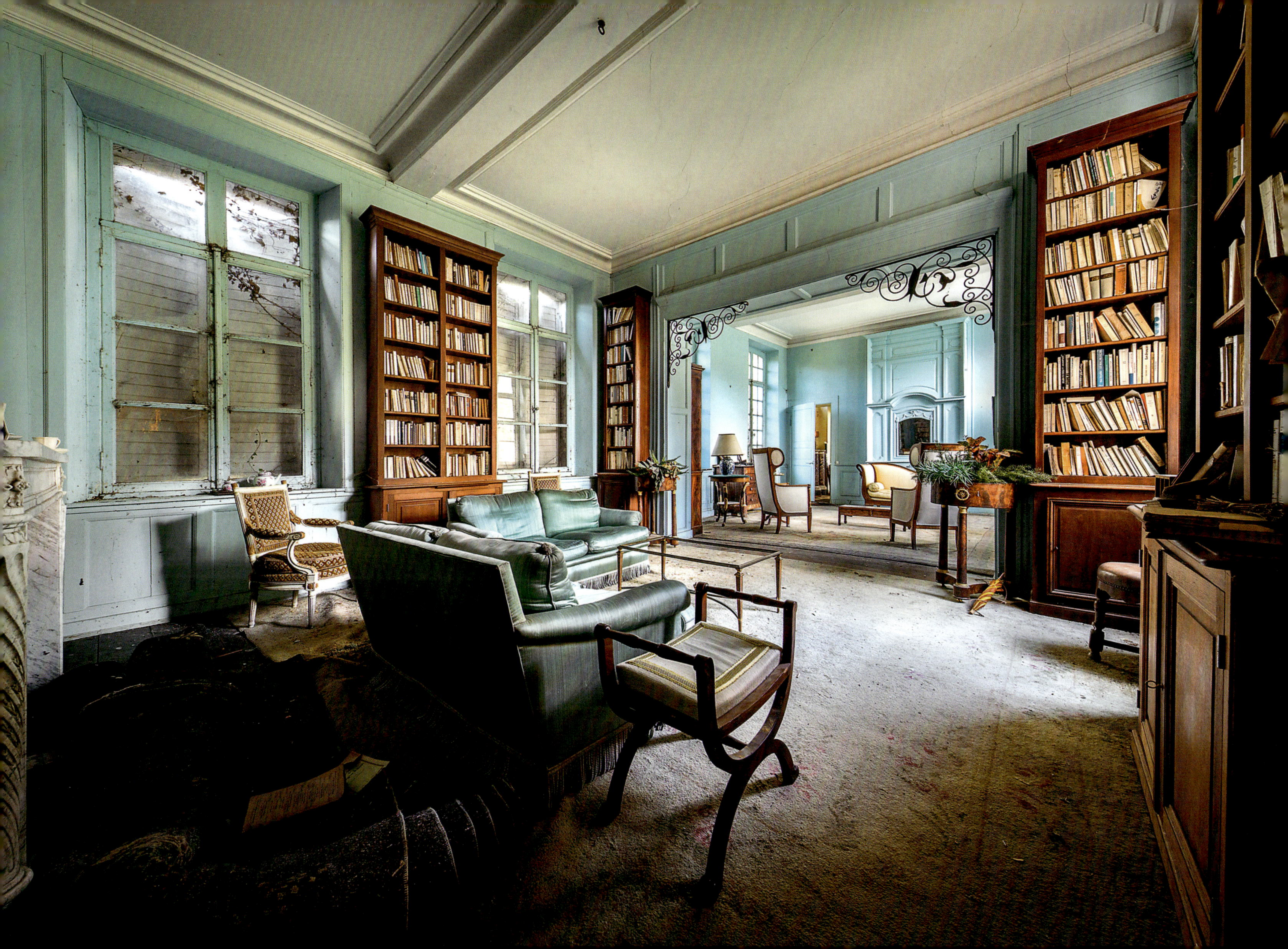

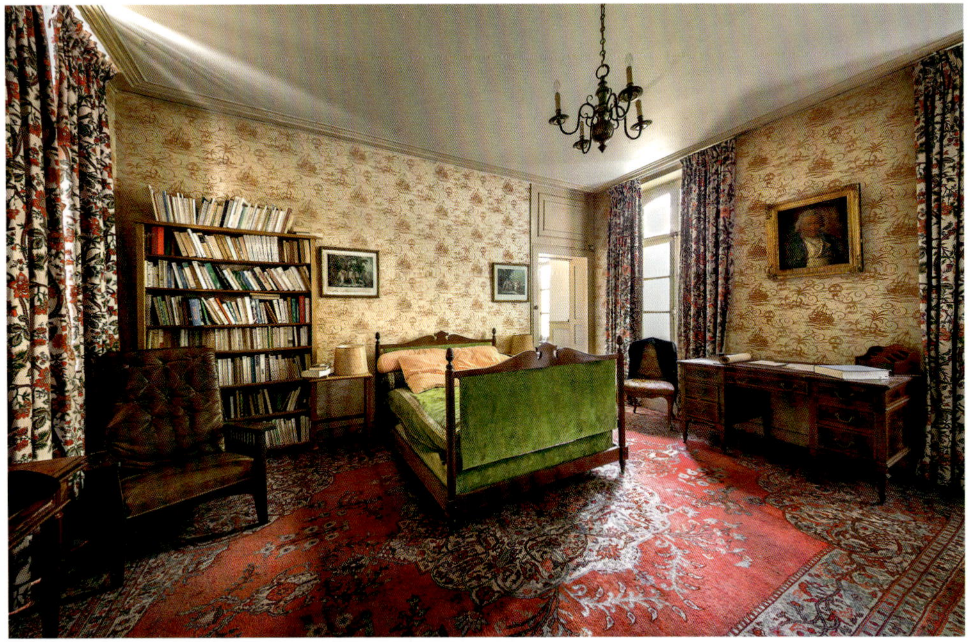

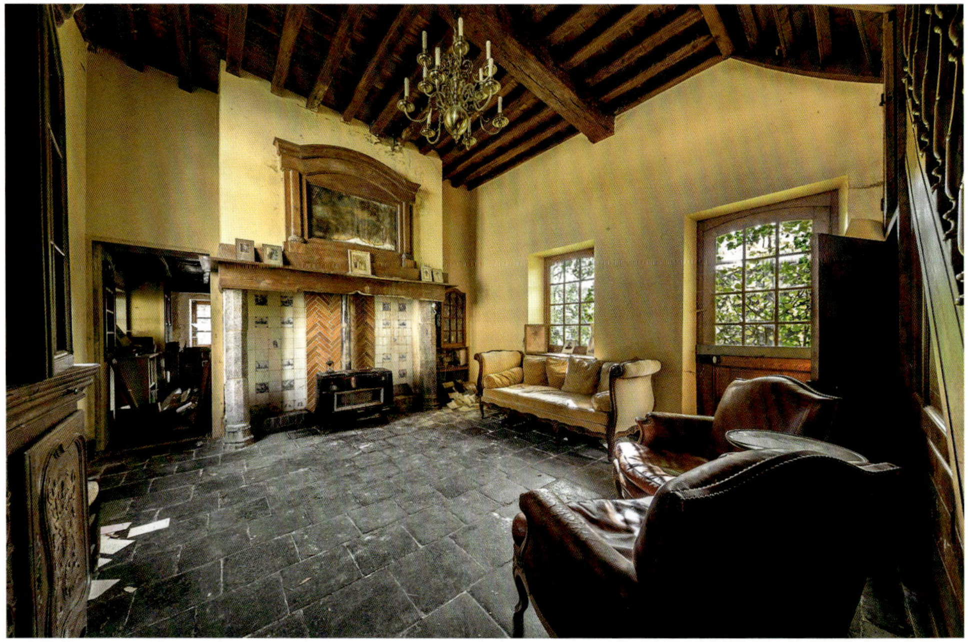

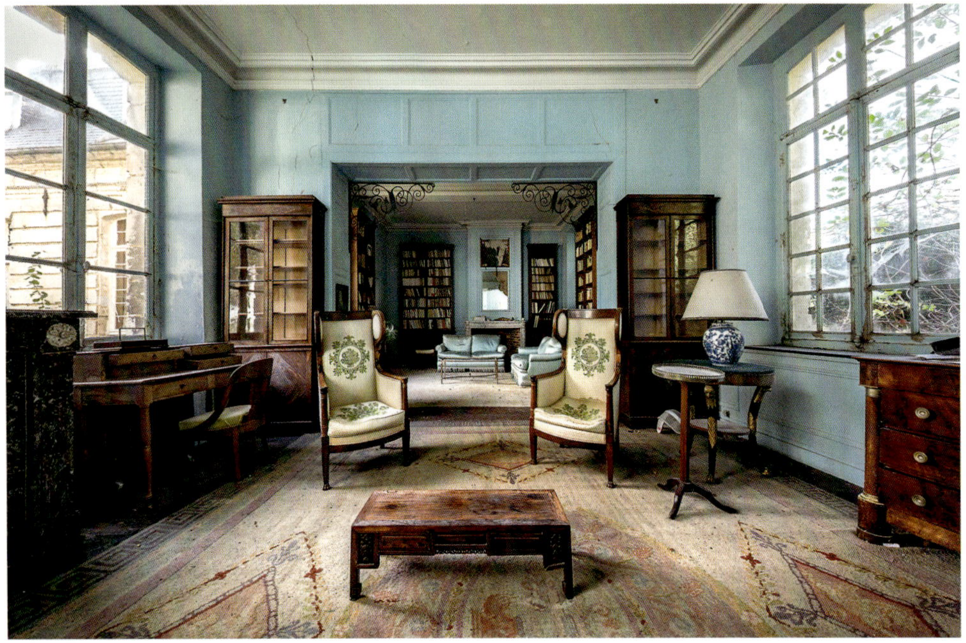

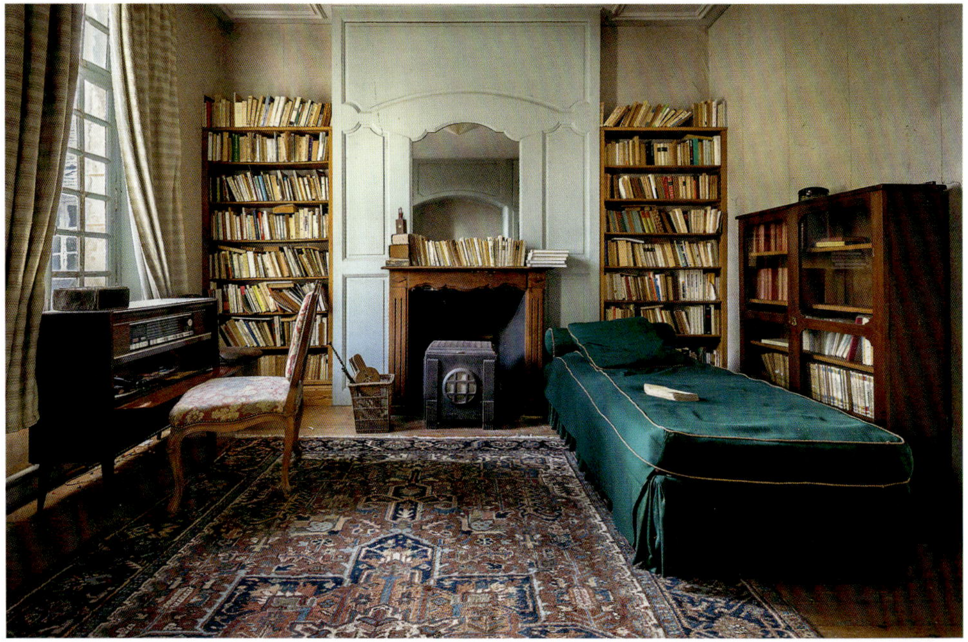

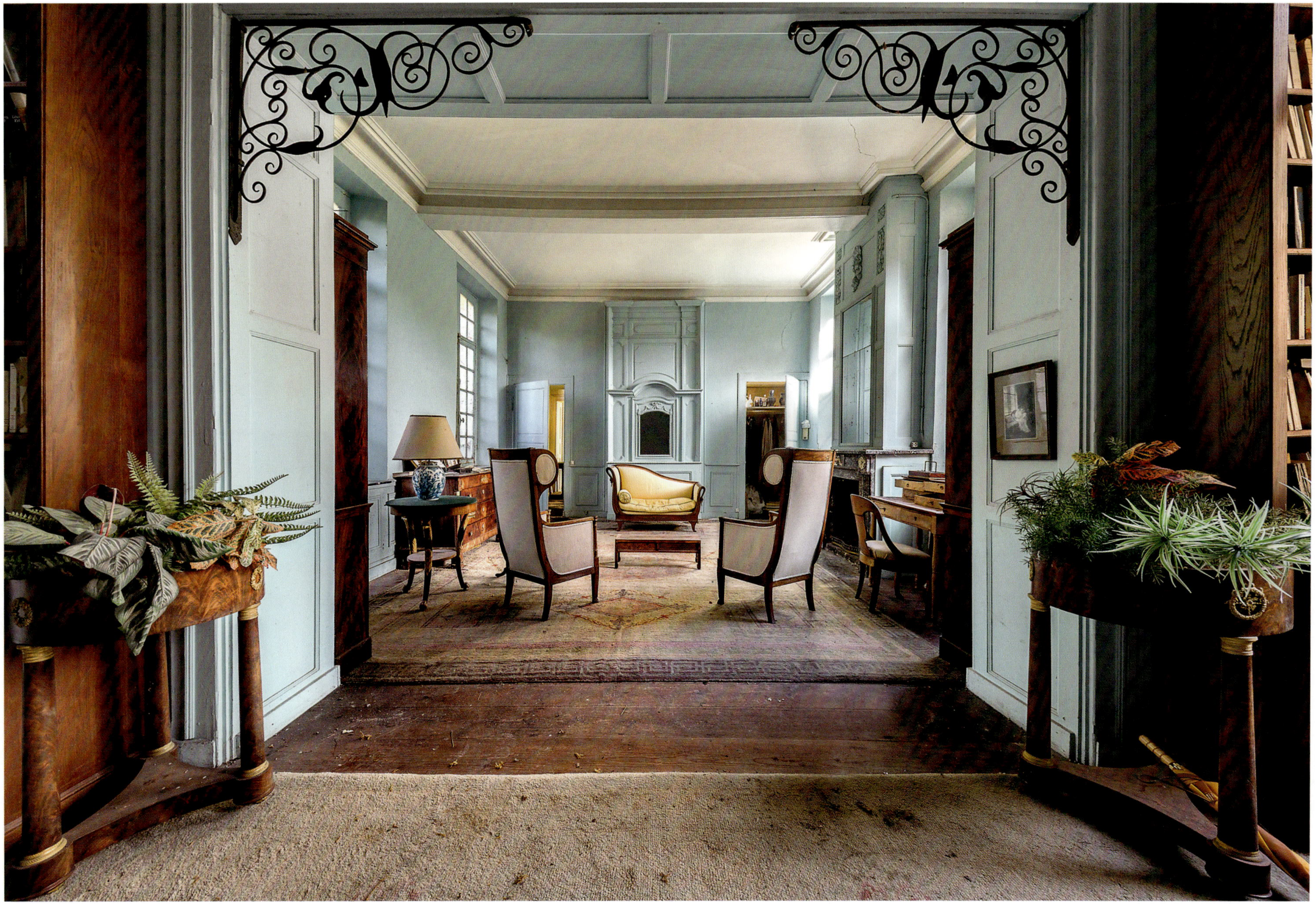

Theatre of Queens • *Hauts-de-France*

I was lucky enough to be granted permission to enter this exceptional art deco jewel well before its renovation. I had an exclusive look at this high room topped with a barrel vault and a large elliptical glass dome. The back wall, with its semi-dome, is the apse of the original chapel. Its frescoes, which follow the curves of the walls and ceilings, tell the story of the city's most important moments. The eventful history of the chapel of the Jesuit College spans from 1624, when the first stones were laid, to the present day. The master builder was the Belgian Jesuit friar Jean du Blocq. Later, the Maubeuge art deco architects Henri and Jean Laffite extended the building by one floor and added a grandiose hallway. This jewel of a building is exceptional because of its quality and rarity. It has two rooms: one dedicated to music on the ground floor and a ballroom on the first floor, accessed by a monumental staircase that crosses and uncrosses its flights of stairs.

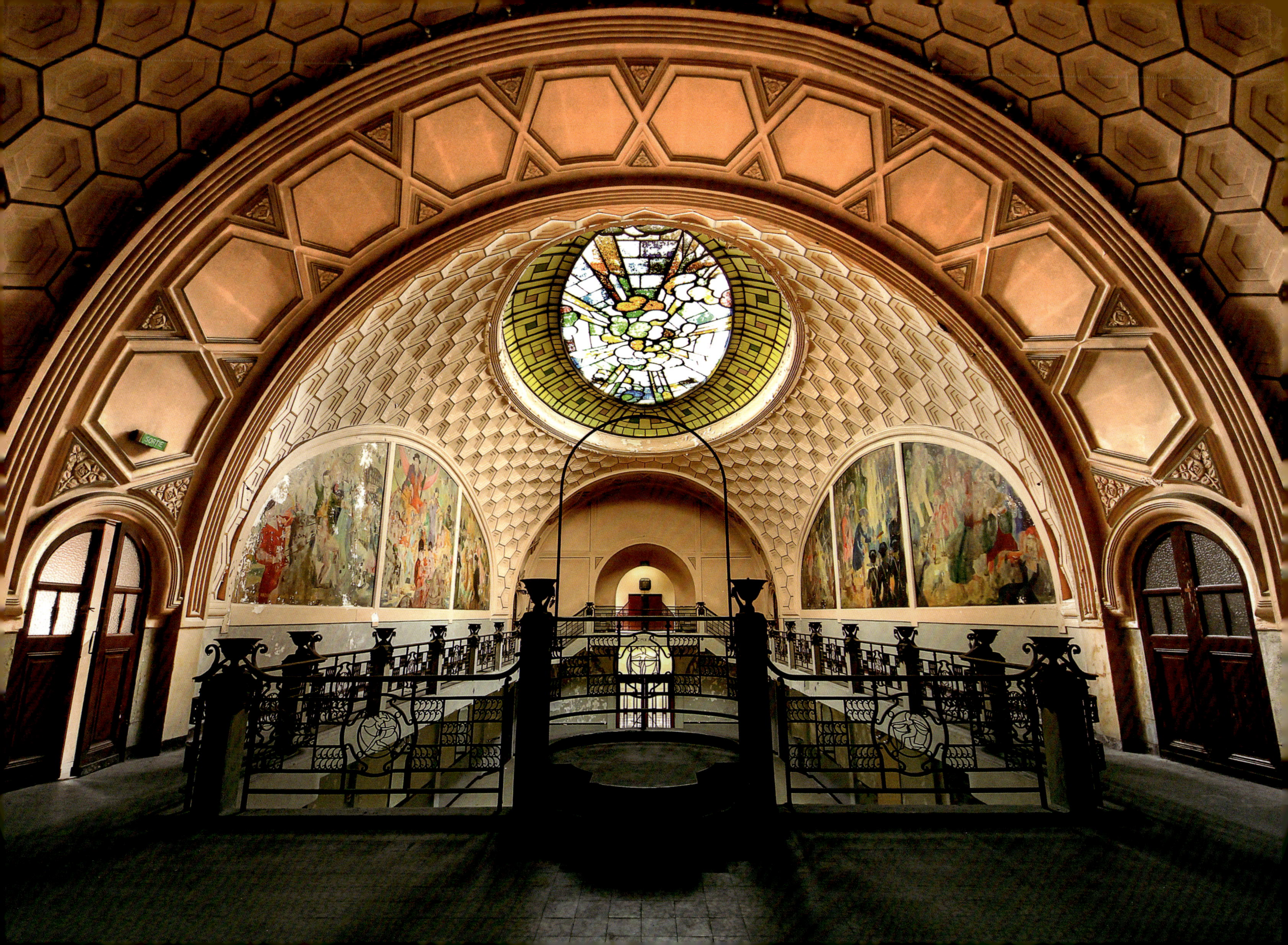
SORTIE

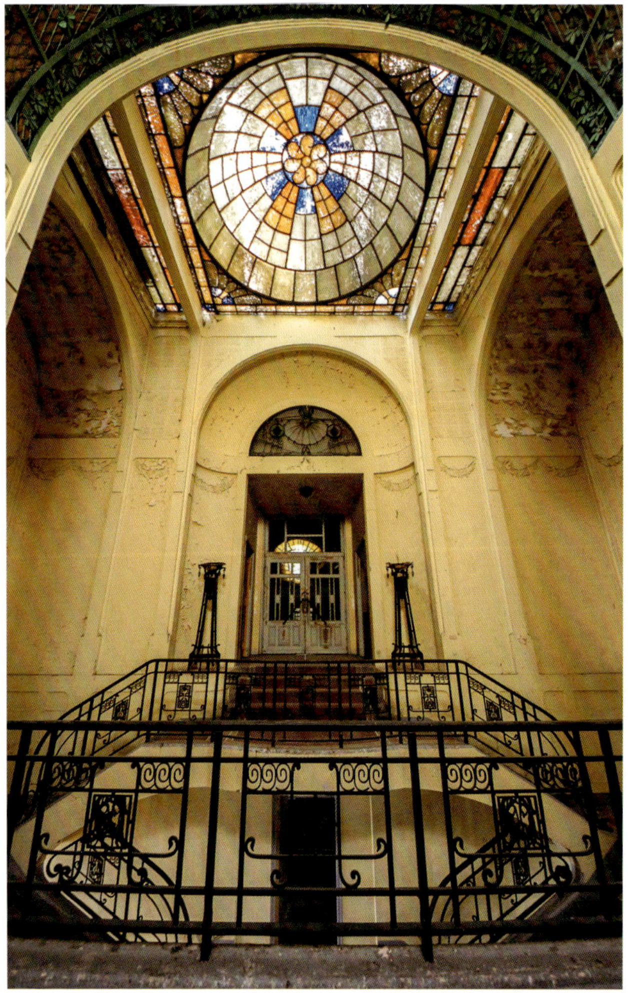

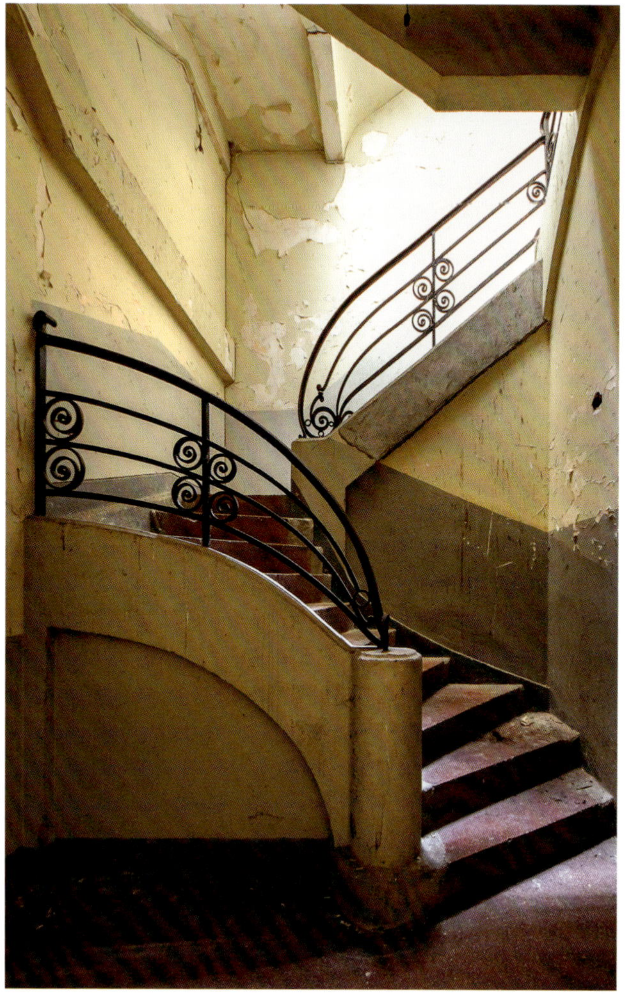

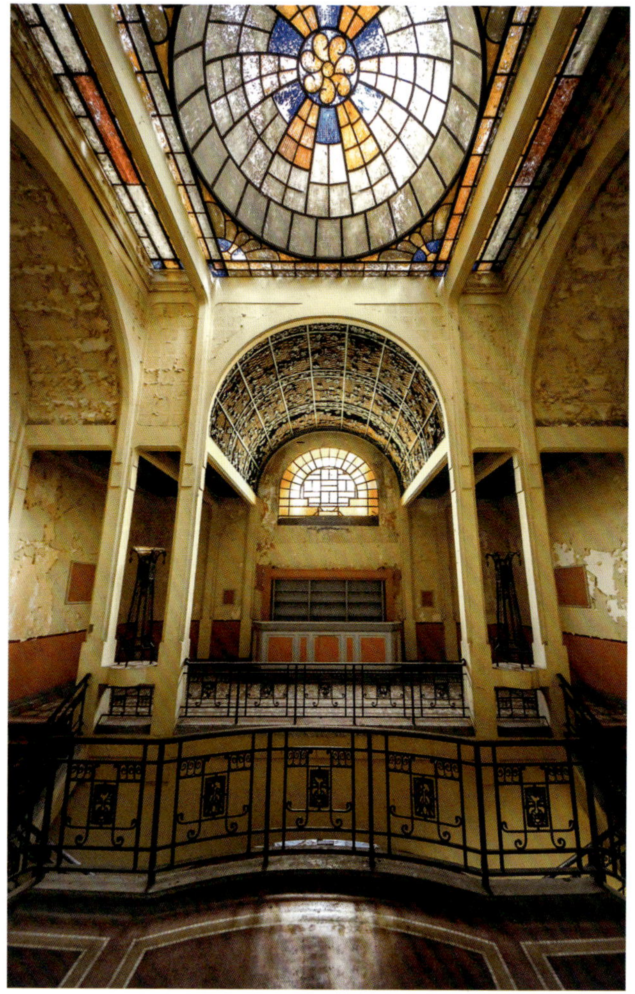

One of the frescoes shows the time when the city of Maubeuge became French again after the second Treaty of Aix-la-Chapelle was signed in October 1748, and a bonfire was held during the night to celebrate this occasion. Another fresco is entitled The Mabuse Party, in honour of the local painter Jean Gossaert.

The chapel was desecrated and converted into a communal building during the French Revolution before it was used as a garrison stable, shop, barracks and museum. It was renamed Salle Sthrau in honour of the little drummer, hero of the nearby battle of Wattignies, and even hosted a grand ball in 1833 in honour of King Louis Philippe. During the Second World War, the stained-glass windows were painted so the light would not betray the presence of people in the building, which miraculously escaped destruction.

The Sthrau Hall has been classified as a historic monument since 2002. In 2017, the municipality of Maubeuge and the French Heritage Foundation joined forces to raise money for the restoration of the building. The renovation was completed at the end of 2018, and the Salle Sthrau is now a cultural space open for exhibitions, artistic activities, and regular concerts. This is an exceptional building that deserved an exceptional restoration.

A taxidermist's chateau • *Hauts-de-France*

At the end of a cobbled path, sheltered from prying eyes, stands a castle. Built between 1680 and 1700, it is mostly forgotten today.

It is the oldest building in the village and was built according to the architectural fashion of the time in brick and limestone for the aristocratic family who commissioned it. A note written in 1973 indicates the current structure of the castle dates from the 19th century, when changes were made to the structure of the original building.

Some of the ceilings collapsed, dragging down the contents of the room above. Papers, newspapers and letters were blown away and scattered around the abandoned rooms.

In the centre of one of the rooms, which has withstood the ravages of time, is a billiard table with a cupboard full of stuffed animals. A heron stares at solitary visitors with its immobile eye, while in other rooms, an eagle frozen in flight and an imposing stag still seem to be watching over the place. But for how much longer?

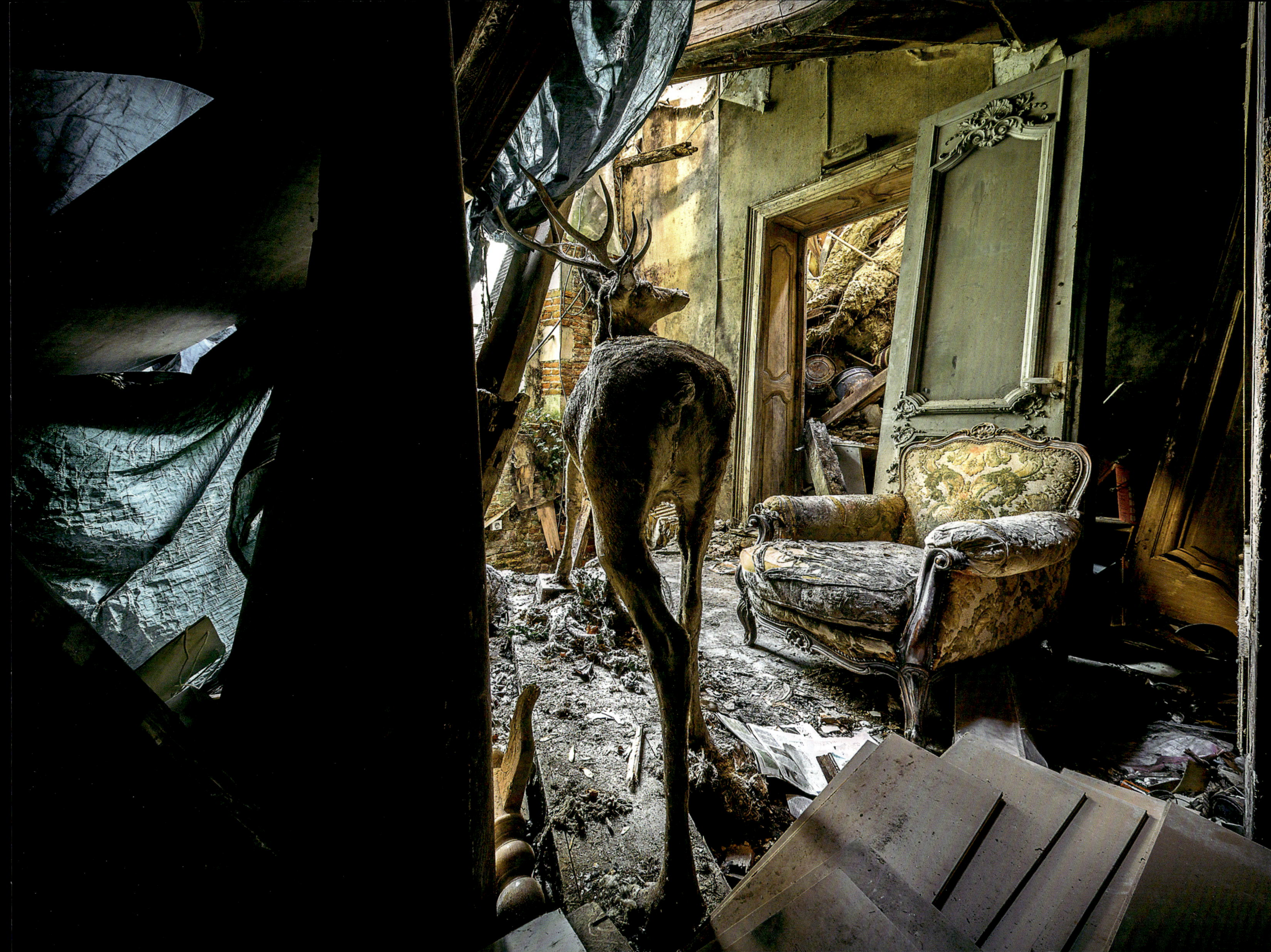

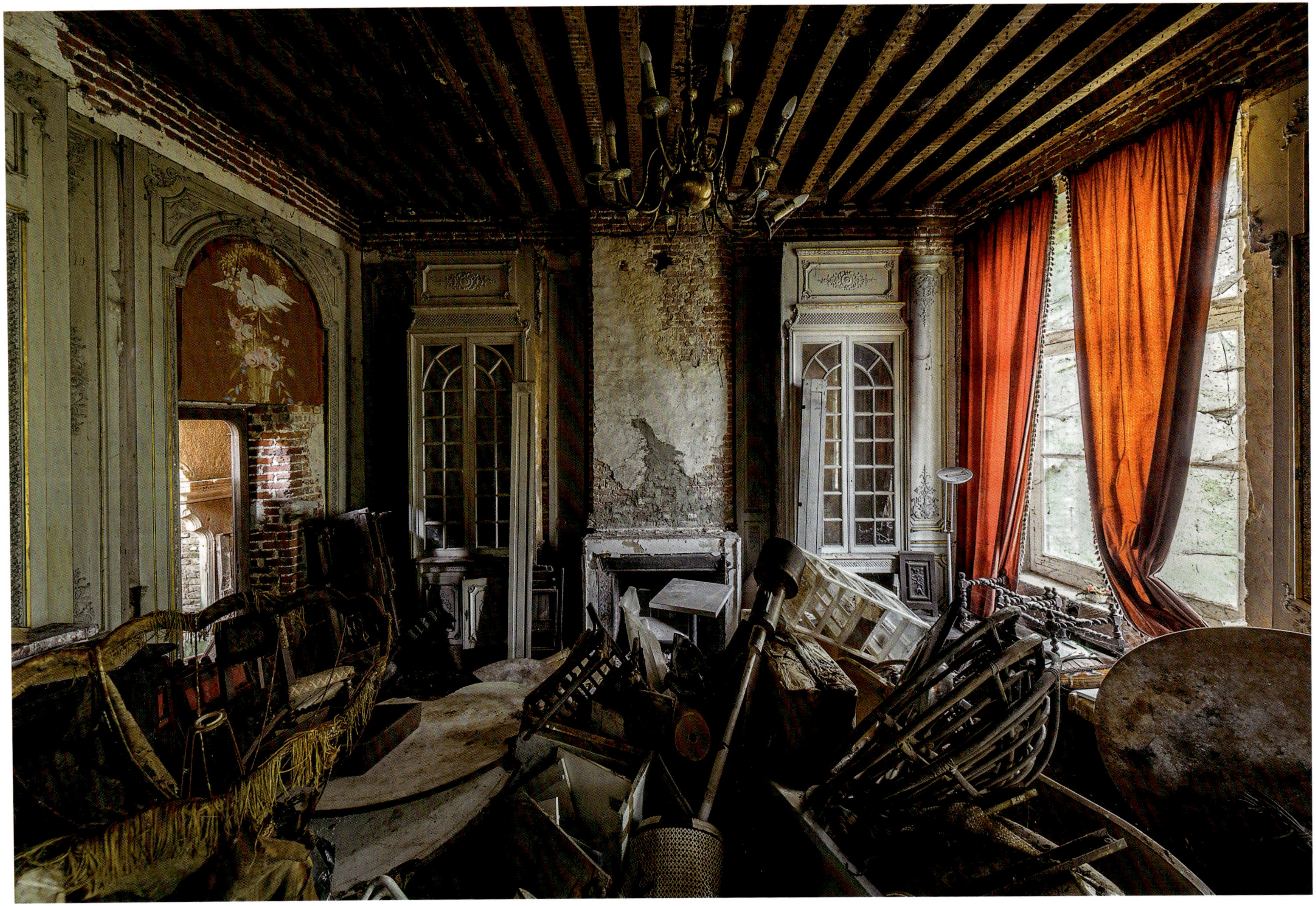

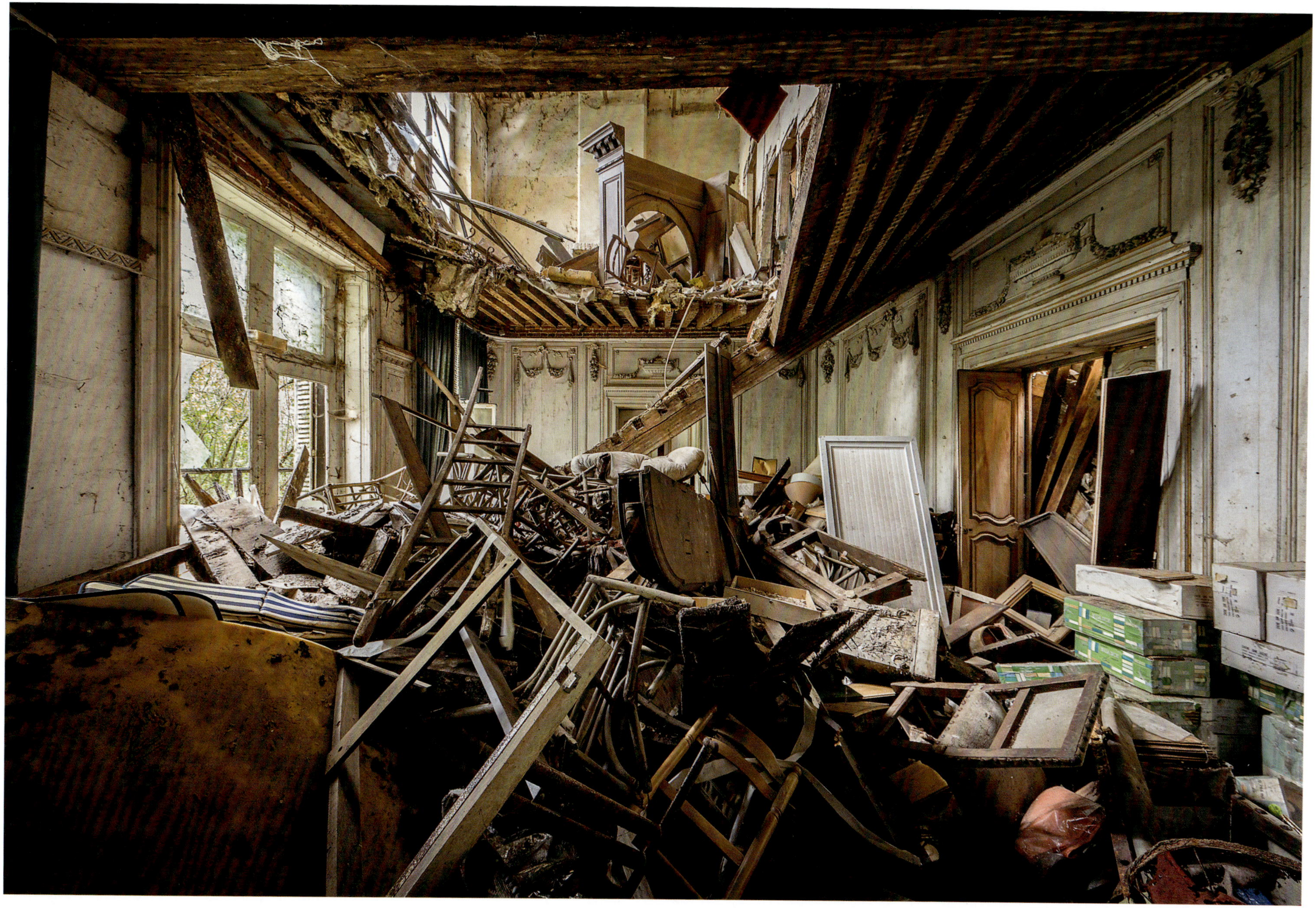

A craftsman's workshop • *Hauts-de-France*

As you enter this dimly lit craftsman's workshop, it is impossible not to marvel at the superb decorative objects made of solid wood, which slowly reveal themselves: from animal sculptures to figurines, ceremonial furniture to decorative shutters, everything is possible with woodwork.

The different types of wood bring unique textures and colours, which give an indisputable richness to these delicately crafted pieces.

Woodcarving requires both patience and skill, acquired over many years. It is a pity these works of art, created with such passion, are not preserved as they deserve.

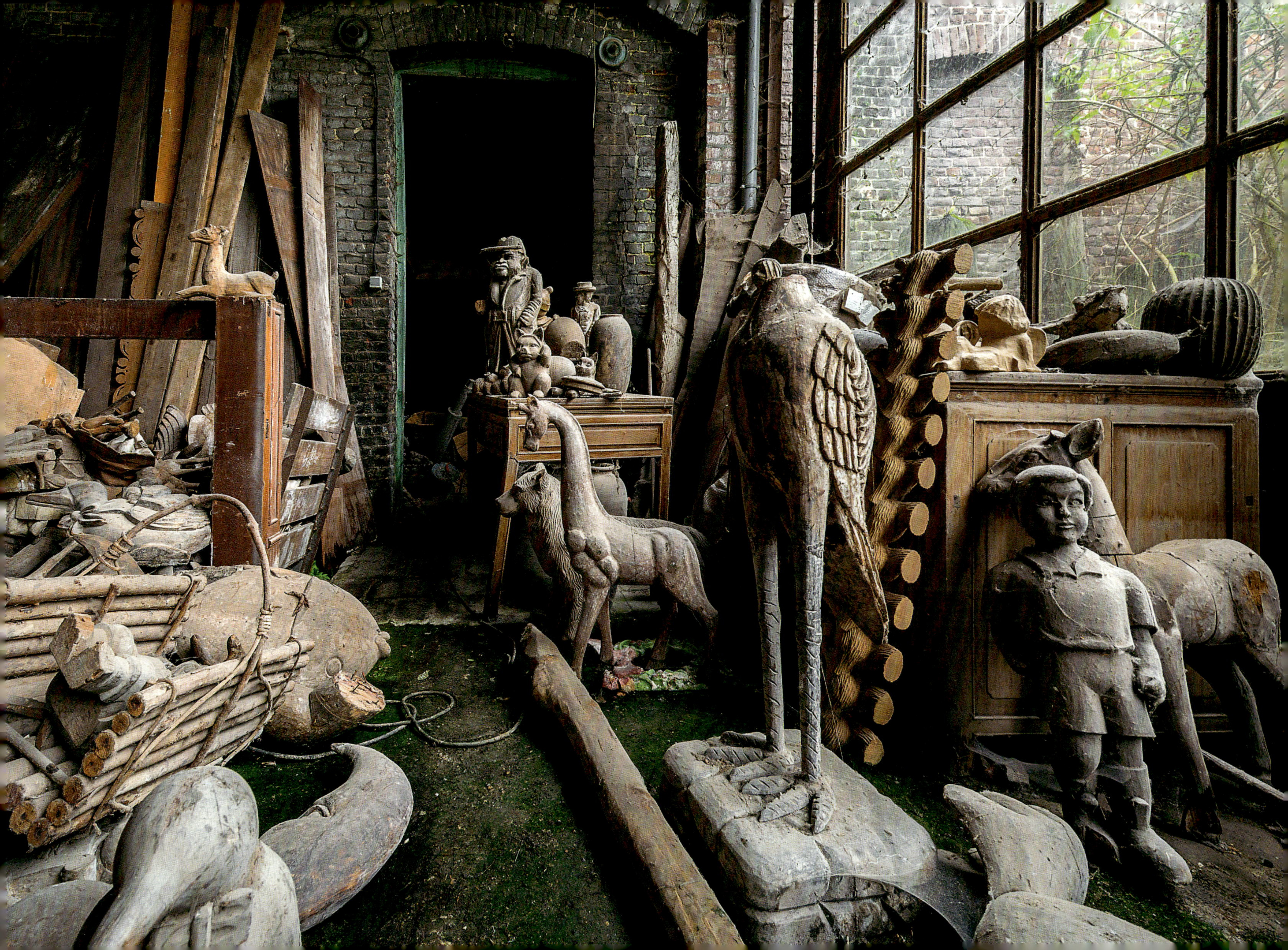

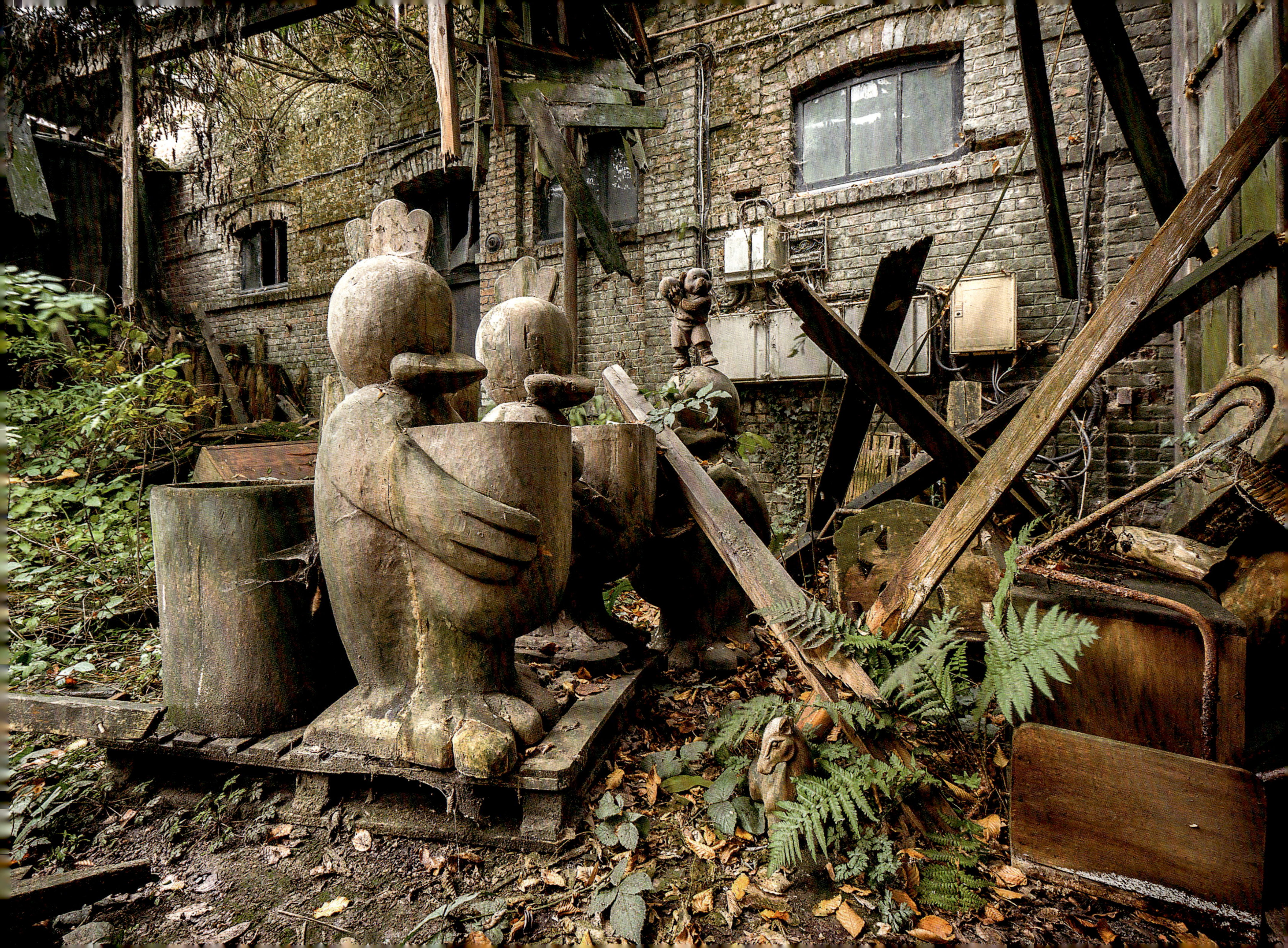

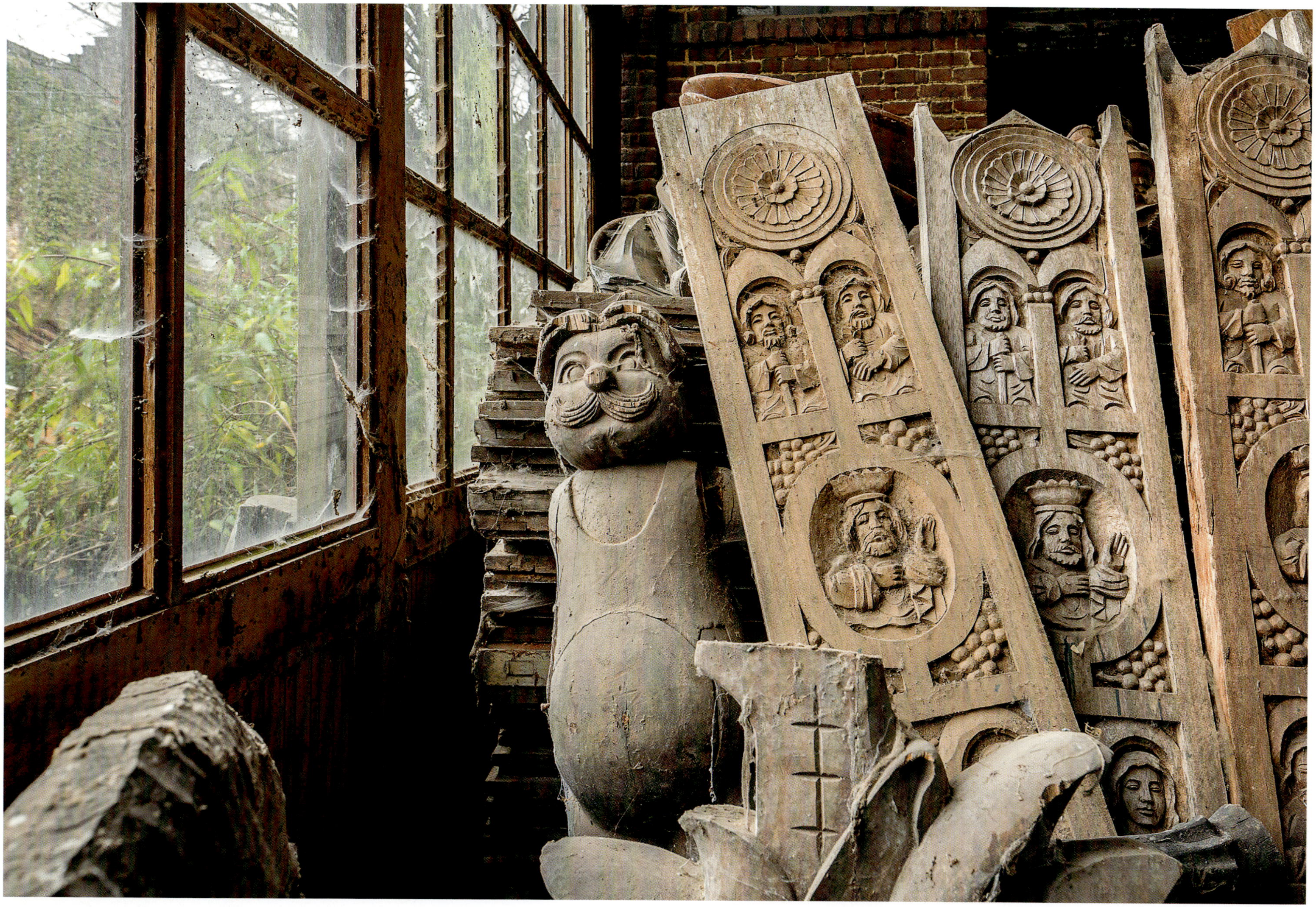

The May swimming pool • *Hauts-de-France*

One year after the poor results of French swimmers at the 1968 Olympic Games, a programme was launched by the Ministry of Youth, Sports and Leisure to give every child the opportunity to learn to swim.

This centre is one of the 183 swimming pools born of this French national programme launched in the early 1970s.

This industrial construction is 25 metres long and 10 metres wide. Its base is a circle 35 metres in diameter. The dome, supported by metal arches, is 6 metres high and opens to 120 degrees.

This is a small wonder where no one dares to venture.

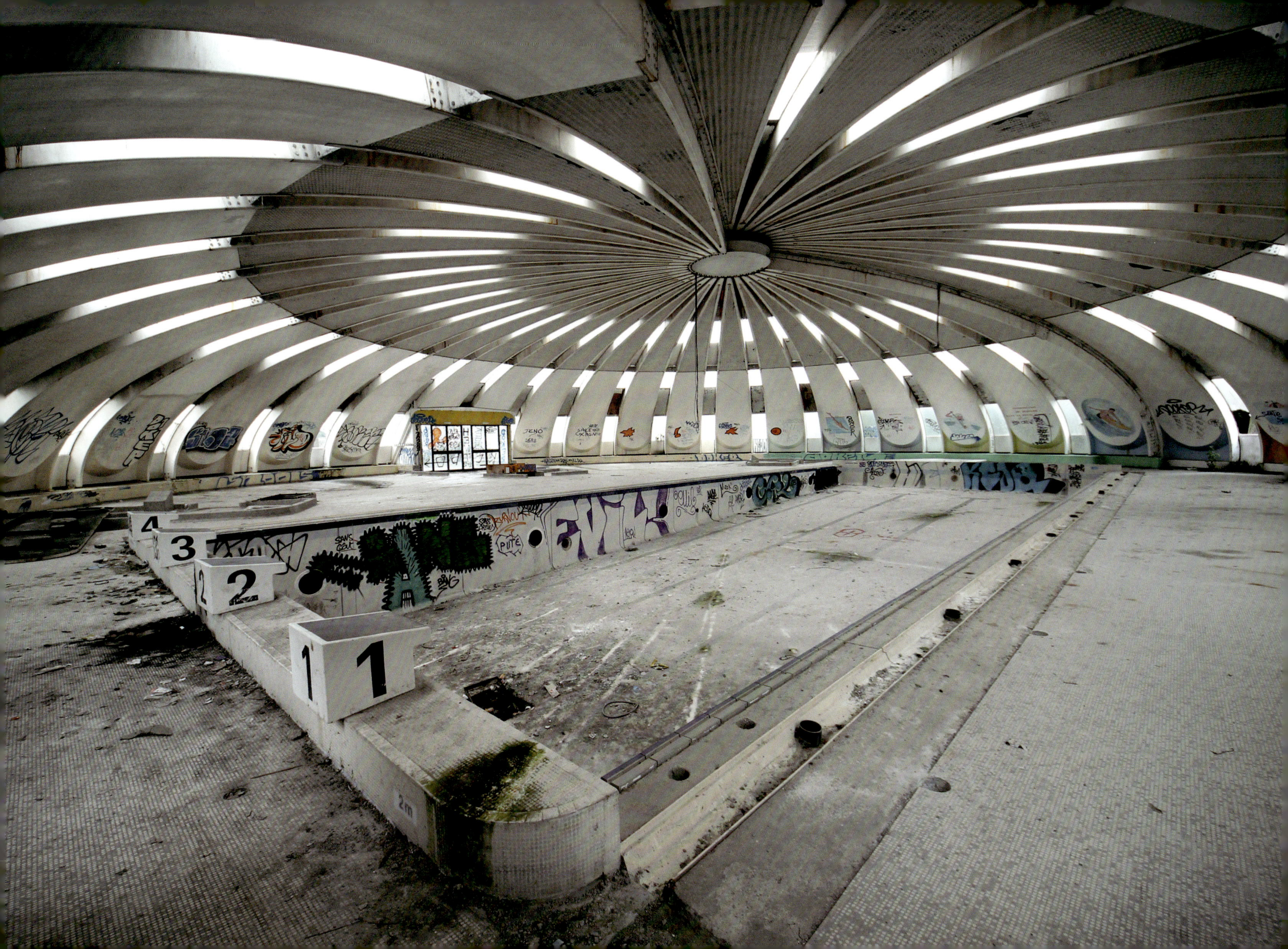
4
3
2
1
2m

The iris university • *Hauts-de-France*

As one of the three faculties of the former University of Humanities, Social Sciences and Professional Studies of Lille, the Faculty of Literature of the region of Hauts-de-France offered classes from 1970 until, one day, it stopped. Reopened in 2017, the building now belongs to Sciences Po. I was able to visit the premises before they were reopened and, like all vast public buildings in France, they are grandiose.

In the second half of the 19th century, Catholic circles in Lille were renowned for the vibrancy of their missions, including the construction of a Catholic university to resurrect an old college. The founders opted for the construction of an architectural complex in the 13th-century Gothic style, reminiscent of Anglo-Saxon buildings, in line with the creations of the time. The brilliant Louis Dutouquet, who specialised in the construction of colleges and religious buildings, contributed greatly to its beauty. The Catholics of the city were awarded the 'Cross of the Order of Pius IX' in recognition of their efforts to build the university, which opened its doors in November 1874. It first offered courses in law and, soon after, the faculties of theology, medicine, science, and literature also opened.

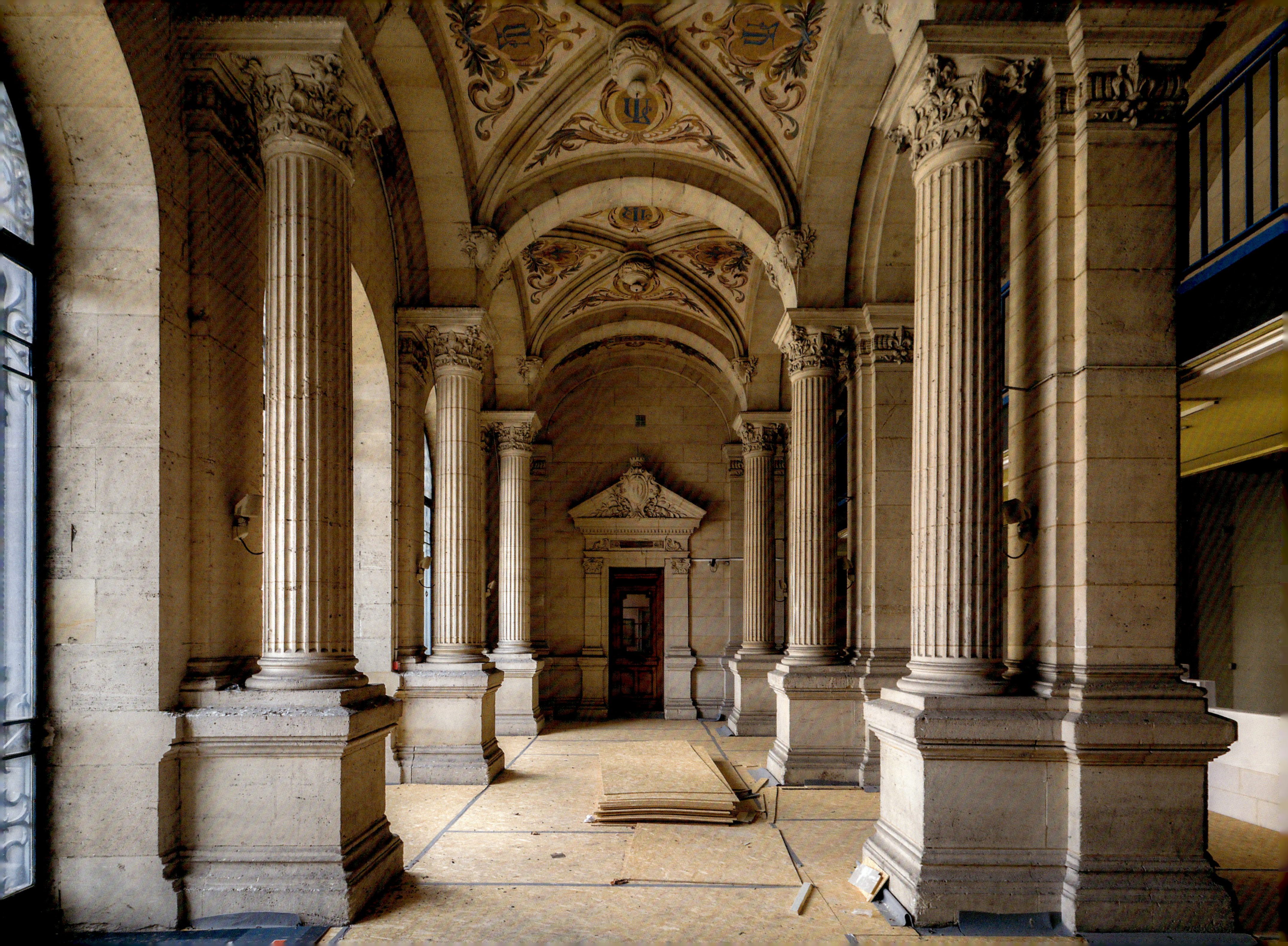

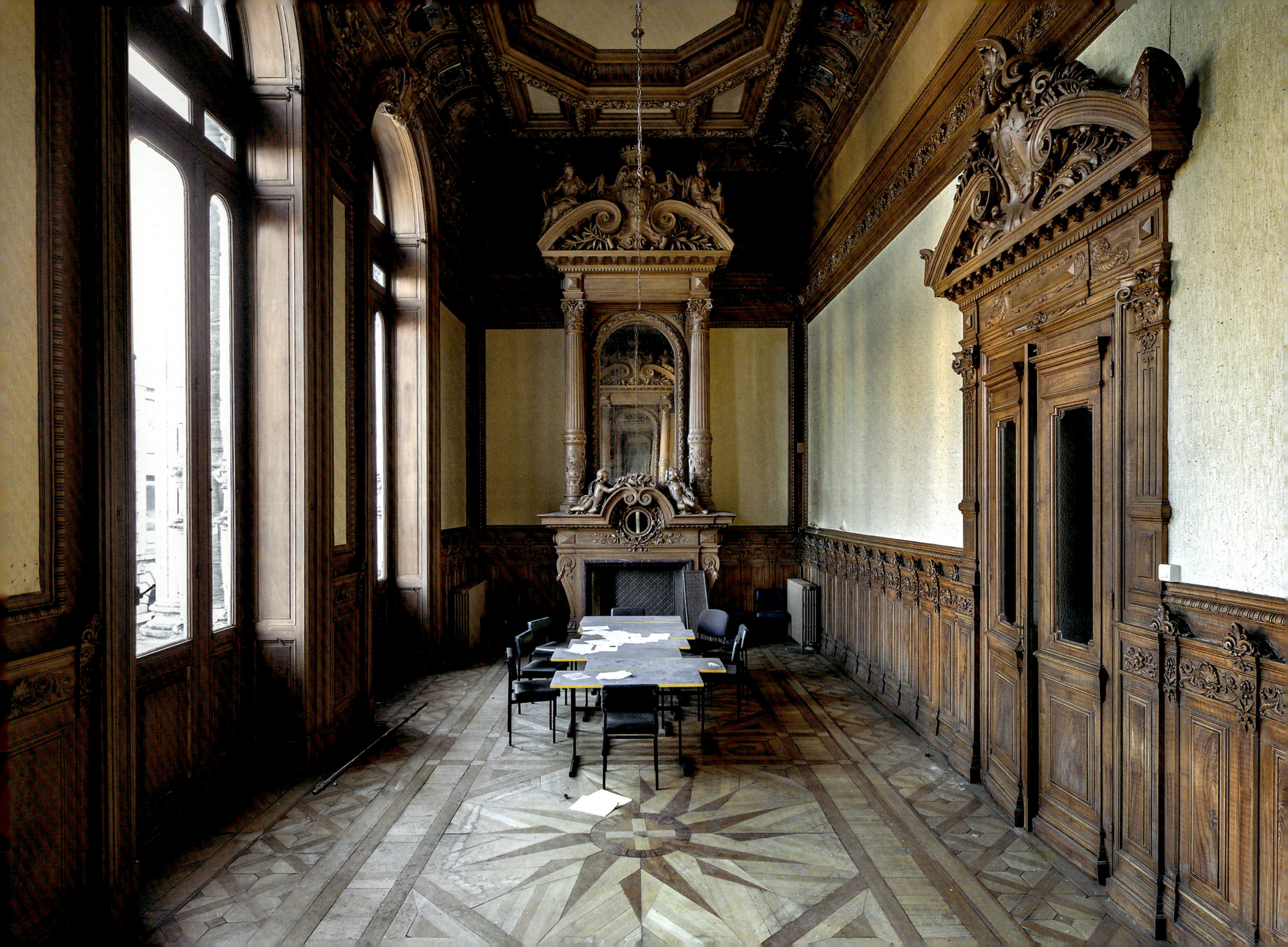

This beautiful building was built in glazed red brick and white stone. Its coat of arms represents an iris flower, not a lily, according to the wishes of Louis XIV. Cast iron pillars support the courtyard and an amphitheatre frames the back of the courtyard. I was unable to see the famous two-storey fresco of teachers, animals and textile mills established in the area, as it was protected for the refurbishment of the building.

A notable feature is the statue of Pasteur on a bluestone pedestal dating from 1895, the year of his death. He was the first dean of the Faculty of Sciences and Literature in Lille, from 1854 to 1858. A physicist, chemist by training, and pioneer in microbiology, he became world-famous for administering the first human vaccines.

With the restoration now complete, classes have resumed, and the building is teeming with students again.

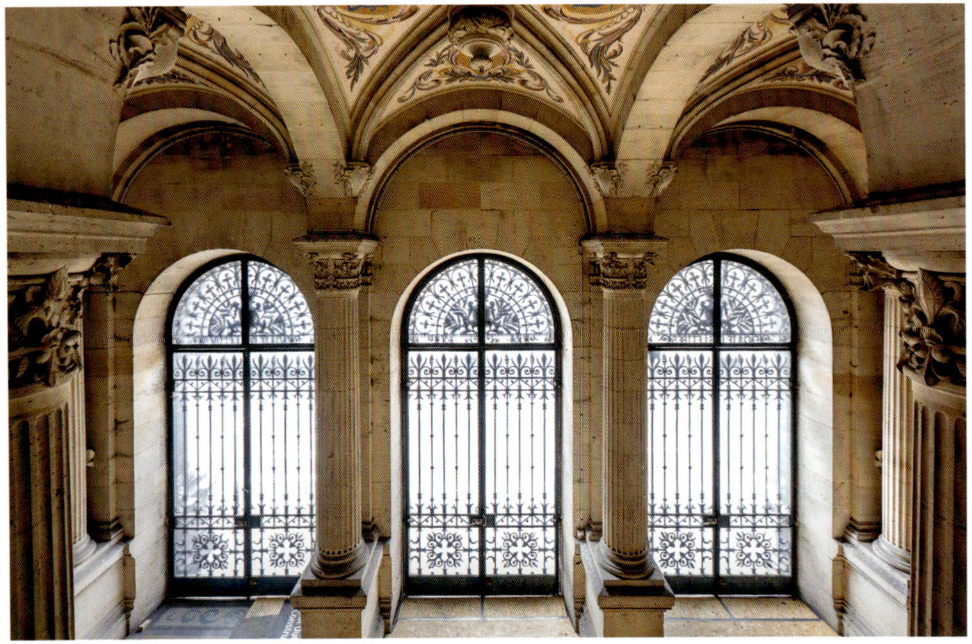

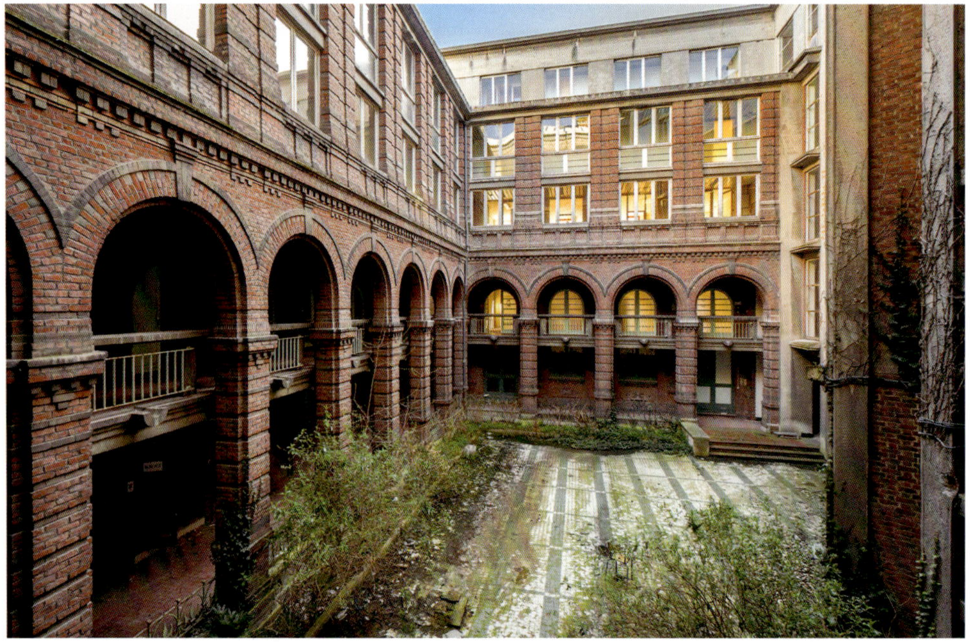

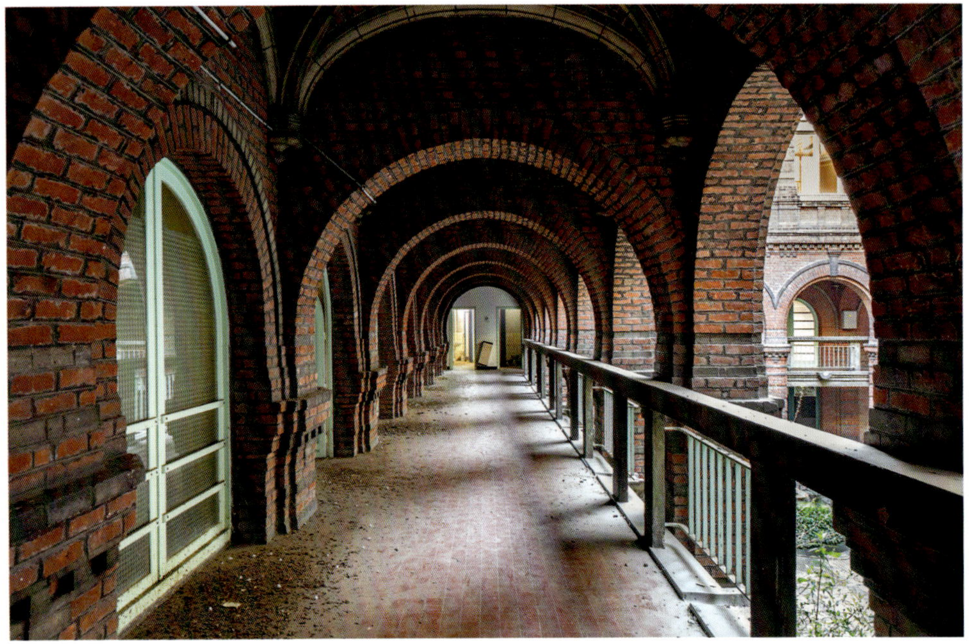

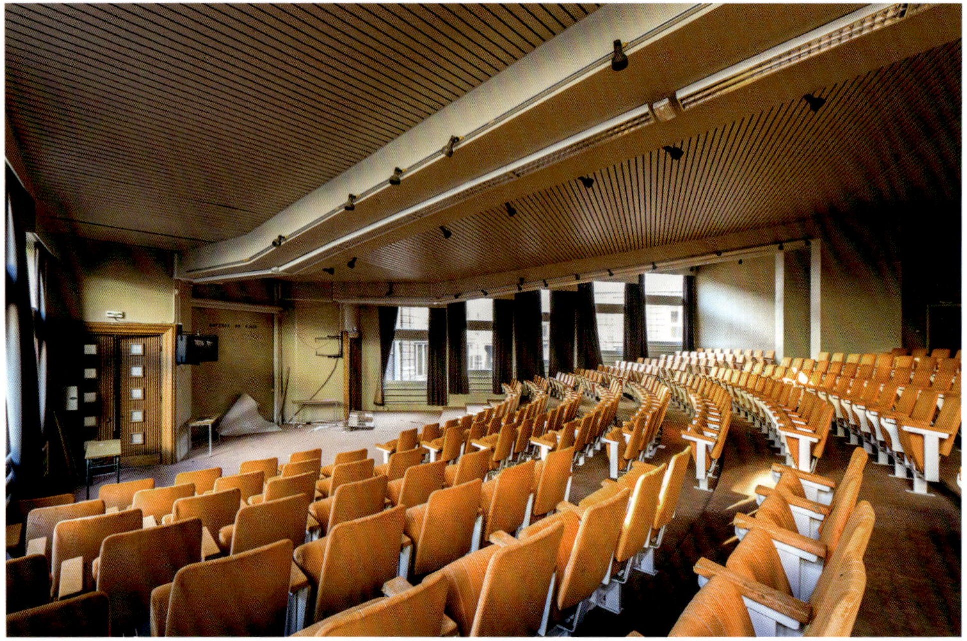

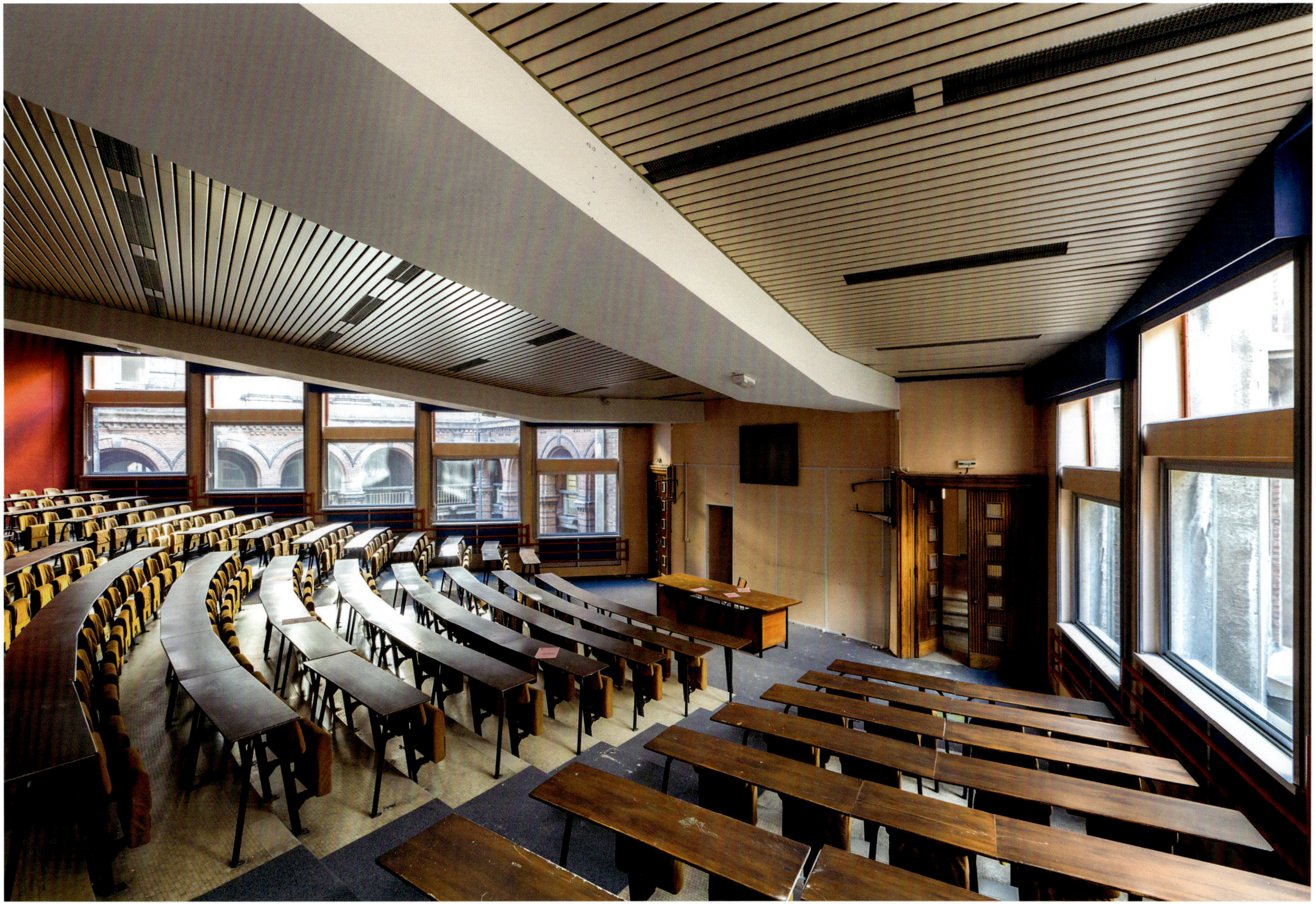

The courthouse in *Remi, Nobody's Boy* • *Hauts-de-France*

This 650-square-metre courthouse, dating from 1843 but disused since 2007 due to the building's endangered structure, has a number of historical and cultural references.

It was in this court that, in March 1898 – amid a national crisis, anarchist attacks, social strikes and the Dreyfus affair – the case of 'Louise Ménard and the Good Judge Magnard' was tried. A destitute mother and her daughter were acquitted after stealing bread from a bakery. Across France, the verdict was widely publicised, and many legal practitioners even adopted this principle of 'defence of necessity'. Located in the town where the poet and fabulist Jean de La Fontaine (1621–1695) was born, the bold building also featured in the film *Remi, Nobody's Boy*, starring French actor Daniel Auteuil.

Numerous projects, sometimes far-fetched, where considered for the courthouse, but they never came to fruition. Today, it is in the benevolent hands of Mr Brest. Passionate about music and old buildings, he has been involved in the local community for 30 years, and bought the building to restore it and dedicate it to his passion: music. The Salle des Pas Perdus, the remarkable courtroom and the council room have been preserved out of love for the place. The beautiful woodwork, the period tapestries, the ceiling roses and the furniture have also been kept in perfect condition. This building benefitted from an honourable enhancement.

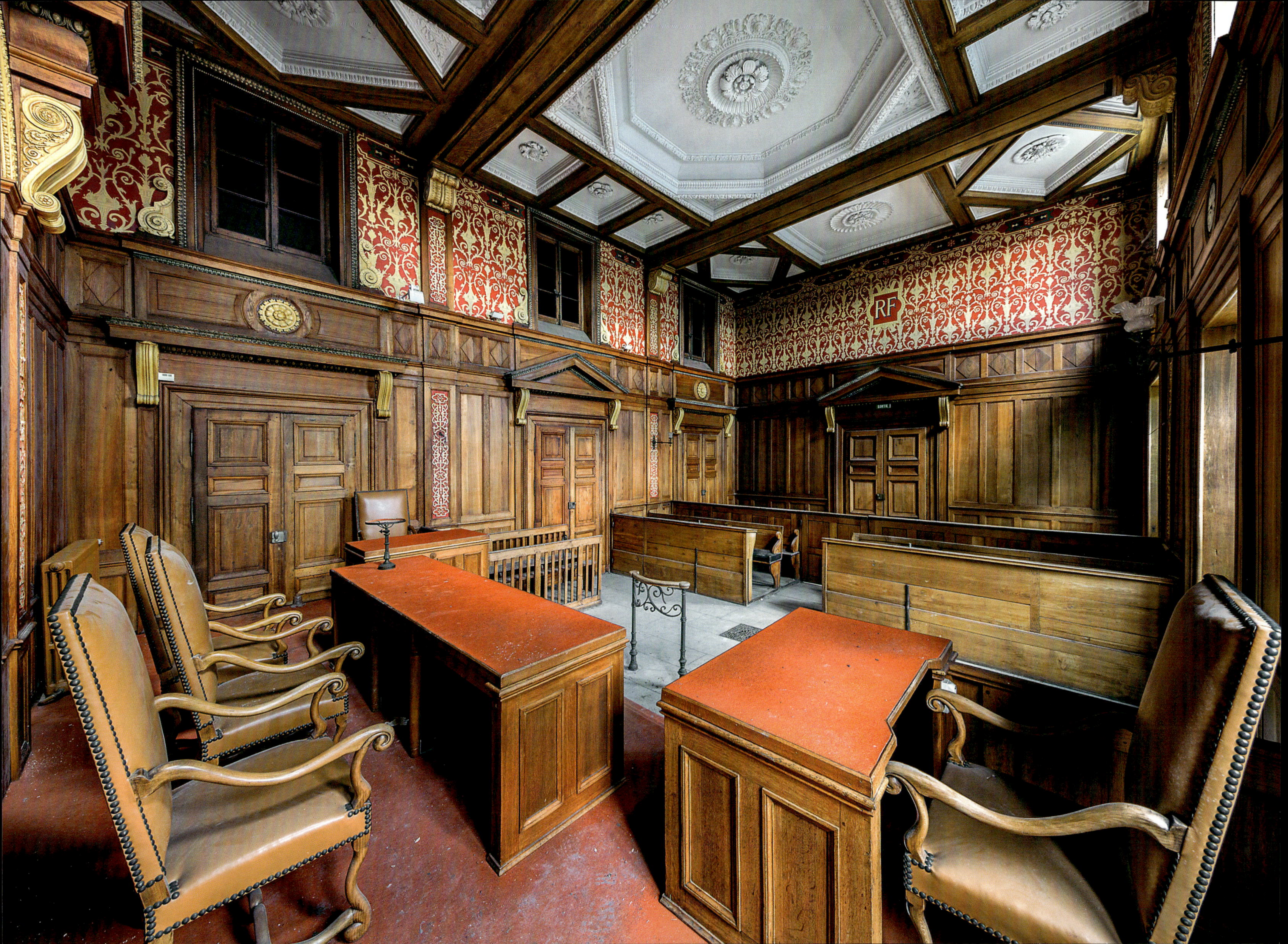
RF

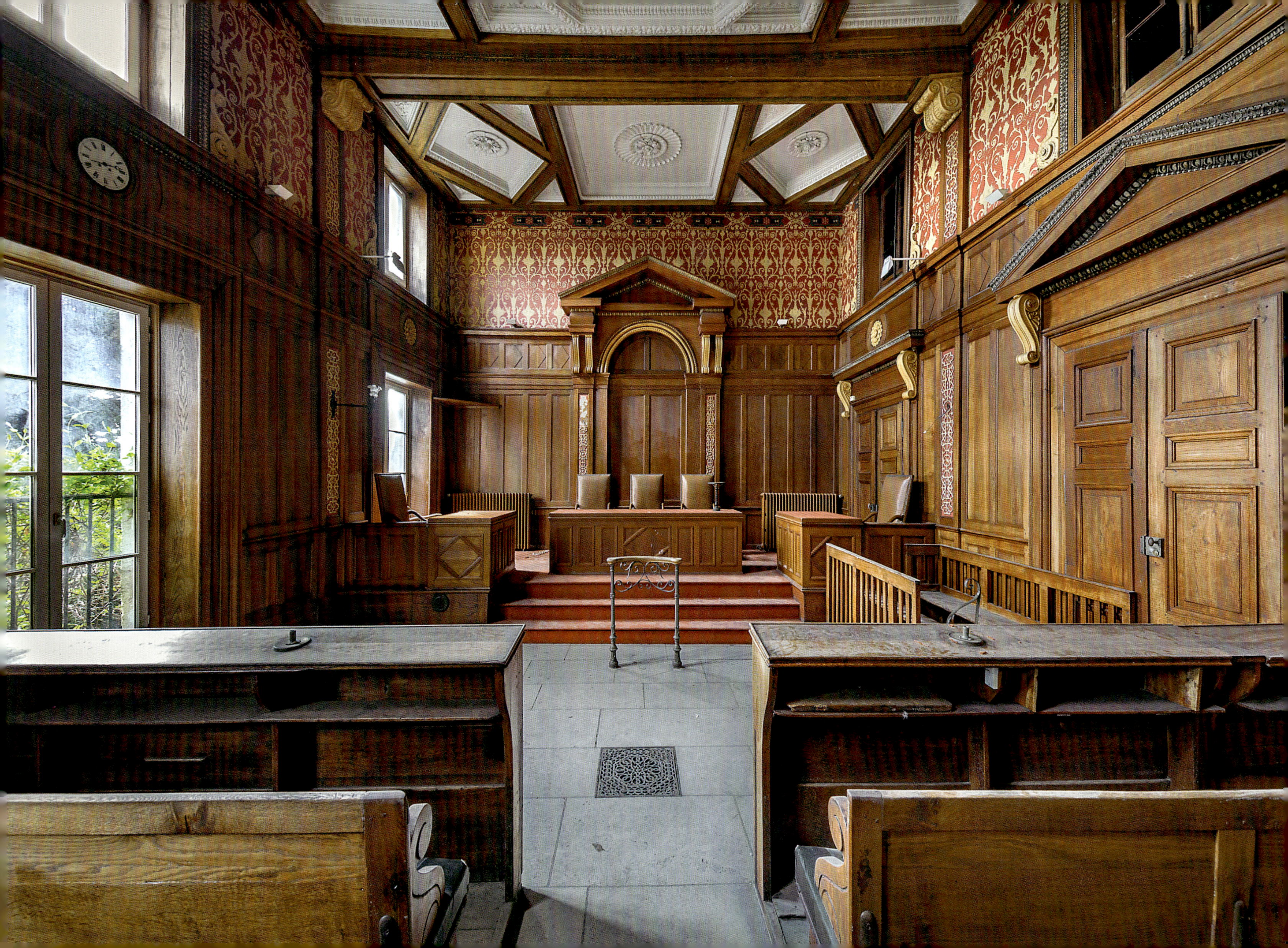

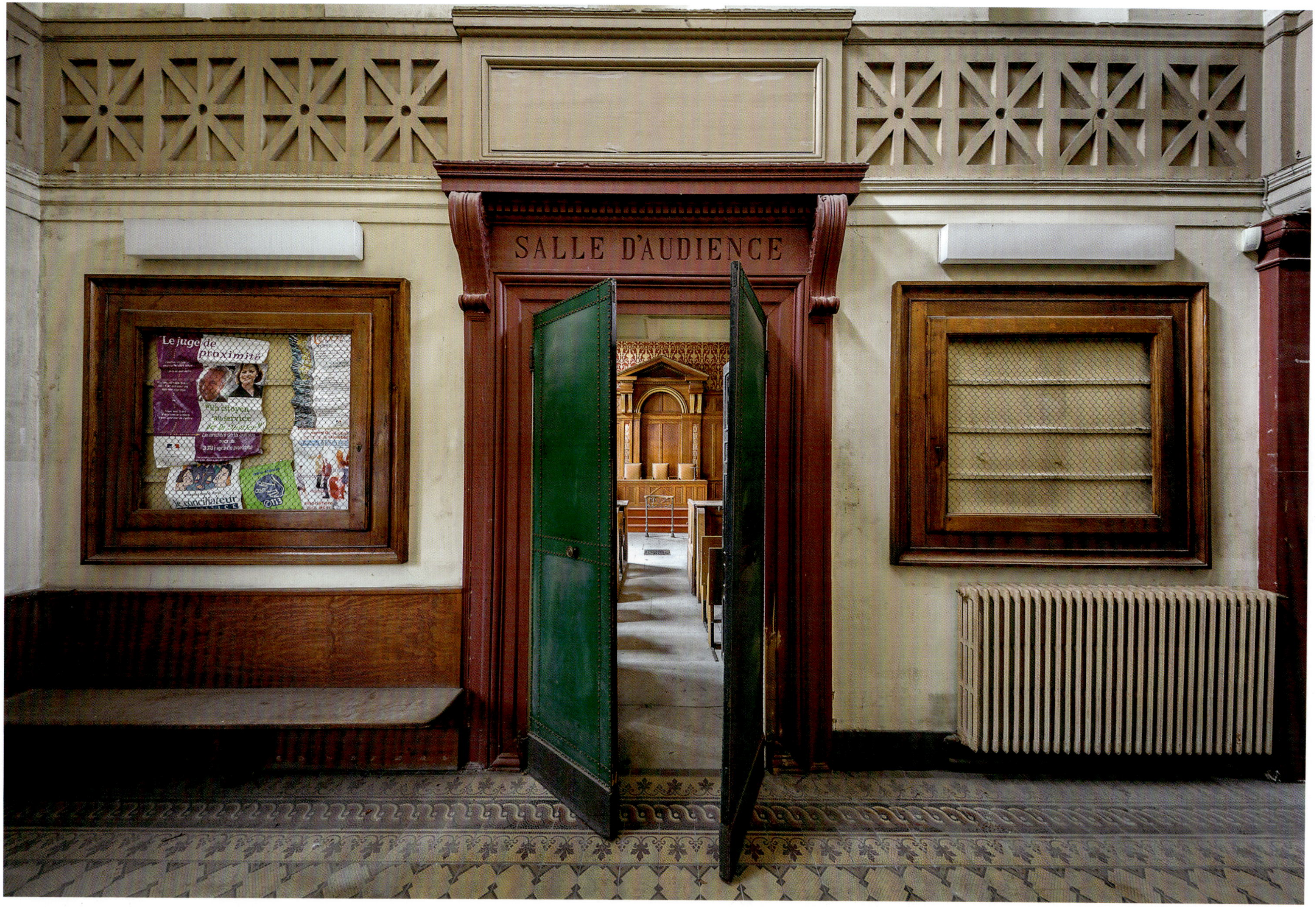
SALLE D'AUDIENCE
Le juge de proximité

Castle of kings • *Île-de-France*

The first indication that a building existed here was in 1377. However, it was not until 1504, when Cardinal Georges I of Amboise acquired the estate, that what used to be a manor house was referred to for the first time as a 'château'. This beautiful building belonged to the greatest families of France, notably the families of Amboise, Montmorency and Rohan, who came here to relax, far from religious and political affairs. The chateau also attracted many illustrious statesmen, including Henri II, Louis XIII, Richelieu and Adolphe Tiers.

After suffering from the ravages of time, it was rebuilt in 1867 in the troubadour style, which remains one of the reasons for its long-standing popularity. More recently, the site was used as a location for several films that are emblematic of the history of French cinema. Among others, *The Great Spy Chase* was almost entirely filmed there, as was the farcical *The Seventh Company Has Been Found* and *The Visitors*, with Jean Réno and Christian Clavier.

The castle and the dozen outbuildings, as well as the unique greenhouses, have been listed as historic monuments by decree since 1984. The interior has an extraordinary atmosphere, full of history and memories. You almost expect to see illustrious people walking through the rooms in period dress. The castle is built on a rectangular island, surrounded by a moat. Unlike the original arrangement where water flowed directly to the foot of the building, a flowerbed now surrounds it. Two bridges connect it to the rest of the estate, with the first squarely facing the forecourt and leading to the main courtyard. The second bridge, in the corner of the island, provides a path to the gardens to the south of the estate. Unfortunately, the foreign group that owns the building has left the estate untended for 15 years now, and a most unwelcome guest has moved in: mould. Although the external shell does not show any signs, the building is in ruins. This remarkable place requires urgent preservation measures.

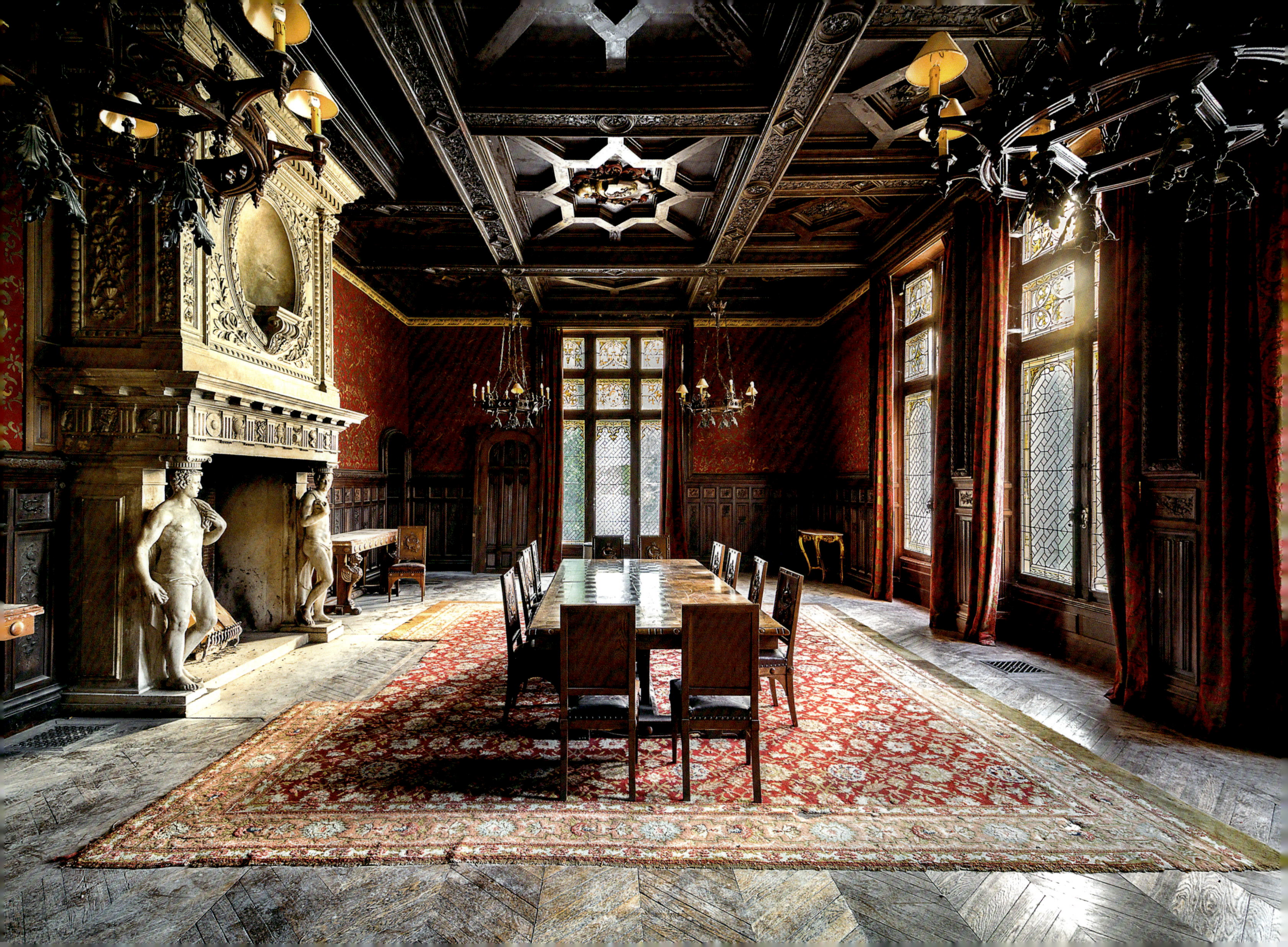

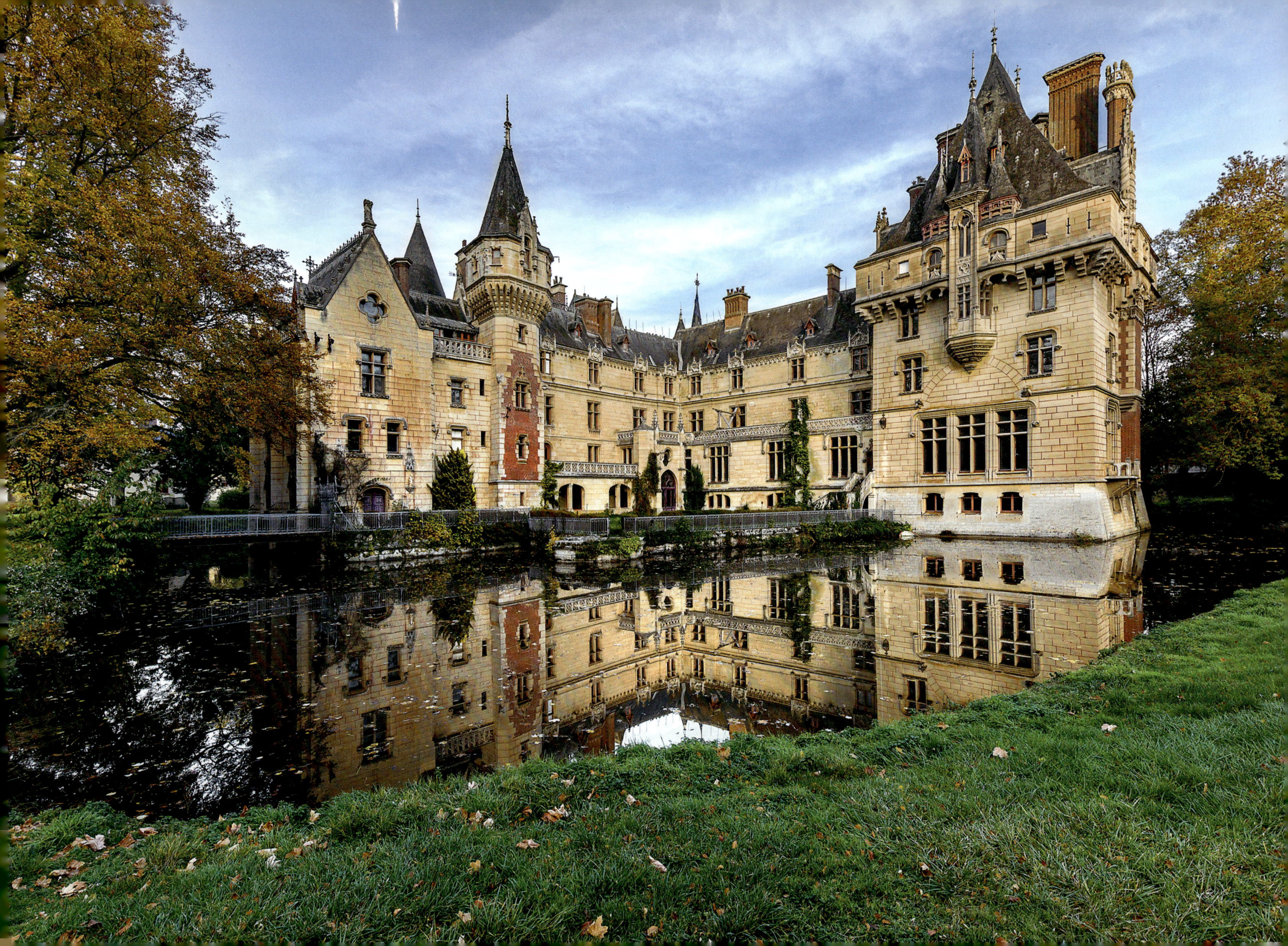

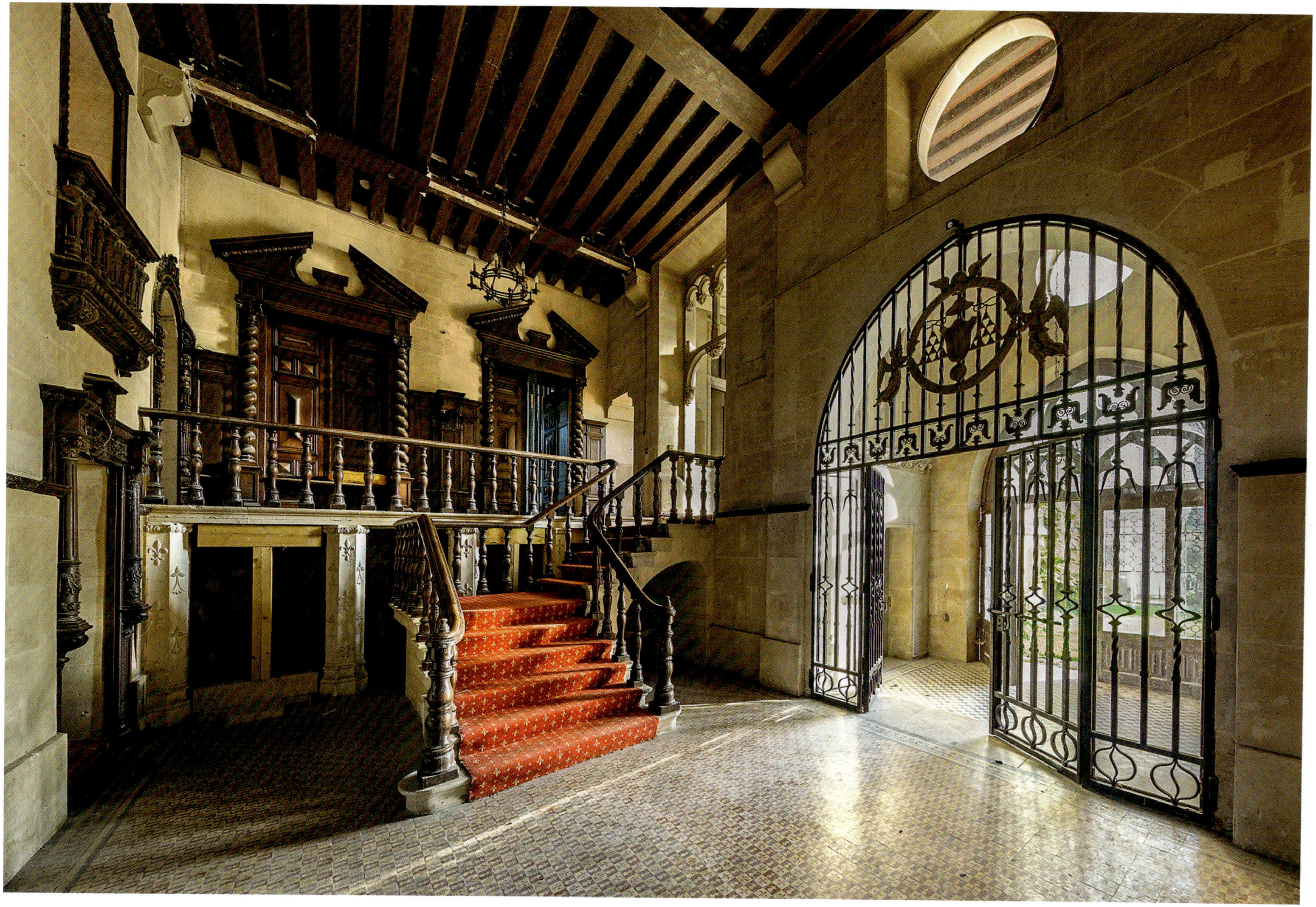

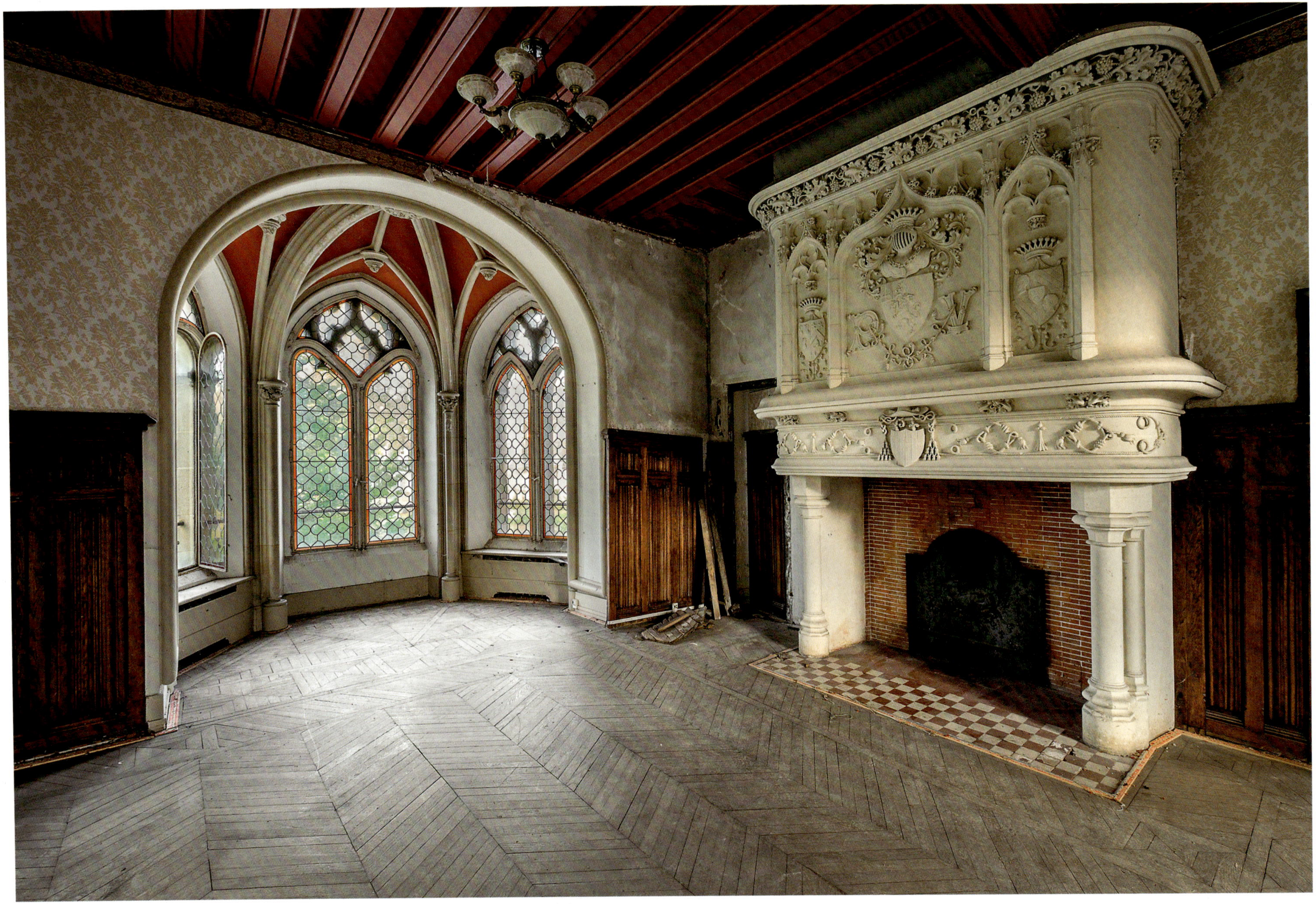

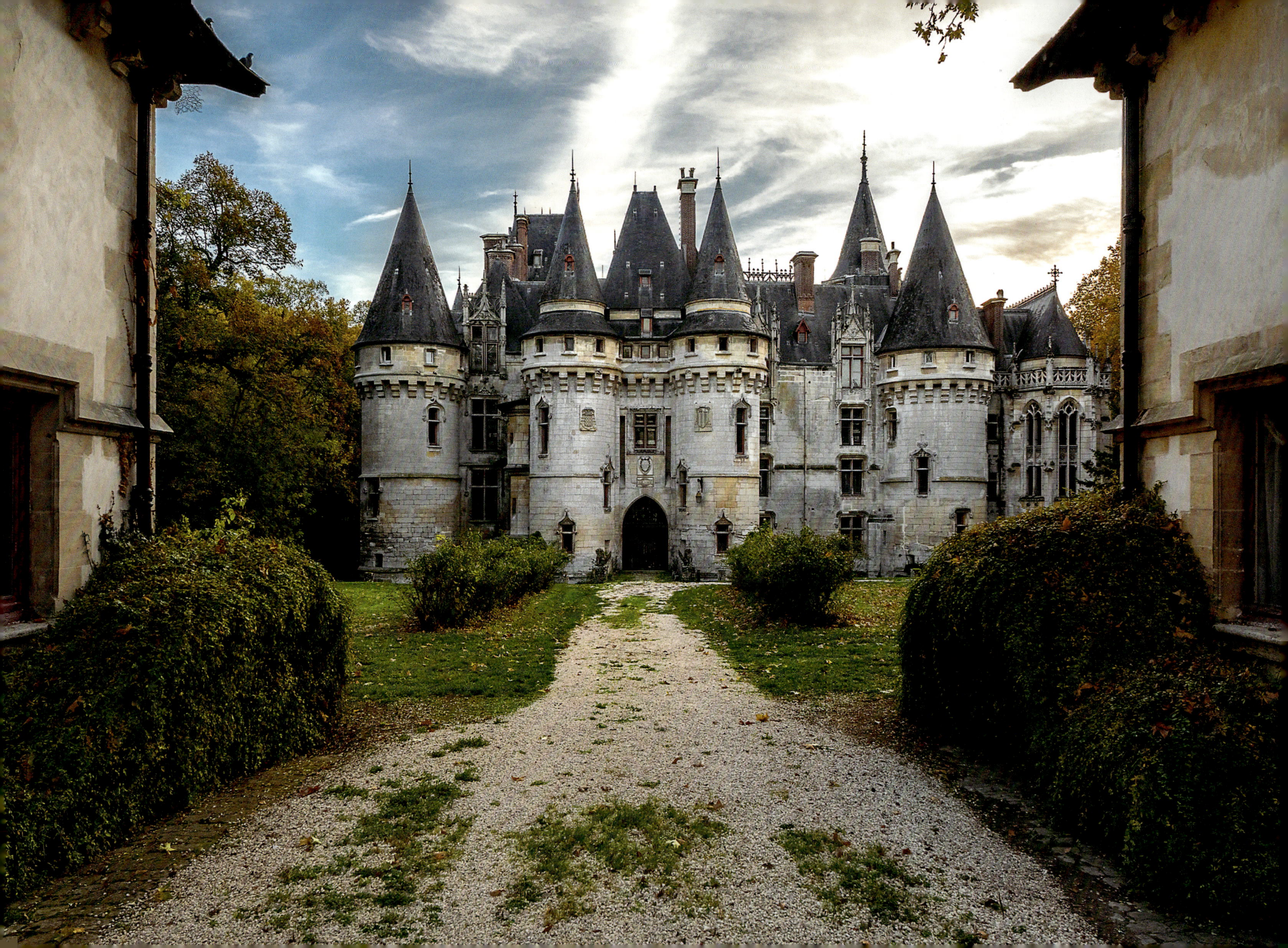

Marlinspike hall • *Île-de-France*

From its central position in a vast wooded park of 40 hectares, this majestic residence, built in the 19th century in the Louis XIII style, was for a time the home of the French School for Fire Service Officers. It remained the property of the Ministry of the Interior until 2007, and I was lucky enough to visit the chateau long before it was reassigned. With its black and white chequered floor tiles and monumental marble staircase that leads up to a gallery with wrought iron balustrades worked in bronze, the entrance is radiant. On the upper storeys, the floors and ceilings are made of inlaid wood, whose honey-coloured hue gives a warm atmosphere.

The residence was bought by enthusiasts in 2019 for more than three million euros. The new buyers, who are passionate about France's artistic and cultural heritage, spent all their weekends, public holidays and many hours after work during the week cleaning the building, clearing the estate and on major work to restore the chateau to its former glory. The estate is now a prestigious place, ideal for company receptions, weddings and other ceremonies.

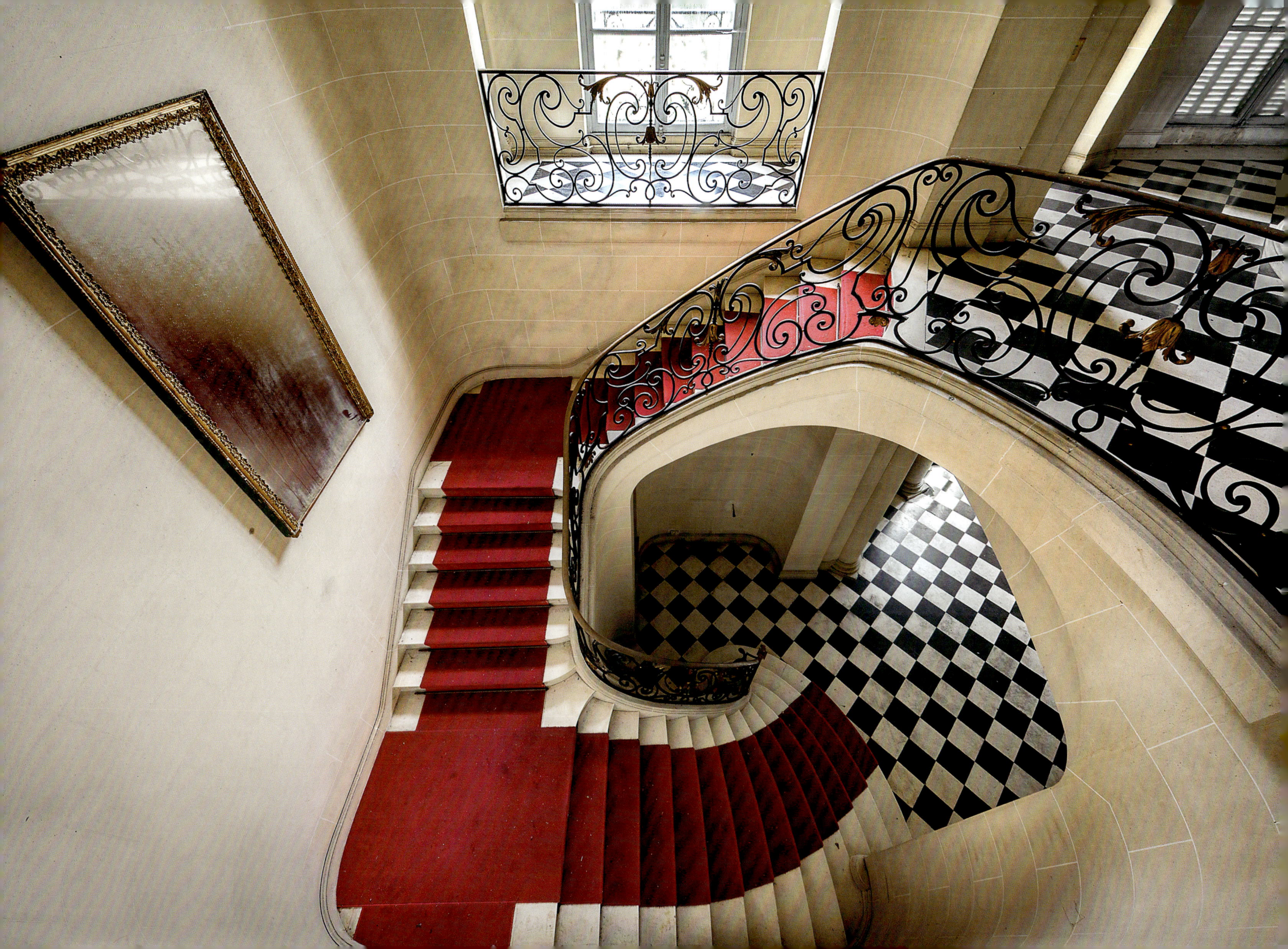

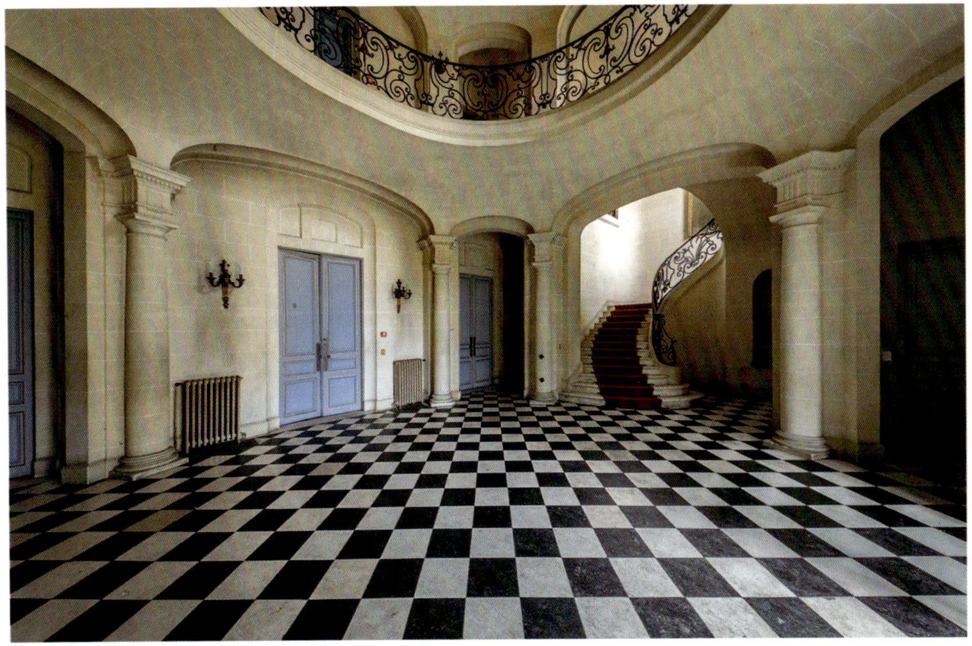

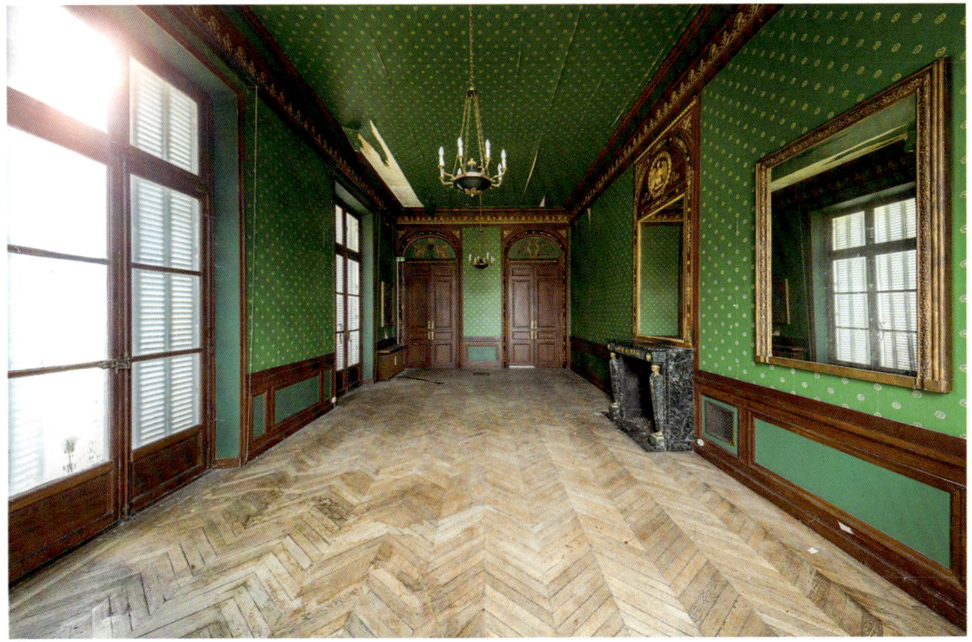

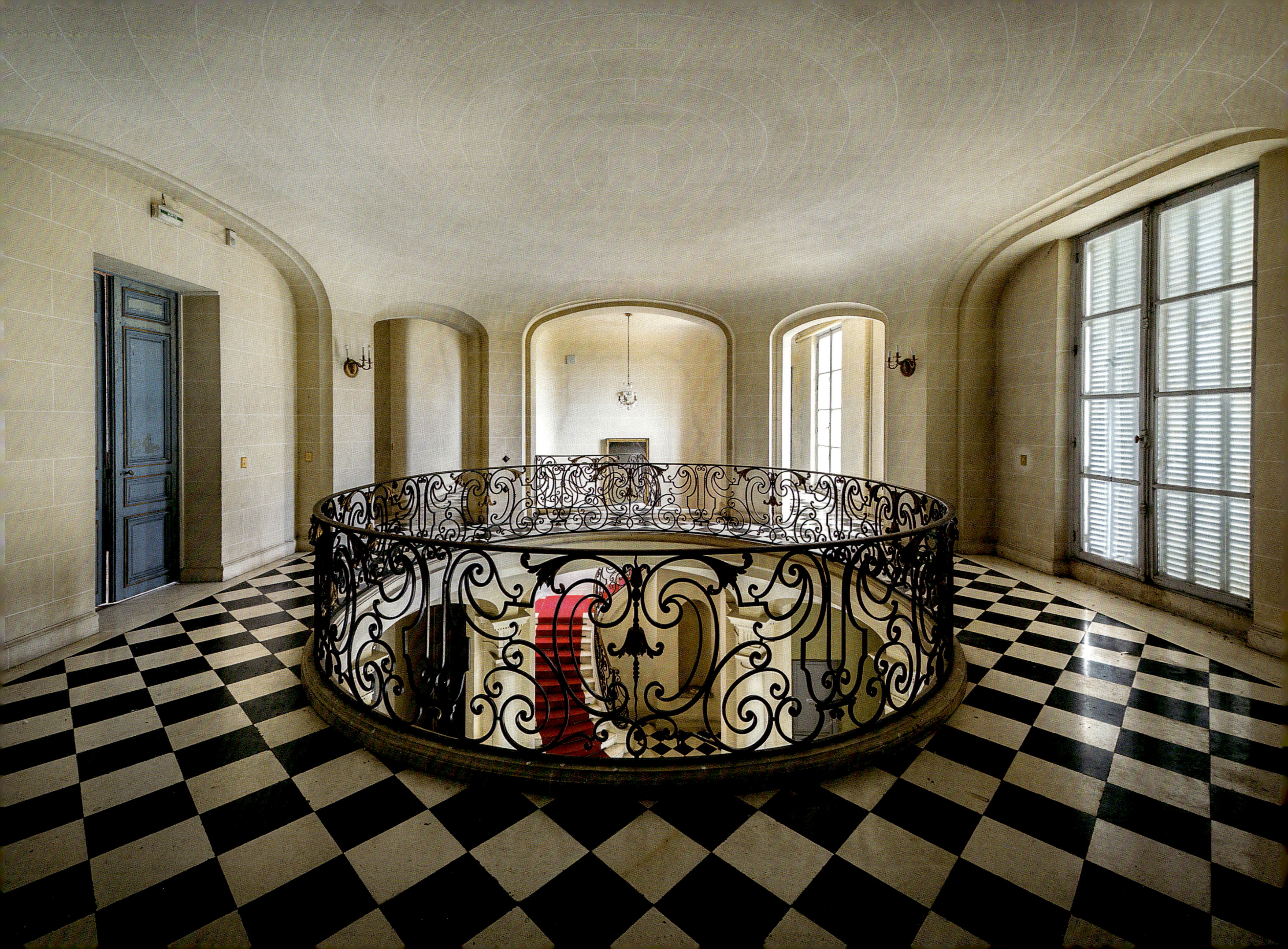

The Cluedo castle • *Île-de-France*

In the 5th century, the Franks founded numerous estates in this region. Traces of several ancient roads and buildings have been unearthed in this hamlet, which dates to the 13th century. In 1760, a large castle was built on the site of an old manor house called *La maison du chemin* (the house on the path), according to the plans of the architect Saget des Louvières. A viscount and several local lords succeeded one another there.

This long and imposing building has one floor and an attic. Surprise awaits as you enter. The decoration of the castle, which has a certain class, is particularly heterogeneous: the walls are covered with a multitude of paintings, grandiose murals grace the walls, imposing mirrors reflect the space, large stuffed birds are placed on the fireplaces and objects appear to have been haphazardly abandoned. The living room is particularly eye-catching. The last owner enjoyed painting on canvas, and dozens of sketches and drafts litter the floor of his studio, with his most successful paintings hung in the various rooms.

No one lives here any more. When I visited, the letterbox was overflowing with mail and a notice of seizure was affixed to the perimeter wall around the house. As I write these lines, the big house has, however, been partly restored and a reception room hosts banquets to raise funds to restore it. For this little gem of a building, this is great news.

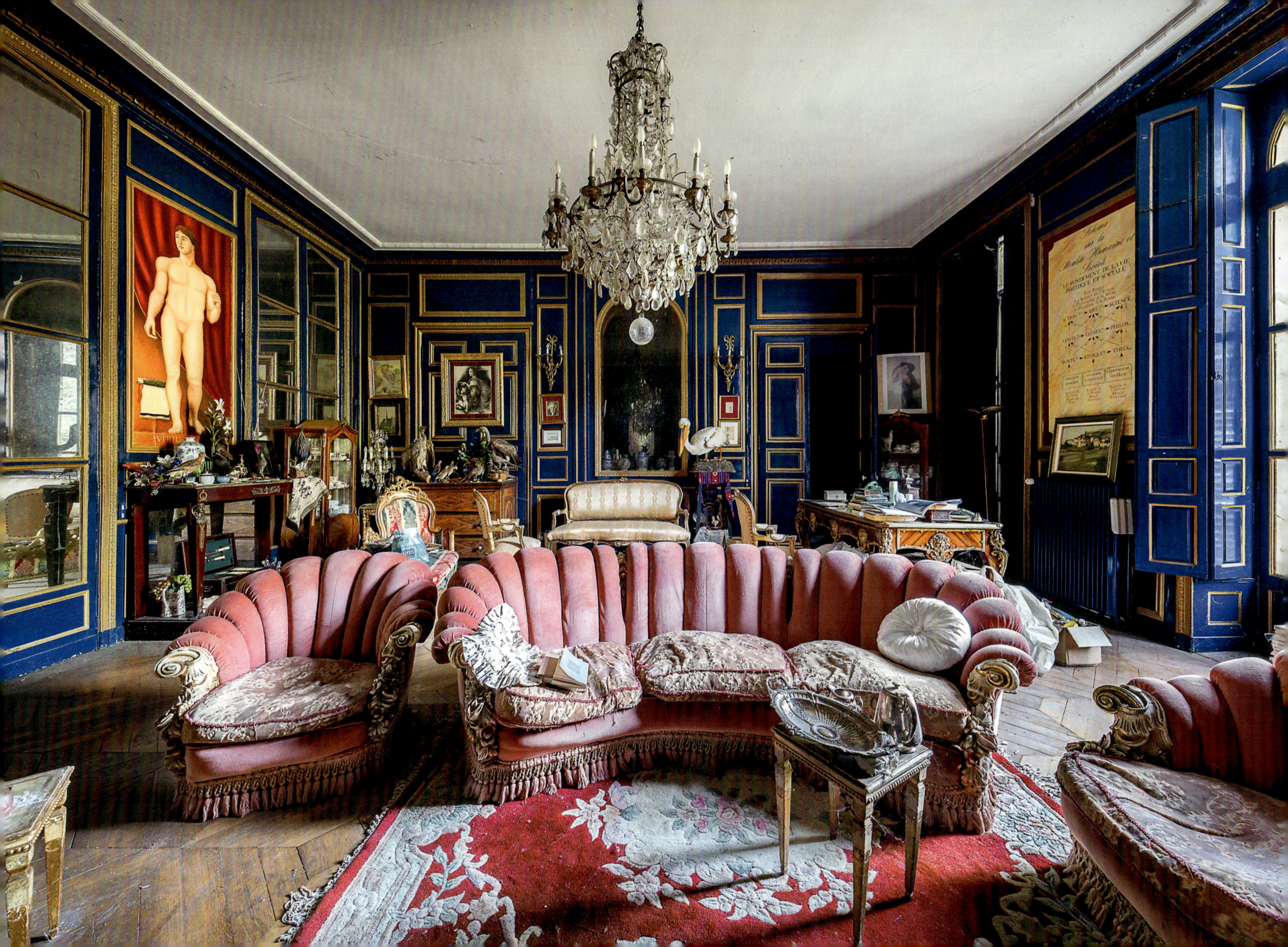
LE FONDEMENT DE LA VIE
PSYCHIQUE ET SOCIALE
ART
SCIENCE
PHILOS.
THEOL.
ETHIQUE

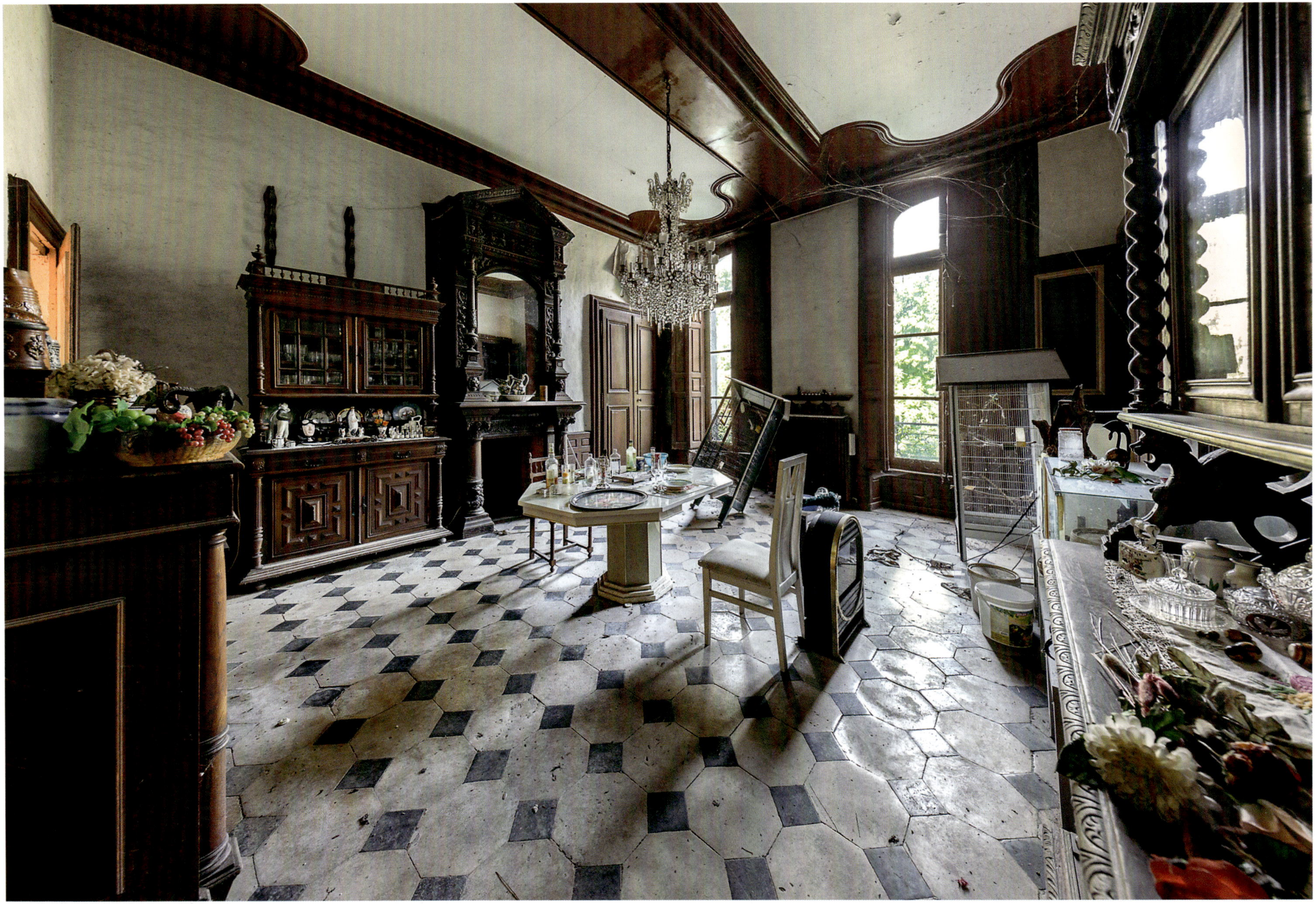

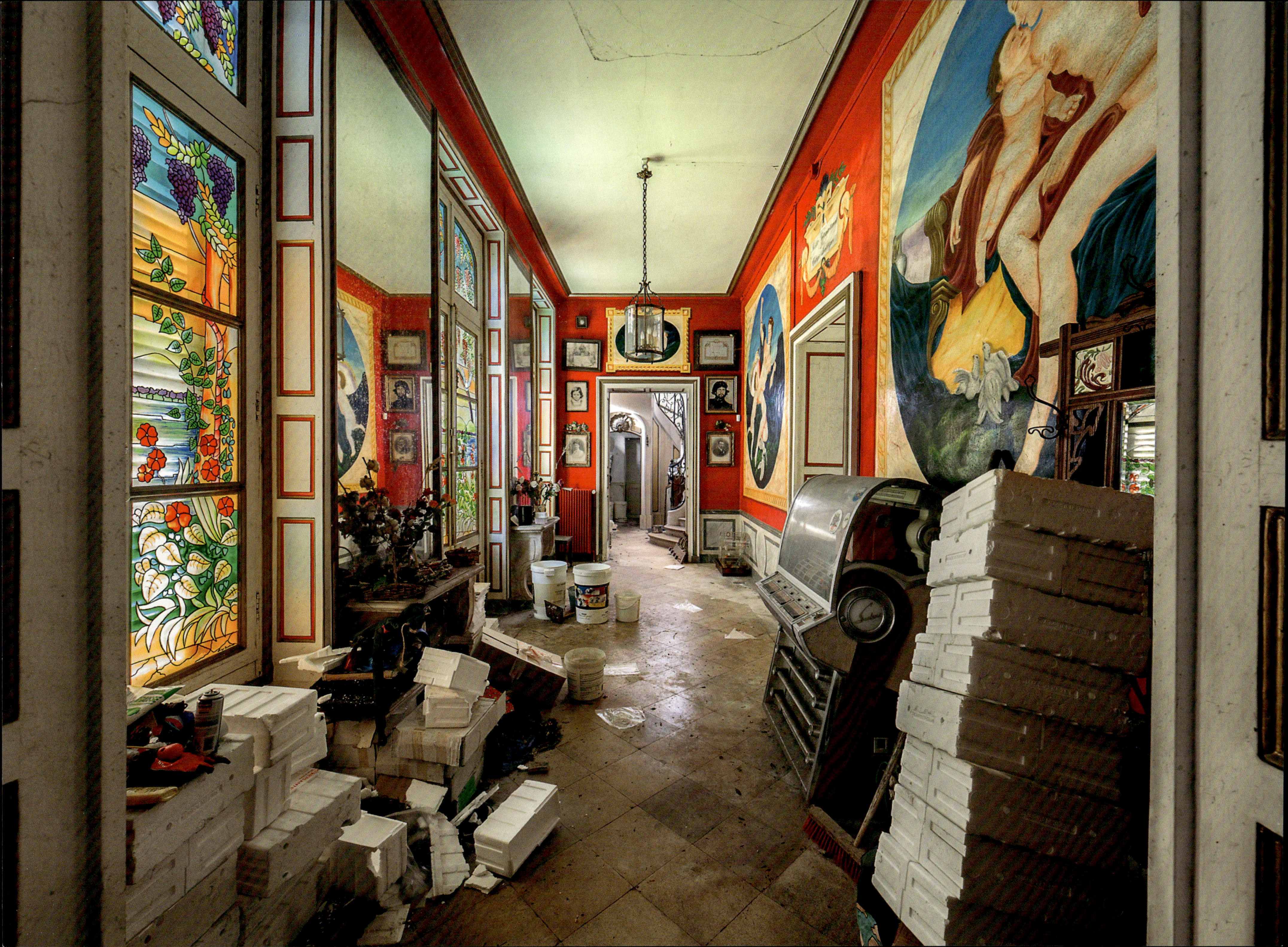

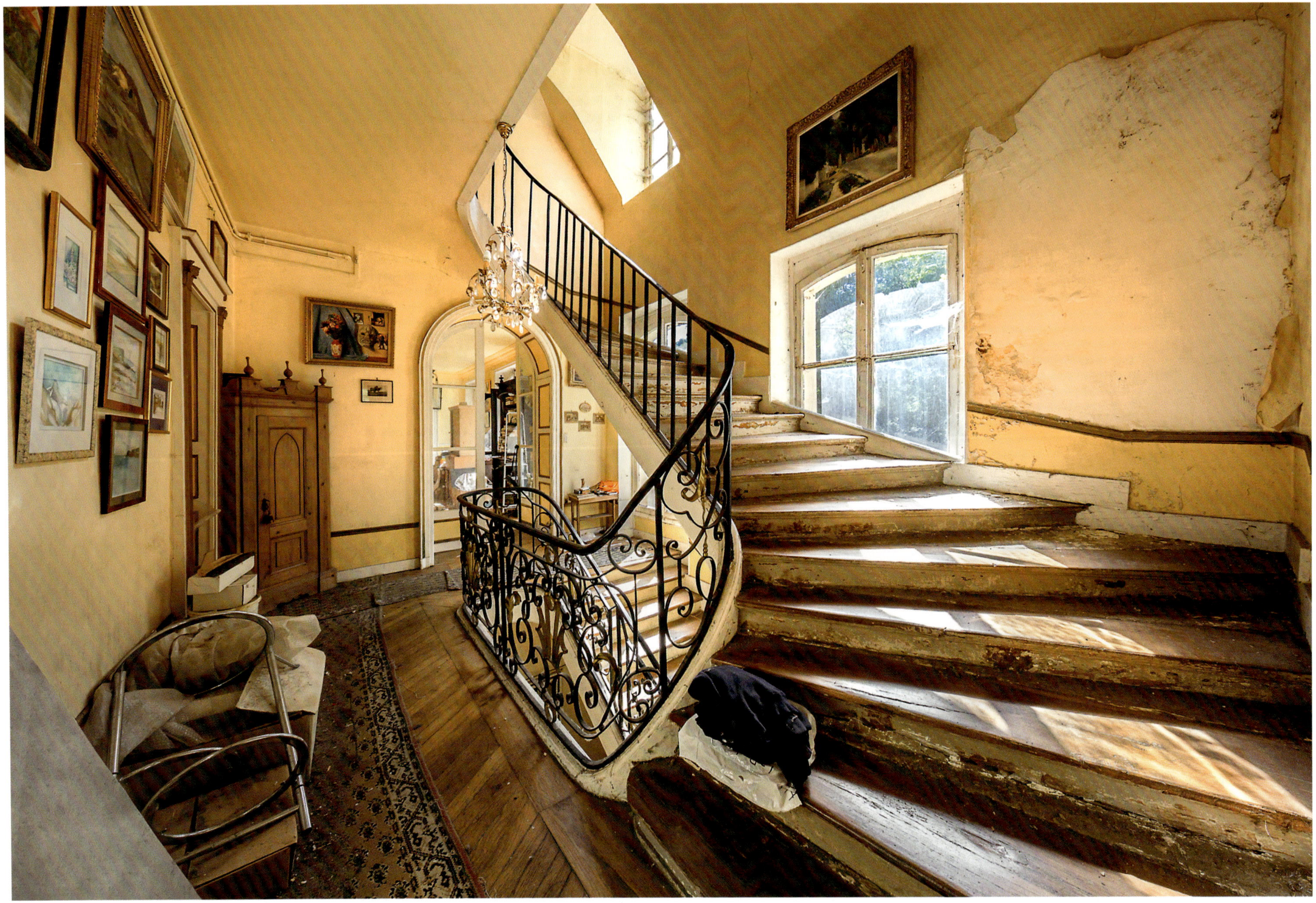

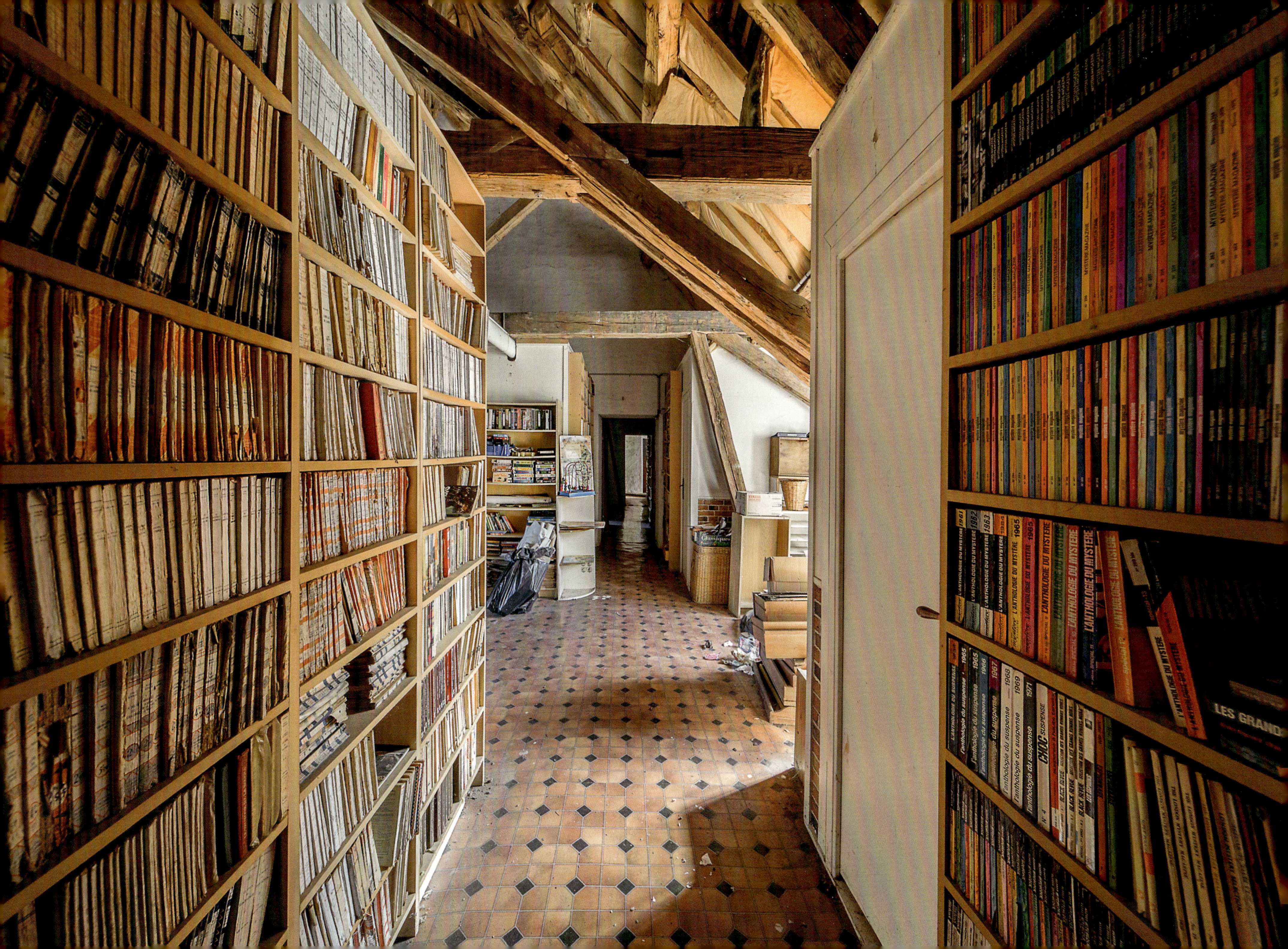
L'ANTHOLOGIE DU MYSTÈRE
l'anthologie du suspense
CHOC SUSPENSE

A flourishing castle • *Île-de-France*

Hidden behind a high wall in an affluent French suburb, this small castle was probably built in the 1930s. It appears to have been forgotten by everyone since the 1990s and is now slowly crumbling and deteriorating amid its lush green surroundings.

The main attraction is the castle's entrance hall, where a dusty old grand piano sits in an alcove under the grand stone staircase. The chandelier has lost its shine and the paint has peeled off after years of neglect, but the sunrays peeking through the set of double-leaf windows cast a beautiful, subtle light on its keys. From the first-floor landing, the view of the instrument is superb, and is set against the black and white chequered floor of the hall and accompanied by the delicately curved silhouette of the wrought iron staircase banister. Rough scaffolding and wooden braces support what is left of the upper floor. Apart from two chairs and tattered curtains, there is no furniture left here. Ceilings have collapsed, rubble is piling up in some rooms, and pigeons have taken over the turrets, so the floor looks like a chicken coop that has never been cleaned.

There have been a few attempts to save it in the past, but it seems to have been abandoned for good. Until the day this beautiful place eventually succumbs to the ravages of time, the only residents will be the pigeons that have made the castle their home.

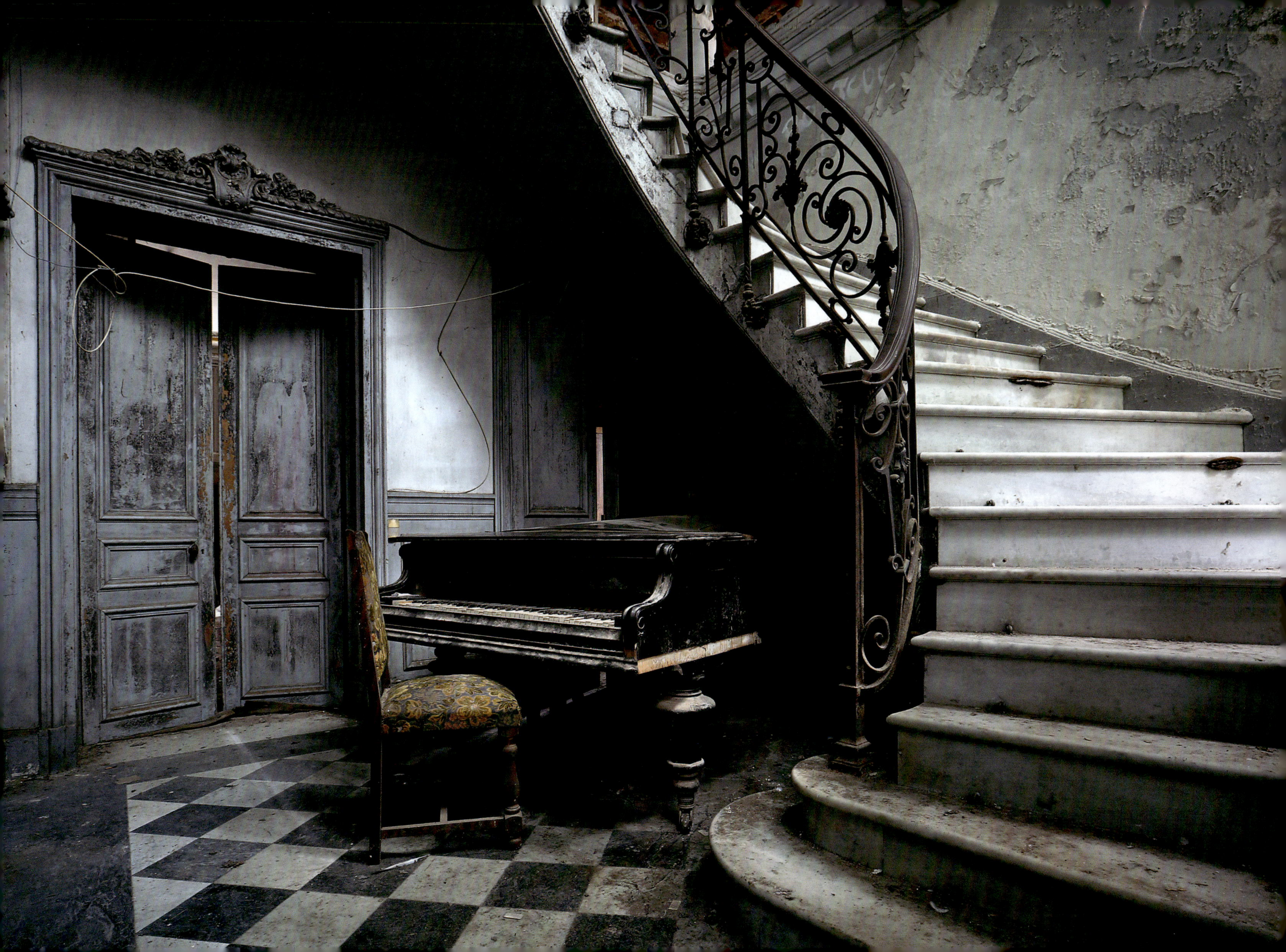

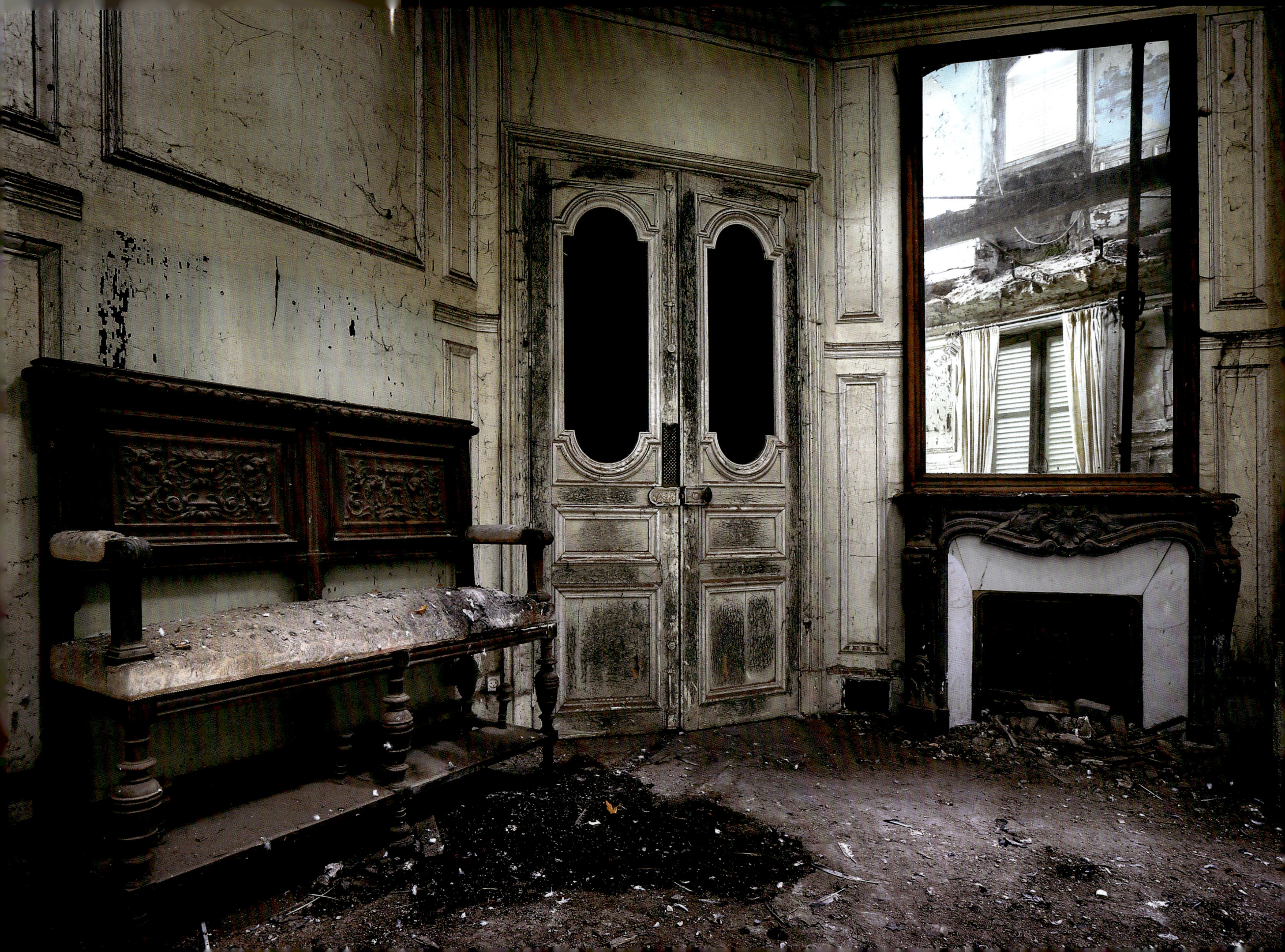

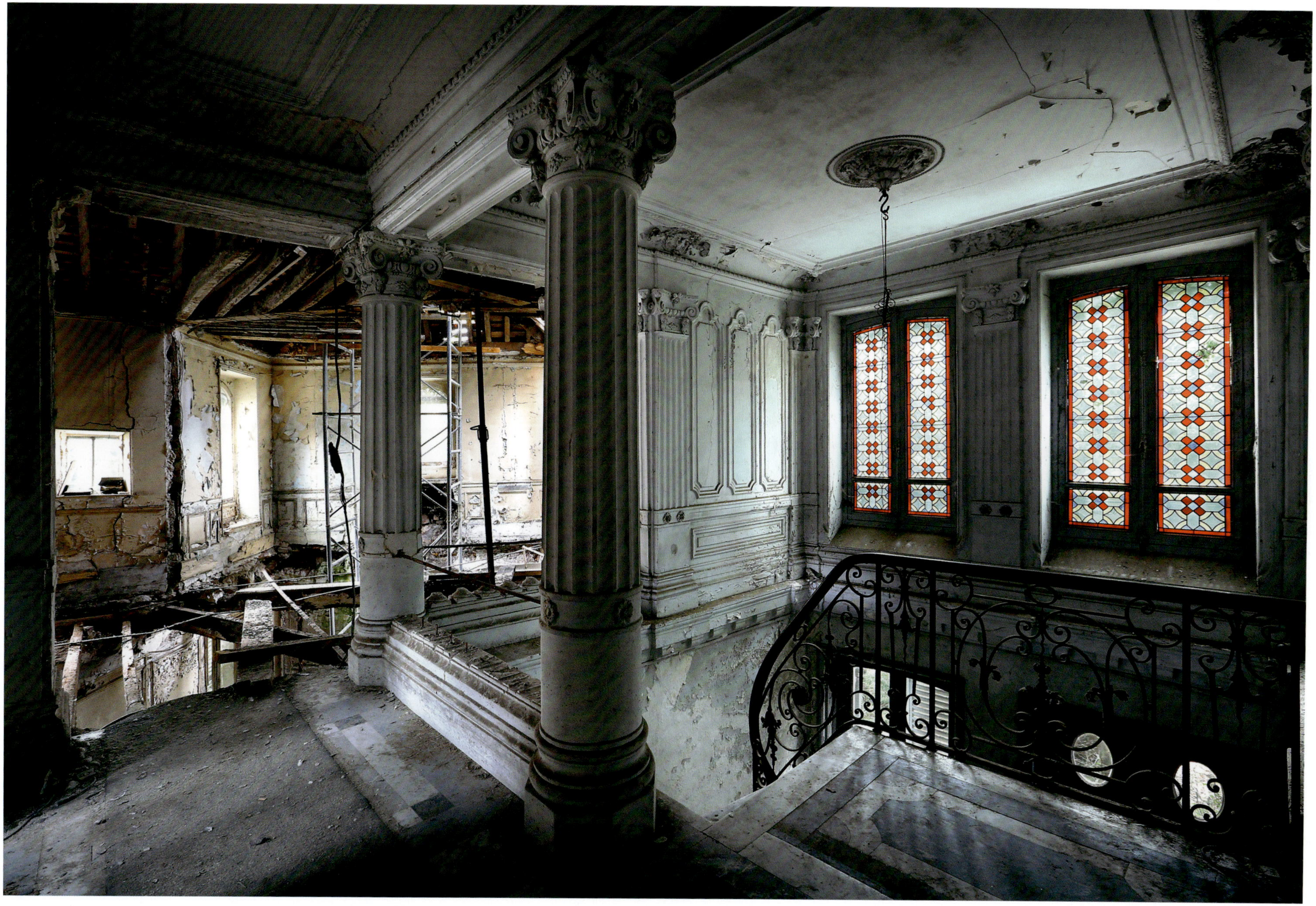

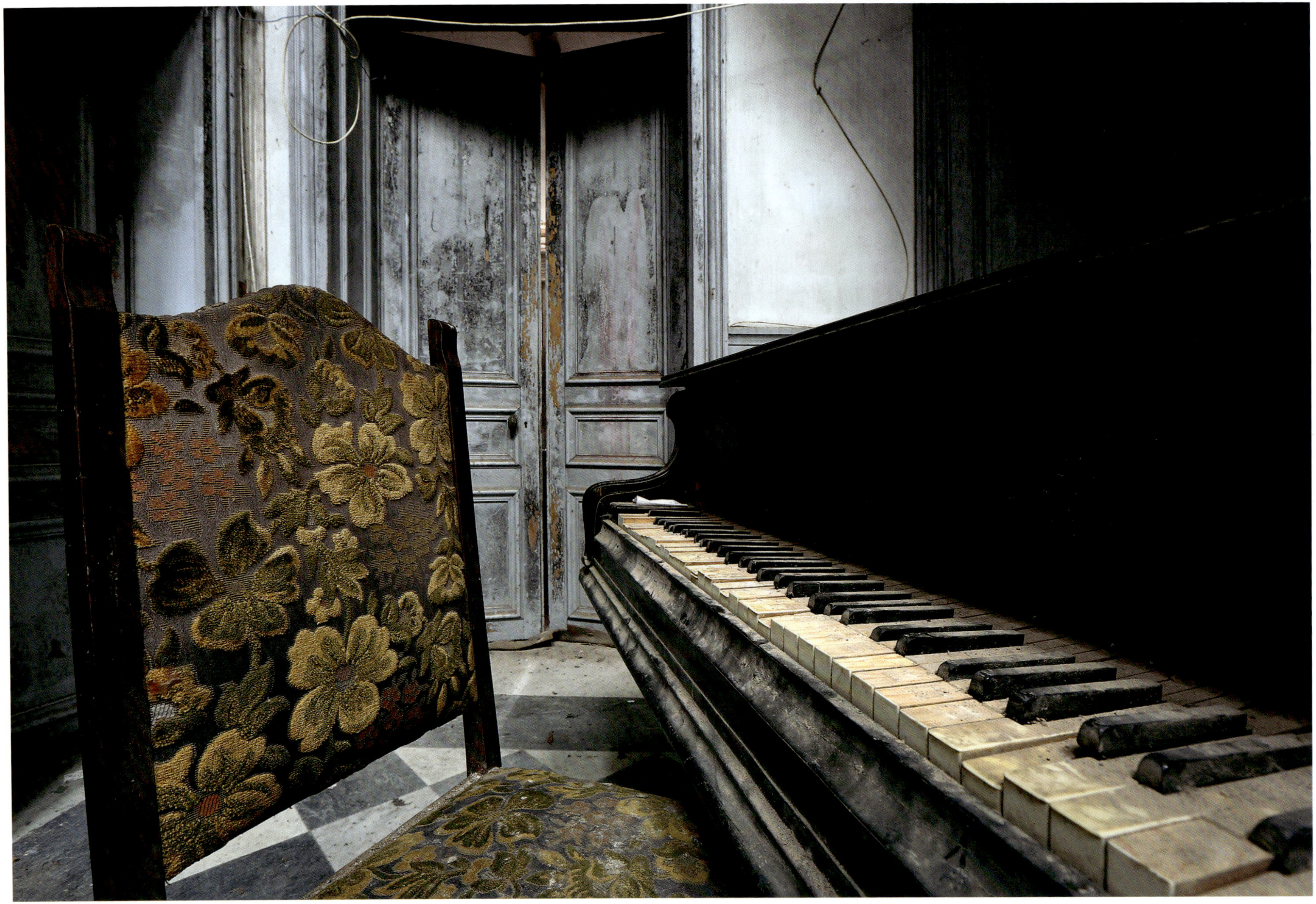

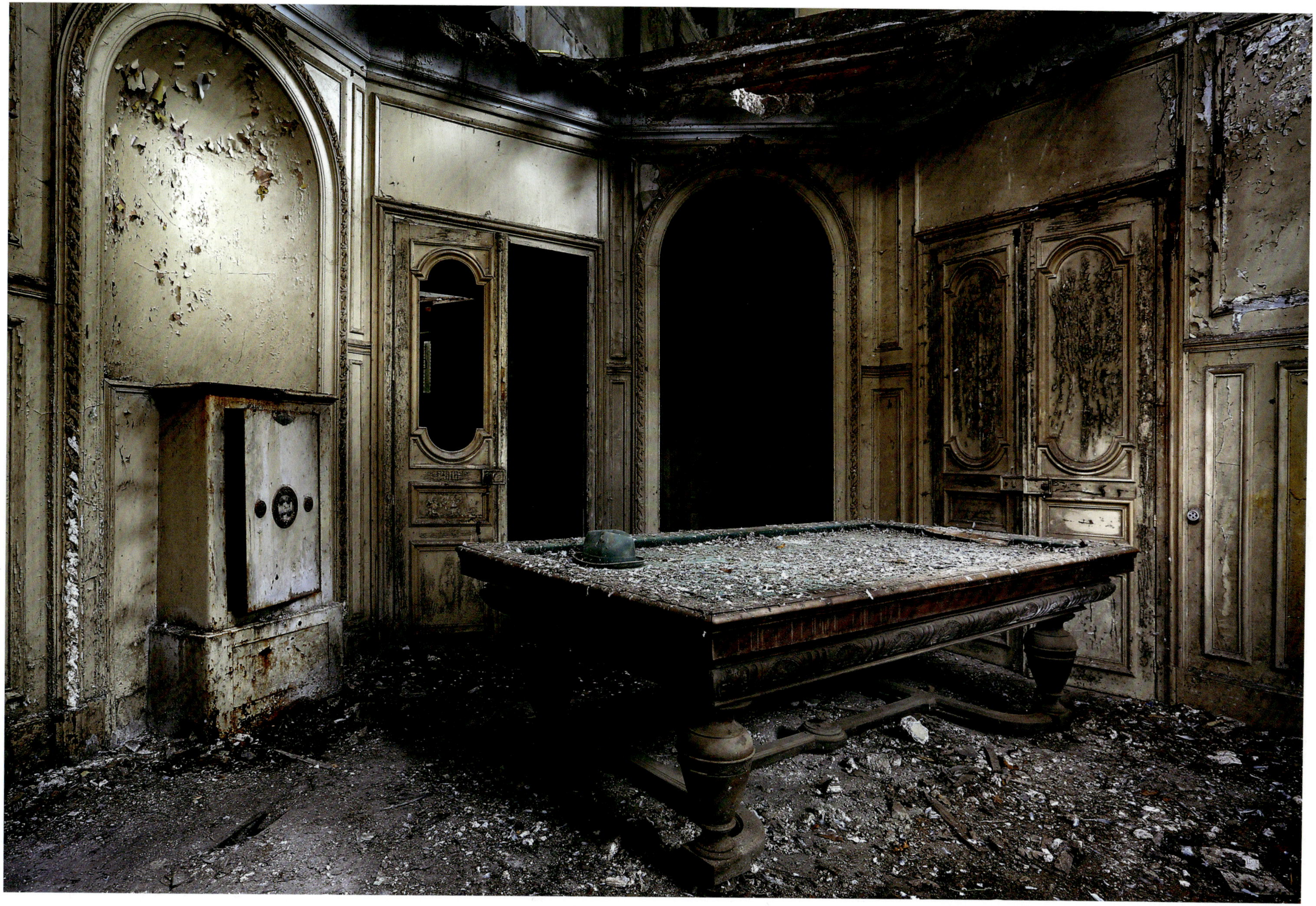

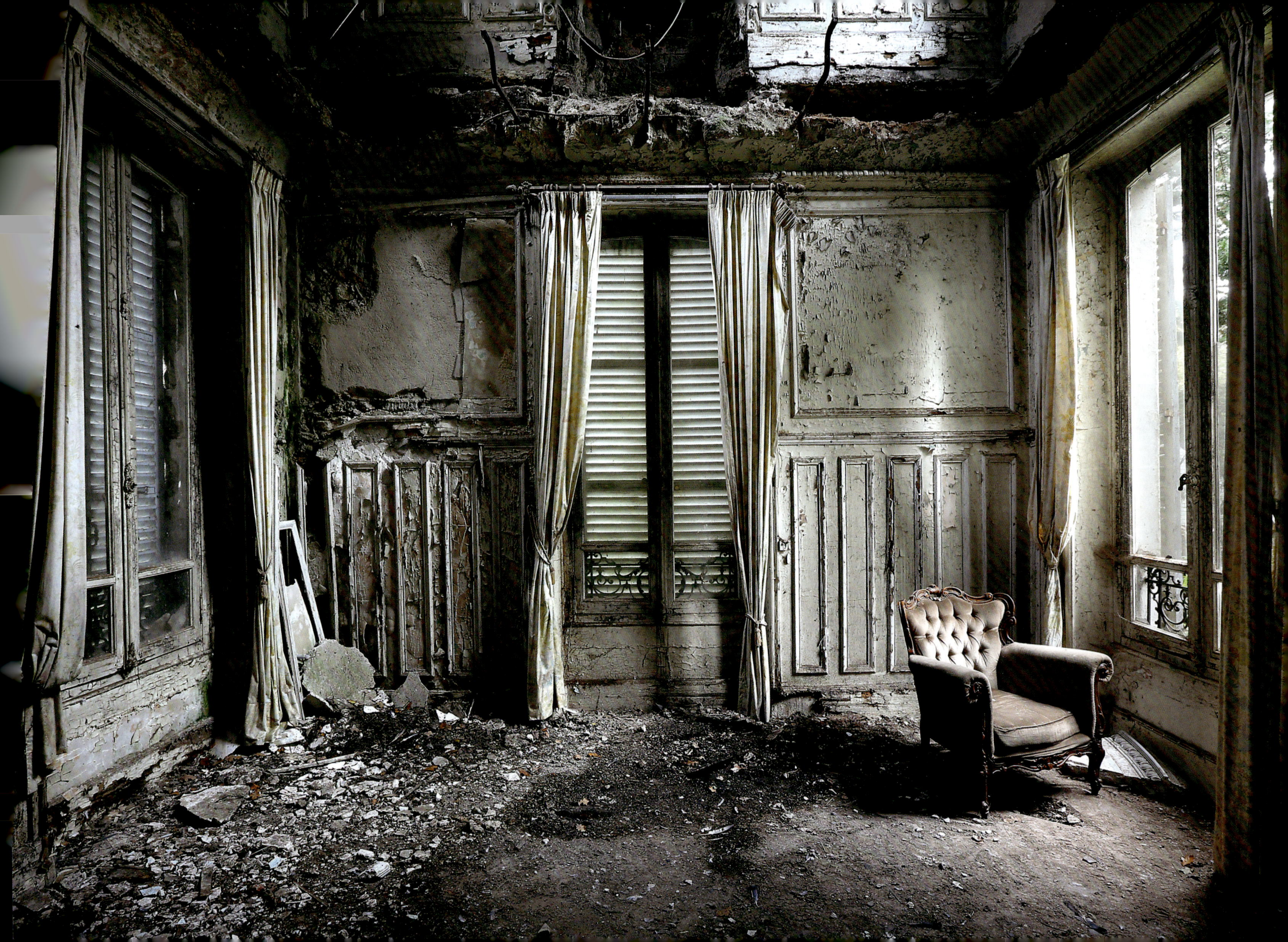

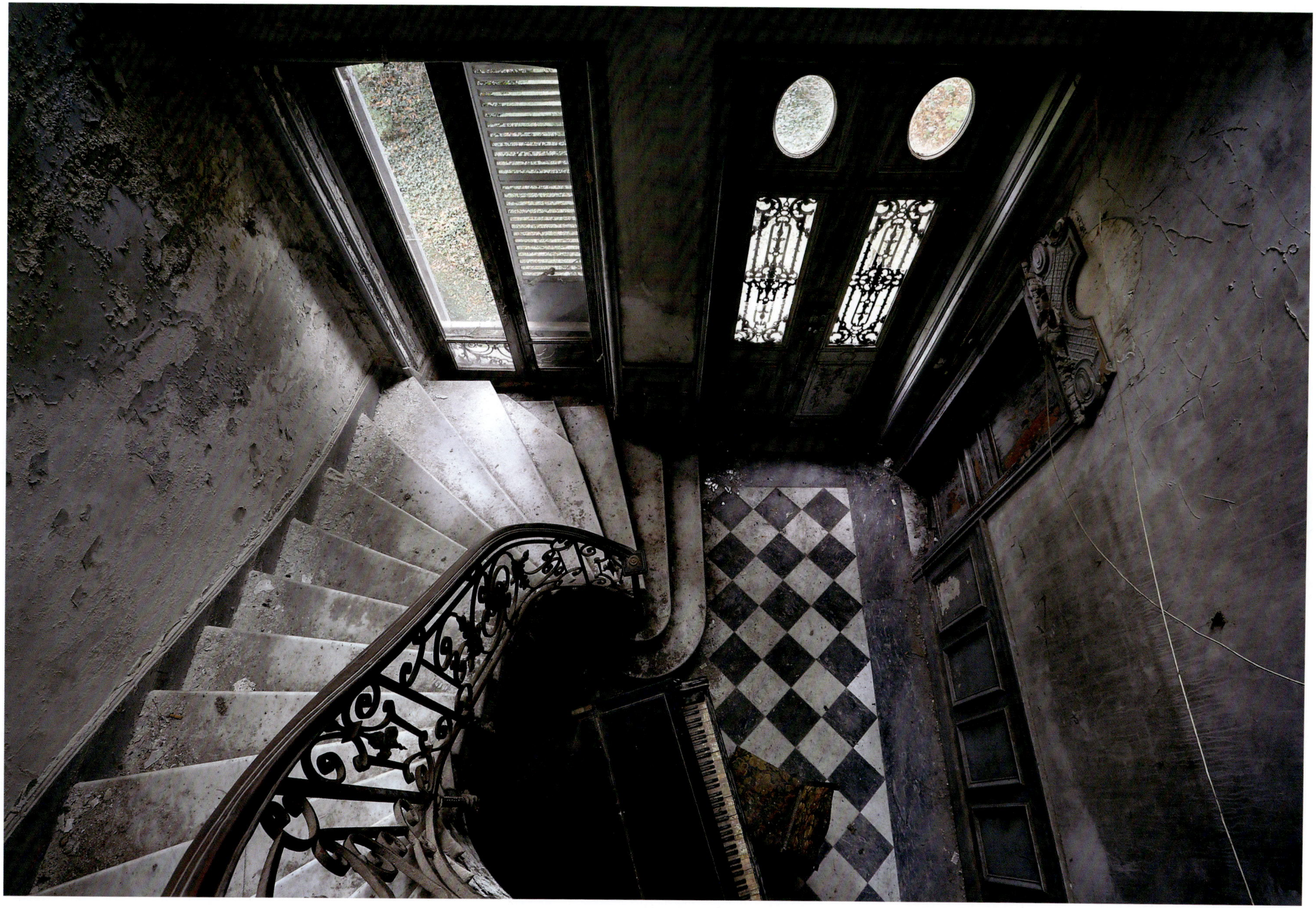

Shooting site of the series A *French village* • *Île-de-France*

The French historical series called *Un village français* (*A French village*), broadcast on the France 3 channel, retraces the stages of the German occupation in a small fictional town in the Jura, not far from the demarcation line separating Occupied France and the Free Zone. The last episodes of the final season were filmed in 2009 on the site of a sawmill still in operation today. There, the decoration team reconstructed workshops and offices from the period. From the fake forge to the locker rooms and workshops, it took them several months to build the set.

It took a team of 20 people ten days to build the teacher's 1943 flat, the police station and, upstairs, a maid's room. All the furniture is period furniture gathered from across the country. There are cupboards that don't open, staircases that don't lead anywhere, concrete walls that are simple wooden panels. The 'wooden' floor is made of linoleum. Some floors have been painted to look like tiles, and the colour of the walls has been artificially aged. On the ceiling there is nothing – except spotlights hanging in the void. It feels like stepping back in time!

As I get a feel for the place, I imagine myself on the set, among the crew, right in the middle of the shooting. As I close my eyes, I can hear the sound of the Wehrmacht soldiers' boots as they pound the asphalt … Lights, camera, action!

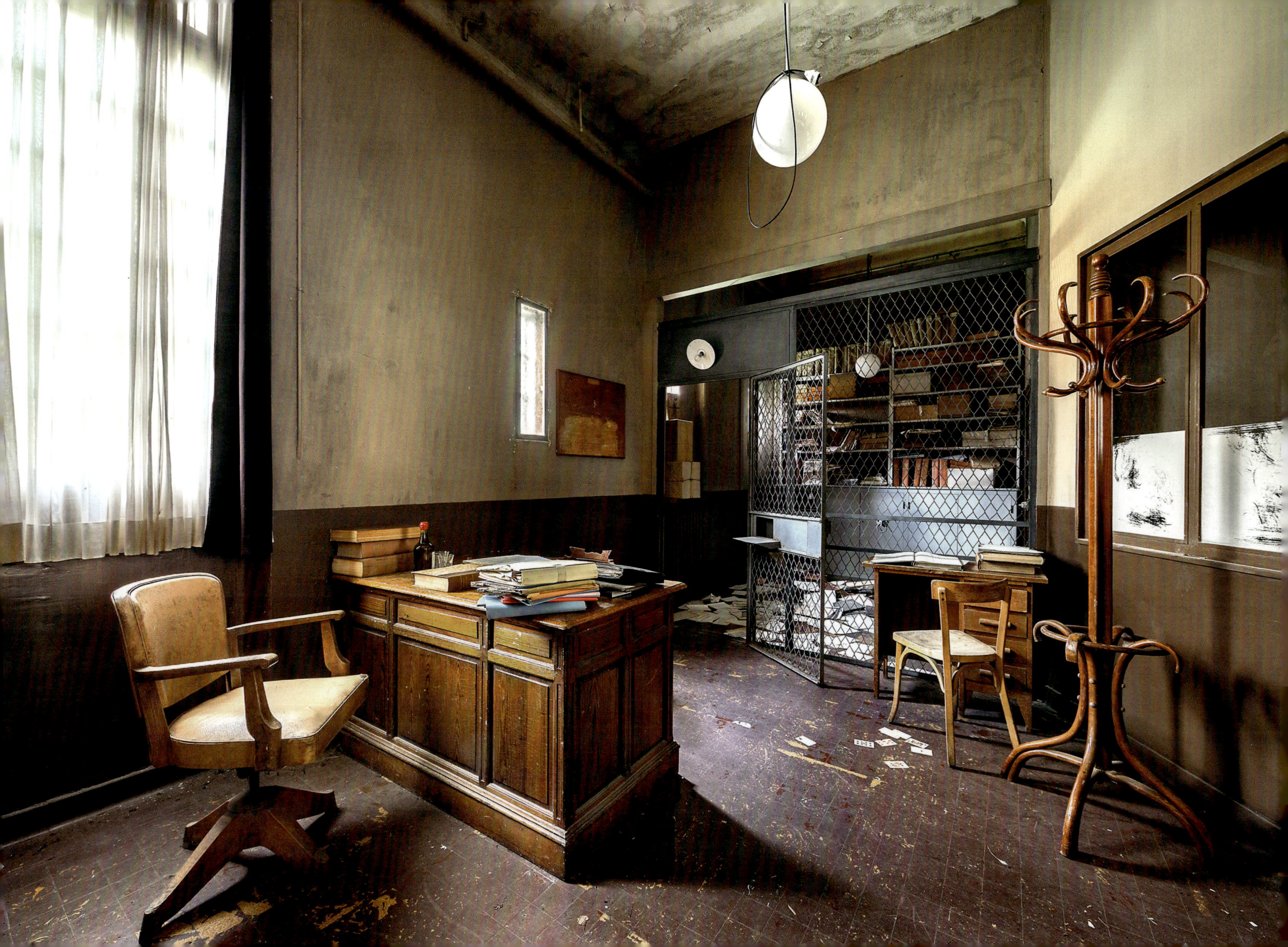

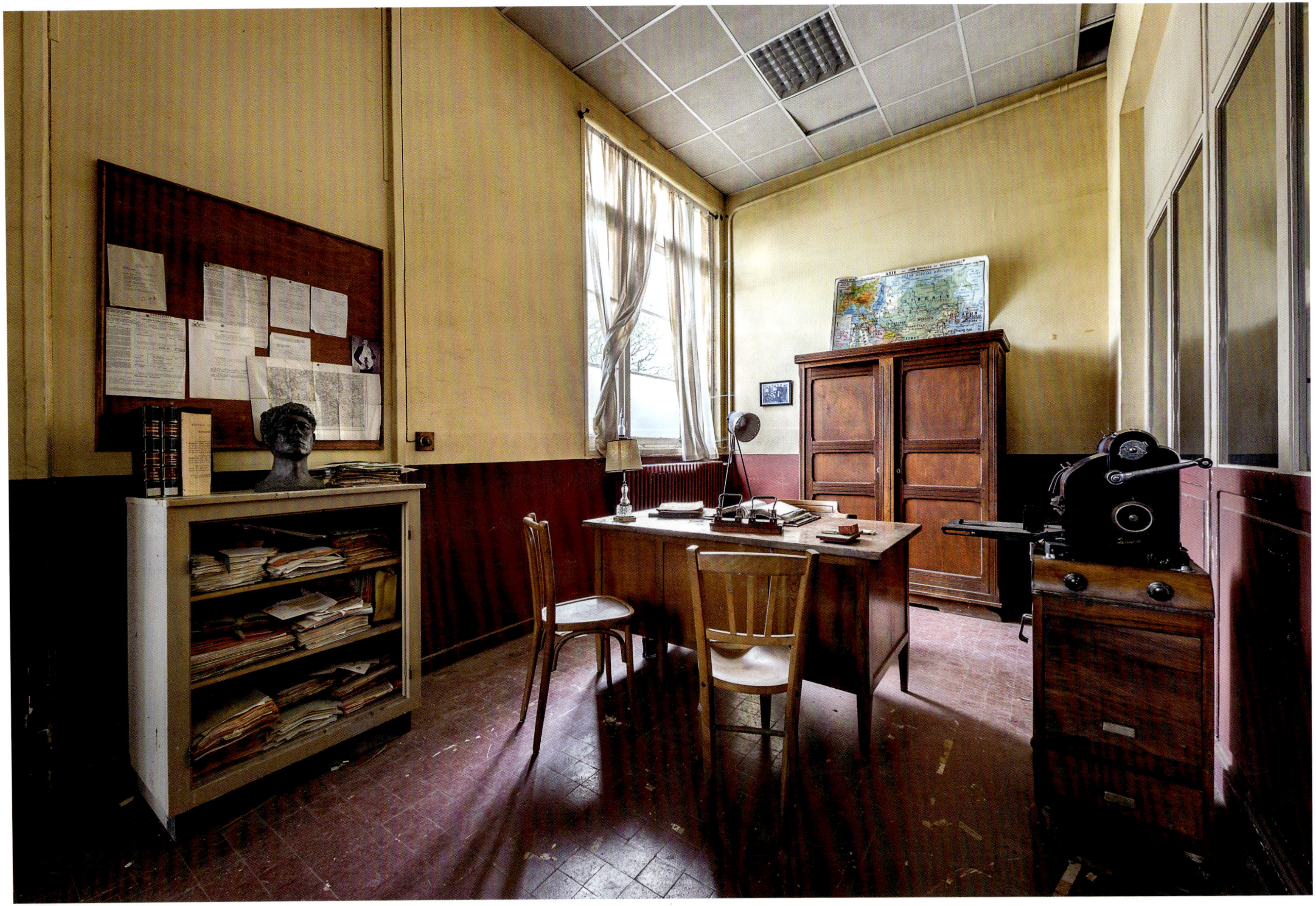

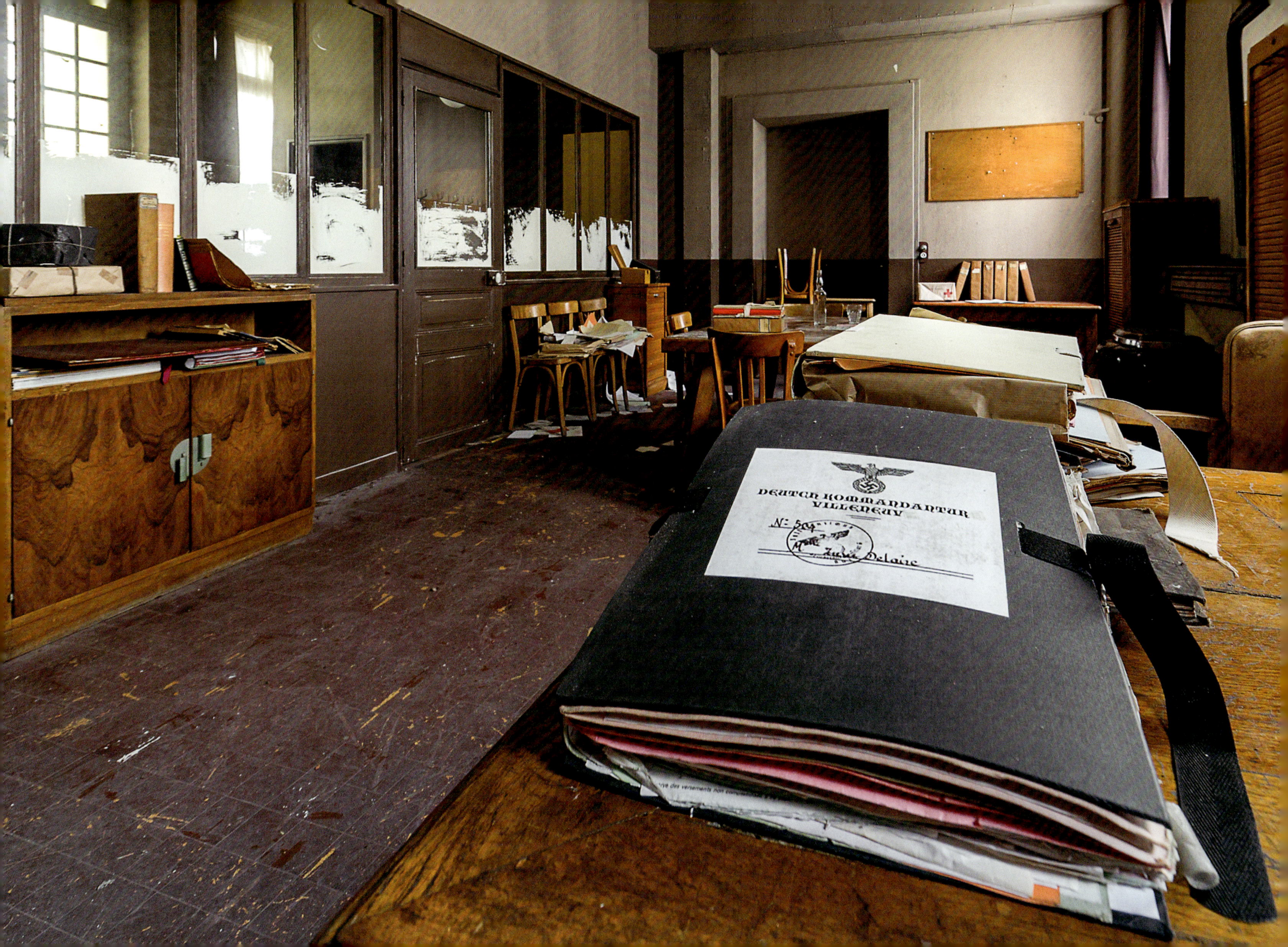
DEUTCH KOMMANDANTUR
VILLENEUV

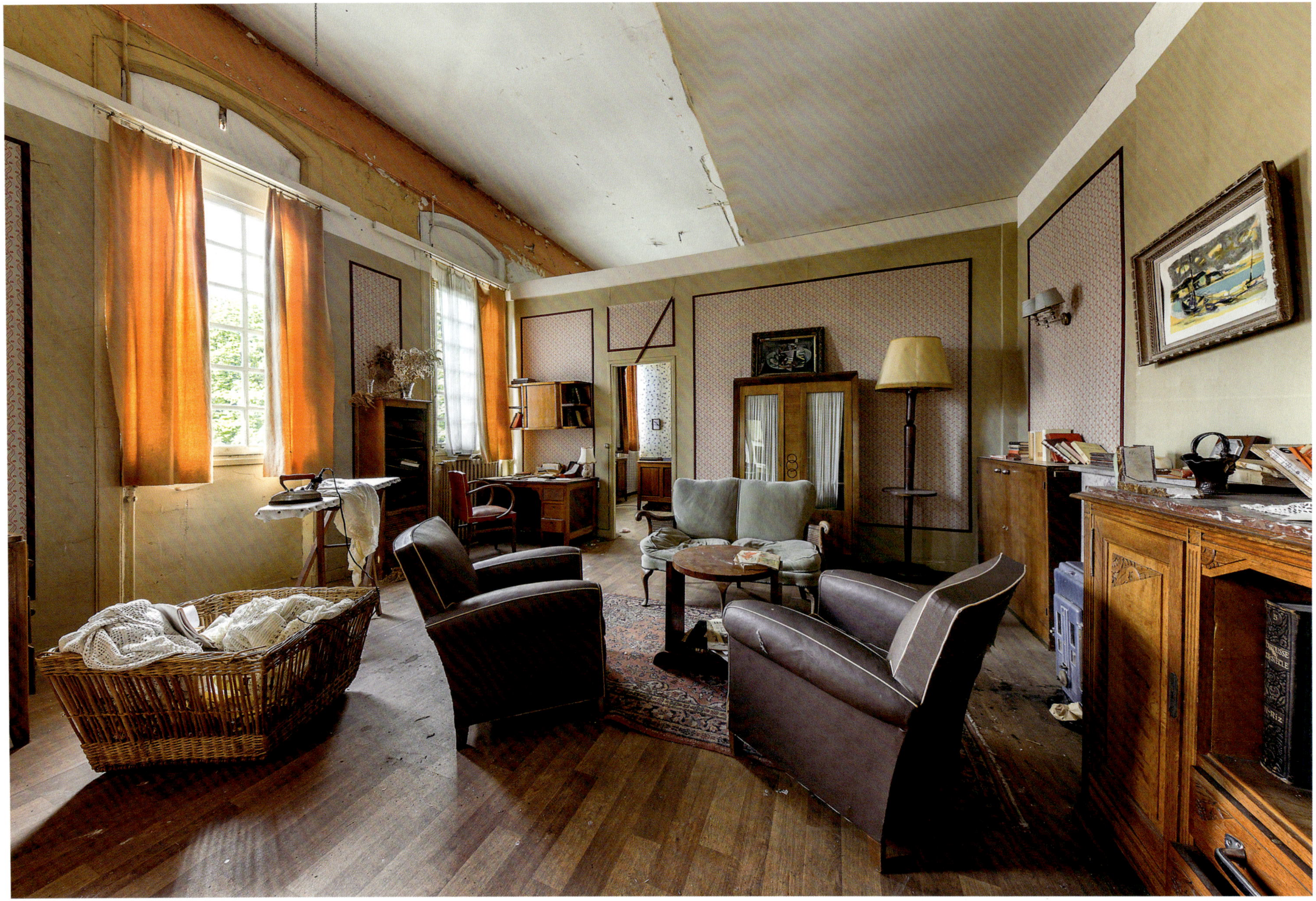

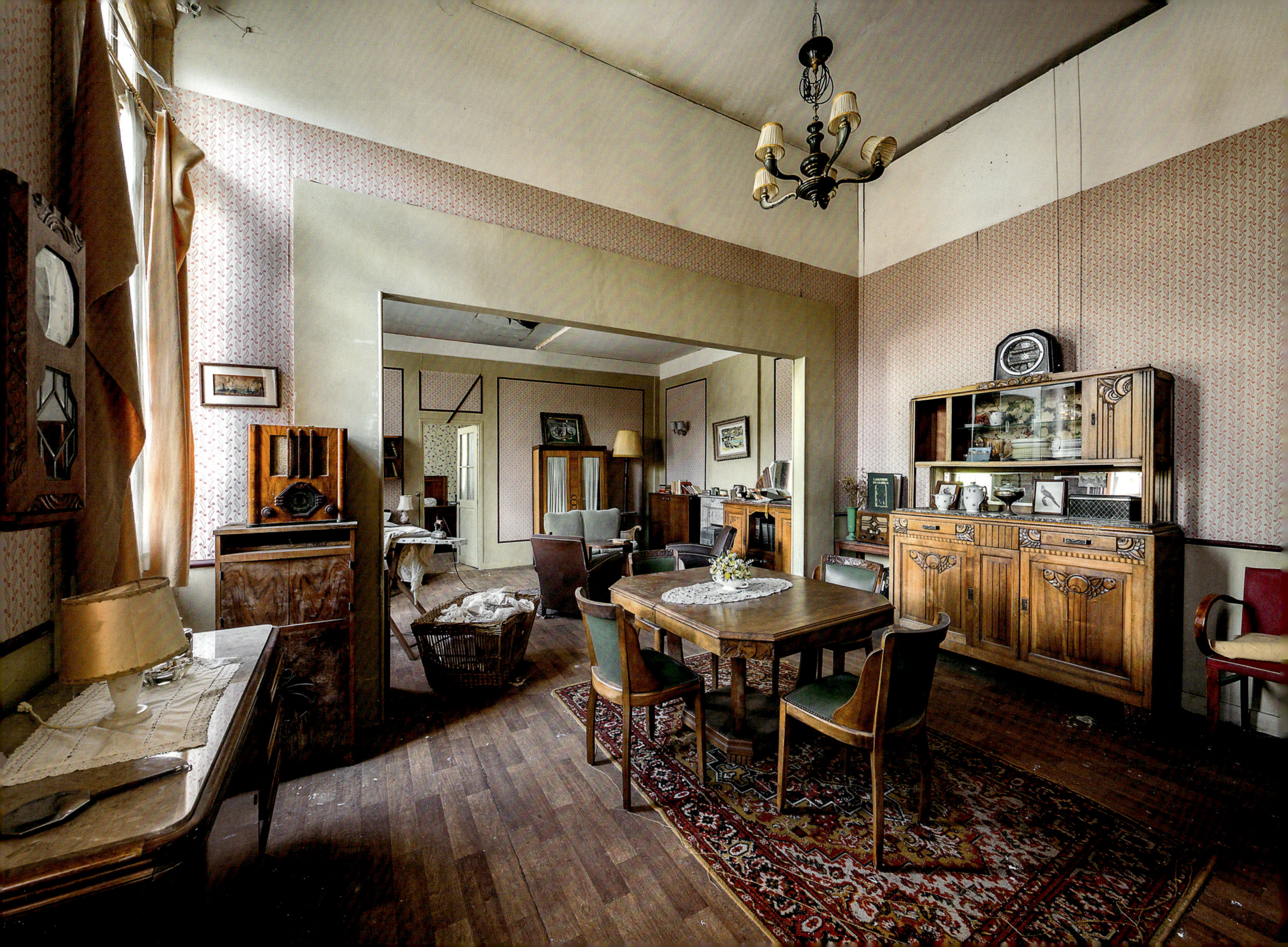

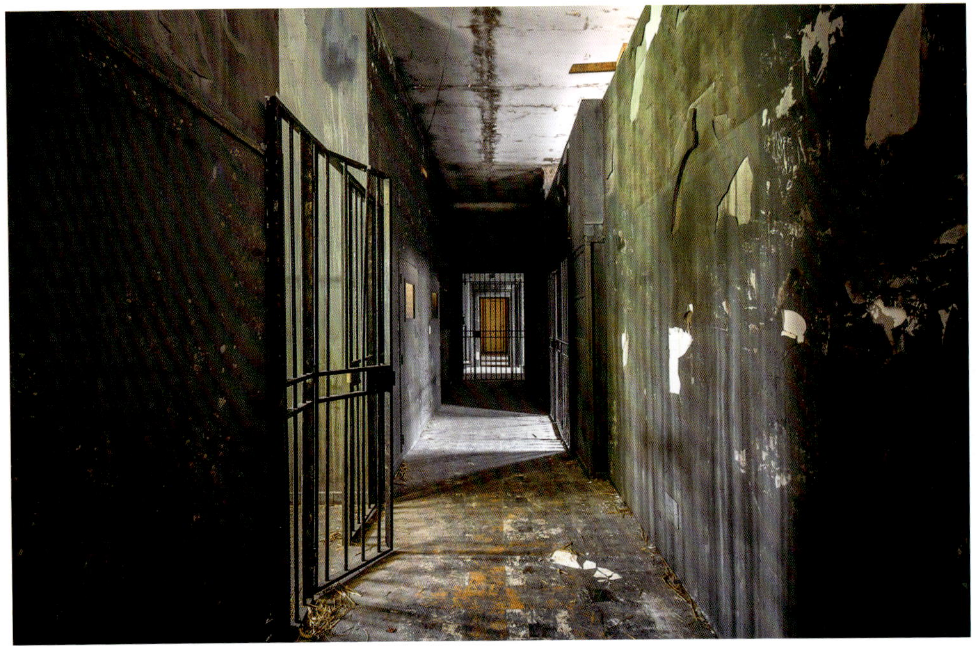

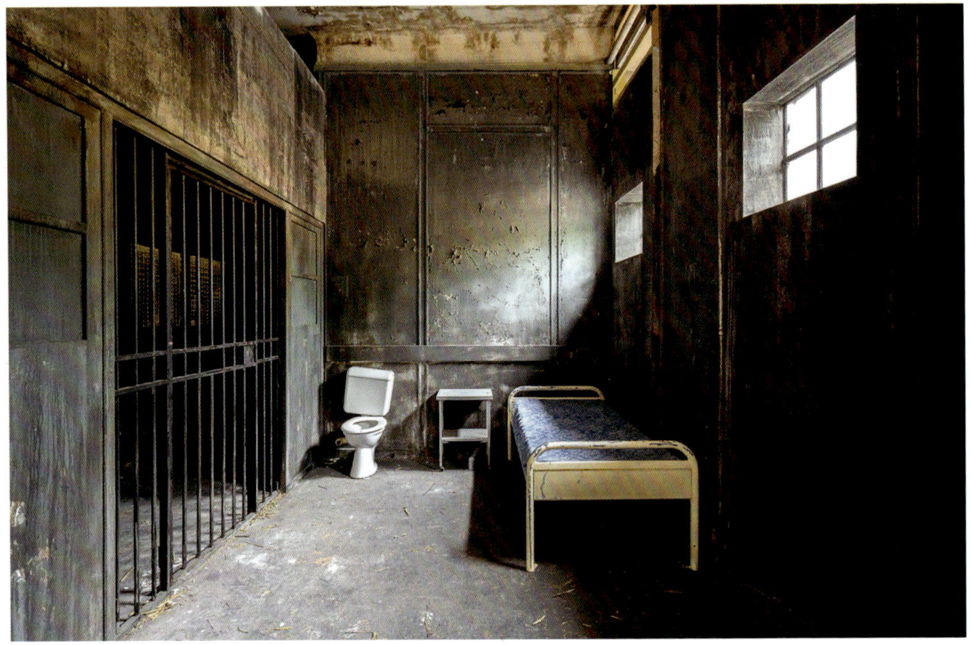

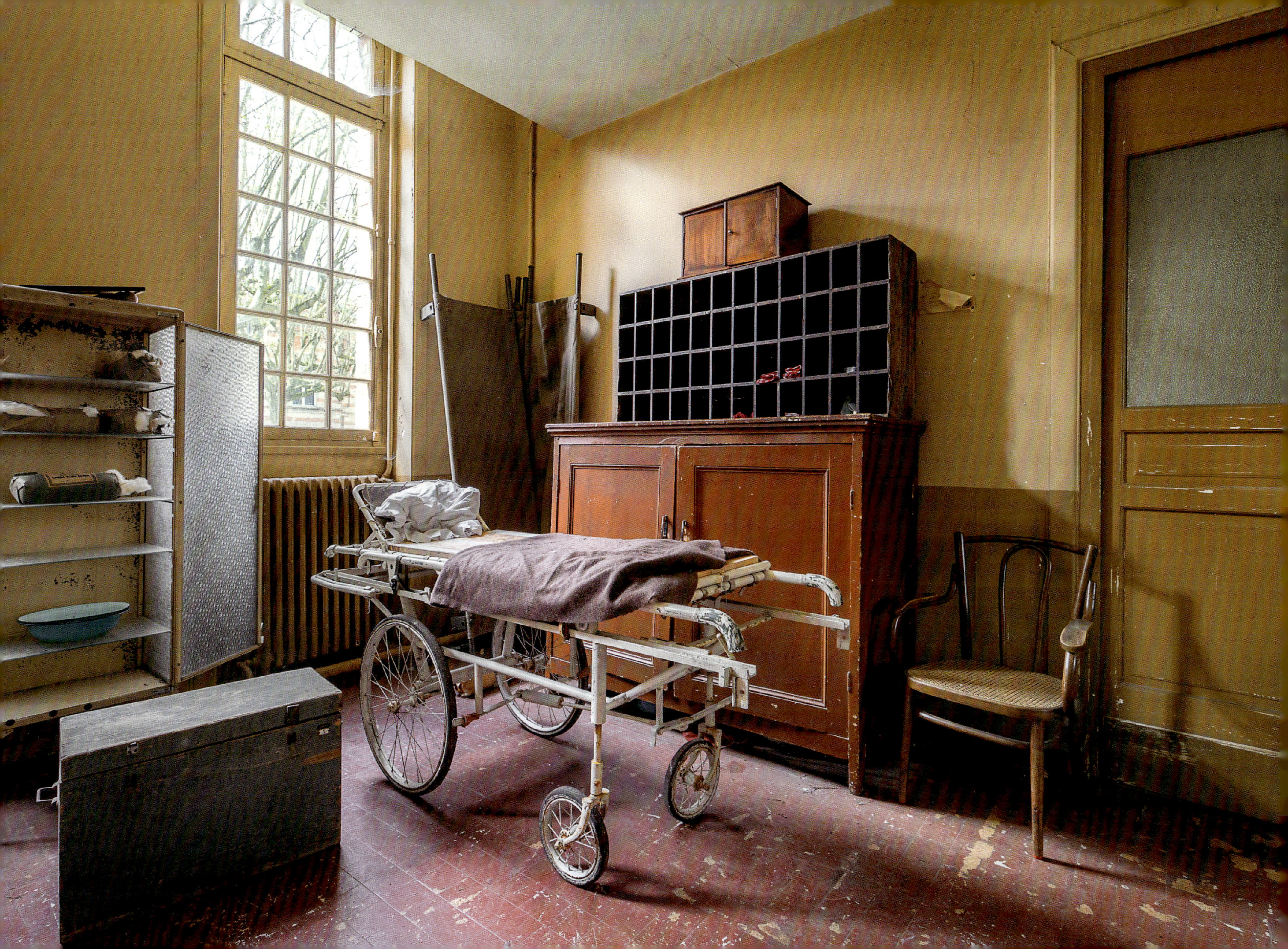

Bibliopolis • *Île-de-France*

Libraries are a privileged place in which to access knowledge and culture. Without them, research would stagnate, and it would be impossible to preserve this heritage of humanity for future generations. The need to pass on this heritage is reflected in this immense library, created to complement the oldest school in France. Hundreds of metres of shelves run along this hall, which has been emptied of its books since the school closed its doors in 2012.

The boarding school and its adjoining oratory were founded in 1638 by order of Louis XIII and, for nearly 400 years, they welcomed generations of students. As a Catholic private school, the establishment has housed pupils from the country's most prominent families, who were taught by the institution's most brilliant teachers. Pupils included illustrious personalities such as Montesquieu and Jean de la Fontaine, Jérôme Bonaparte – Napoleon's brother – for the most prestigious of them, and more recently Philippe Noiret, Claude Brasseur, Jean-Pierre Castaldi (actors), Michel Polnareff (a singer-songwriter), Michel Hidalgo (a football player) and even Jacques Mesrine (a famous French criminal).

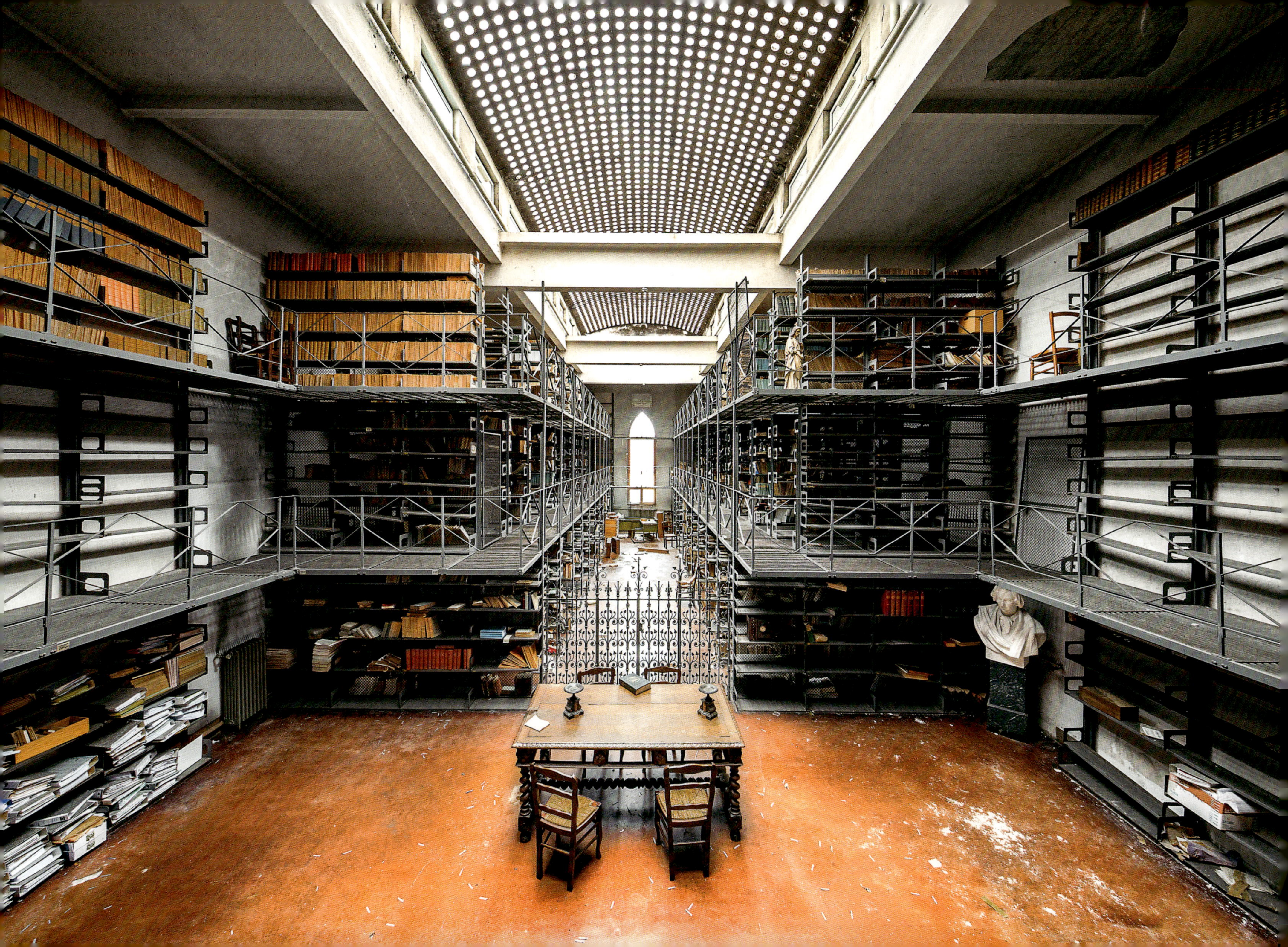

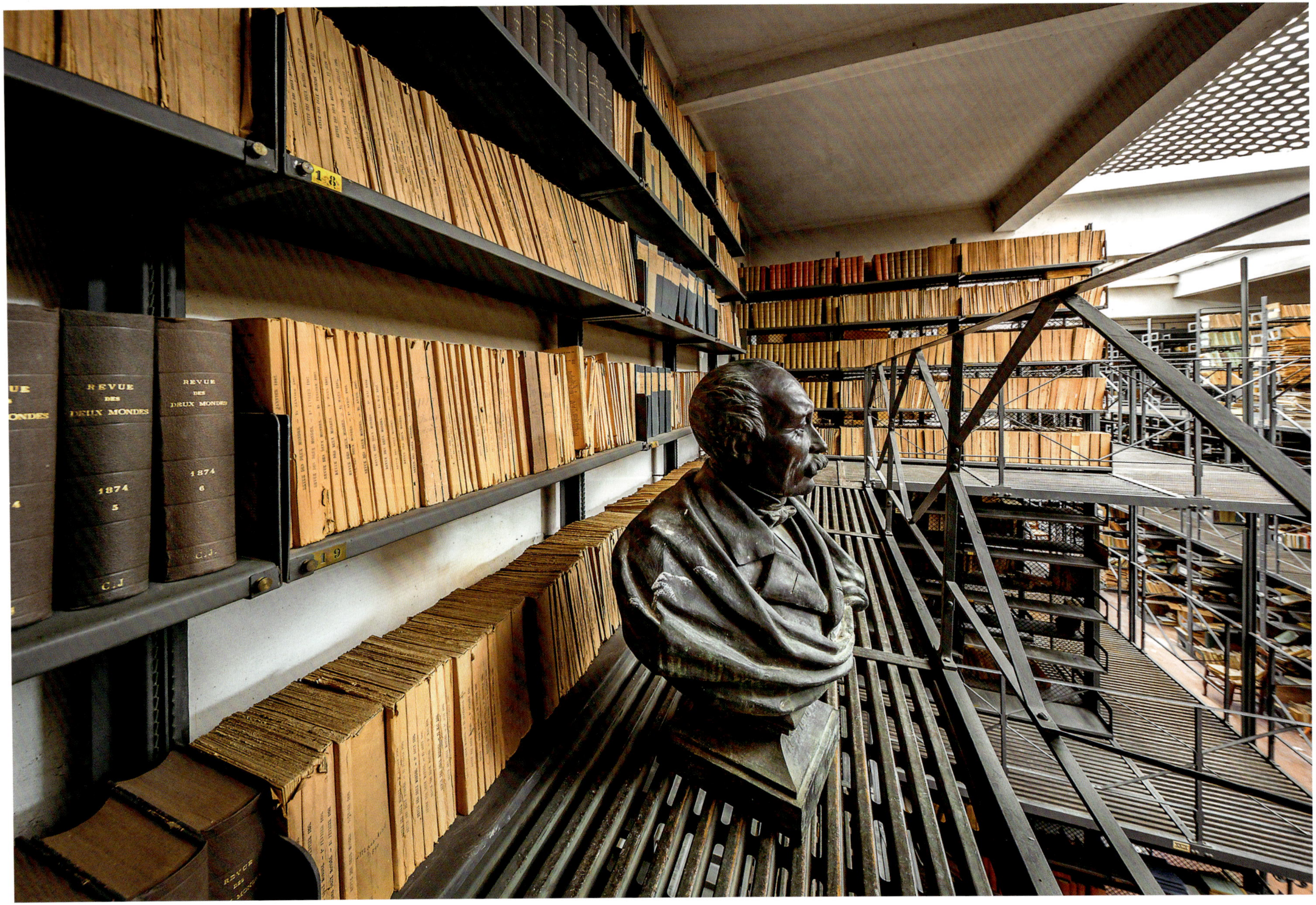
18
REVUE DES DEUX MONDES 1874 5 C.J
REVUE DES DEUX MONDES 1874 6 C.J.
19

To ensure the stewardship of the boarding school, the Oratory initiated several extensions and made improvements to the premises, adding large buildings, a refectory, and the gigantic library. However, during and after the French Revolution, the boarding school experienced difficulties. After serving as a hospital for the wounded in the army, it became a high school under Napoleon I. With the fall of the Empire, it lived through all the vicissitudes of French history.

Abandoned since 2012, its condition has been deteriorating ever since. To continue to write its history, a project to rehabilitate this historical and architectural jewel has been proposed to develop 217 exceptional homes to bring the emblematic place back to life. Work should begin under the supervision of the Architectes des Bâtiments de France (the national association of building architects of France).

The supersonic Concorde – test machine • *Île-de-France*

This is the cockpit of one of the two Franco-British supersonic Concorde airliners to have been produced: the 102. Designed jointly by Sud-Aviation (now Aérospatiale) and the British Aircraft Corporation (now British Aerospace), it was equipped with wings known as 'gothic delta' and a turbojet engine with afterburner. The Concorde made its maiden flight on 10 January 1973. Its cruising speed of Mach 2.02 (about 2,145 km/h) defies belief.

There are only 20 of these aircraft in existence. Six were used for development and 14 for commercial flights. There were two prototypes (001 and 002), two pre-production aircraft (101 and 102) and 16 production aircraft (201 to 216), of which 14 made intercontinental commercial flights and were still in service in April 2003.

The Concorde 102 F-WTSA had the shortest active life, just three years, but it participated in numerous demonstrations to promote supersonic passenger flights. It featured a new tail geometry and vertical tailplane, and a new secondary nozzle design, with increased length and span. From 1973 to 1975, it made 311 flights, totalling 642 hours and 28 minutes, of which 280 hours and 19 minutes were supersonic. It proved very useful throughout the programme.

Commercial flights began in 1976 and ended 27 years later in 2003. High fuel consumption made the Concorde unprofitable. Its decline was hastened by the only accident in its history, in July 2000 on Air France Flight 4590, which killed 113 people after a piece of metal on the runway collided with one of its fuel tanks. Despite this incident, the Concorde remains a wonderful machine.

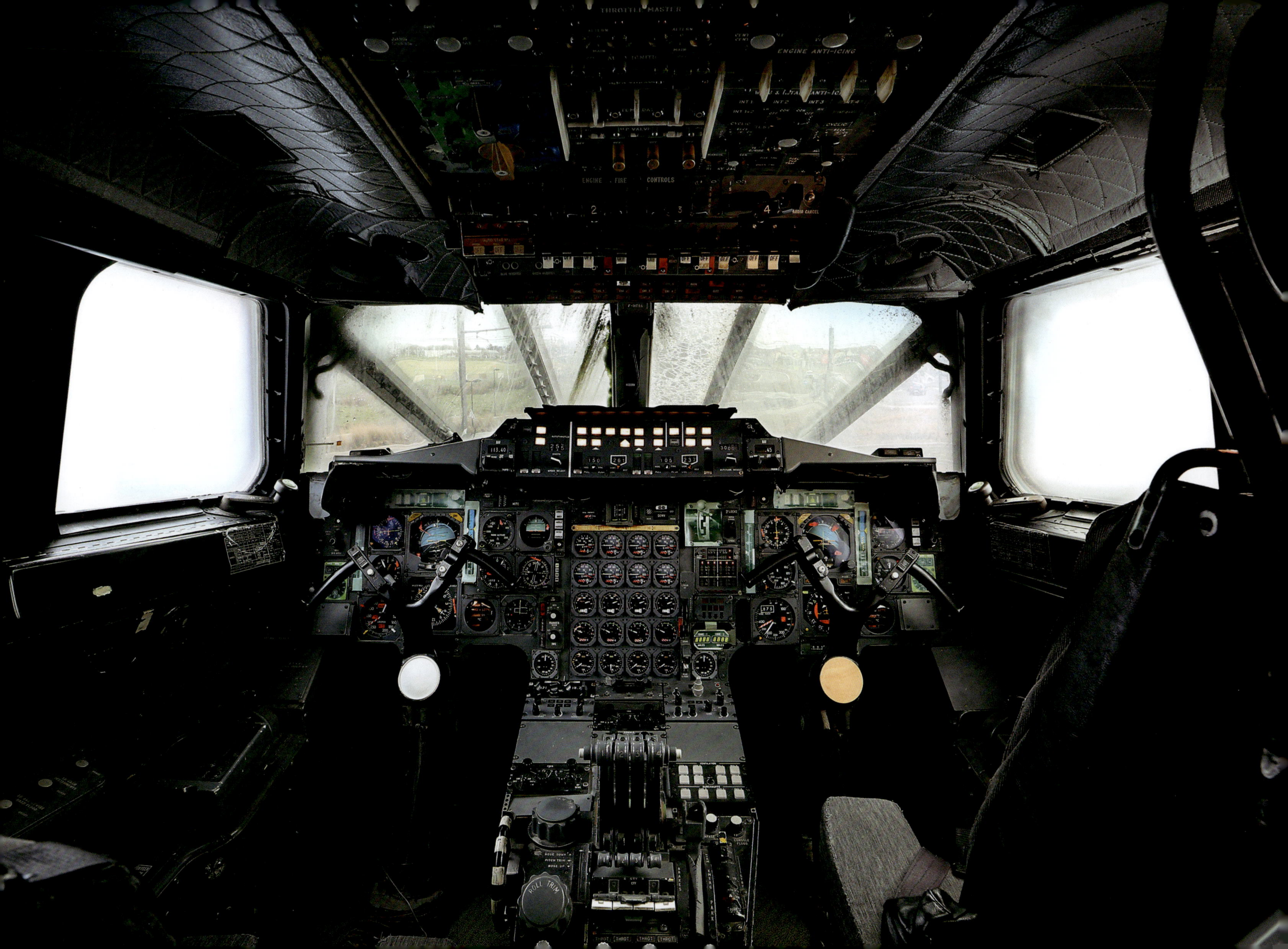
THROTTLE MASTER
ENGINE ANTI-ICING
ENGINE FIRE CONTROLS
AUDIO CANCEL
ROLL TRIM

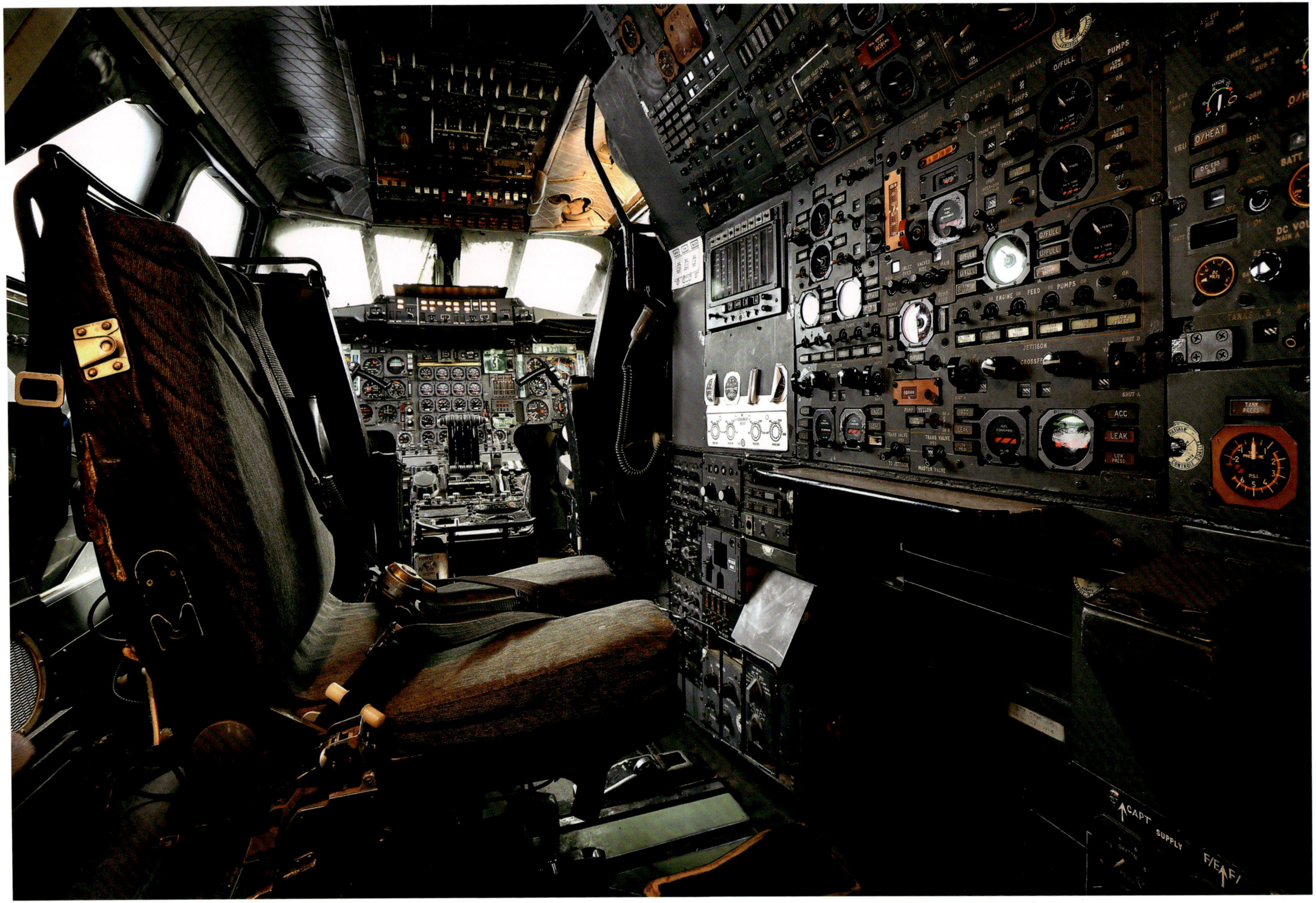
O/HEAT
ACC
LEAK
CAPT SUPPLY

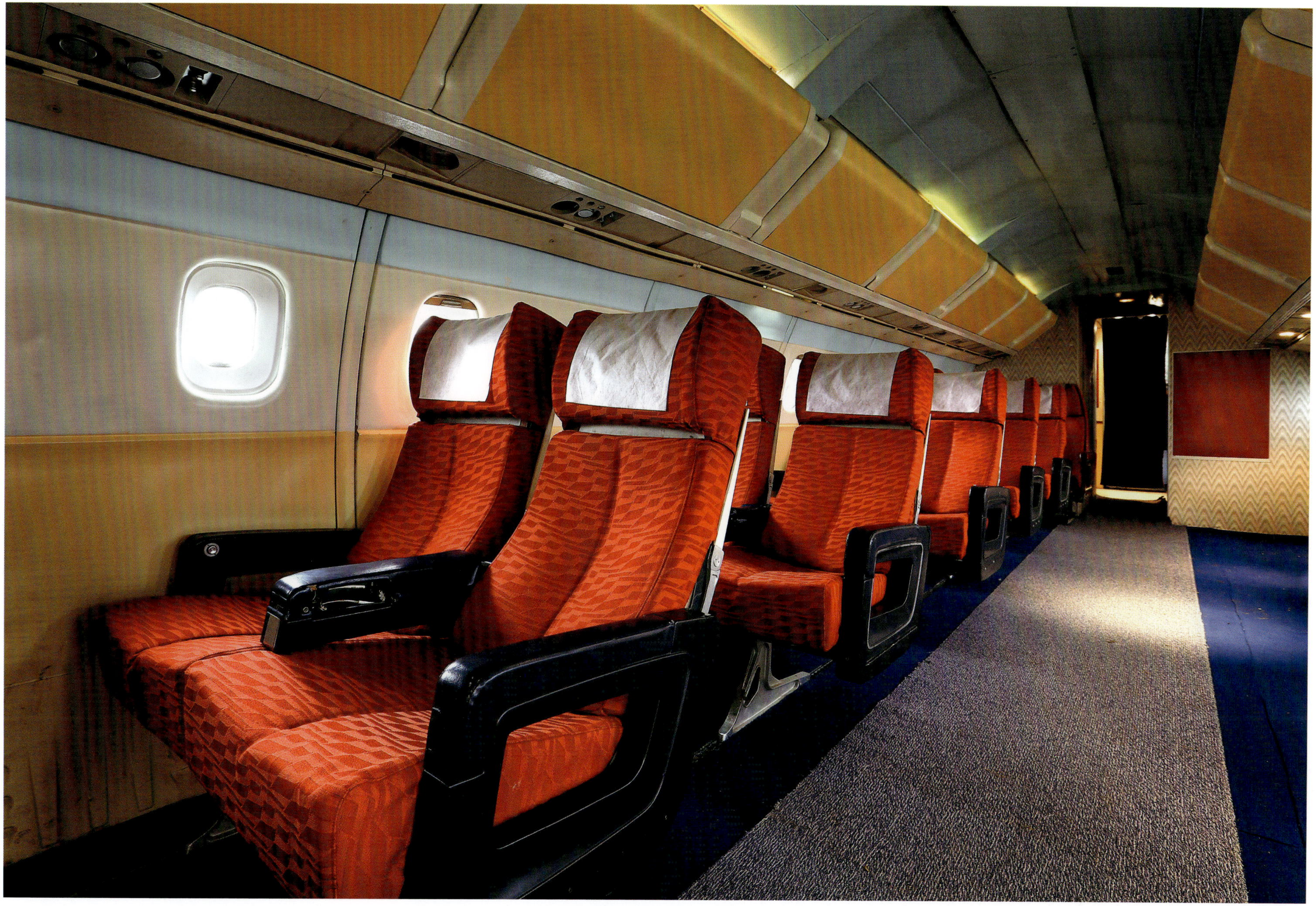

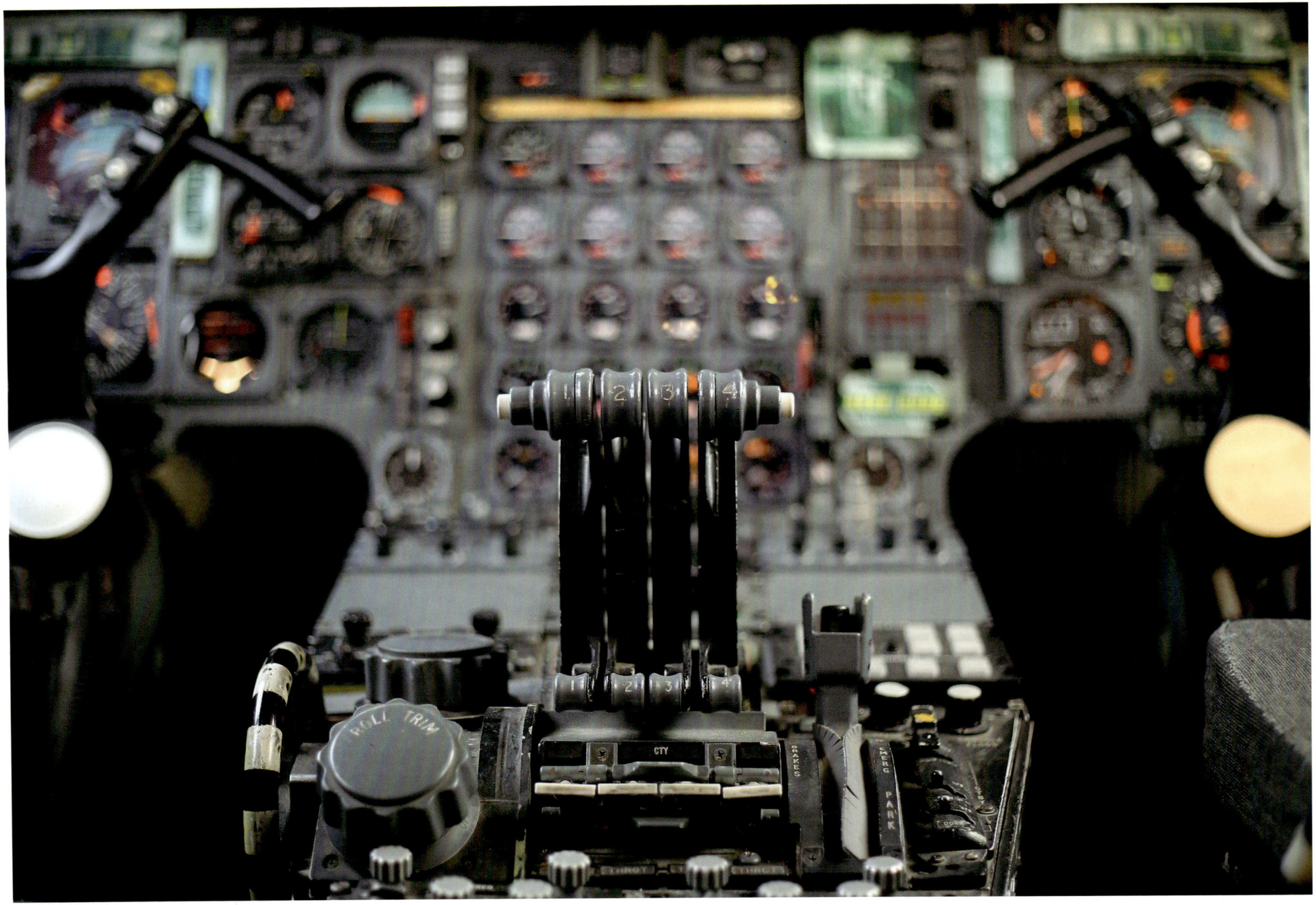
ROLL TRIM
CTY
BRAKES
EMERG
PARK

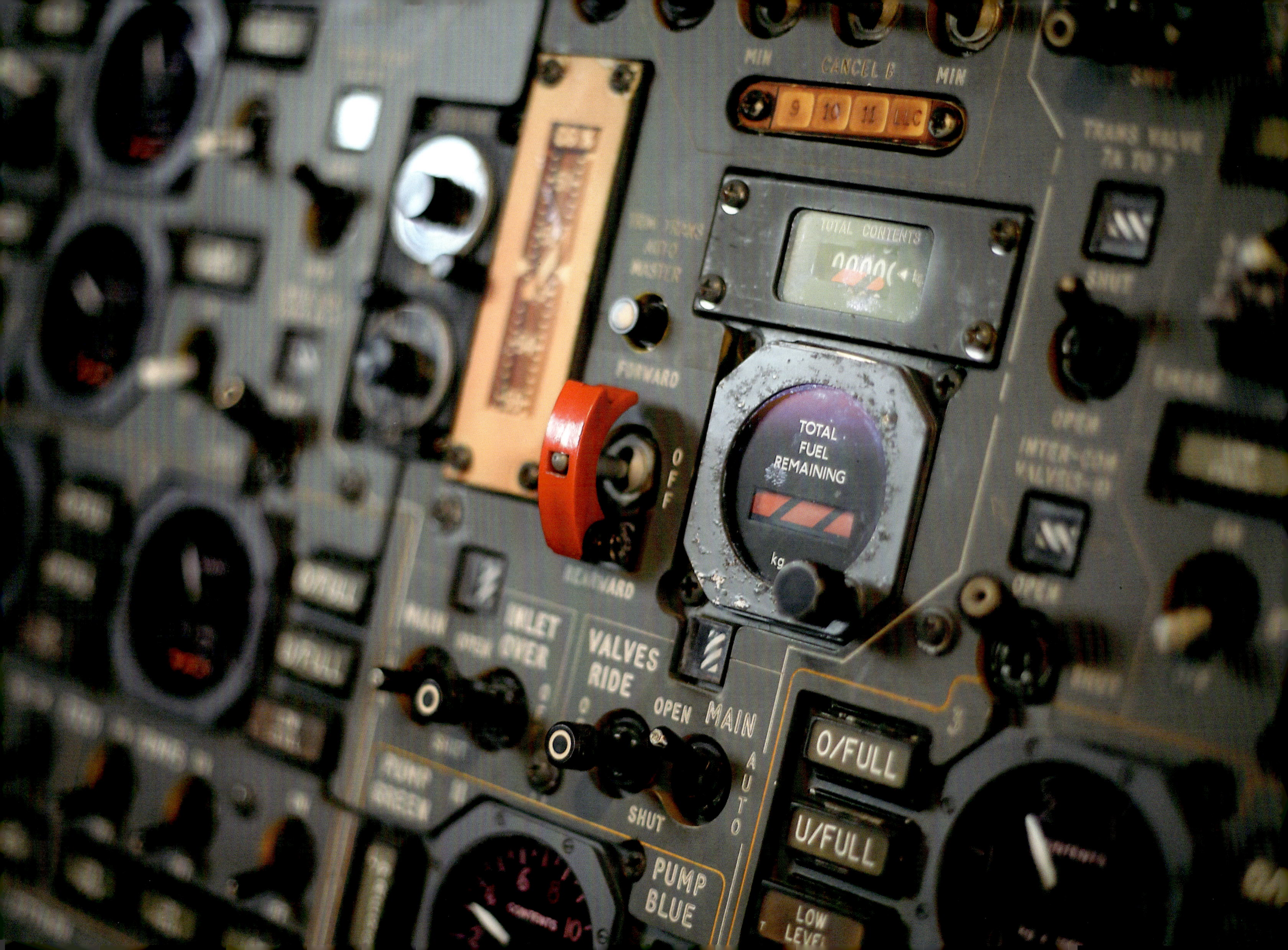
MIN
CANCEL B
MIN
9
10
11
TOTAL CONTENTS
FORWARD
OFF
TOTAL
FUEL
REMAINING
kg
VALVES
RIDE
OPEN
MAIN
SHUT
AUTO
O/FULL
U/FULL
LOW
LEVEL
PUMP
BLUE

A hovertrain 'Made in France' • *Île-de-France*

Some 25 years before the TGV (France's high-speed train) was invented, the Aérotrain, or hovertrain, was the remarkable technological innovation and design of its time.

During tests in February 1966, the 01 prototype of the *Aérotrain*, mounted on an air cushion, reached 200 km/h. Two years later, an experimental monorail test track entirely dedicated to this new type of transport was built south of Paris by the French engineer Jean Bertin at Gometz-la-Ville. The *Aérotrain* was designed to be part of a future Paris-Orléans route connecting the two cities in just 20 minutes. In 1969, tests of the 02 prototype were carried out on the track, where the train's engine and rockets managed speeds of 422 km/h. From 1969 to 1974, this track was used mainly for the I80-250 and I80-HV prototypes, the latter reaching the world speed record for guided transport of 430.4 km/h, on 5 March 1974.

Despite keen interest in this invention, which aroused the enthusiasm of some 20 countries including the United States, the project was finally abandoned in favour of the high-speed train (the current TGV), which pushed the business of the visionary Bertin into bankruptcy. Capable of equivalent speeds, the TGV had the double advantage of running on electricity rather than hydrocarbons, and on the existing rail network. However, it did not reach a speed of 380 km/h until 1981, and 551.3 km/h in 1990.

About 20 years ago, Thierry Farges, a mechanics enthusiast mainly interested in preserving military vehicles from the D-Day landings, narrowly managed to salvage the I80-250 and I80-HV prototypes that were destined for scrap, from the grassy car park of the former Bertin company. They were restored by Farges, who can't stop talking about the air-cushion technology and propulsion performance.

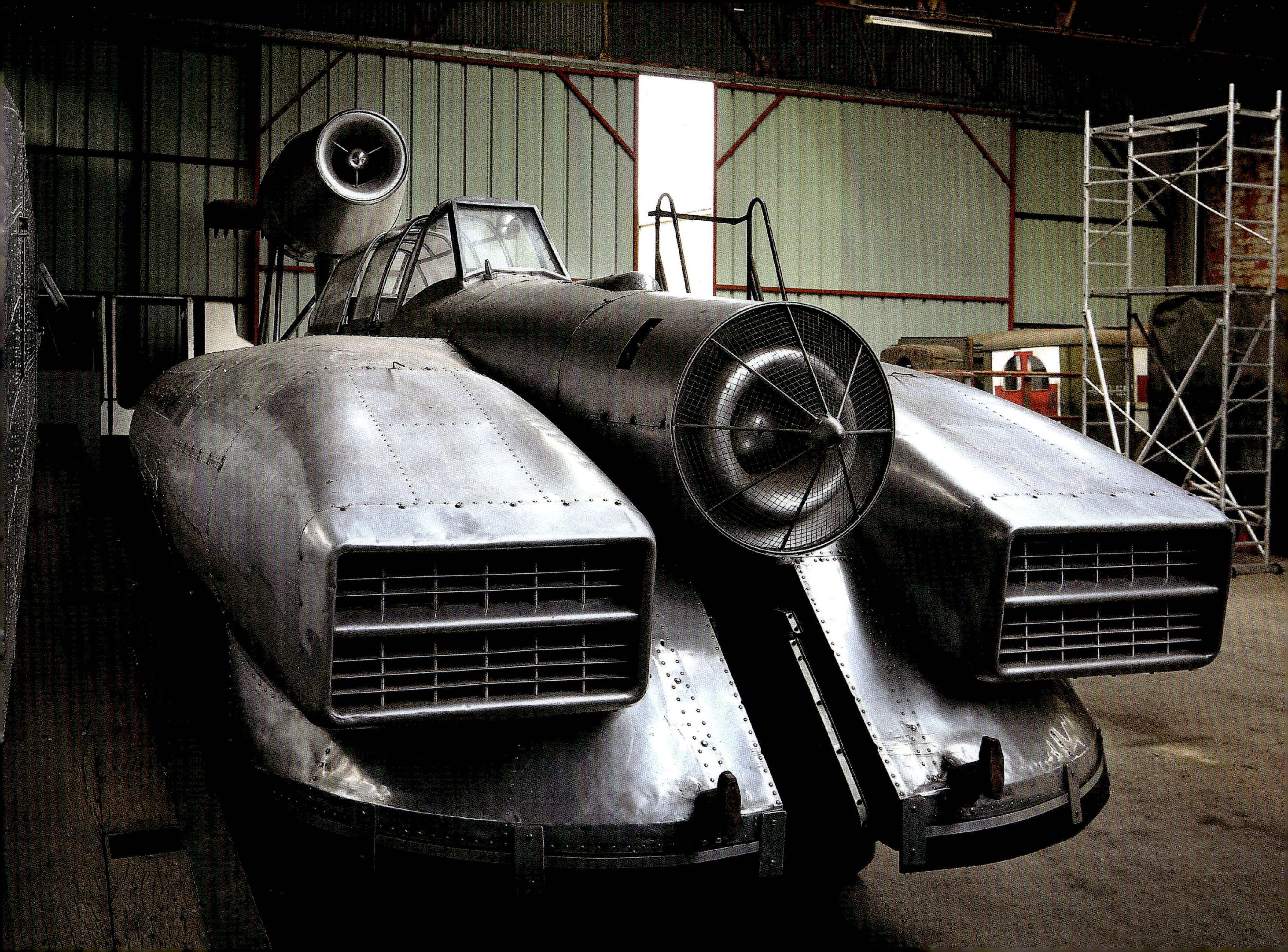

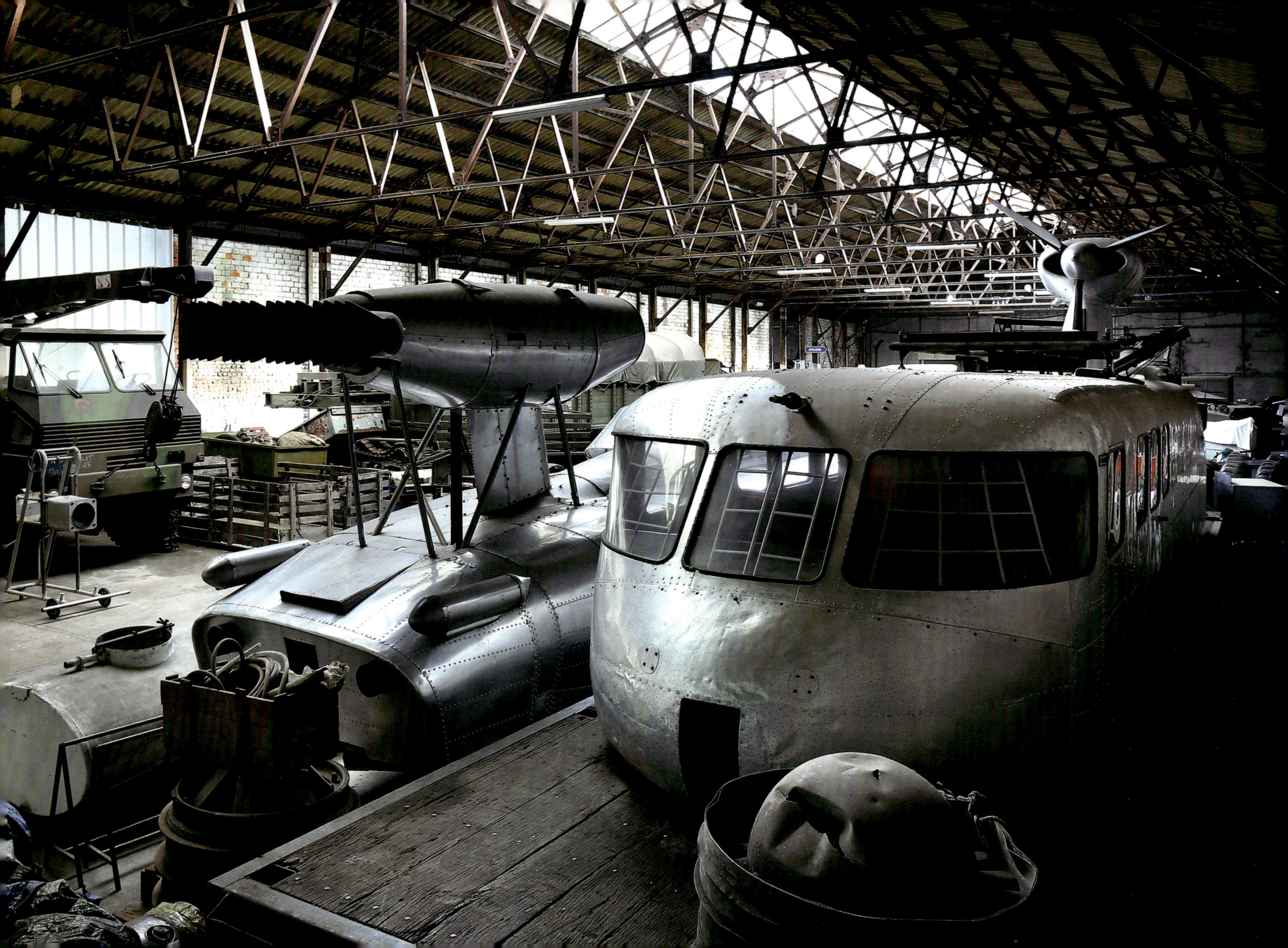

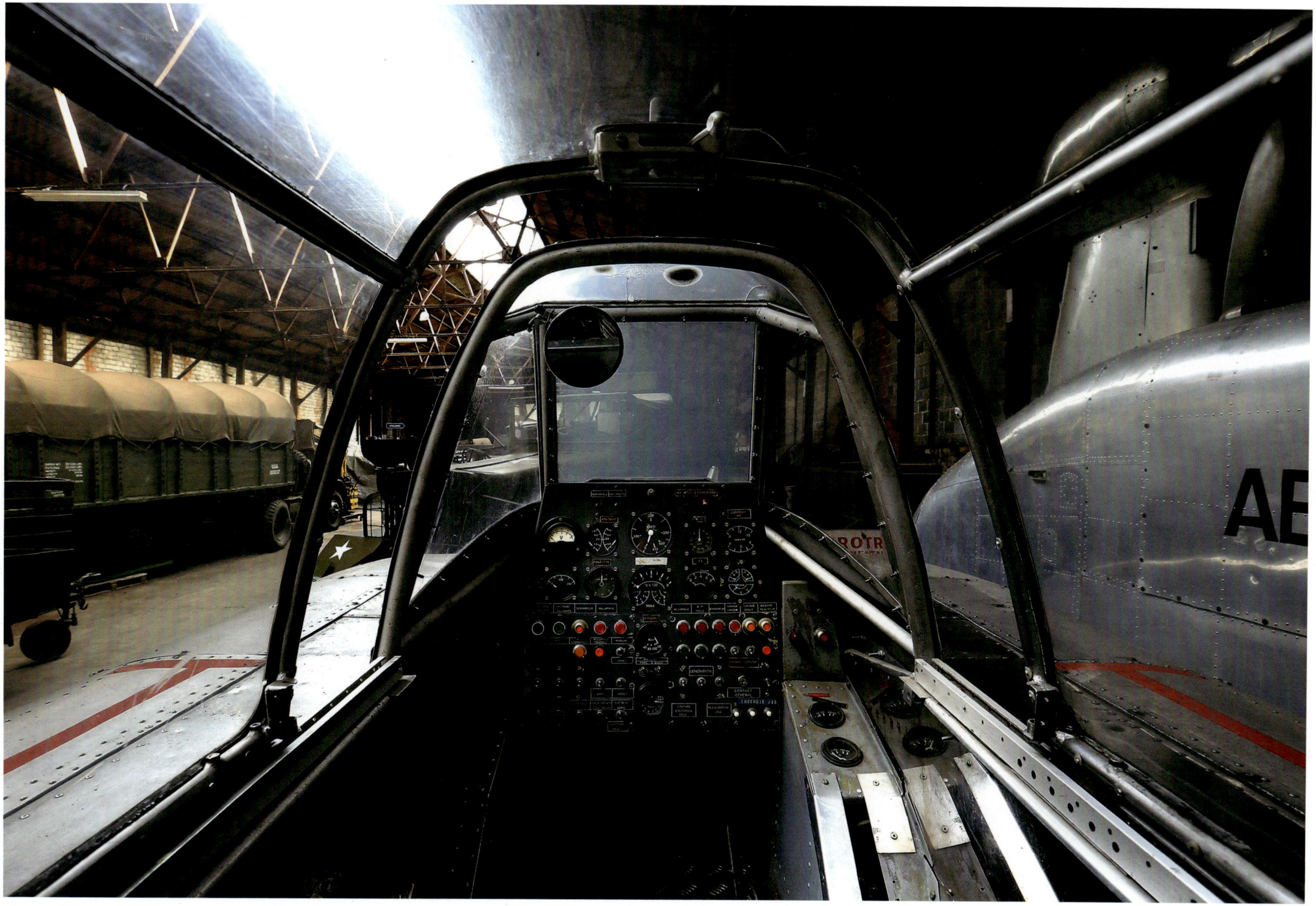
AE

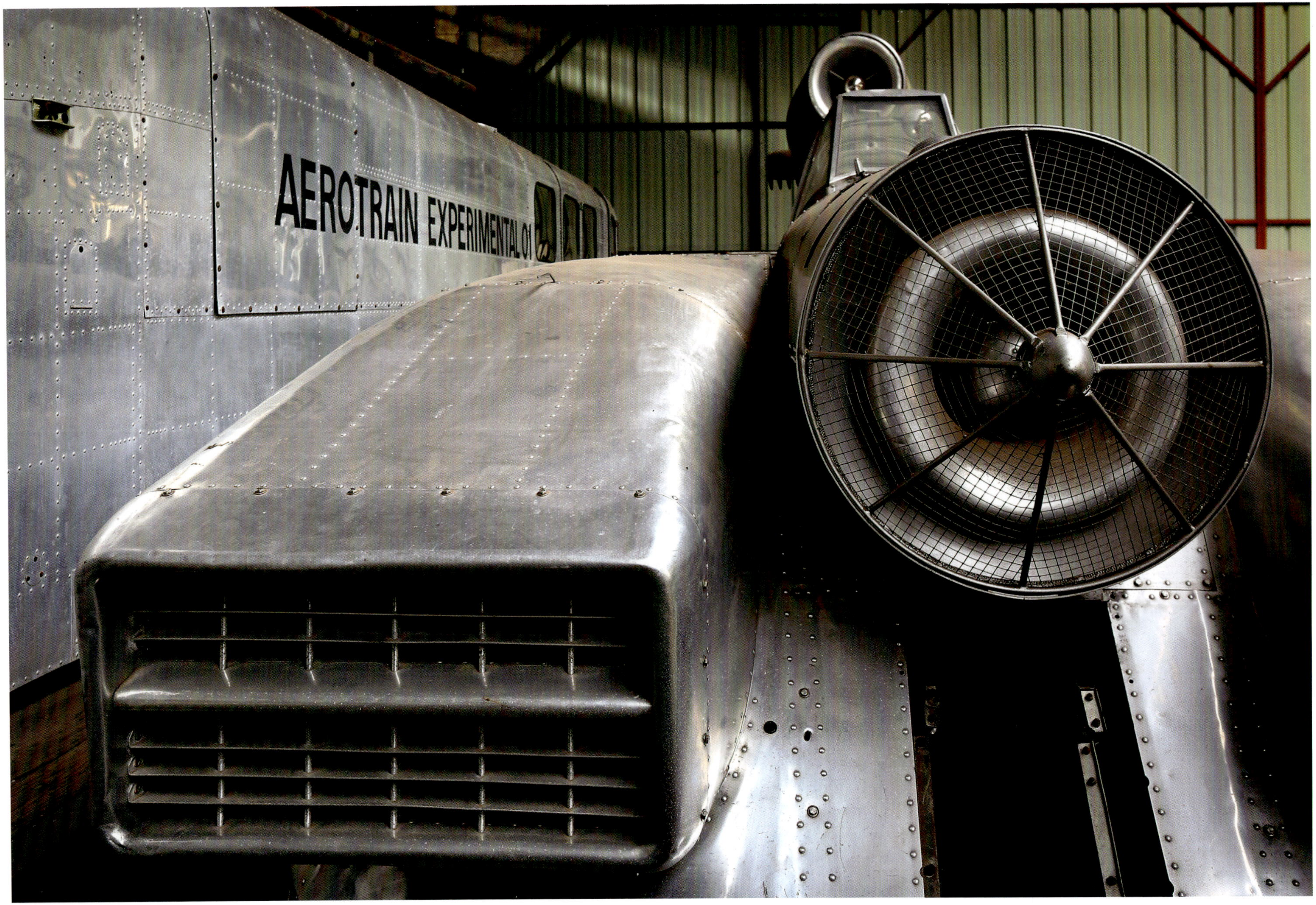
AEROTRAIN EXPERIMENTAL 01

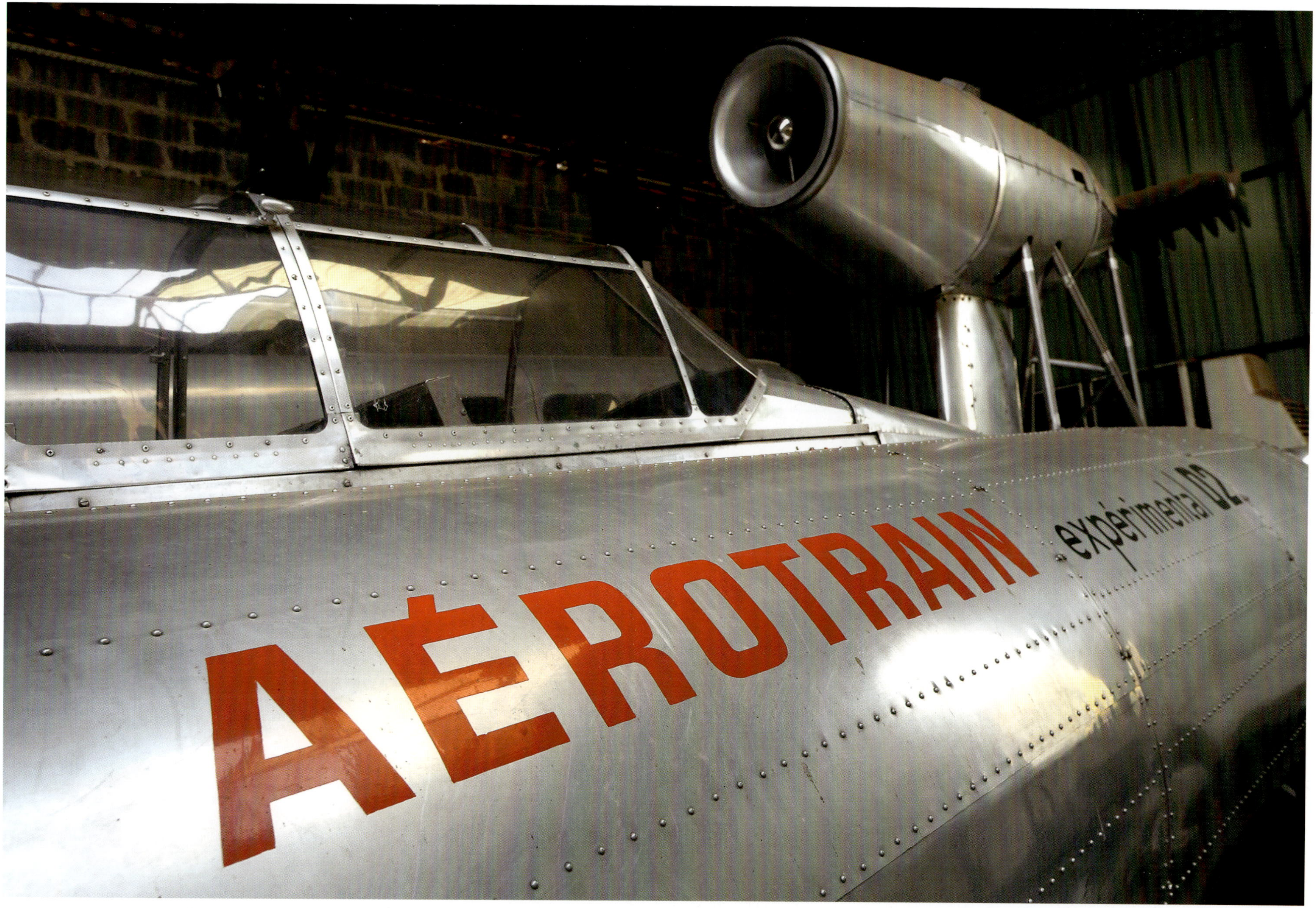
AÉROTRAIN
expérimental 02

A pastel prison • *Île-de-France*

This former prison, built during the Second Empire, is particularly representative of its era. This imposing building is made of brown millstone, a very resistant, cavernous rock which possessed good insulation properties. The stone, sourced in the Île-de-France region, was widely used until 1880. Inaugurated in 1857, the prison had individual cells and could accommodate about 50 prisoners, although their stays were quite short because they were destined for the penal colony. Abandoned since it closed in 2005, the prison is now only a shadow of its former self. The windows are broken from wear and tear and squatting, and the plastered walls have faded and cracked under the weight of time. The paradox of the soft pastel tones on the walls of this emotionally charged place is all the more striking. It is a sad sight.

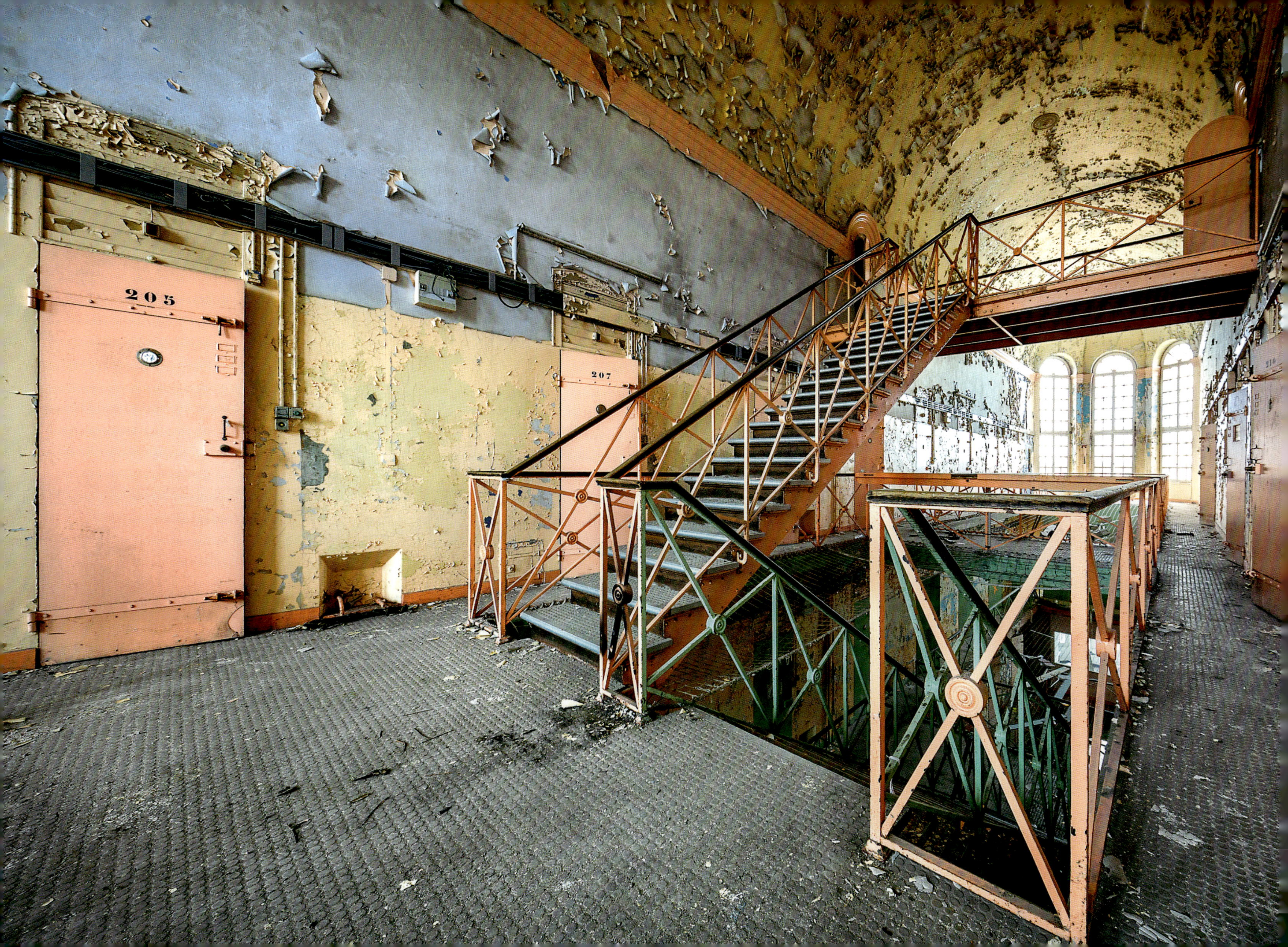
205
207

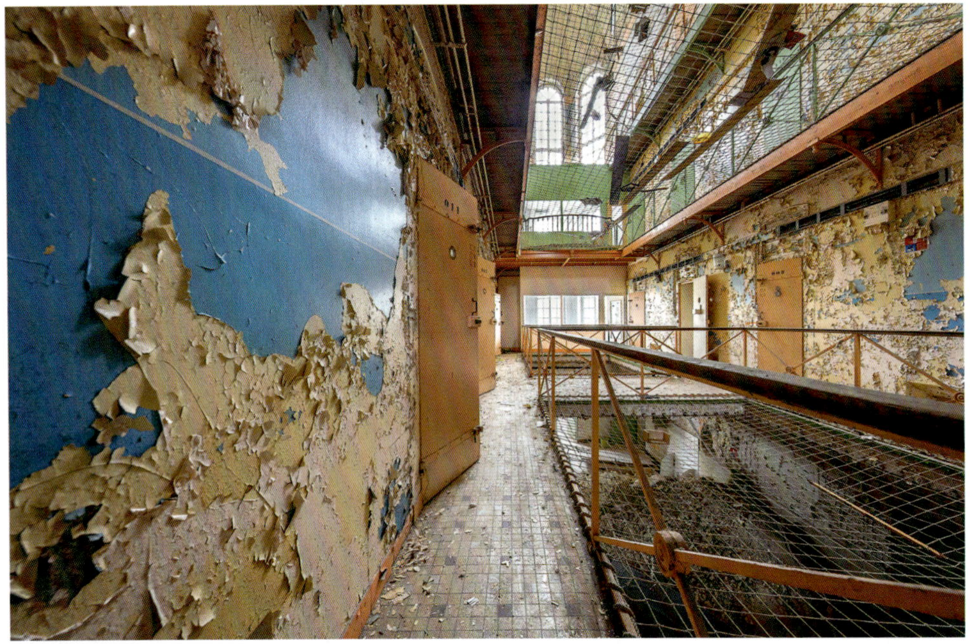

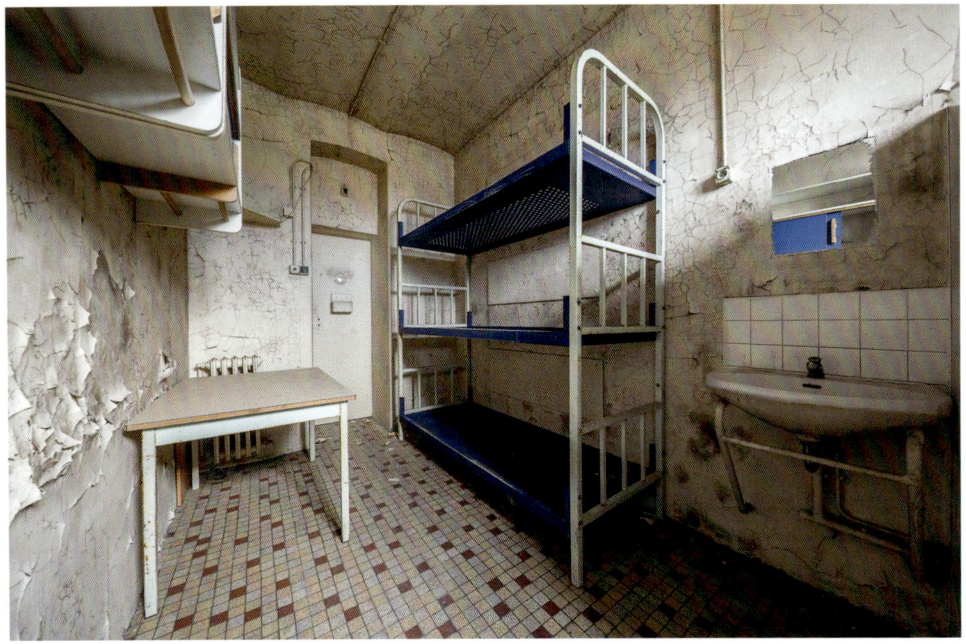

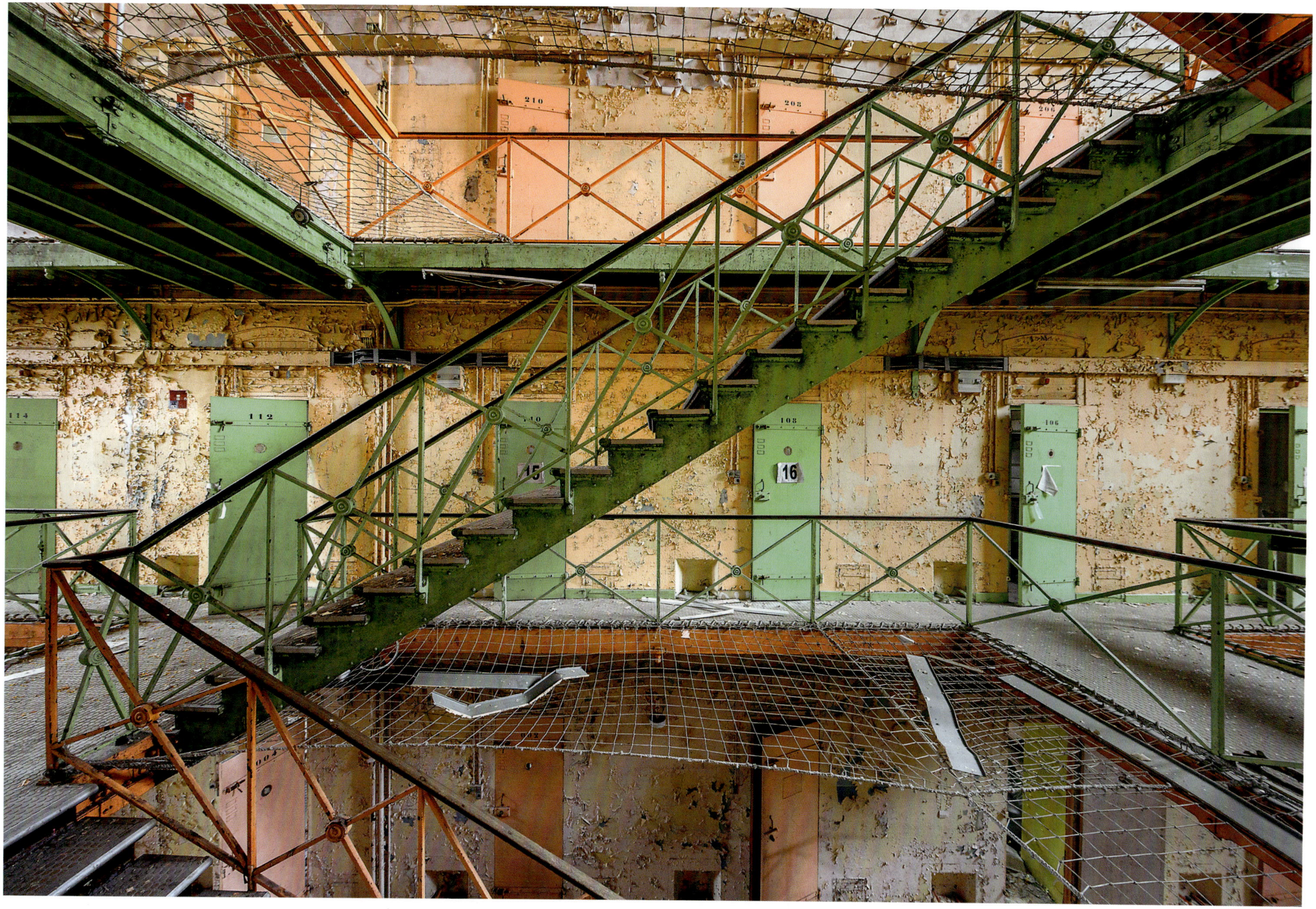
210
208
112
108
16

The manor with many busts • *Normandy*

Tucked away in the Normandy countryside, this magnificent 17th-century manor may have been abandoned for decades, but the surprise that awaits visitors inside its walls is sizeable: the atmosphere of this chateau is as surreal as it is striking.

Although it is abandoned, the magnificent manor is still fully furnished with lavish decorations typical of the great residences of the past. Looking at the photographs of the various rooms, it feels like the occupants left the place in a hurry. The everyday belongings of the manor make the place feel alive, even though it is uninhabited: the former owner's hat and scarf are hanging on the coat rack, books are stacked carelessly on the table as if they are begging to be read, the sumptuous grand piano seems to be waiting for a pianist to play a tune again, busts sit proudly on their pedestal and their models are even represented in some paintings.

In some parts, nature has reclaimed its rights, and this long-preserved place has recently been vandalised and stripped of its furniture by unscrupulous visitors. The manor's atmosphere is destined to fade.

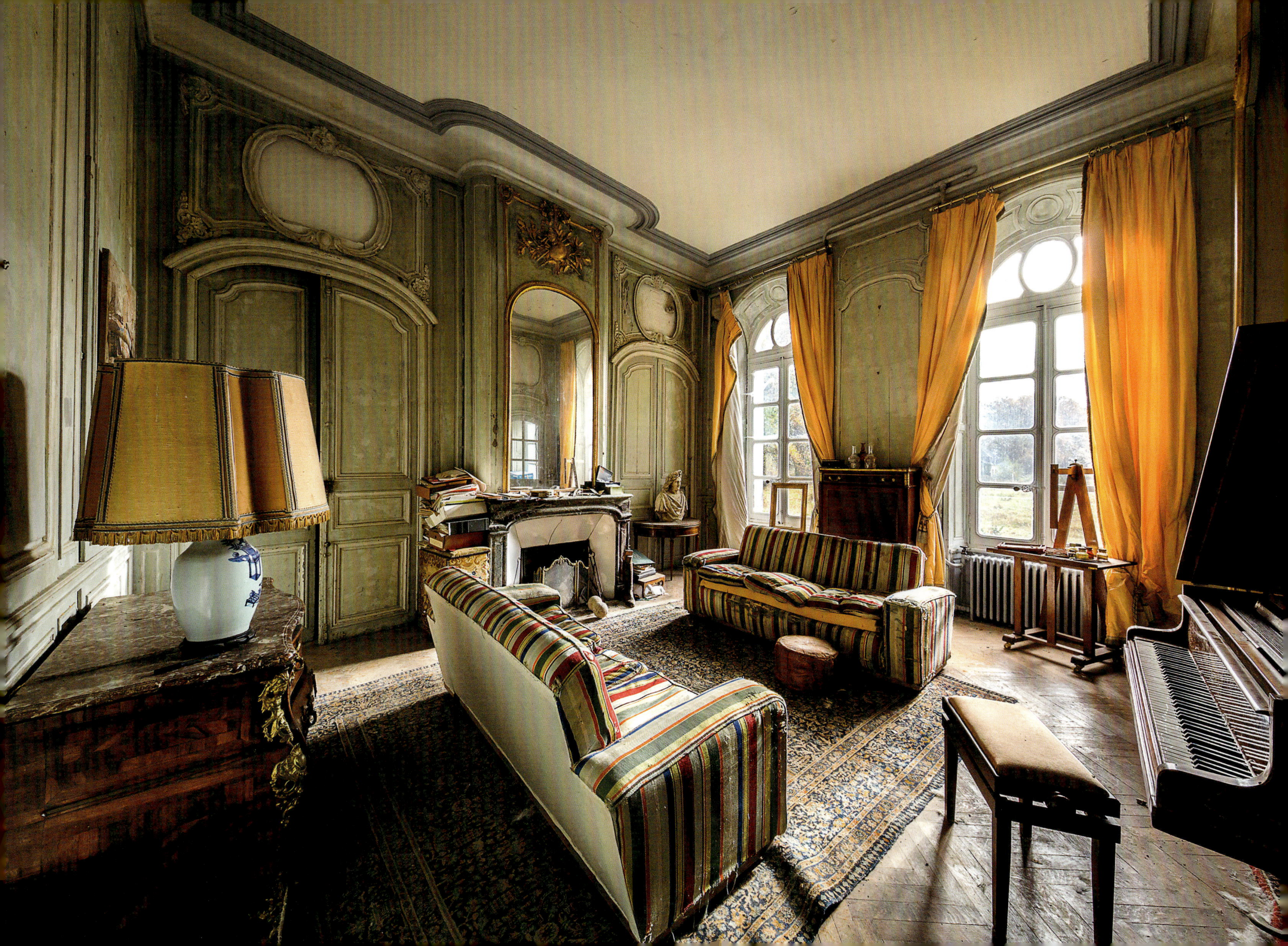

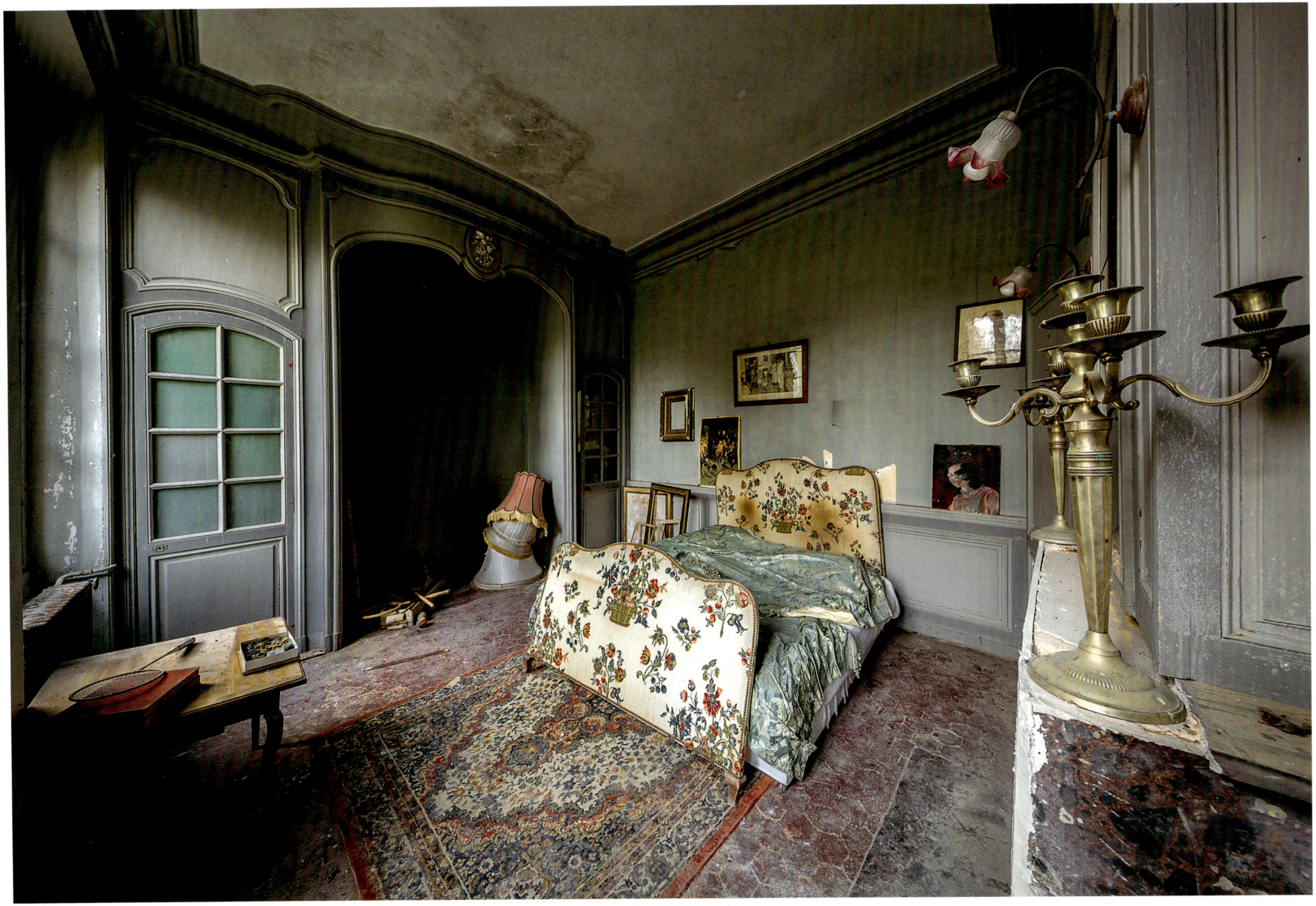

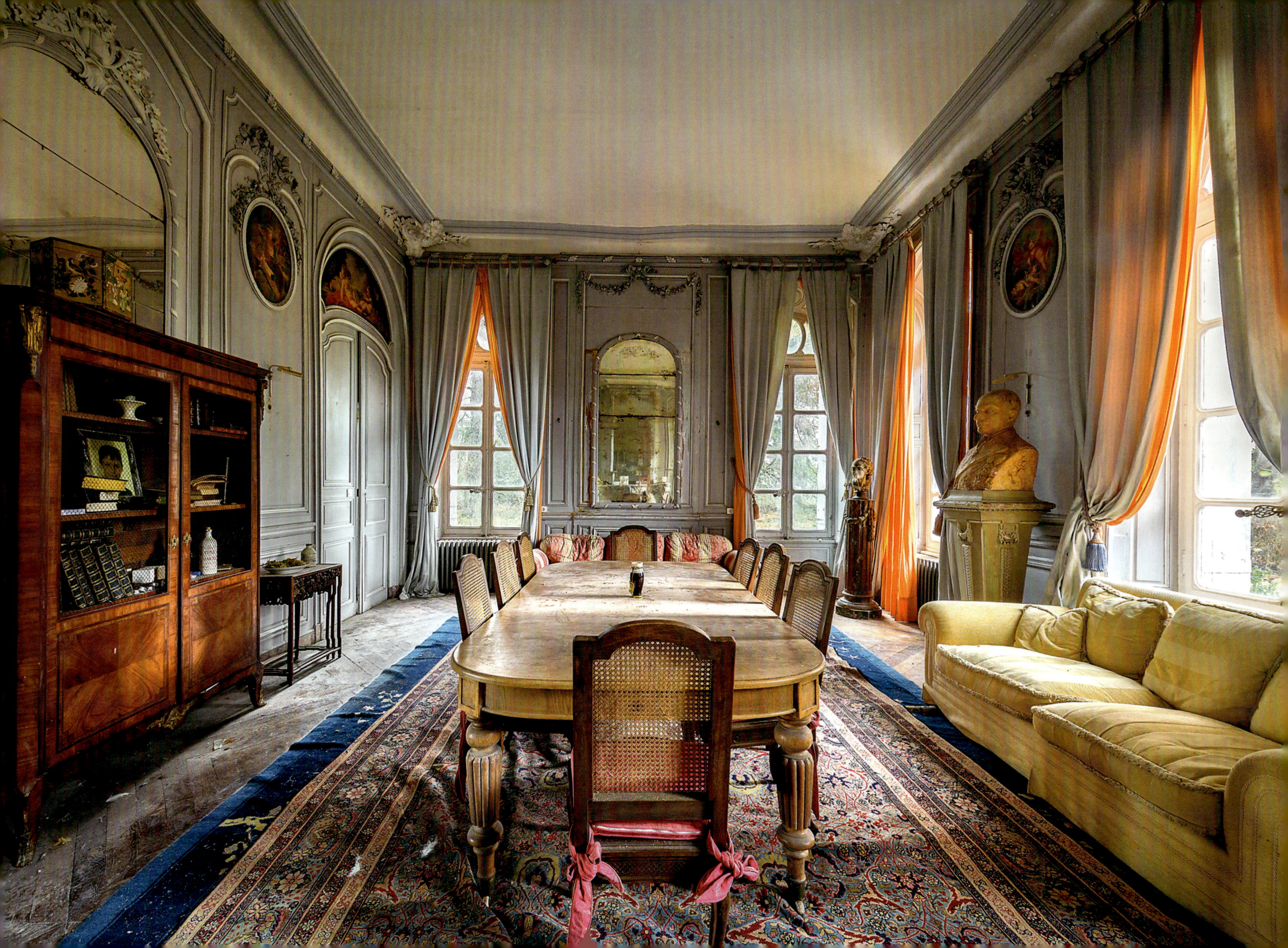

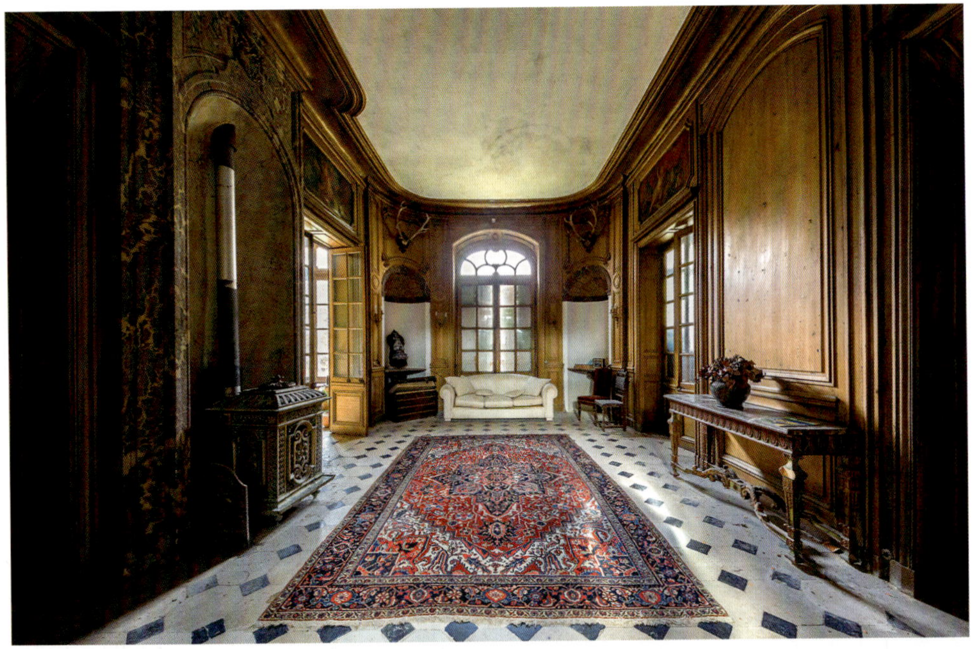

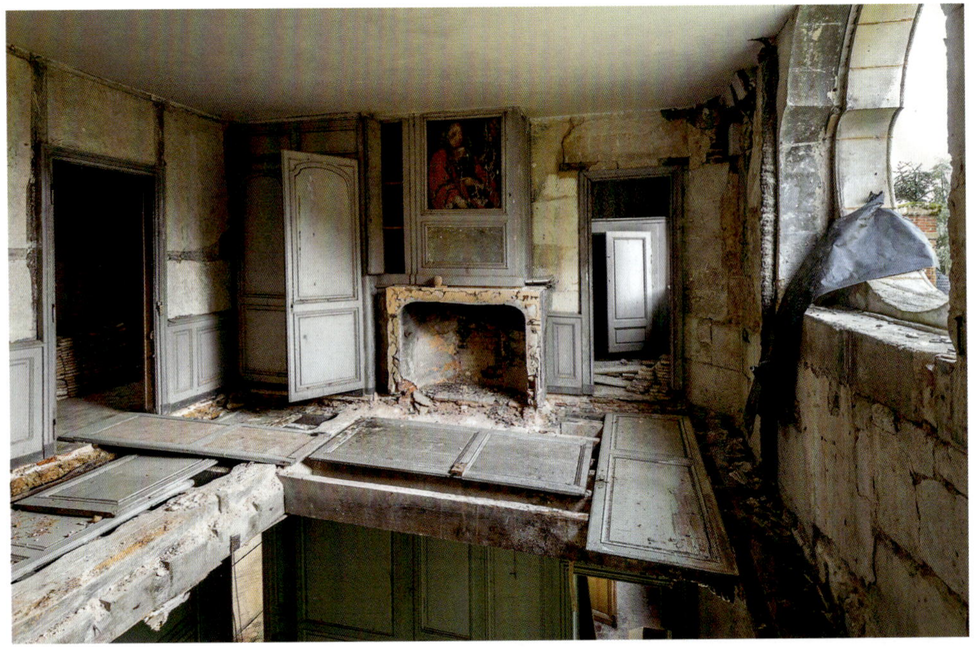

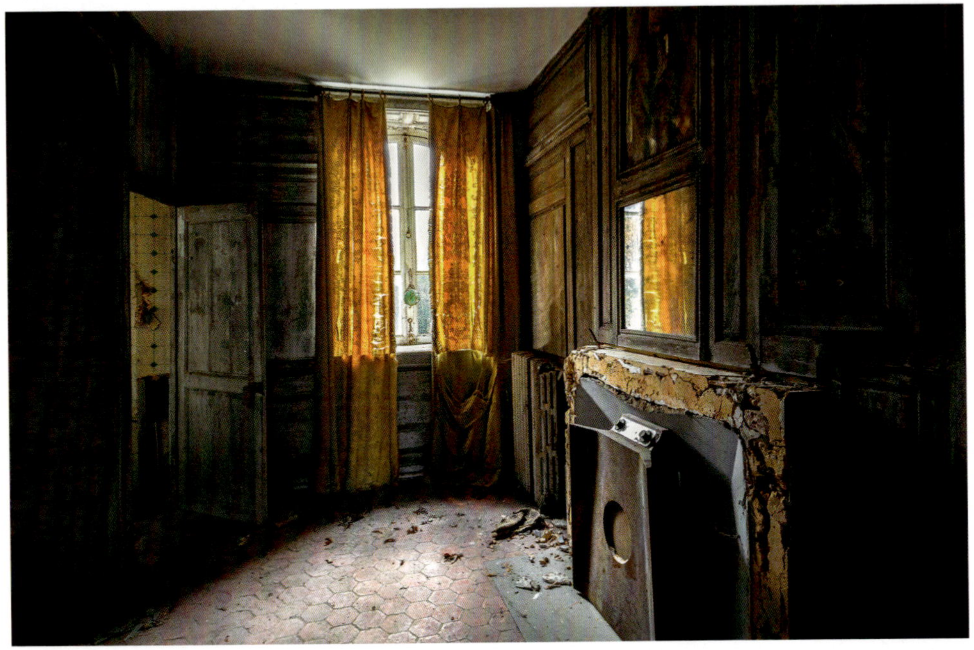

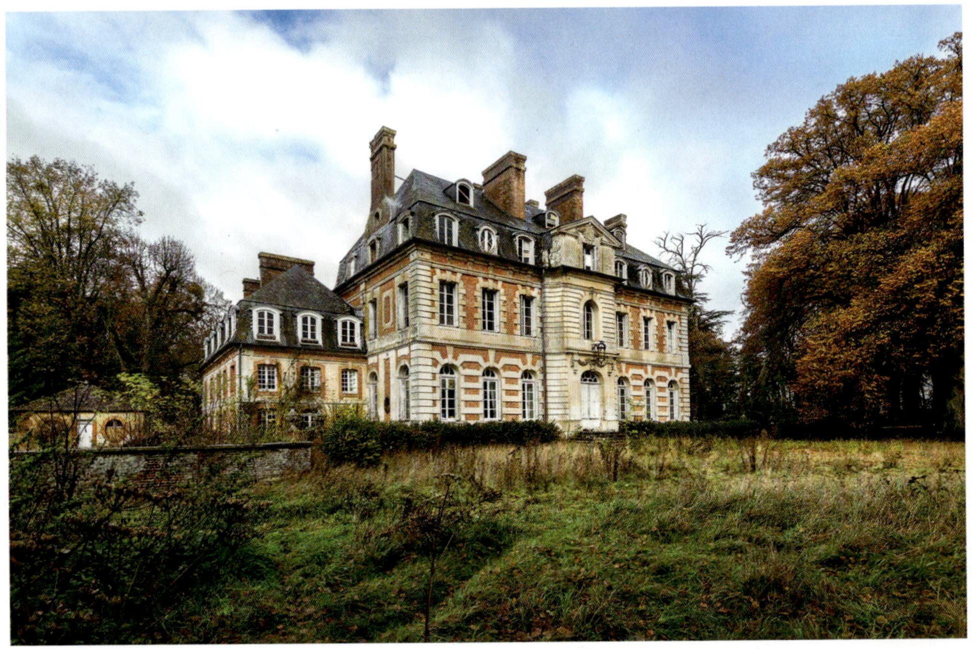

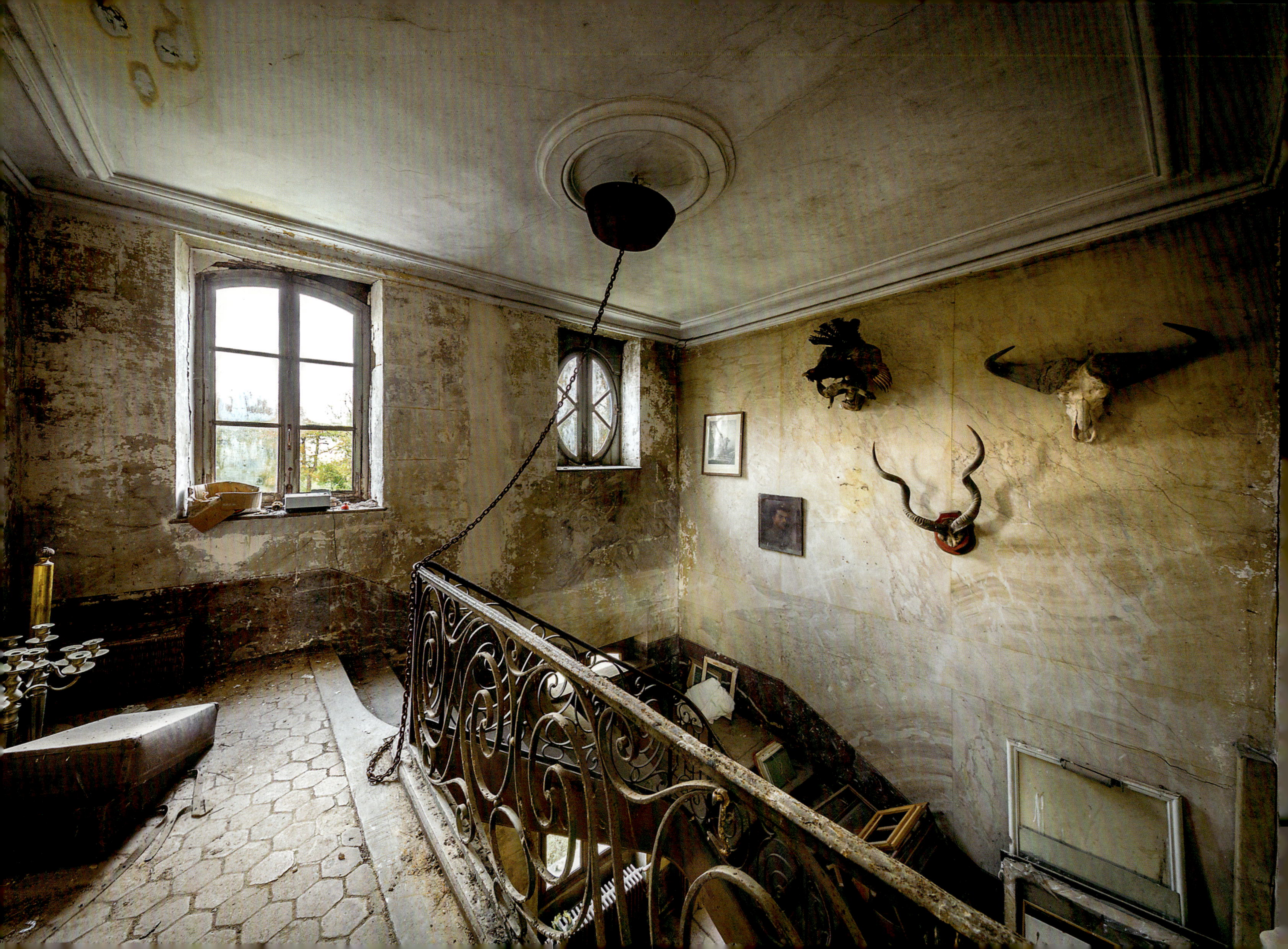

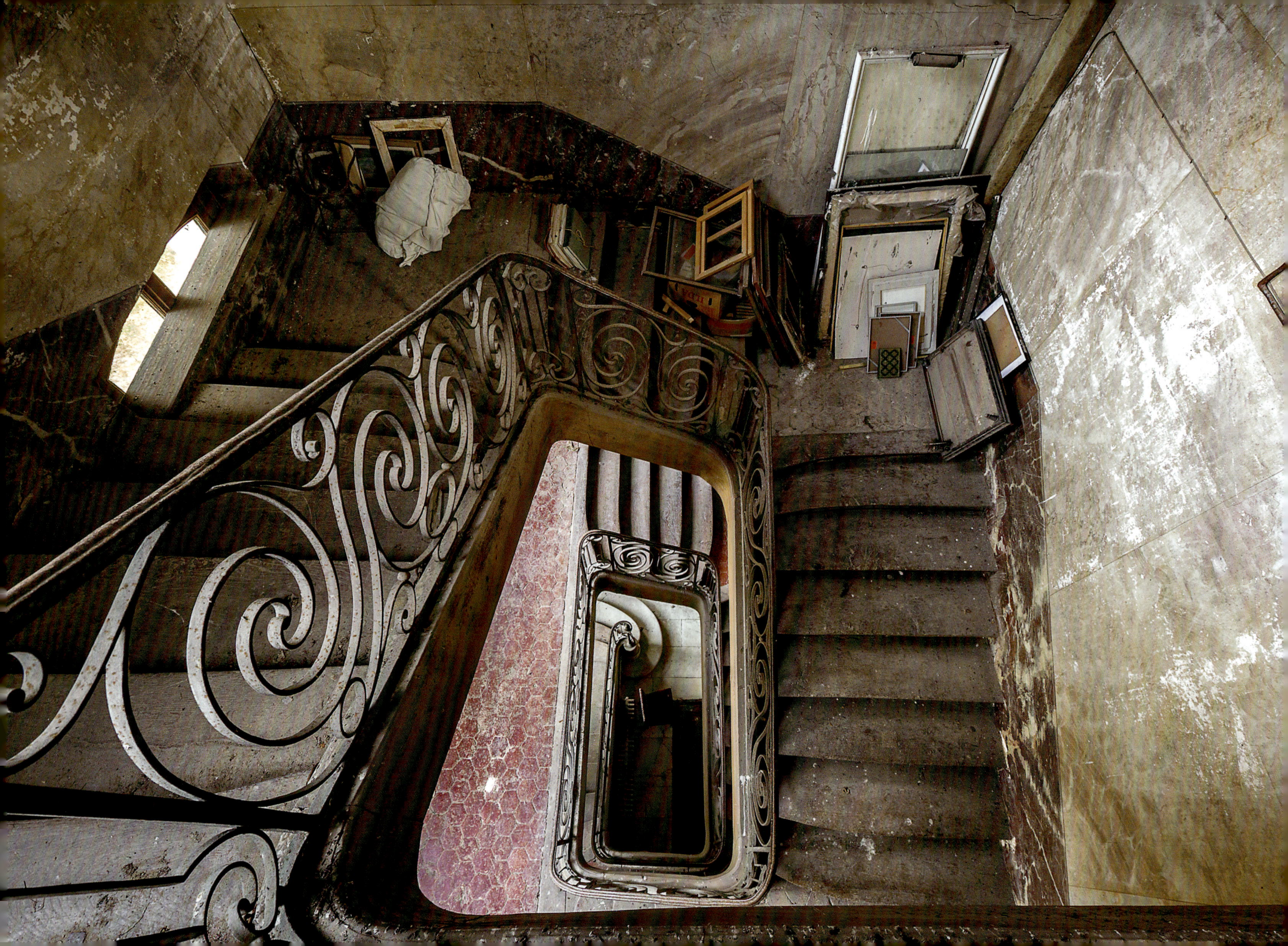

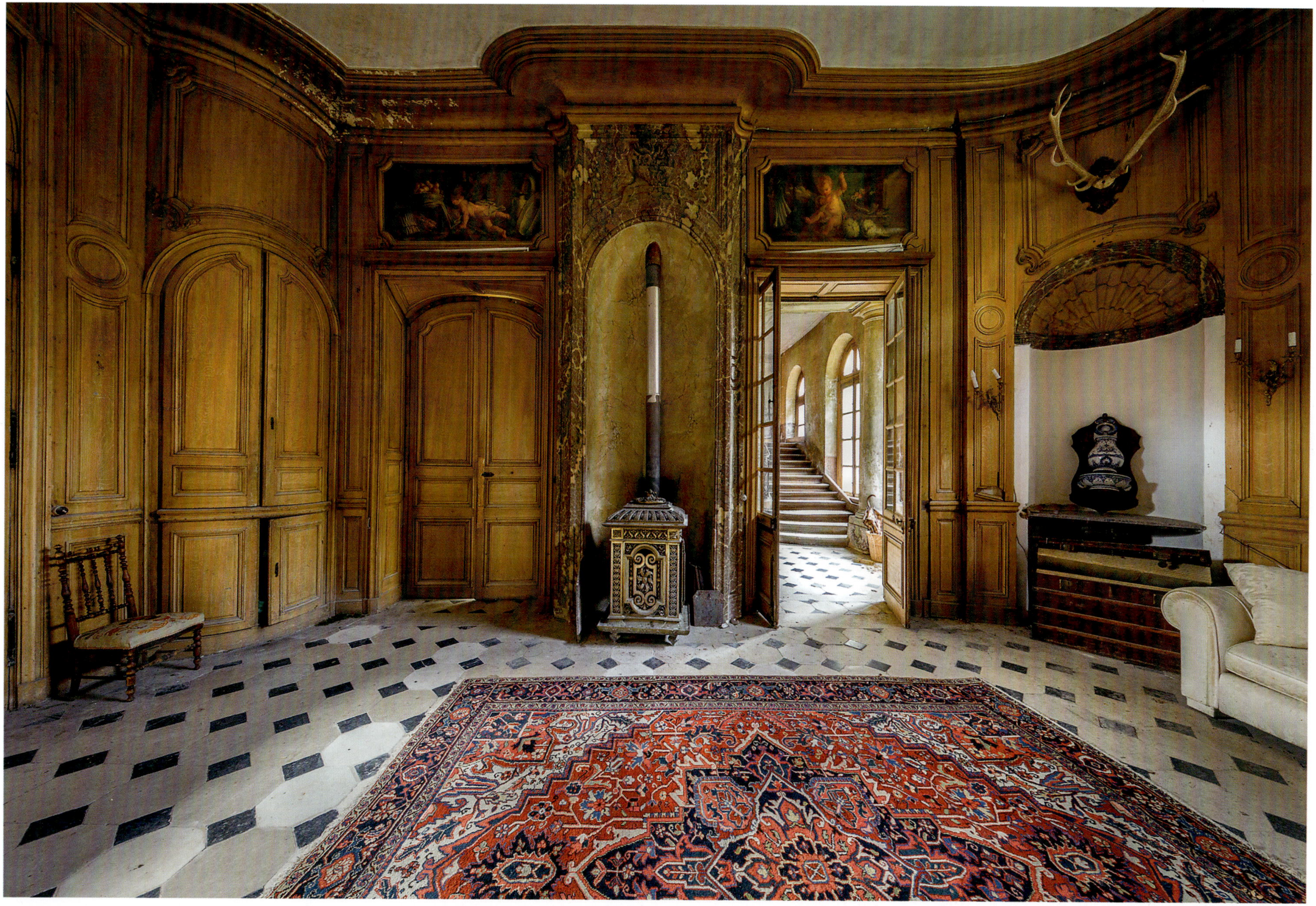

A chateau beneath the clouds • *Normandy*

This lavish 19th-century manor is a private property that was commissioned by a rich family of master dyers whose successful business spanned three generations. Tastefully furnished, the delightful manor was designed by the famous architect Juste Lisch, whose work included the restoration of prestigious castles, courthouses and religious buildings. Unfortunately, during the fourth generation, the young Arthur became an orphan at the age of 9 and was unable to take over the business and manage the house. It was left abandoned until 1990, when it was bought back, in an advanced state of dilapidation. It cost millions of francs to restore the building. The new owner carried out major renovations, bought furniture in beautiful wood from prestigious manufacturers, decorated the floors with oriental carpets, restored the entire park and installed a swimming pool, tennis court, and a rose garden on the island. The castle, which is now a bed and breakfast, was featured on the cover of the brochure Bienvenue au château (Welcome to the castle), which lists popular private chateaux and manors in the region. The owner still has fond memories of this wonderful place but was forced to put it up for sale in 2000.

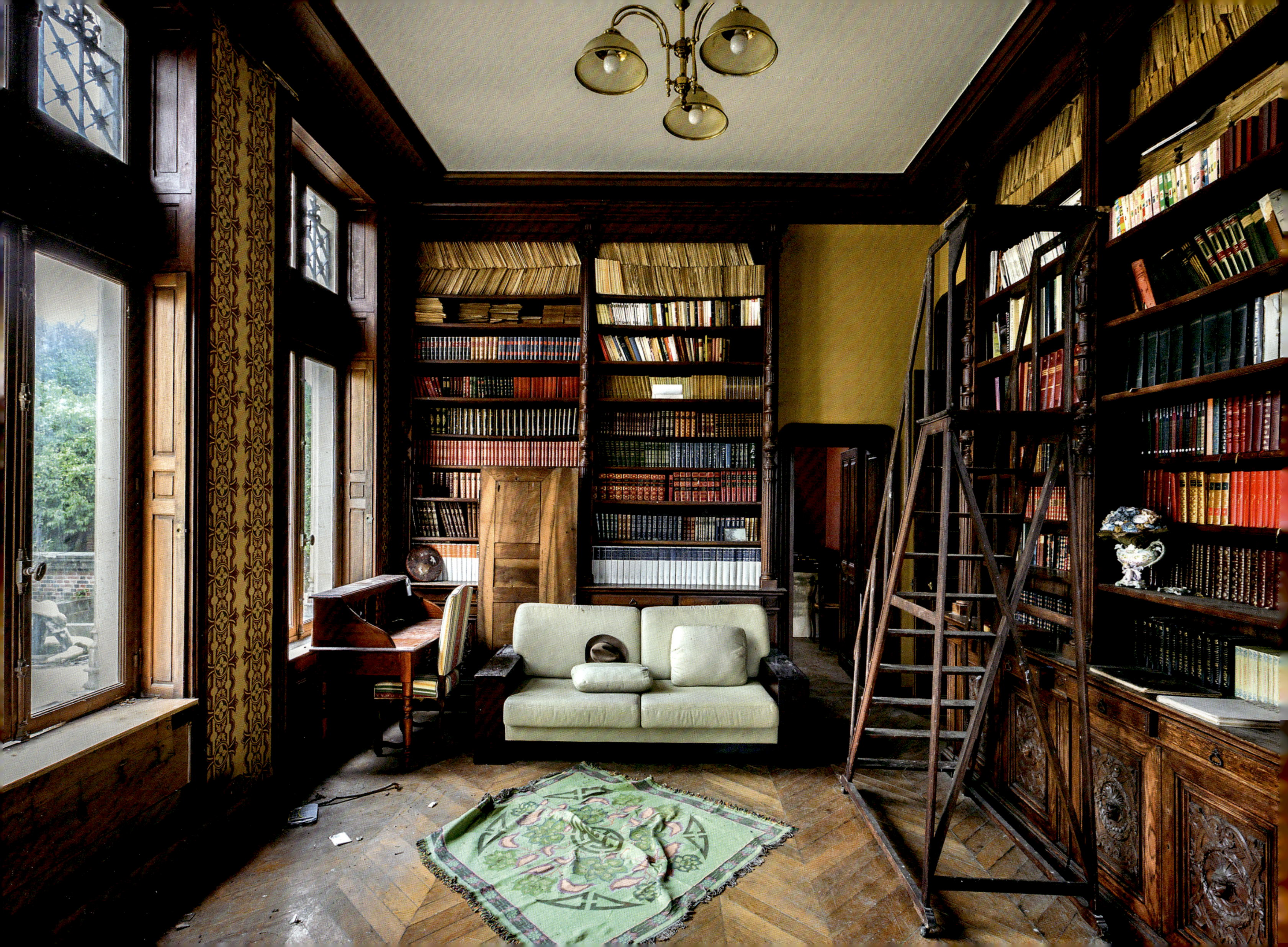

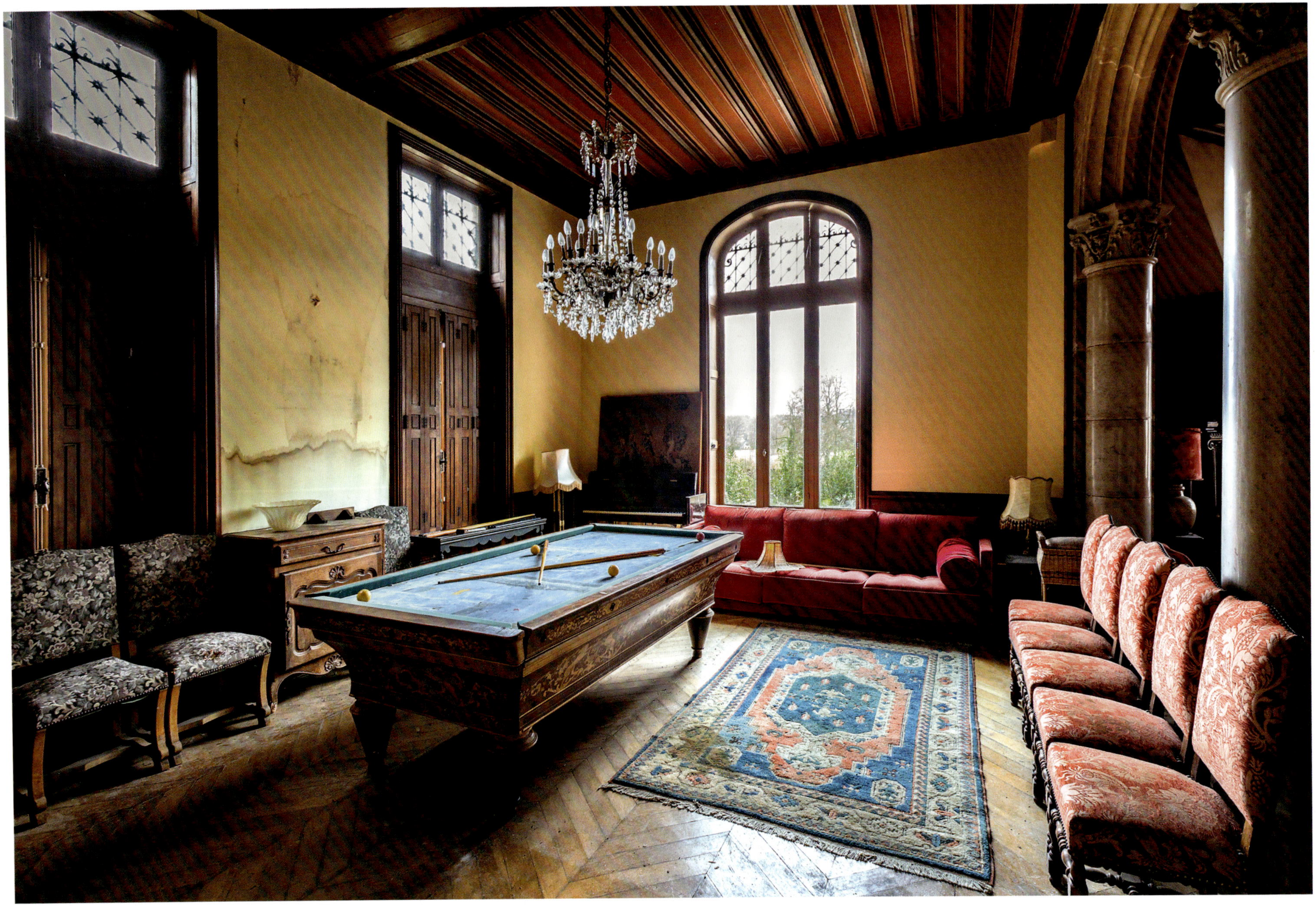

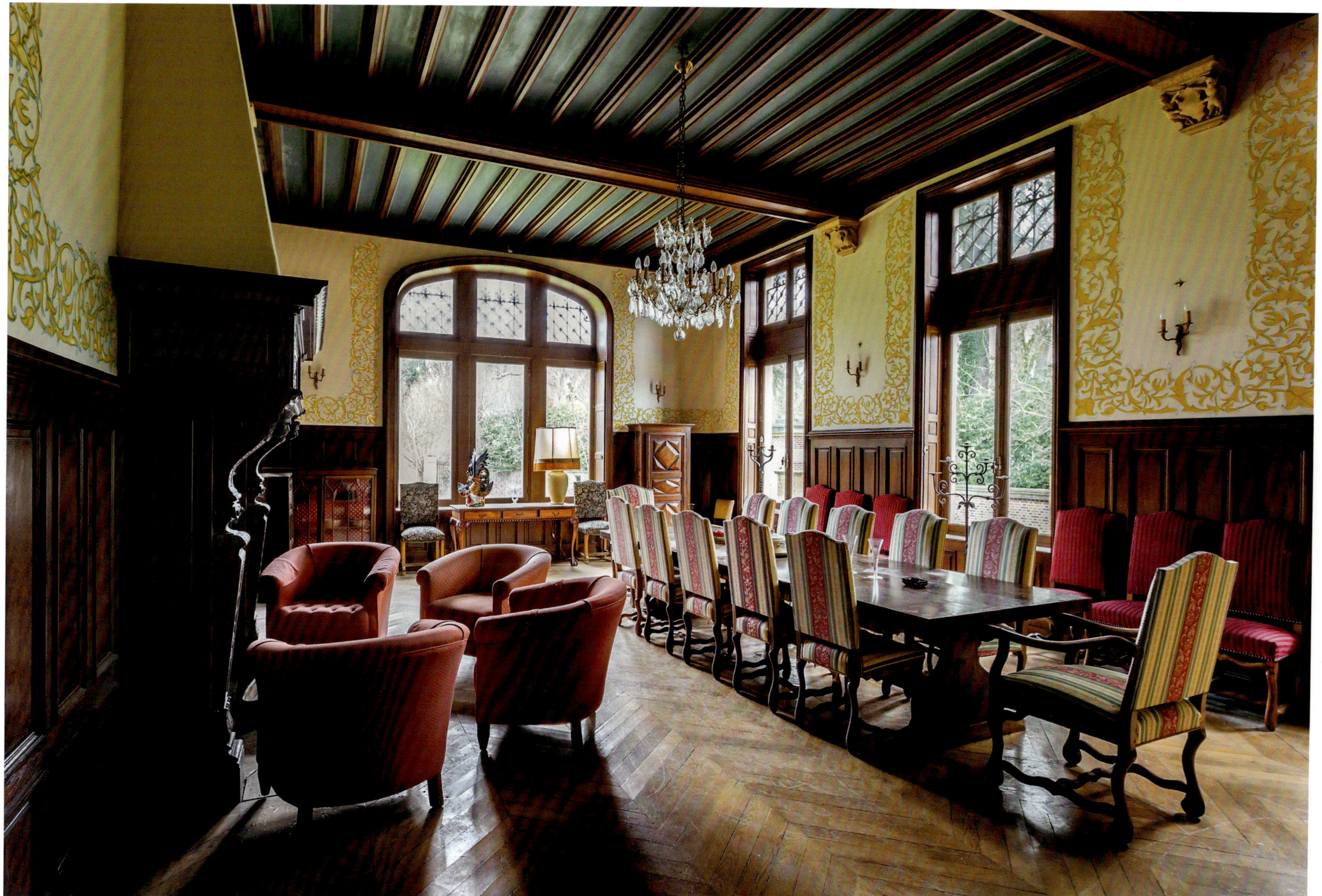

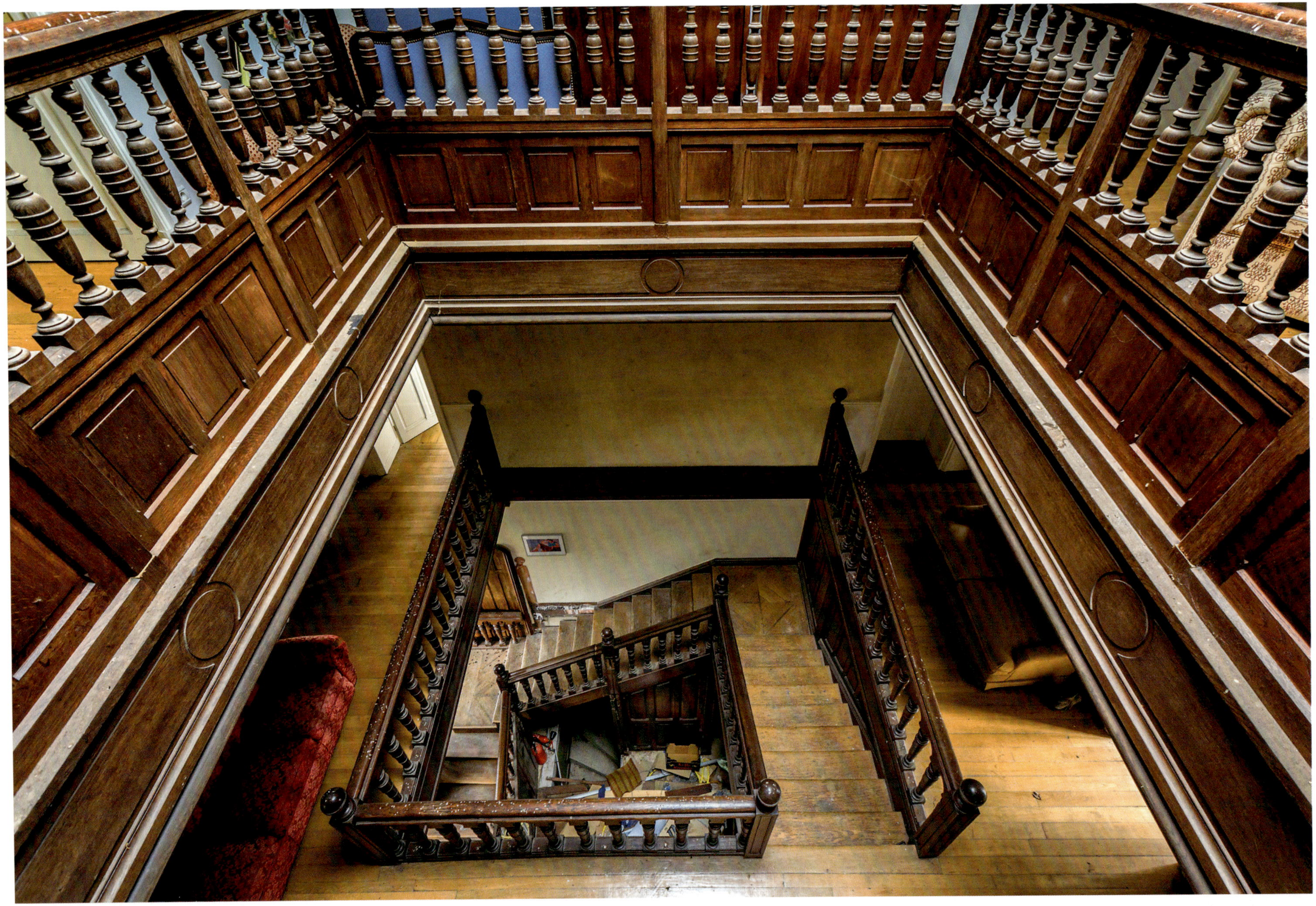

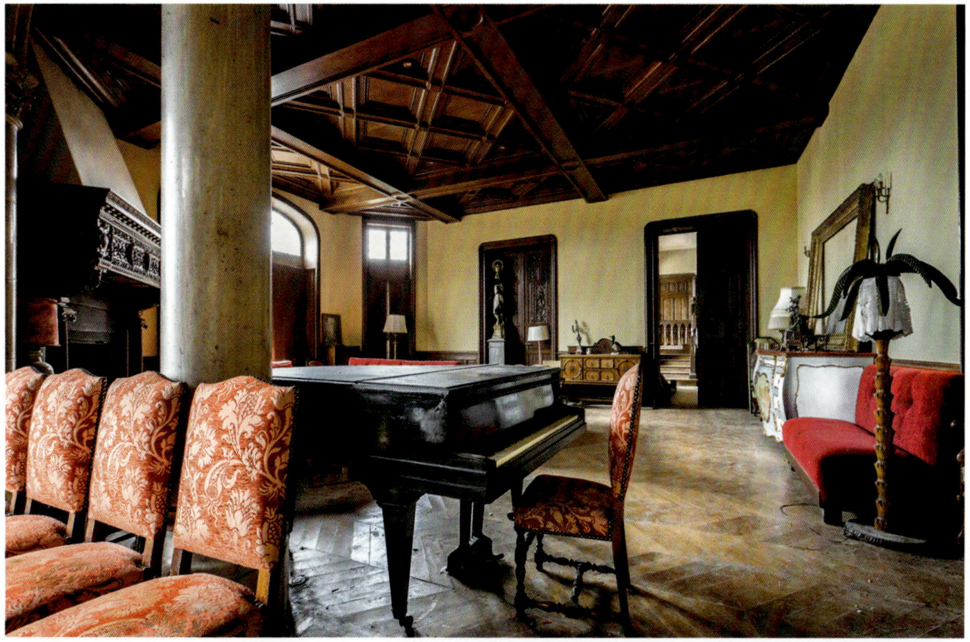

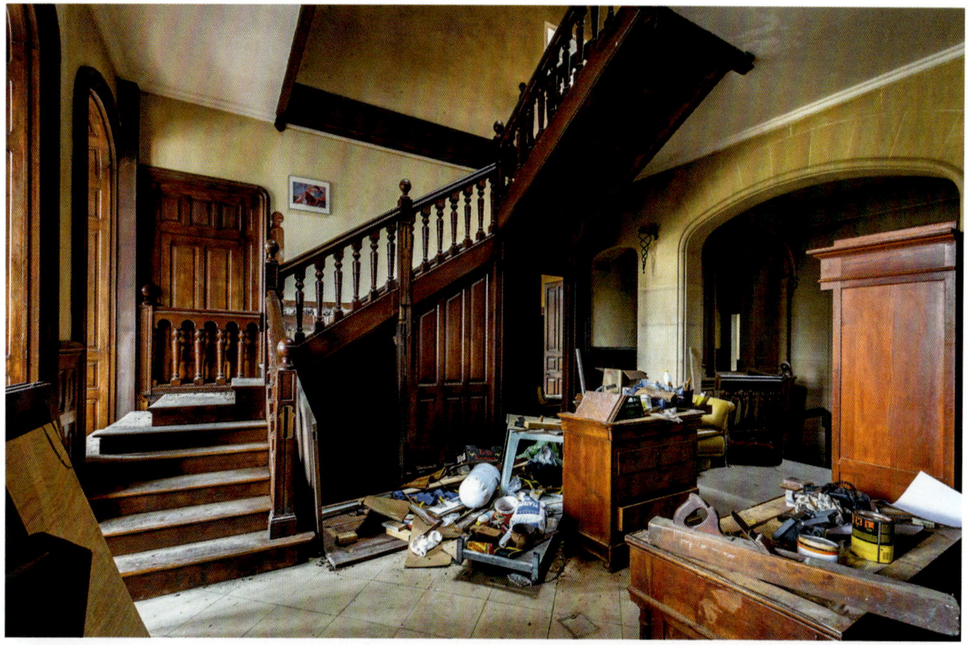

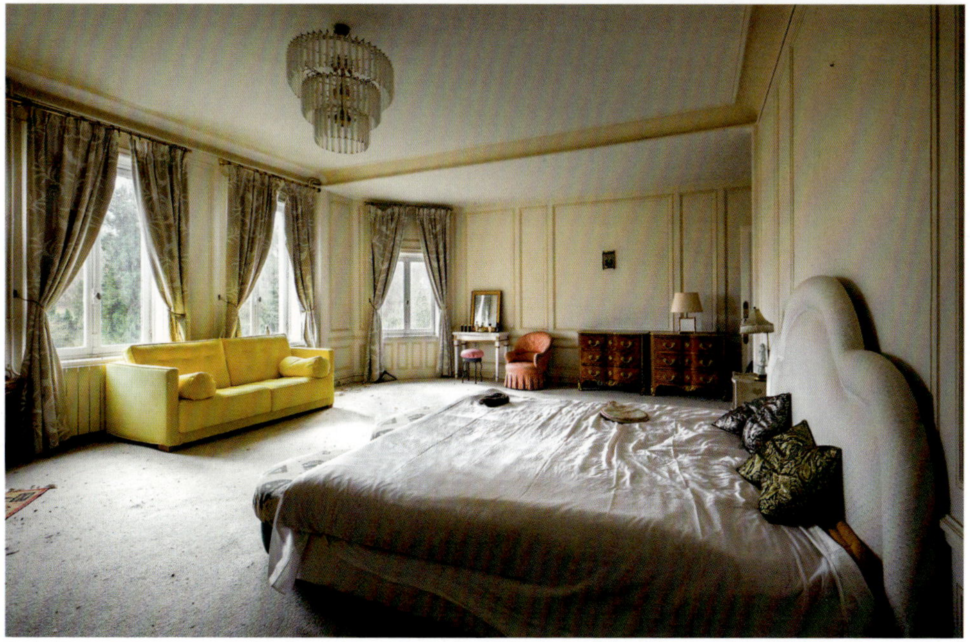

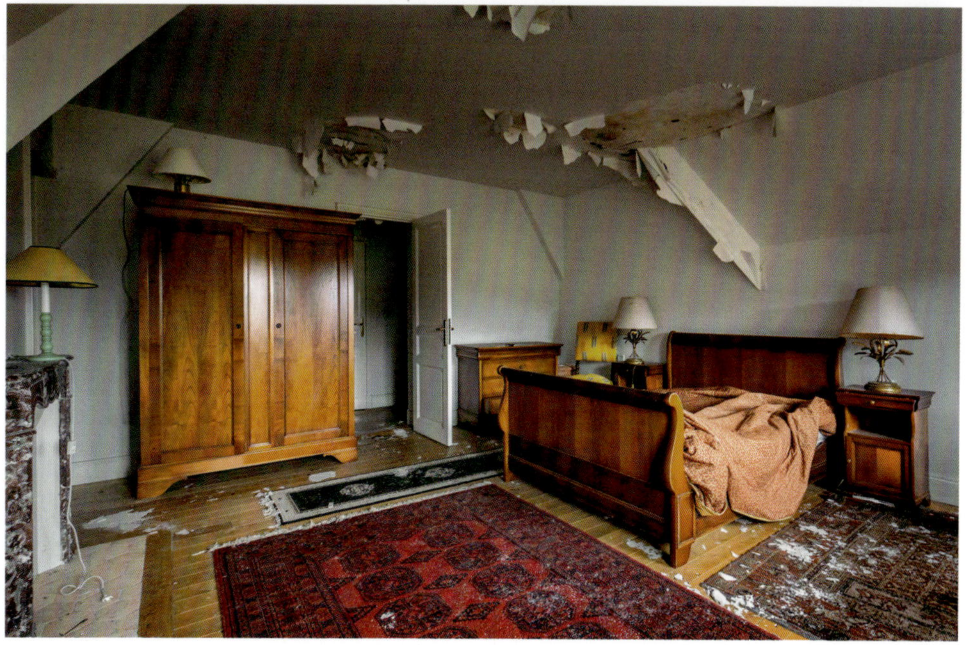

The manor house with the bouquets • *Normandy*

In a pretty, fortified village of France, where life goes on and everyone knows each other, it is still possible to find the remains of a 13th-century wall and tour.

Behind the imposing wall is a manor house overgrown with luxuriant vegetation. Ivy has crept in through the beautiful glass roof, which has suffered from the passing of time, and the wallpaper is falling to pieces from the humidity that seeps through the walls. Huge spiderwebs make up the manor's rather unusual decor that gives the place a certain charm. It is impossible not to notice all the vases filled with bouquets of dried or artificial flowers that adorn every room.

No one knows the history of this grand mansion, which has been neglected for many years. As is often the case, the building has suffered from a problem of inheritance or a lack of funds to maintain and repair it.

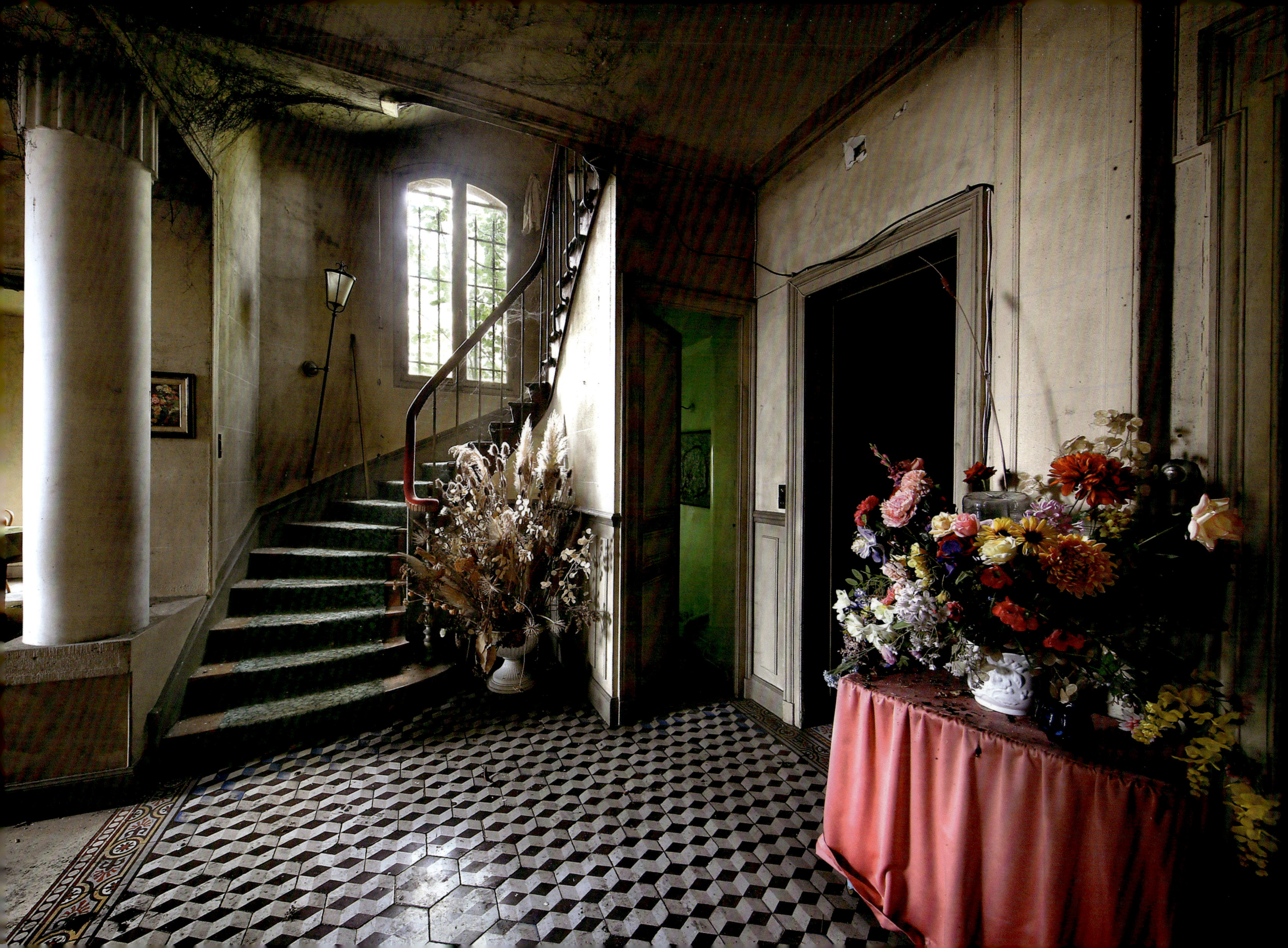

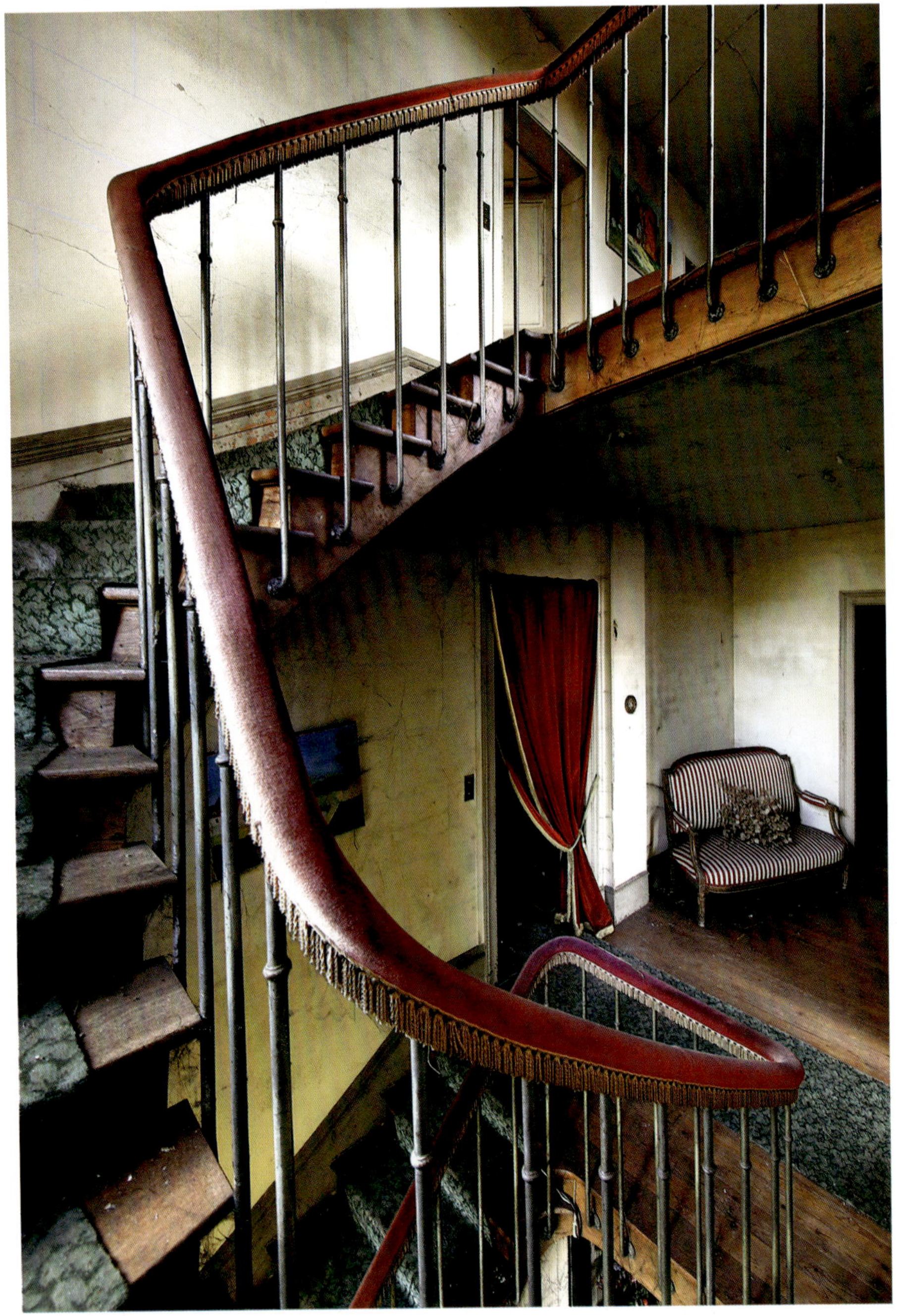

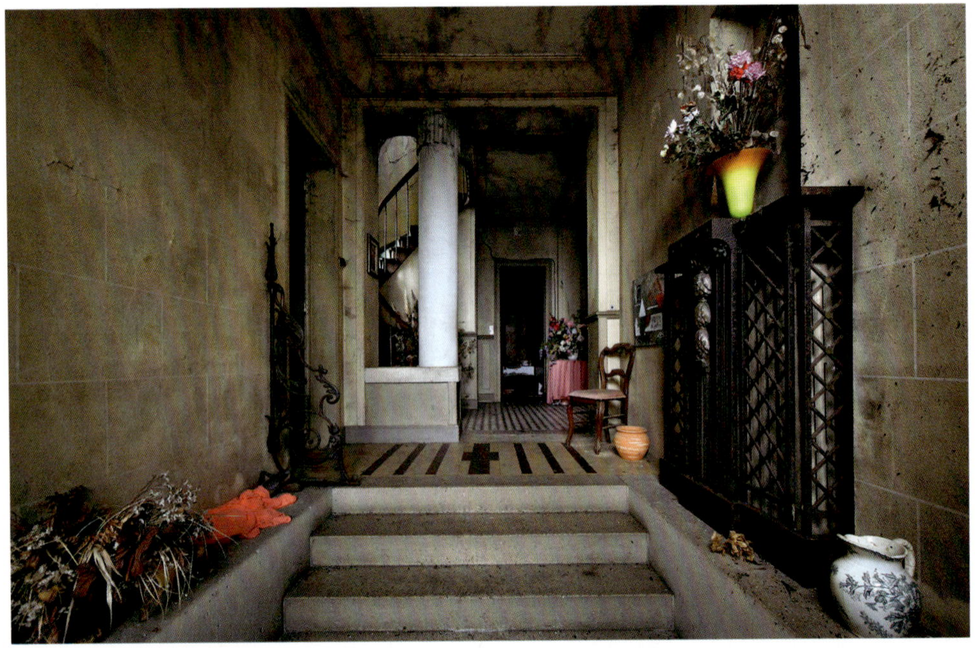

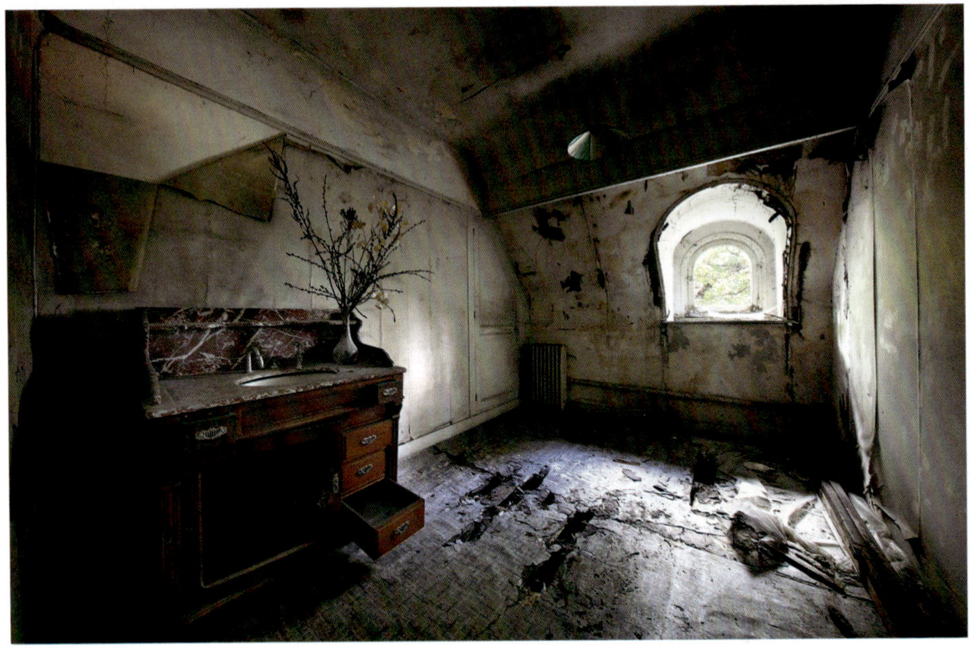

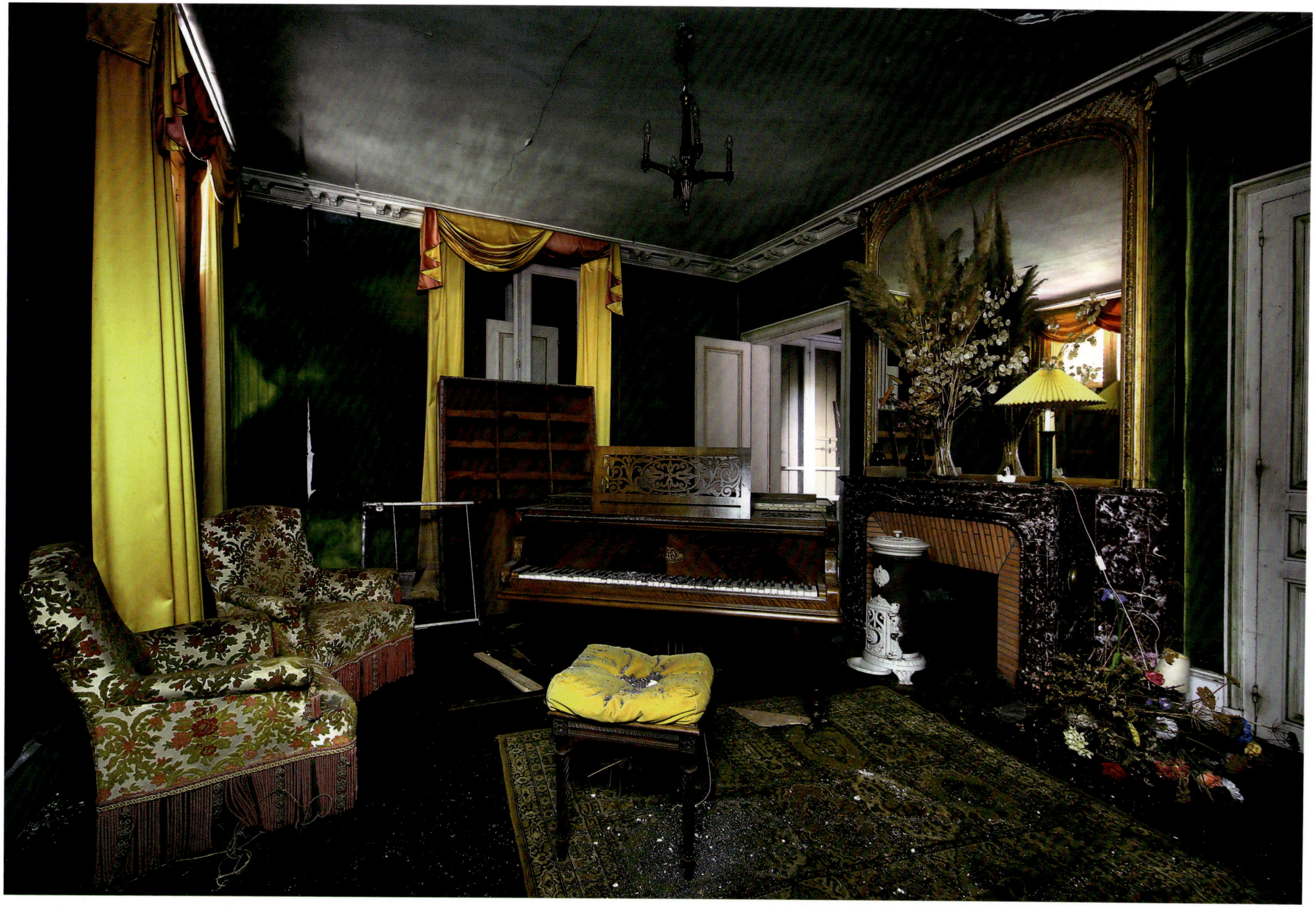

The barracks of Sainte-Barbe • *Normandy*

This warehouse, which seems to have been abandoned since 1994, is home to a dazzling and exceptional collection of fire engines, which were used by the brave firemen and are still in excellent condition today. Dating from the 1930s to the 1970s, they include mostly French trucks such as Saviem (1955–1978), which was a merger of Latil (the heavyweight vehicle division of Renault) and Somua, but also Citroën, Berliet, Peugeot and Delahaye.

The diversity of shapes makes these truck models unique. The equipment of the trucks differed greatly and depended on the type of emergency they had to attend to, whether the emergency was for an illness, burns, wounds, road accidents, sports accidents, at home or at work. Each truck was equipped with specific features that impacted its appearance, setting them apart from the traditional rescue vehicles with their large ladders well known to the general public.

The only thing that unites them is the typical red colour that all trucks have shared since the 19th century. At that time, the Paris fire brigade imported vermilion fire pumps from England. It was noticed that the colour was more eye-catching and had a greater effect on the population, so the French fire brigade decided to keep it for their own vehicles.

The collection is now being restored before being put on display in a museum and given a new lease of life. This is a very welcome project, especially as some models have become particularly rare.

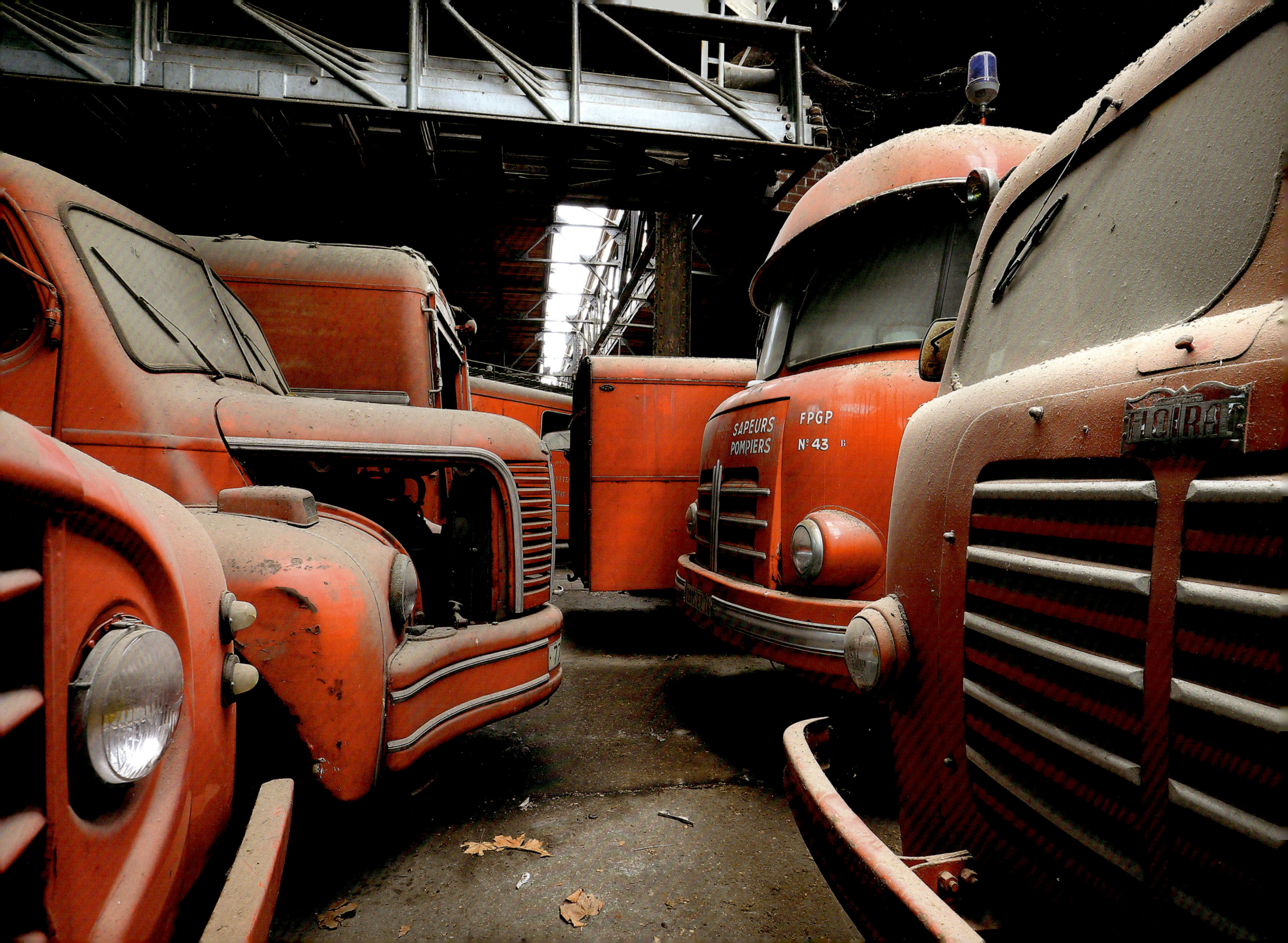
SAPEURS
POMPIERS
FPGP
N° 43
B

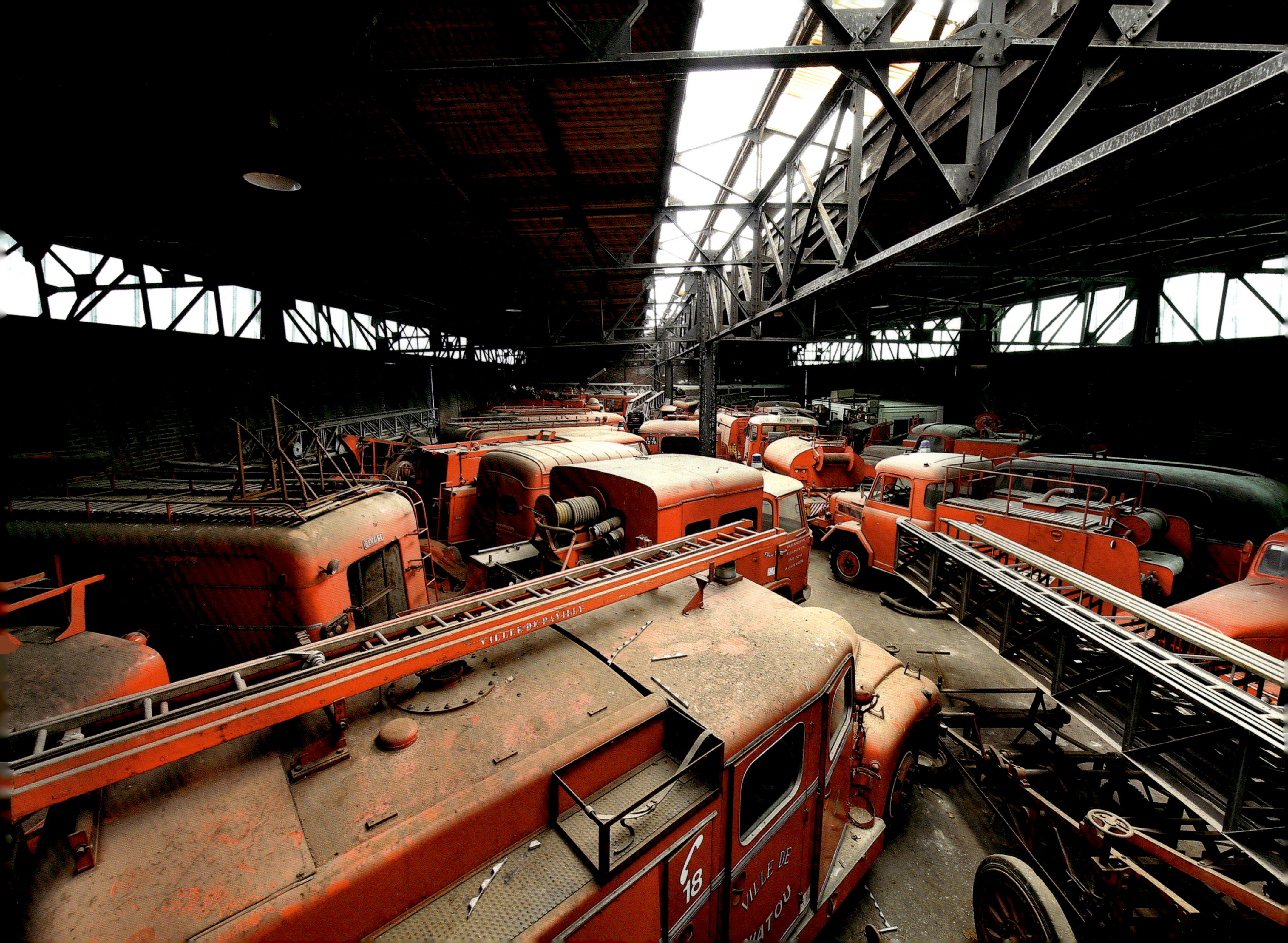
VILLE-DE-PAVILLY
18
VILLE DE

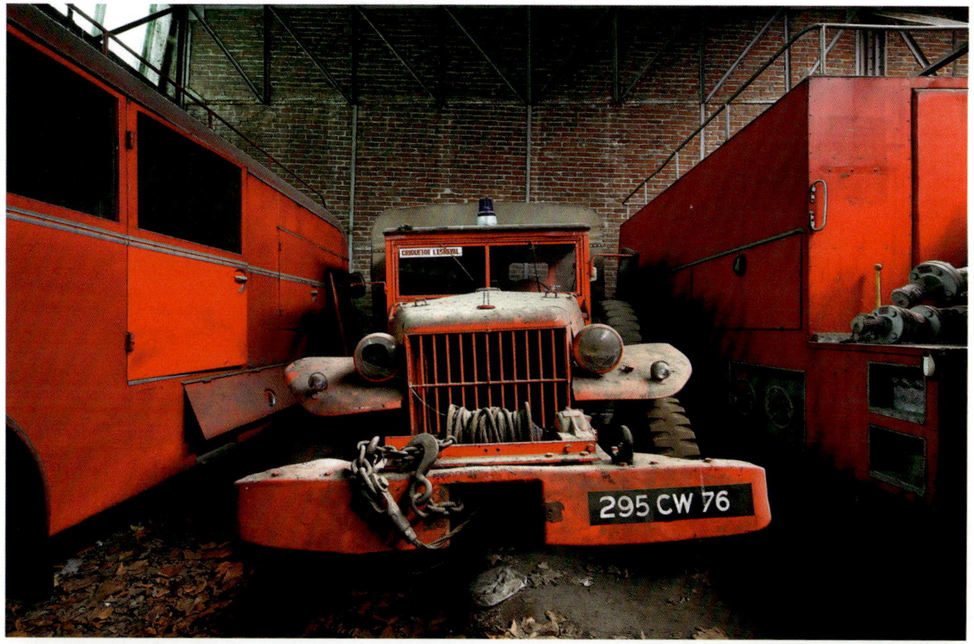
295 CW 76

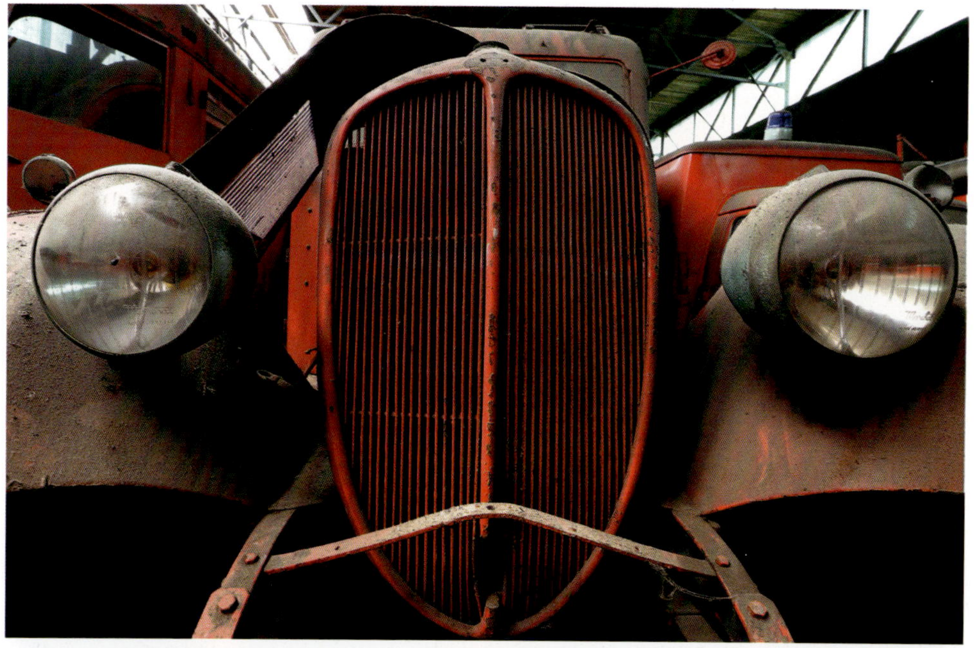

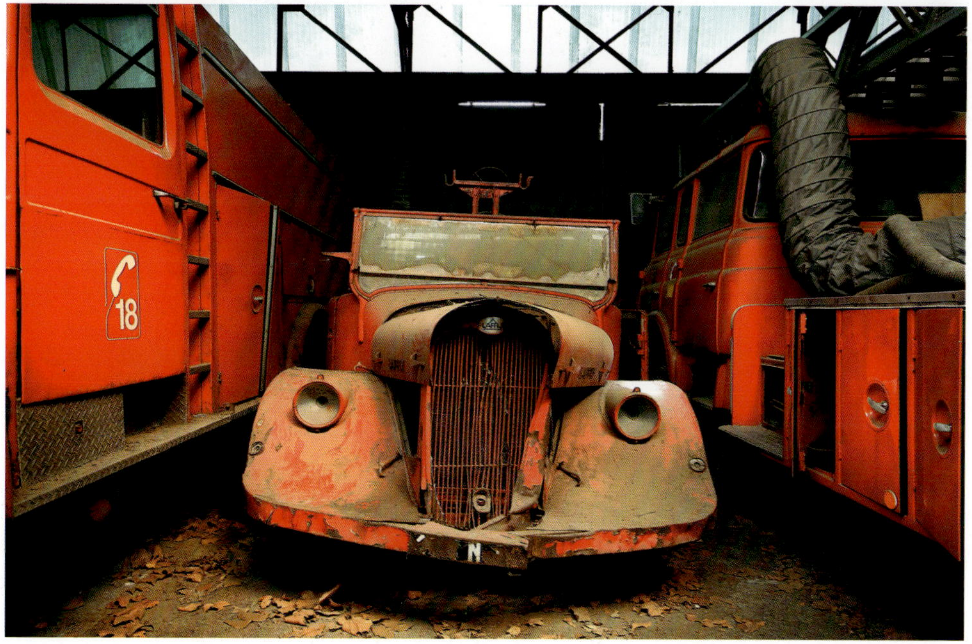
18

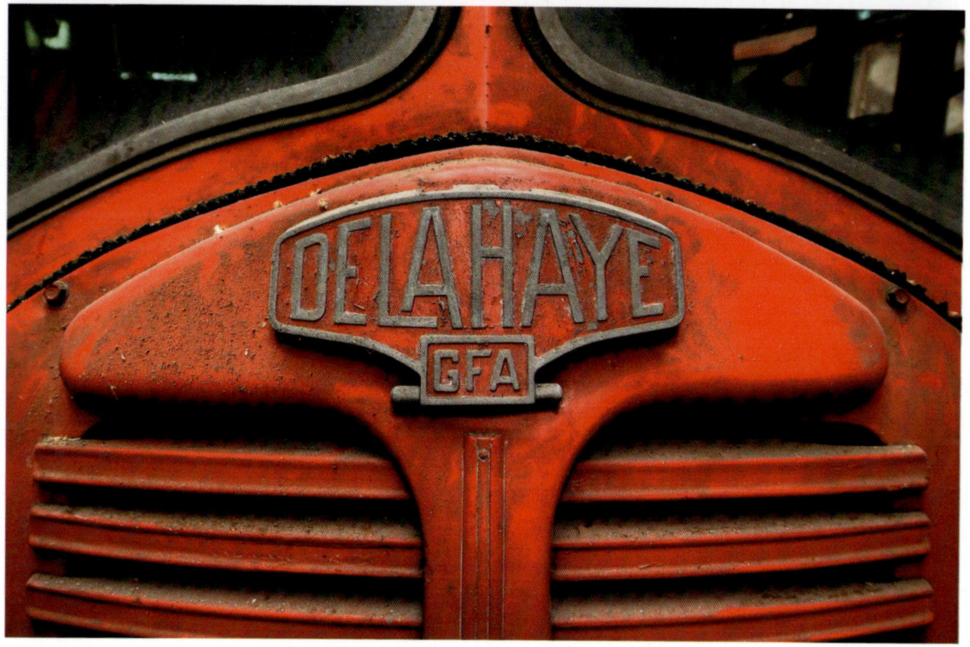
DELAHAYE
GFA

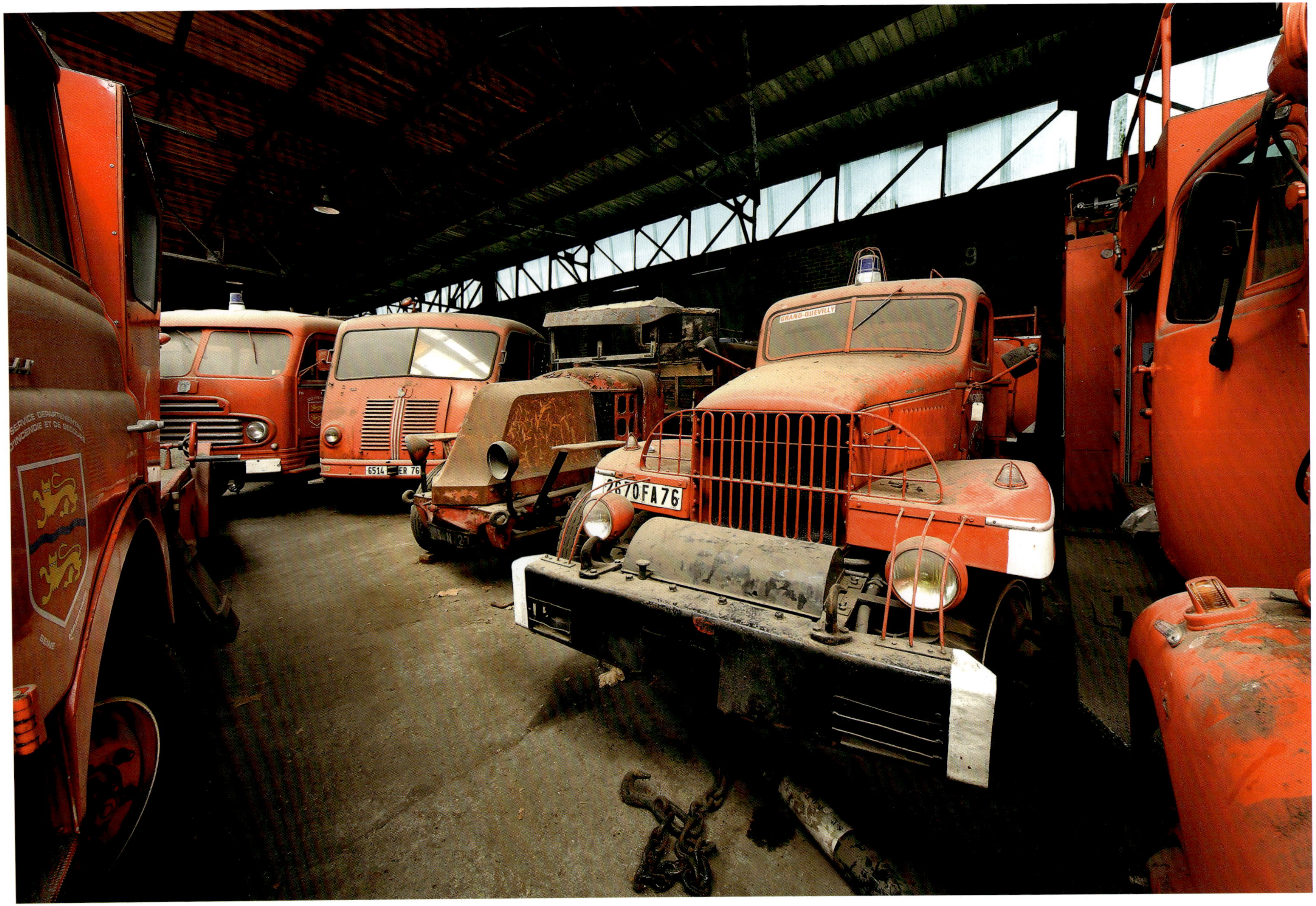
GRAND-QUEVILLY
2670FA76
6514 ER 76

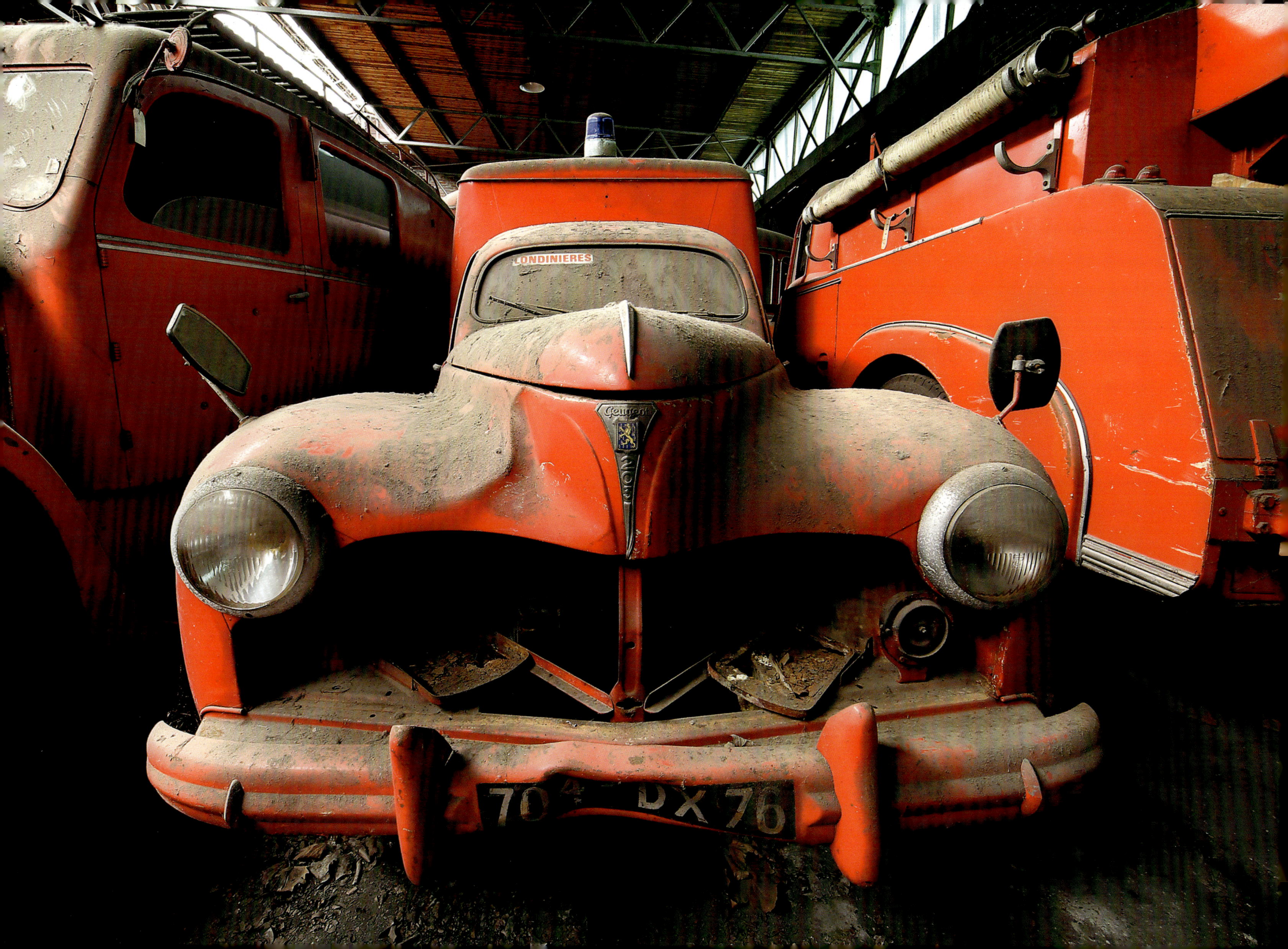
LONDINIERES

Sleeping trains • *Normandy*

Embark on a real time machine! Travel with me at a gentle pace back through the history of French railways, along a section of the old track between Rouen and Orléans. Let yourself be transported back in time: the ticket offices, the scales, the goods warehouse ... All the features that made a station one of the most important economic activities of a region.

Clad in red and white, the ABJ 4 railcar was built by Renault in 1948. Classified as a historical monument, it is the only one still in service. This railcar, which was only for first class, was equipped with a 300 HP engine and ran at 120 km/h on the south-west lines.

For many years, the postal service in France used train carriages known as mail wagons. They were designed to transport dispatches and mail, which was sorted by PTT (post, telegraph and telephone) agents, and were generally attached to passenger trains. There were daytime transport services known as 'primos' and overnight services known as 'secondos', which eventually disappeared in 1995. The first mail wagon for sorting operations ran on 1 August 1845 on the line from Paris to Rouen. It was a 4.80-metre-long wagon with two axles and a wooden frame. Individuals could deposit a letter in the letterbox of the sorting car when the train stopped. The letter was then stamped by the mobile postal service. Today, these stamps are very sought after by some philatelists.

Dozens of trains from different eras are maintained by enthusiasts who bring these beautiful machines back to life. Talking to them took me back to my childhood days.

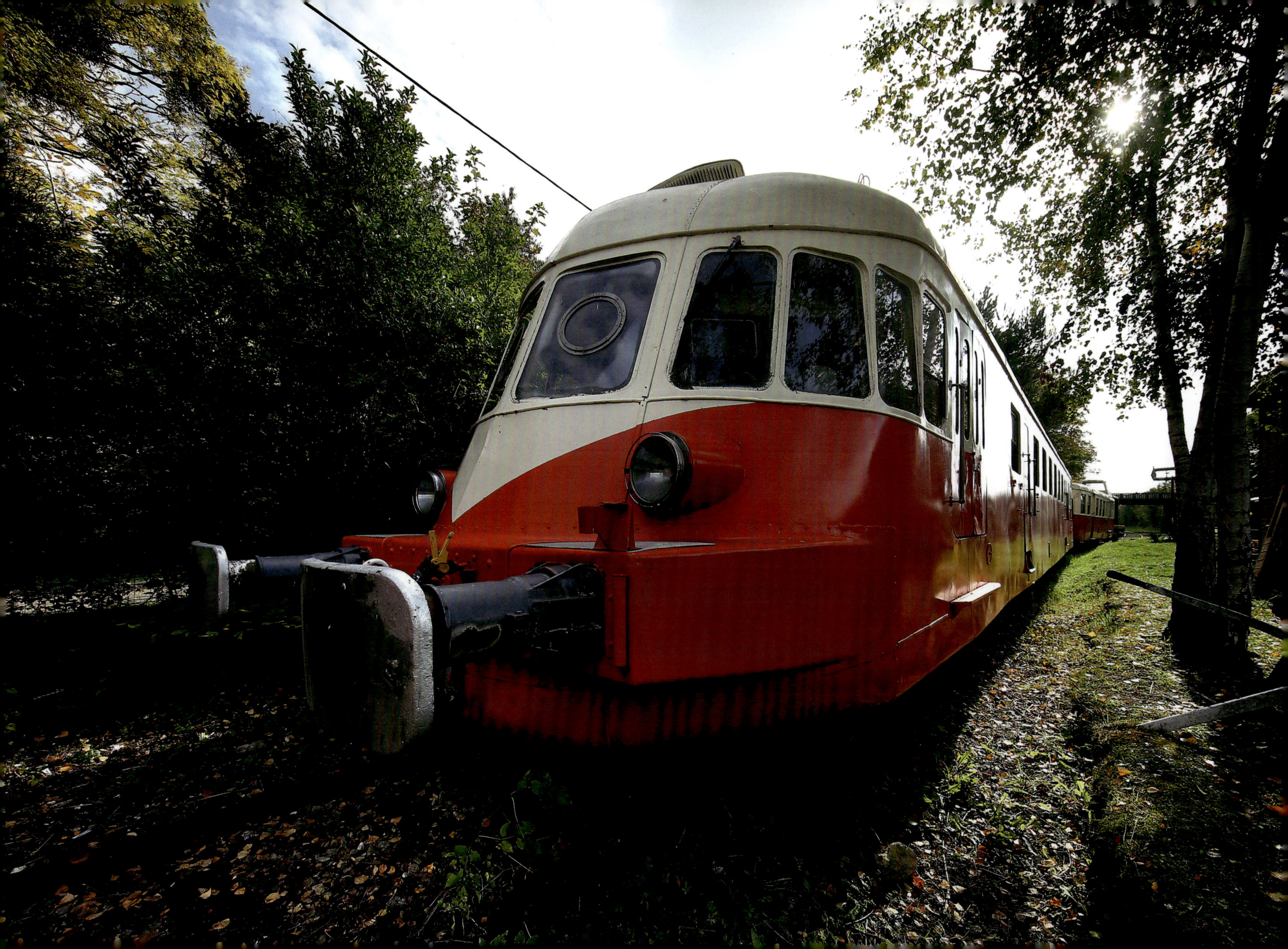

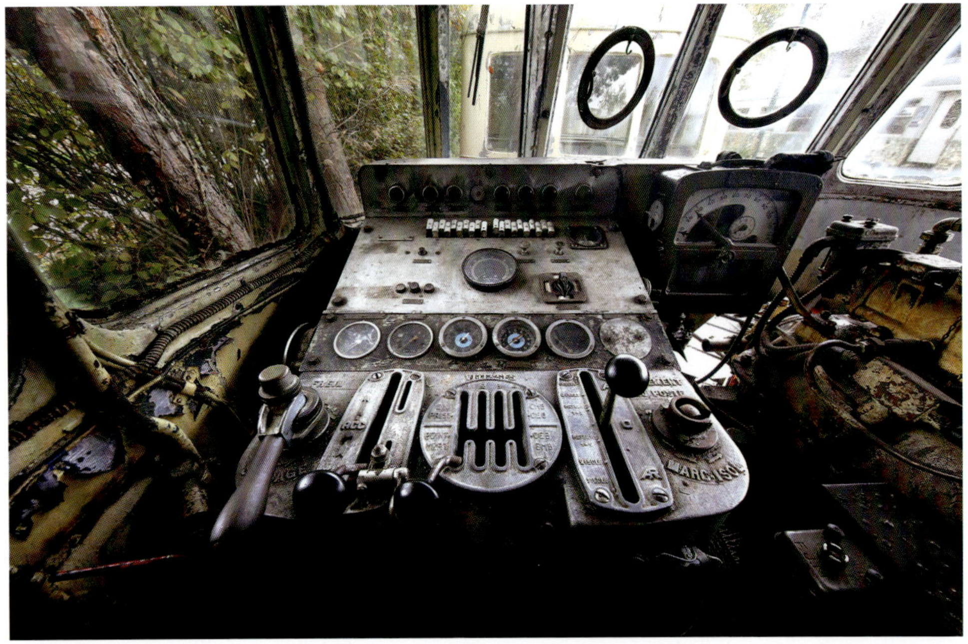

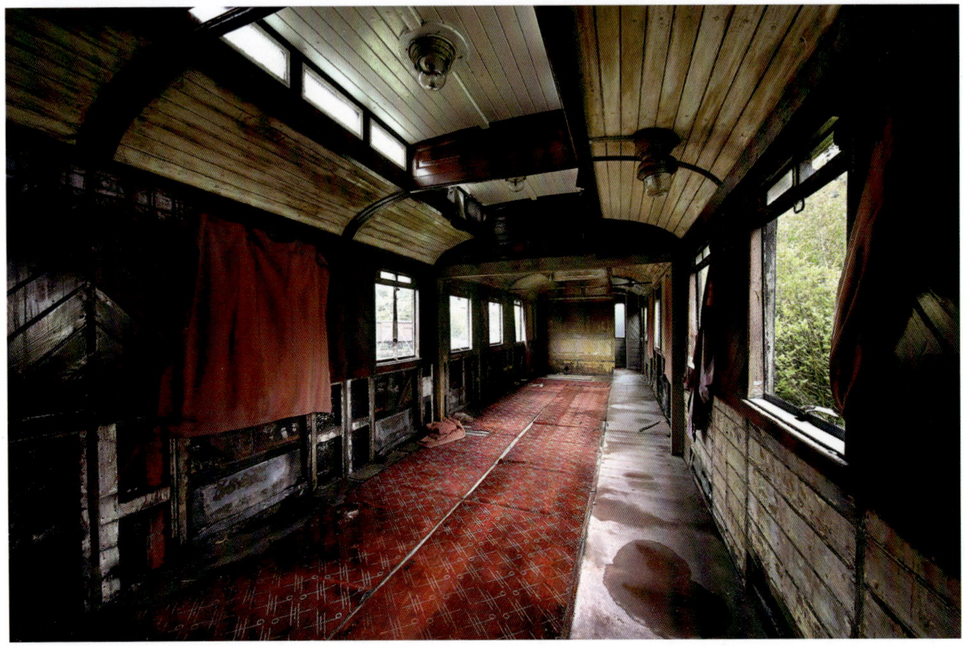

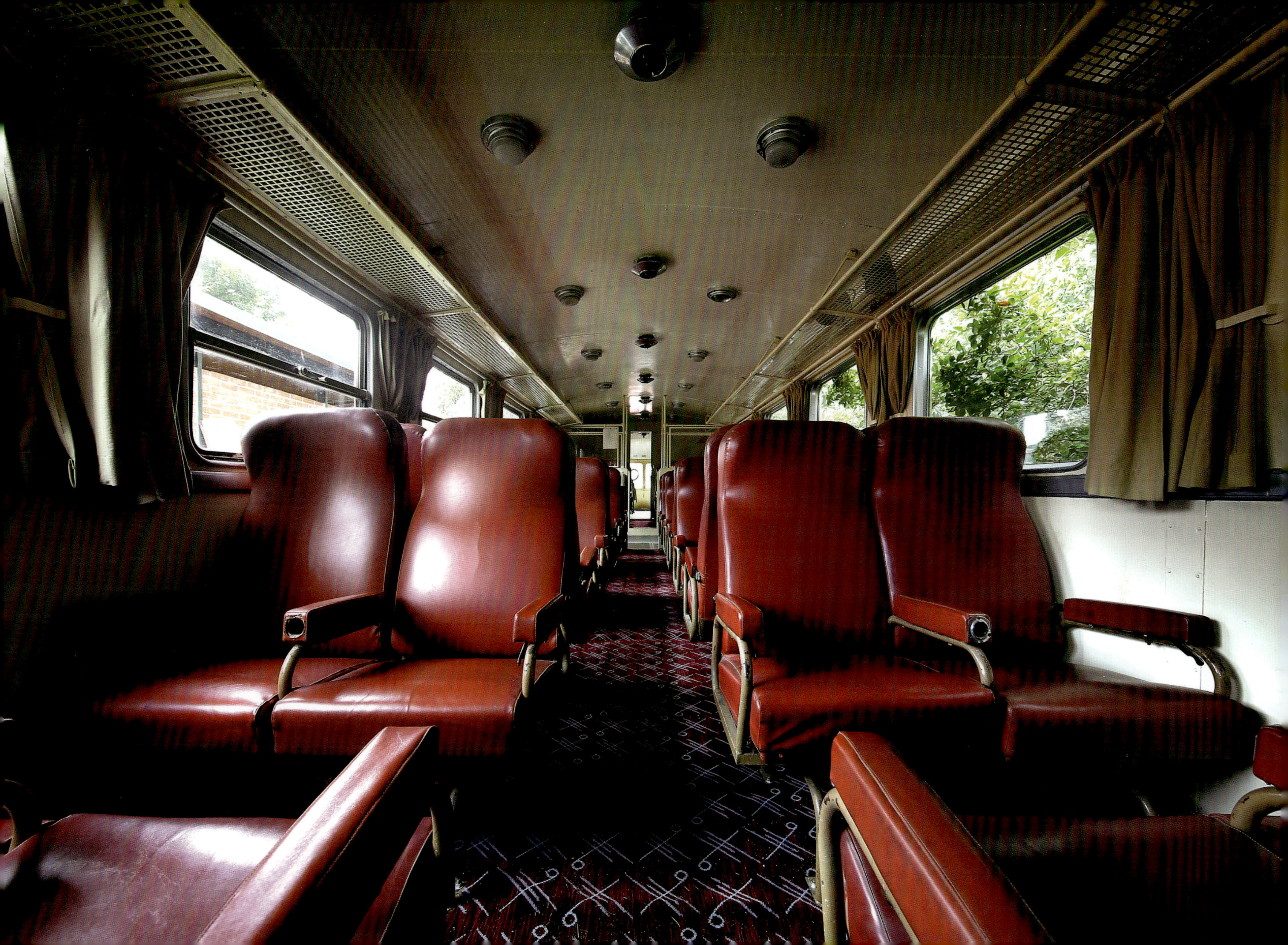

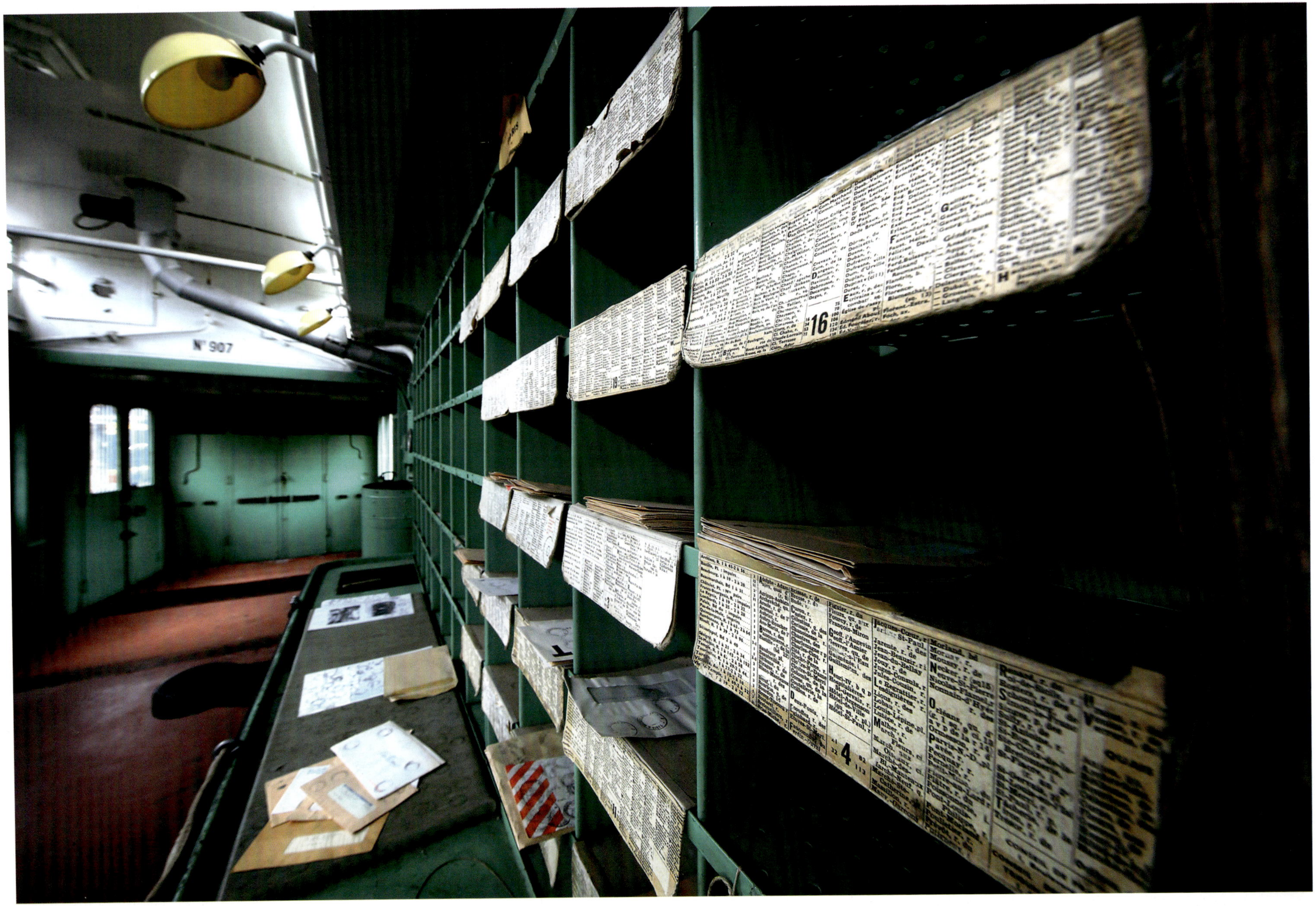
N° 907

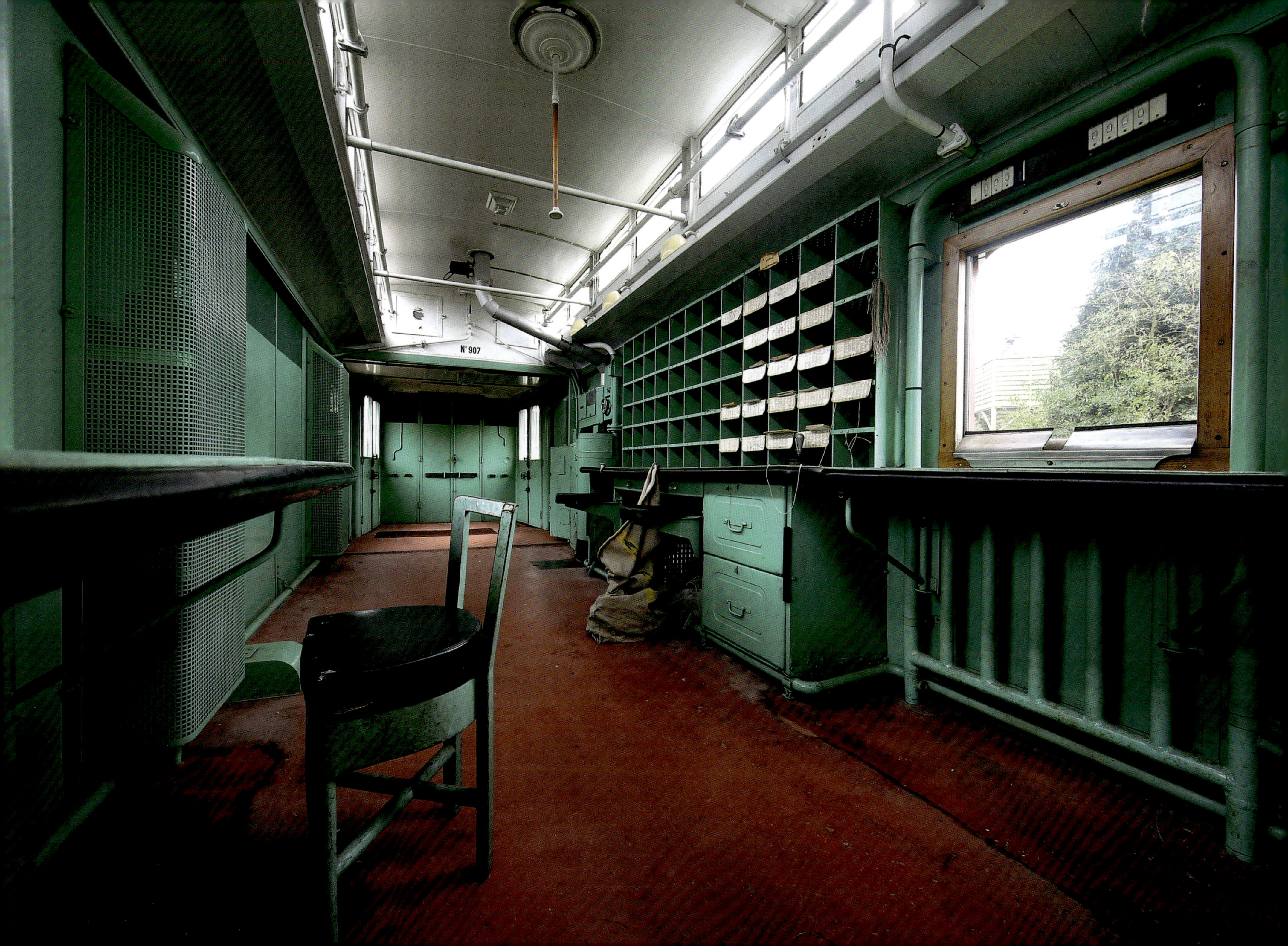
N° 907

Diamond Palace • *Normandy*

This monumental neoclassical building, which is listed as a historical monument in the town, was built between 1783 and 1866. It was mainly built in stone from the Calvados region, since ashlar had been used on a large scale since the 11th century.

The building was built on a hexagonal plan and supported by 10 monumental columns of Ionic order opening onto a busy square. However, the decision to preserve a 15th-century city tower – the 'Châtimoine Tower' that had been used as a prison – gives it an unusual, truncated diamond shape at its northern and southern ends. On the eve of the Revolution, only the prison, the bailiwick and the royal court were completed. Work resumed in 1809 under the direction of the architect Jean-Baptiste Harou-Romain. The large courtroom was designed by architect Léon Marcotte and built in 1866. The court of appeal (known as the 'bees' room') and its exceptional decoration have been largely preserved, as the premises of the regional court were substantially modified during the 20th century.

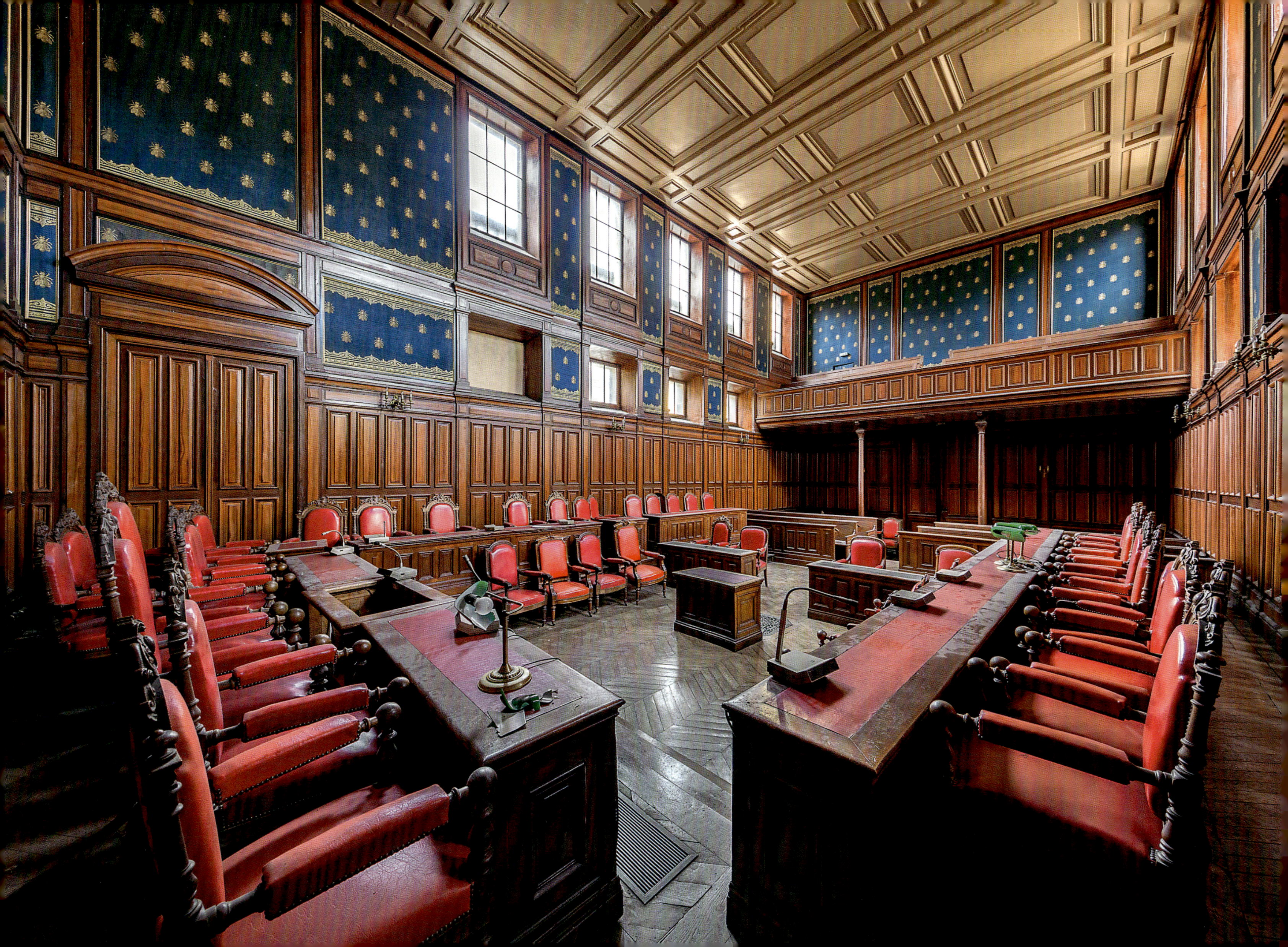

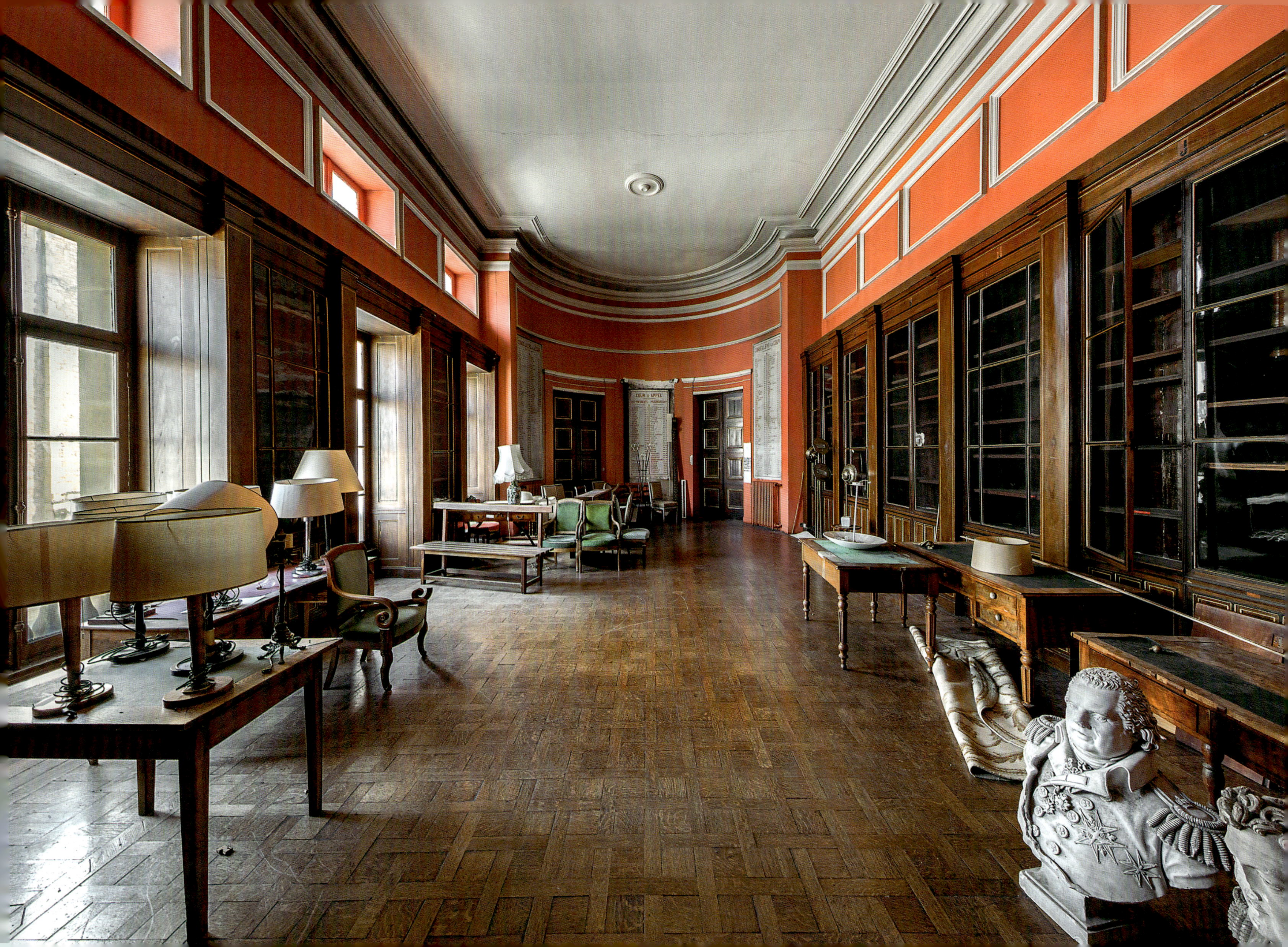
COUR D'APPEL

A reconstruction project was launched in 1978 by Armand Lefèbvre – an engineer from the Ponts et Chaussées institution of higher education – to establish a 'temple of justice' which would bring together a criminal and civil courthouse, a commercial court, court of appeal, labour court, an assize court and a court of first and second instance. The building was abandoned and has remained unused since July 2015. Given its long history, the old building is a miracle survivor. It was spared by the bombs in 1944, but has been enlarged, modified, and sometimes mistreated. According to the mayor of Caen, it is 'the only 18th-century courthouse still standing in France'. There are plans for the former courthouse to be transformed into a top-of-the-range Marriott hotel with a business centre that can seat more than 500 people, and a dazzling 400-square-metre brasserie. This majestic work of art is finally being preserved.

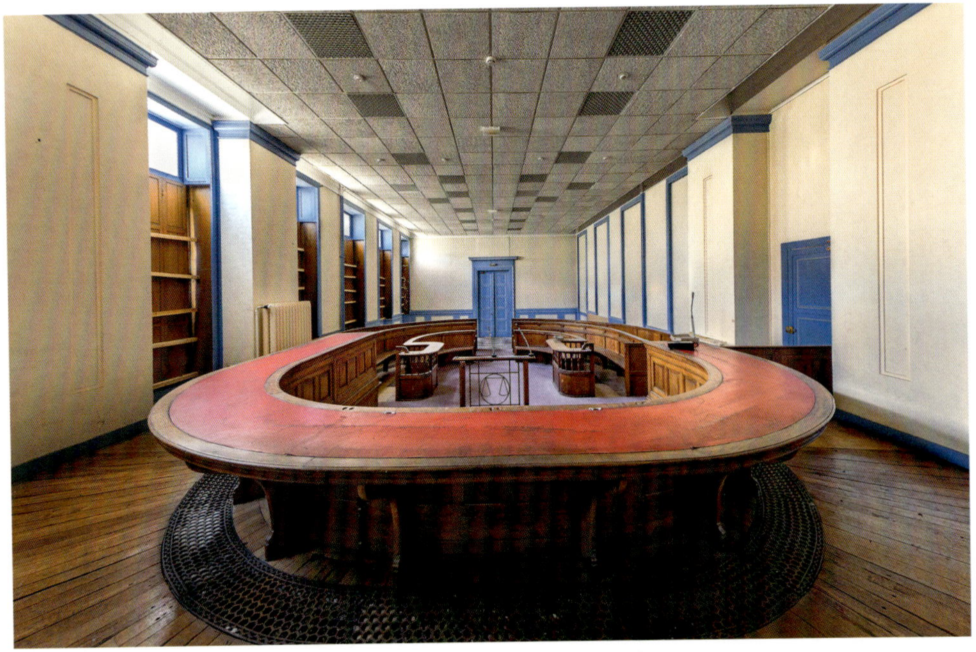
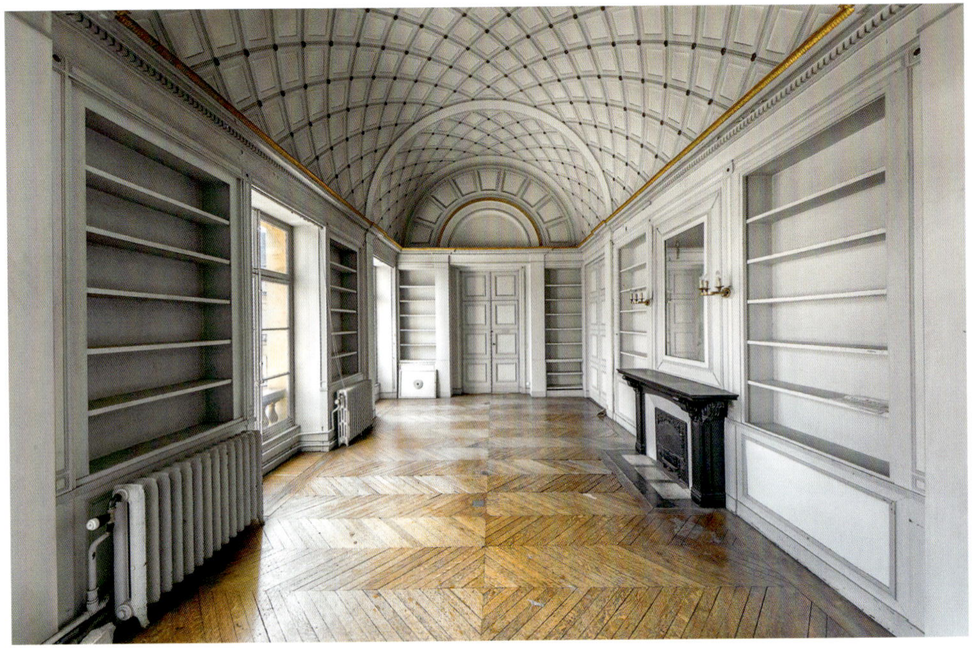
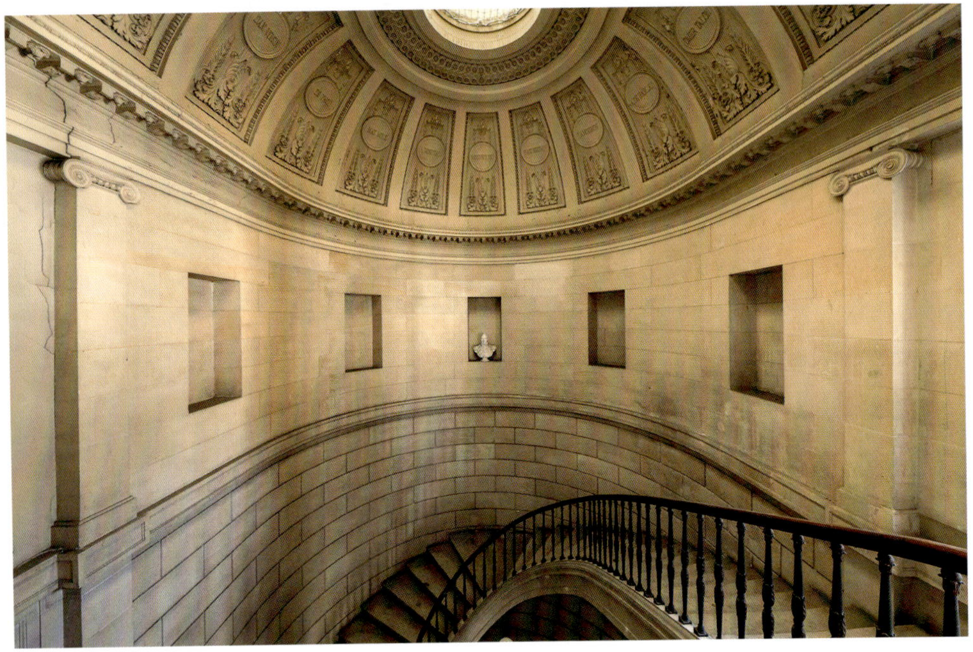
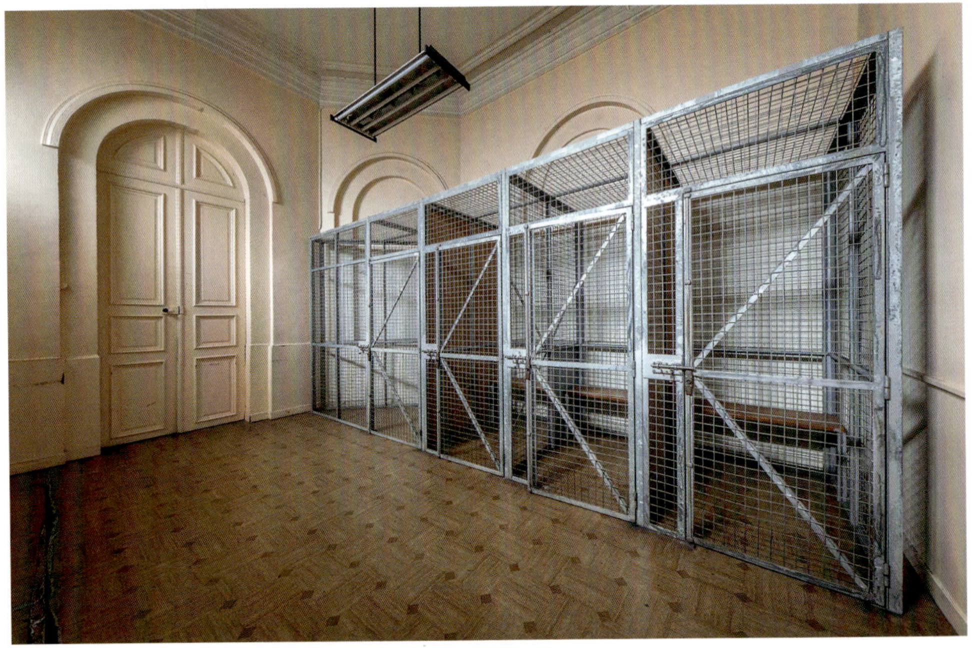

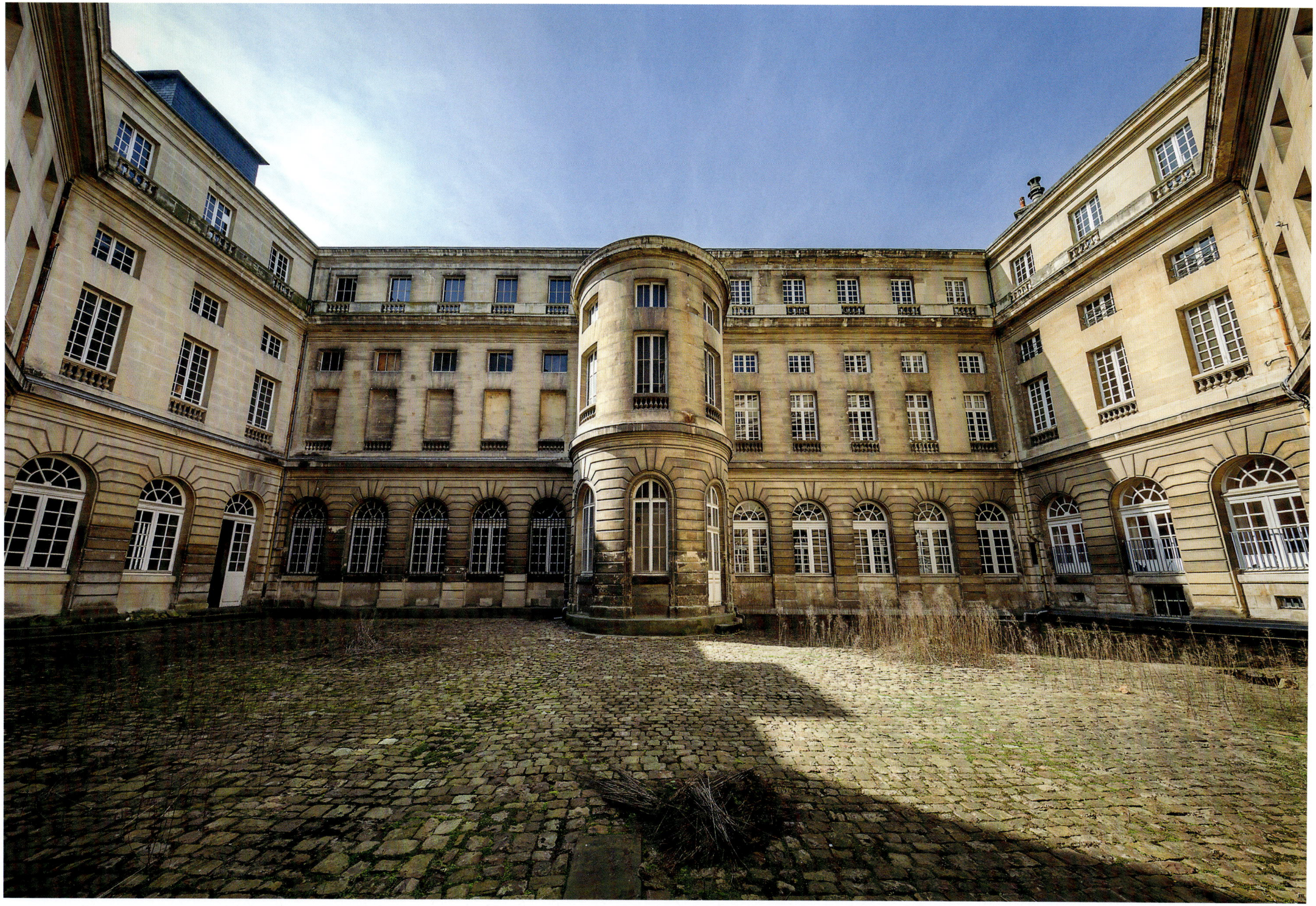

The Jumanji castle • *Centre-Val de Loire*

As early as the Renaissance, princes and lords had hunting lodges built on their forest estates to practise this leisure activity, which was an extremely popular way of life.
Though rustic in appearance, this beautiful secondary residence has all the comforts and decor worthy of the rank of the personalities of the time and was built by renowned architects attached to the court. The hall decorated with hunting trophies opens onto a sensational staircase that celebrates creativity, architecture and beauty in a style steeped in history. Hunters used to gather to feast with friends in this dining room that offers a warm, country atmosphere.
We wish this beautiful, well-preserved place a long life.

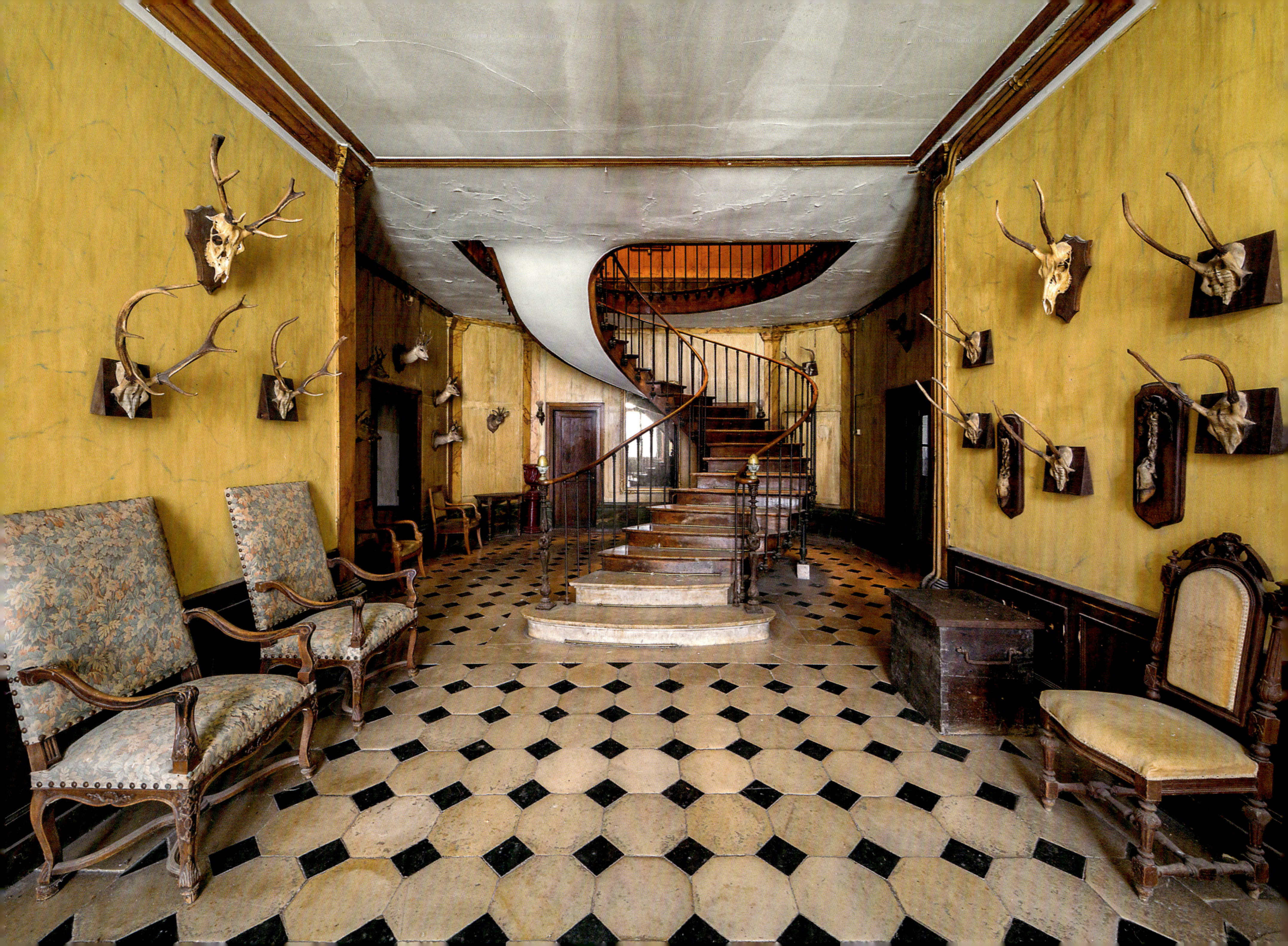

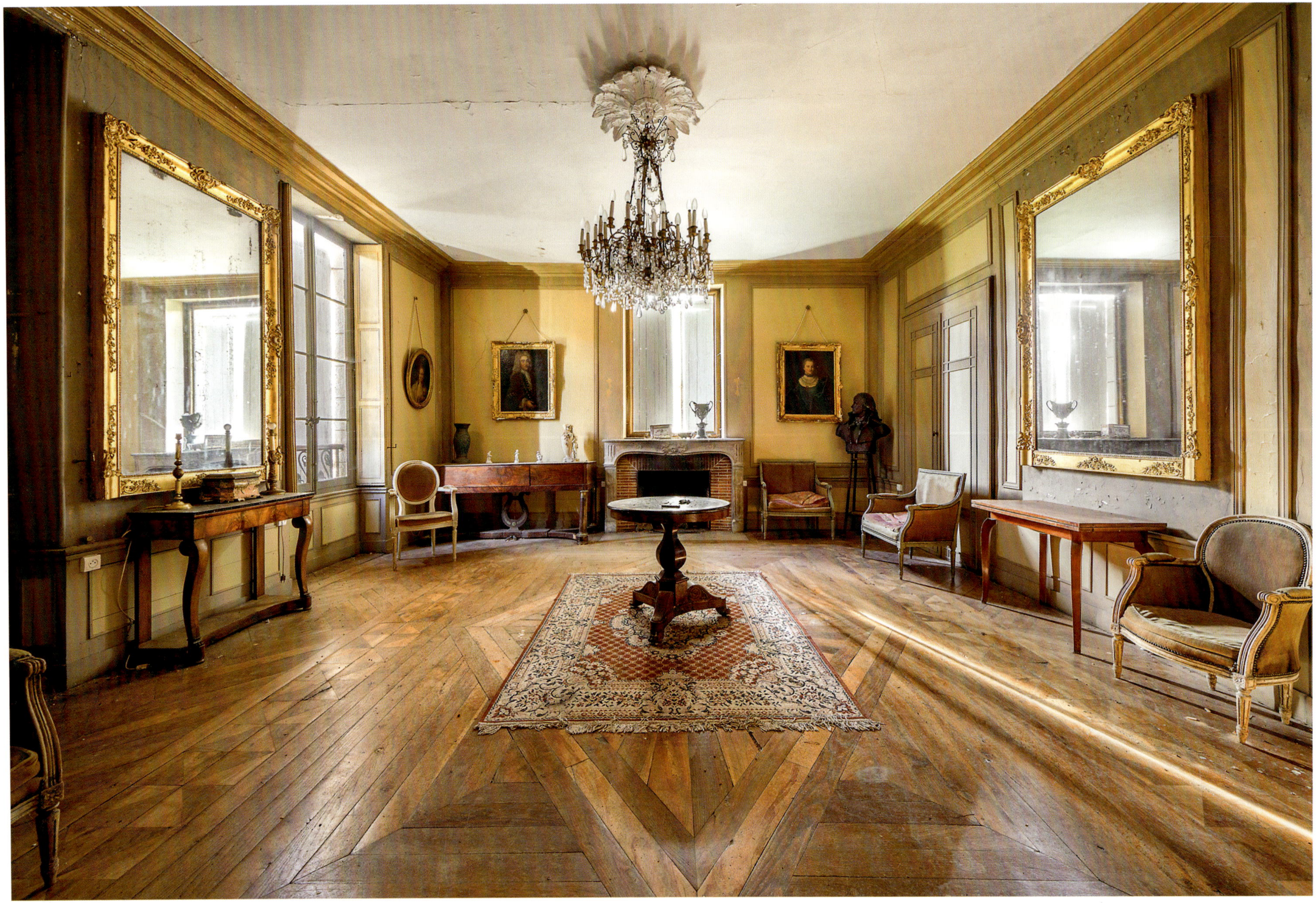

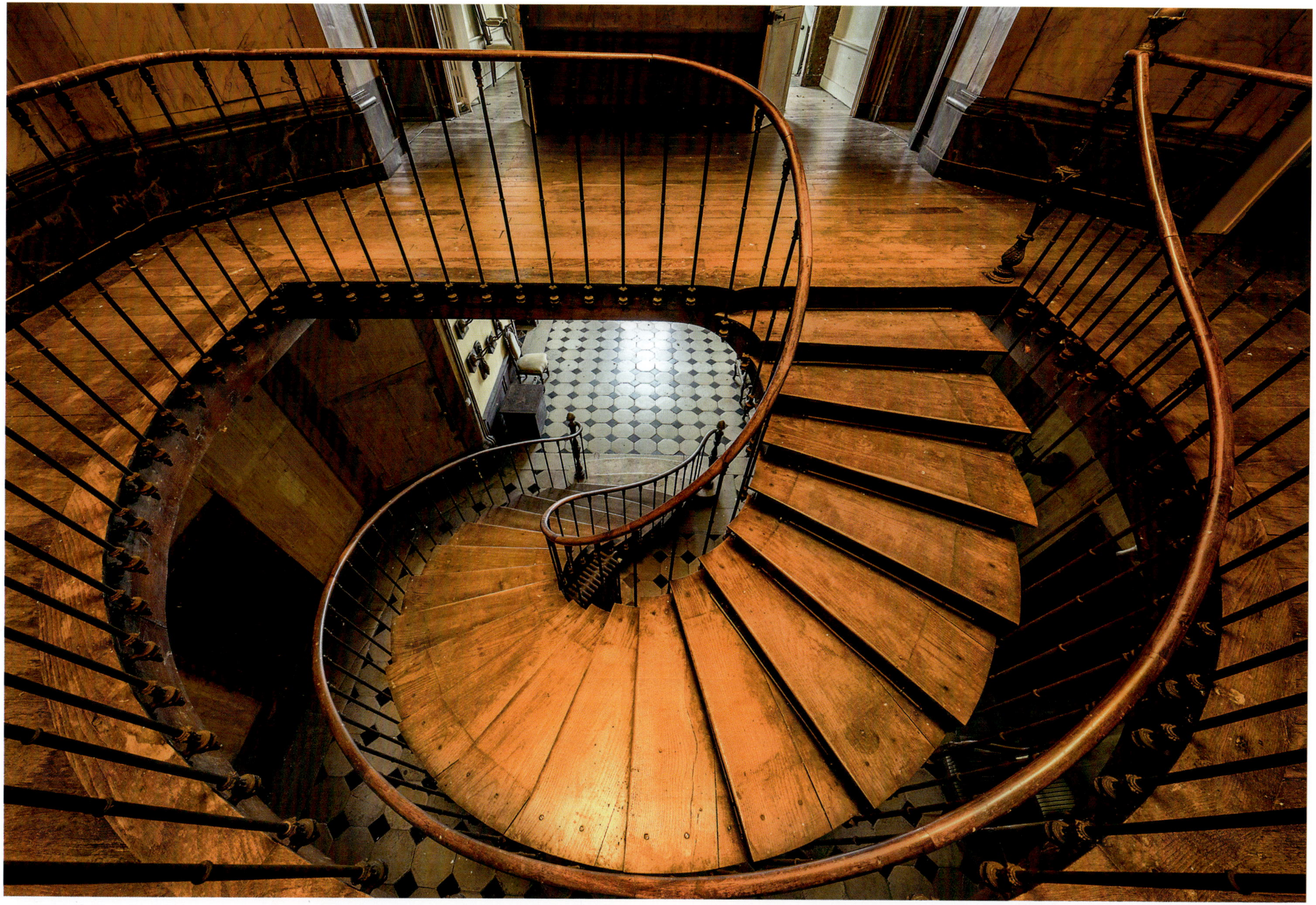

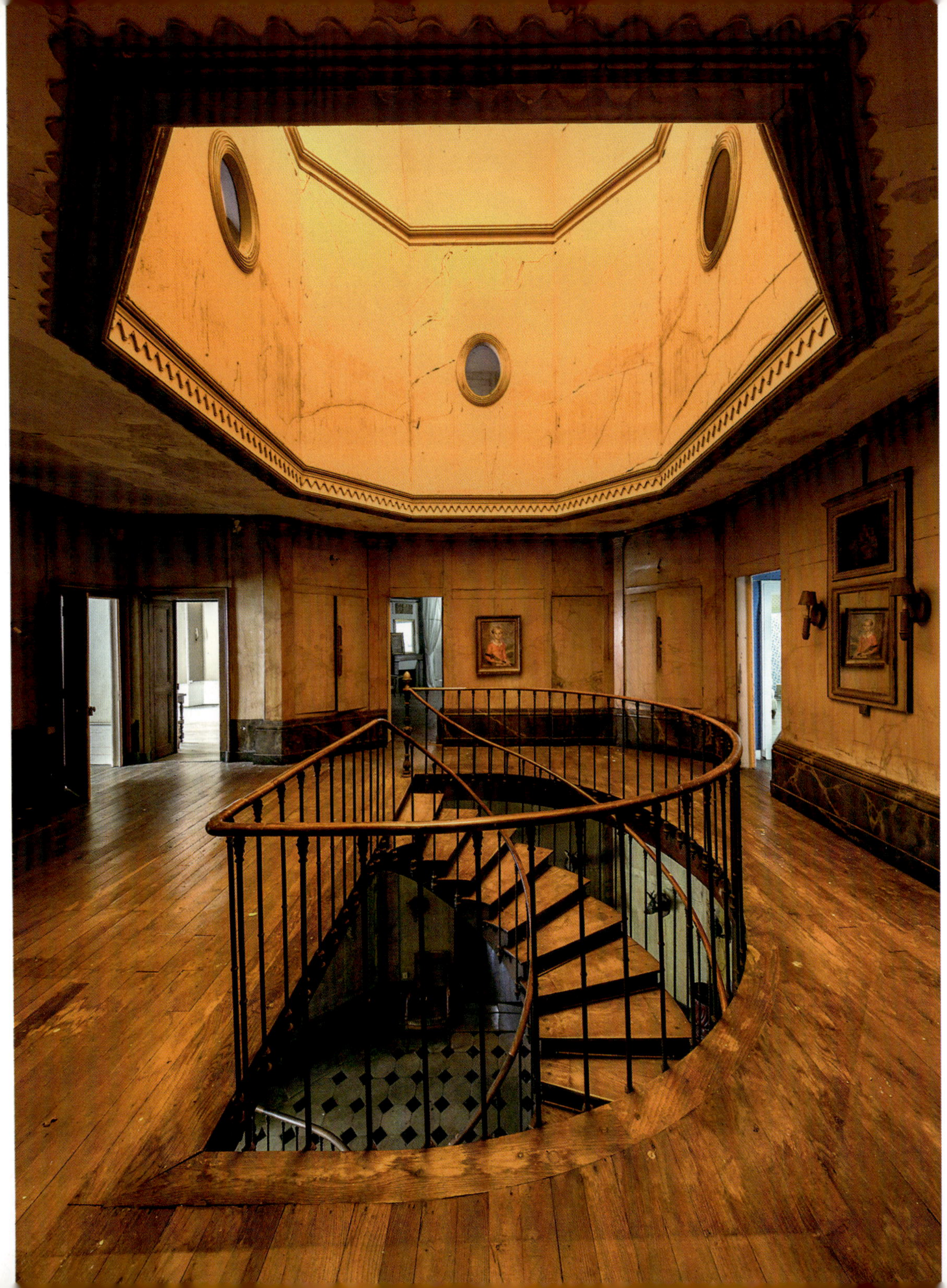

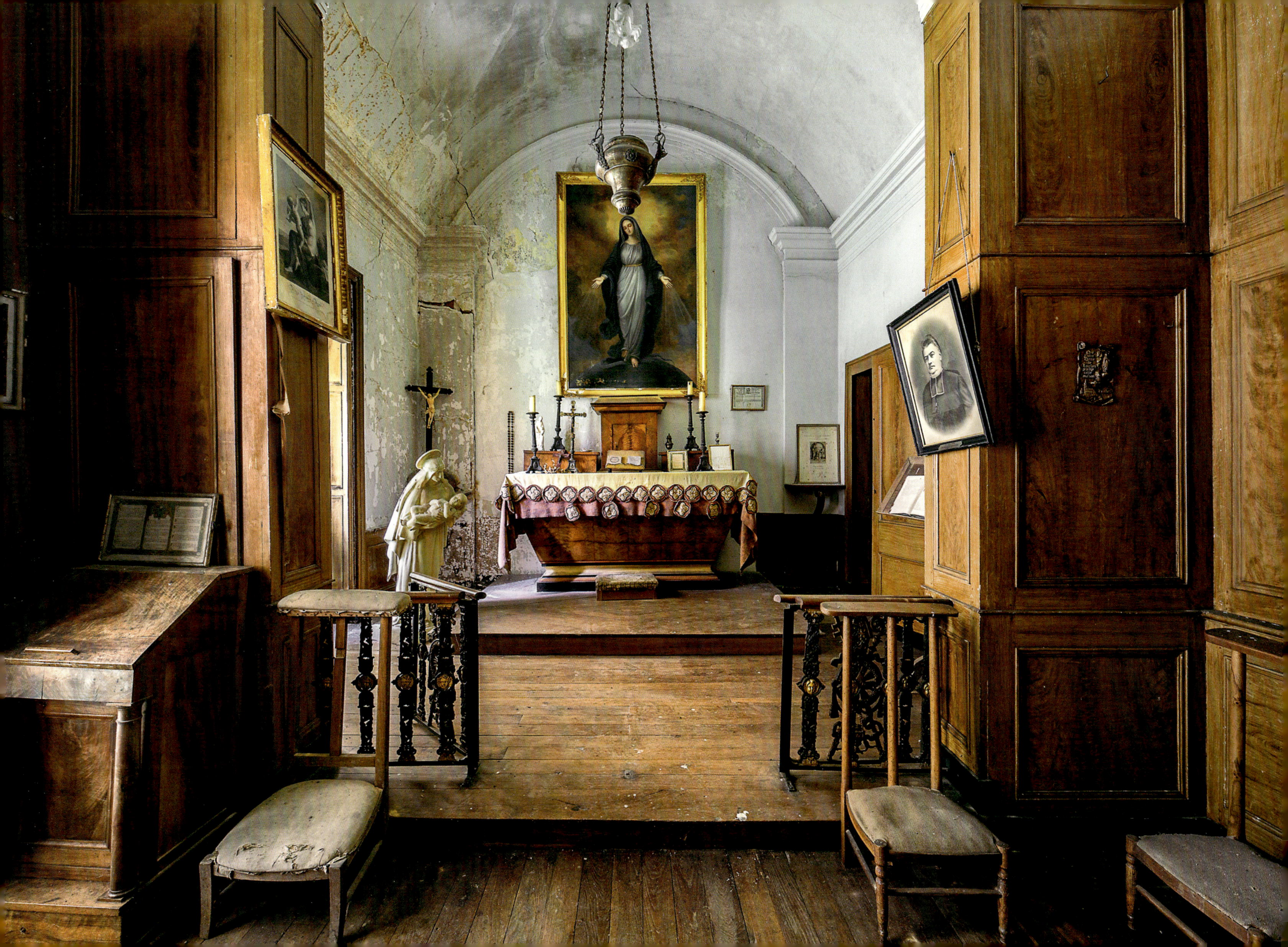

A royalist castle • *Grand-Est*

There are castles that leave a pleasant and warm impression.

In the heart of a small, country village, a castle built on the foundations of a feudal building in the 17th century is surrounded by dense woods. The large building is reached after a few minutes' walk along an avenue of gigantic cypress trees. The once tended gardens have given way to weeds and overgrown bushes. The interior is spacious, with many rooms still fully furnished.

It is said that Napoleon Bonaparte stayed here during the French campaign of 1814. But it was a wealthy 20th-century industrialist and executive of the French far-right political party who made the chateau his home for more than 40 years. His ambition was to preserve it and recreate the French gardens in its park.

The castle seemed to have been pleasantly spared from theft and looting, but perhaps that was because I was lucky enough to visit it before the rough treatment it received in the following weeks.

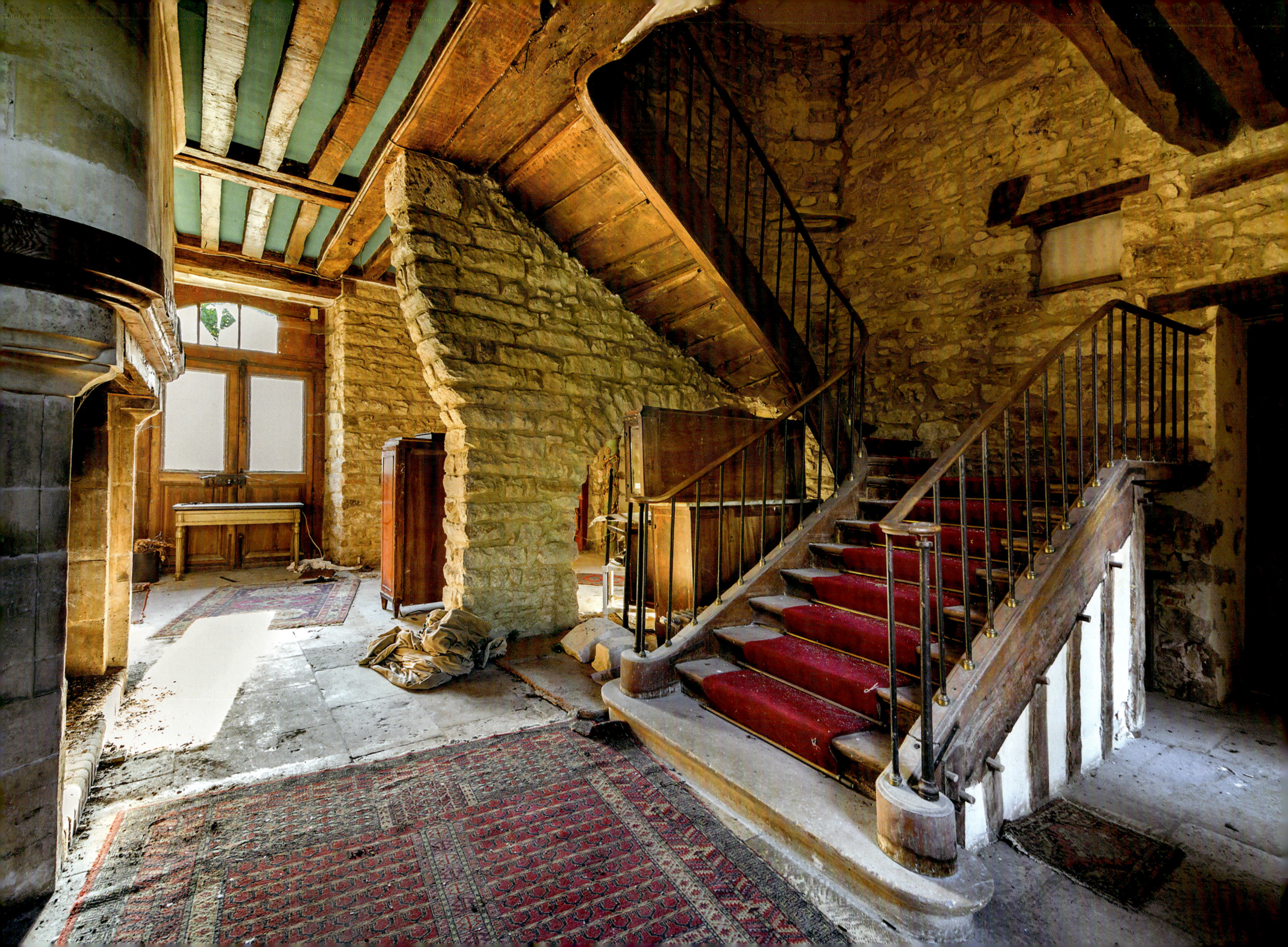

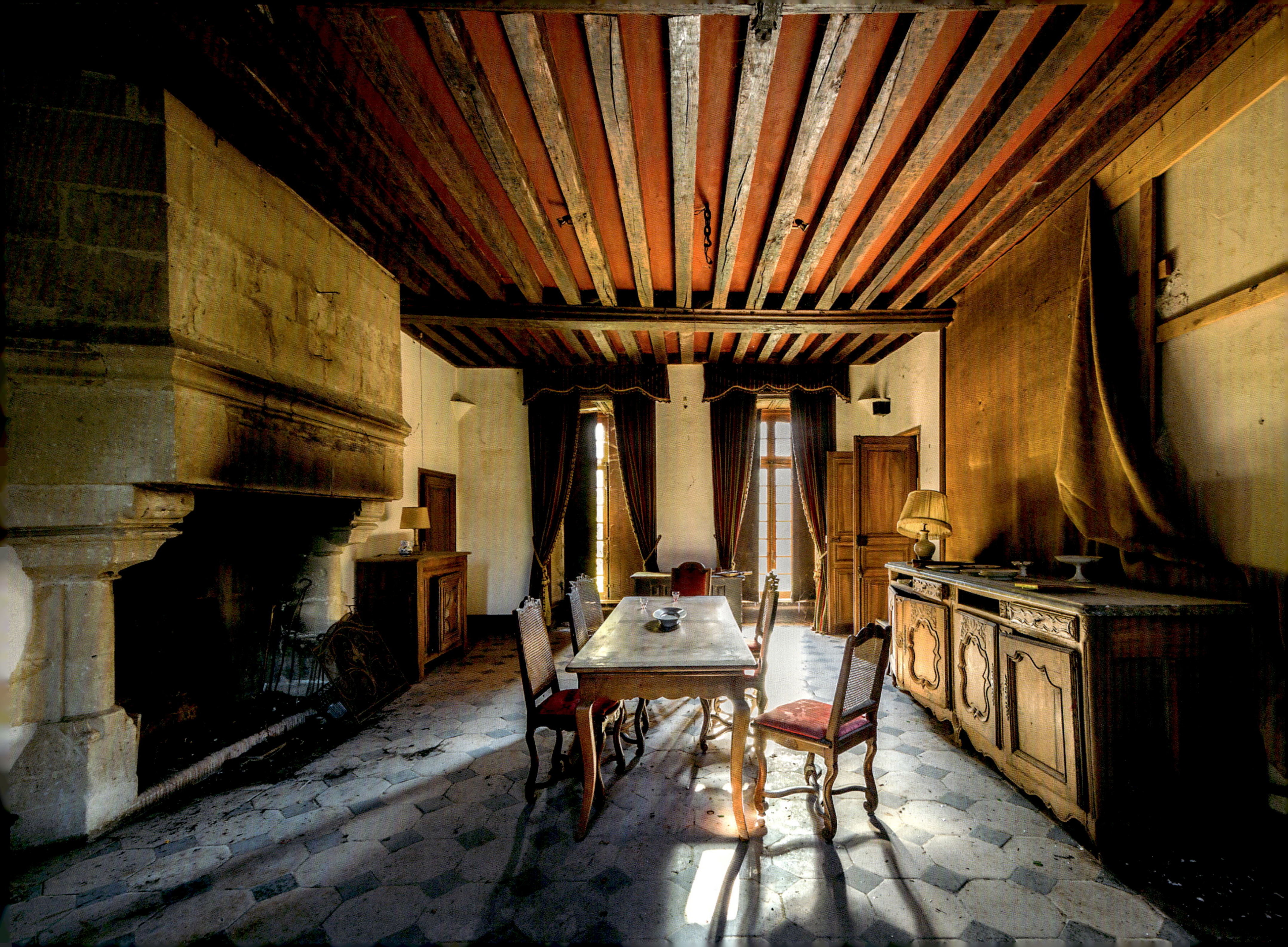

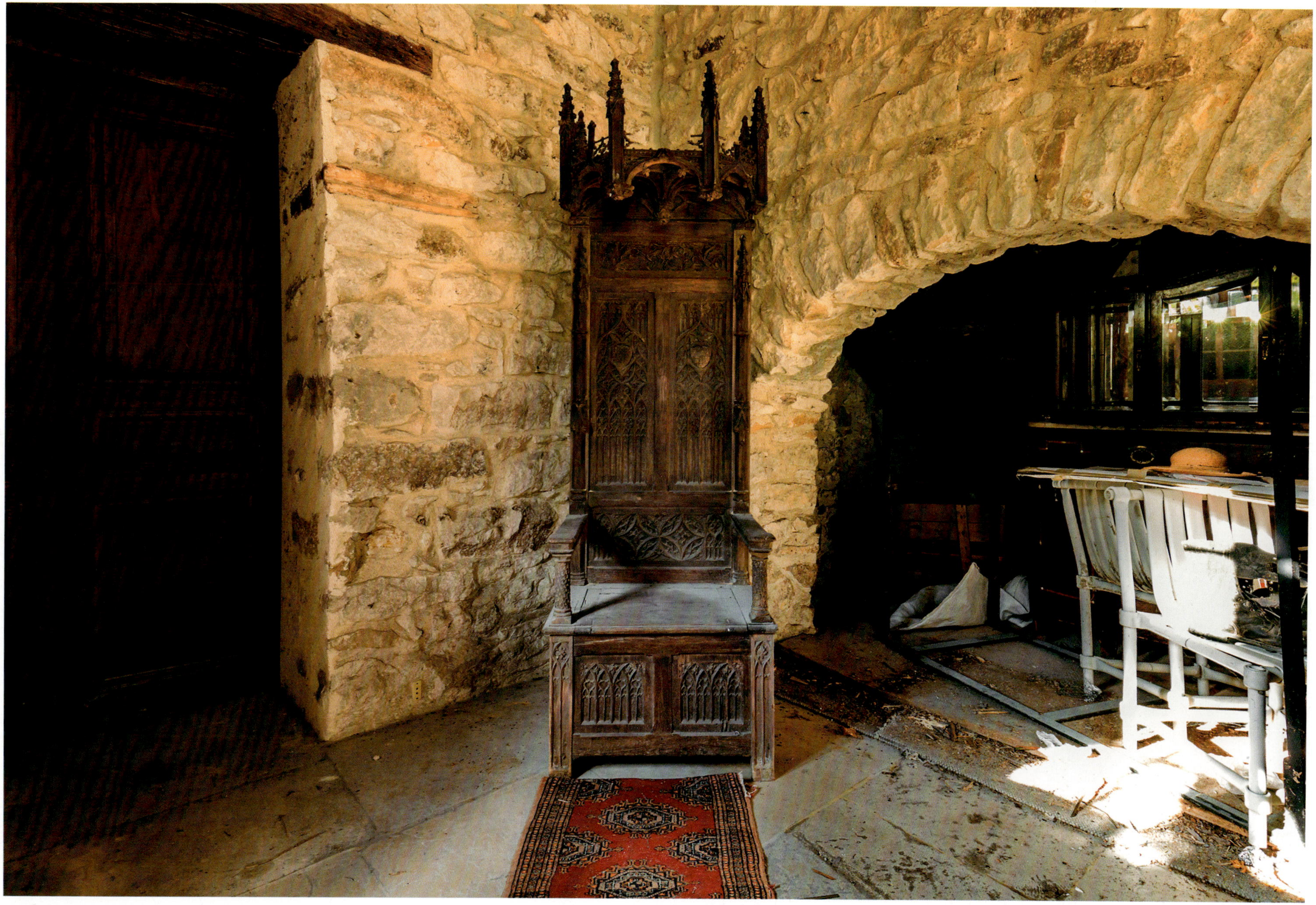

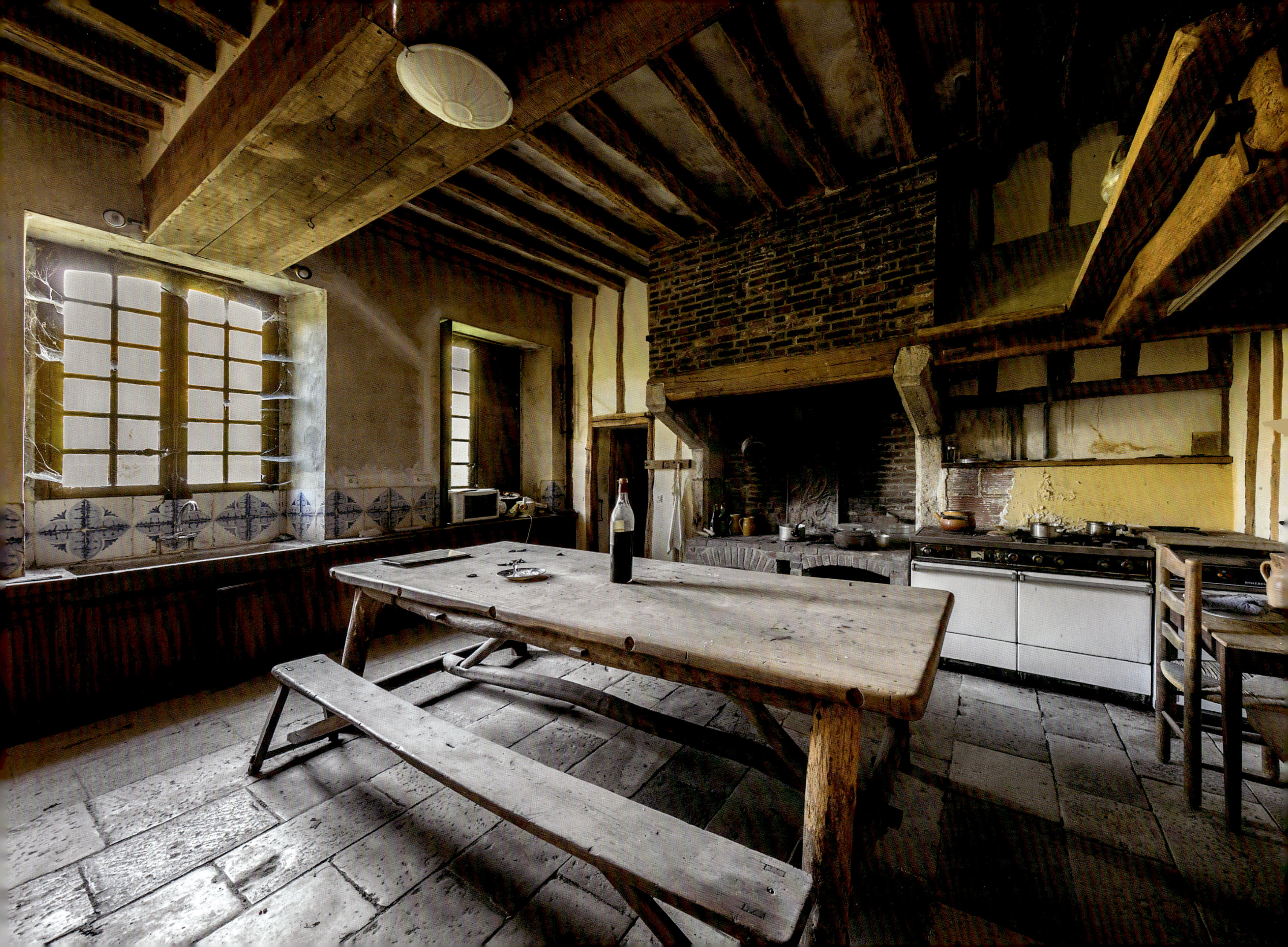

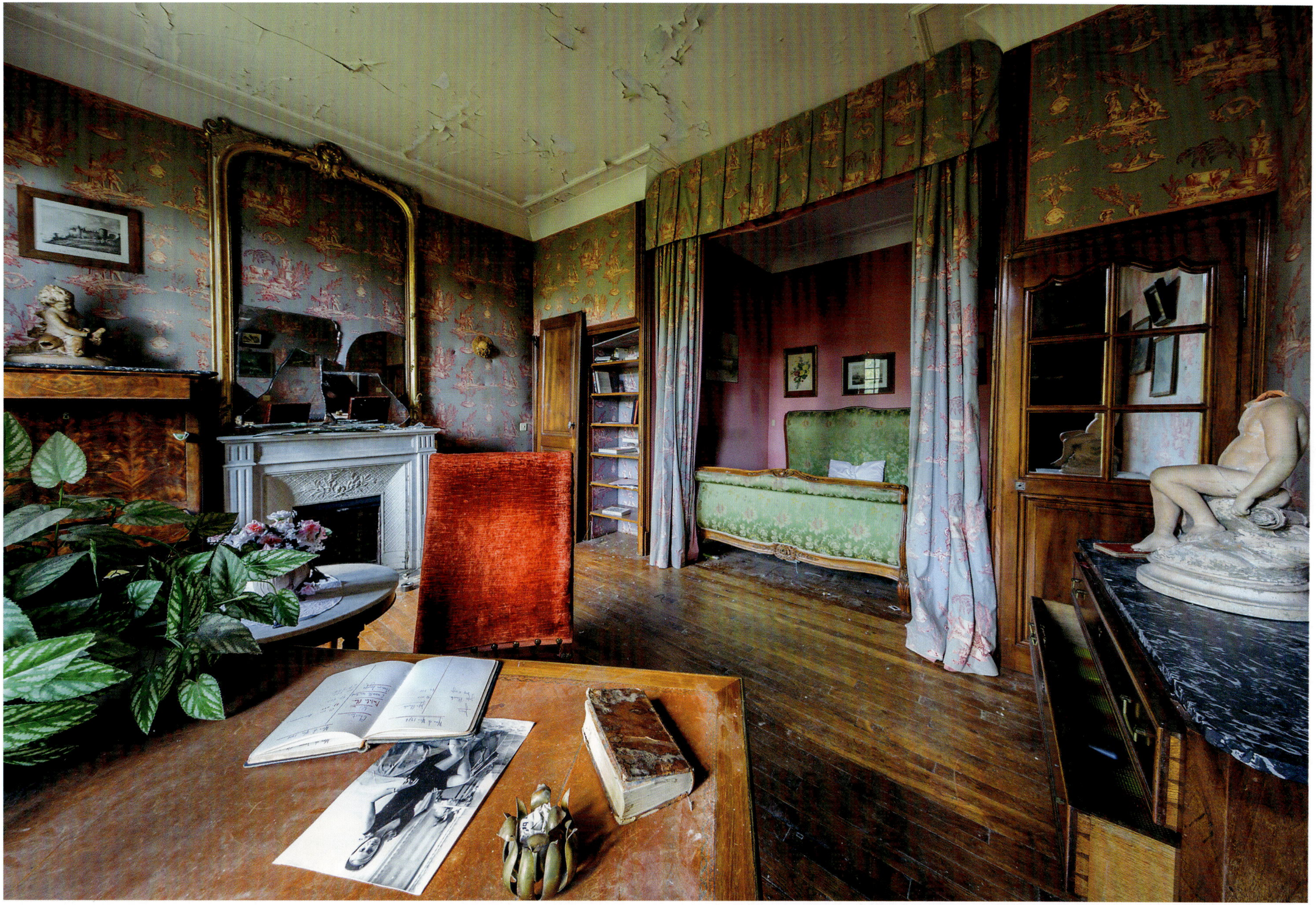

The chapel of the dead • *Grand-Est*

In a tiny hamlet, a humble 13th-century Catholic church is now closed to the public because its structure is unsafe, and the bell tower is in danger of collapsing. The building is shabby on the outside, but surprising on the inside. It was in this fertile agricultural and wine-growing region of France, on what was originally a Gallo-Roman estate on the Langres-Boulogne road, that Benedictine monks established their priory. Over time, Benedictine tombs were erected around the church, making it an even more special place.

It is said that future emperor Napoleon Bonaparte was 9 when he came to the nearby school run by the local nuns and attended mass in this church. Since 1983, the church and its cemetery have been listed as historic monuments. Structural stabilisation works are vital to save this beautiful, luminous building.

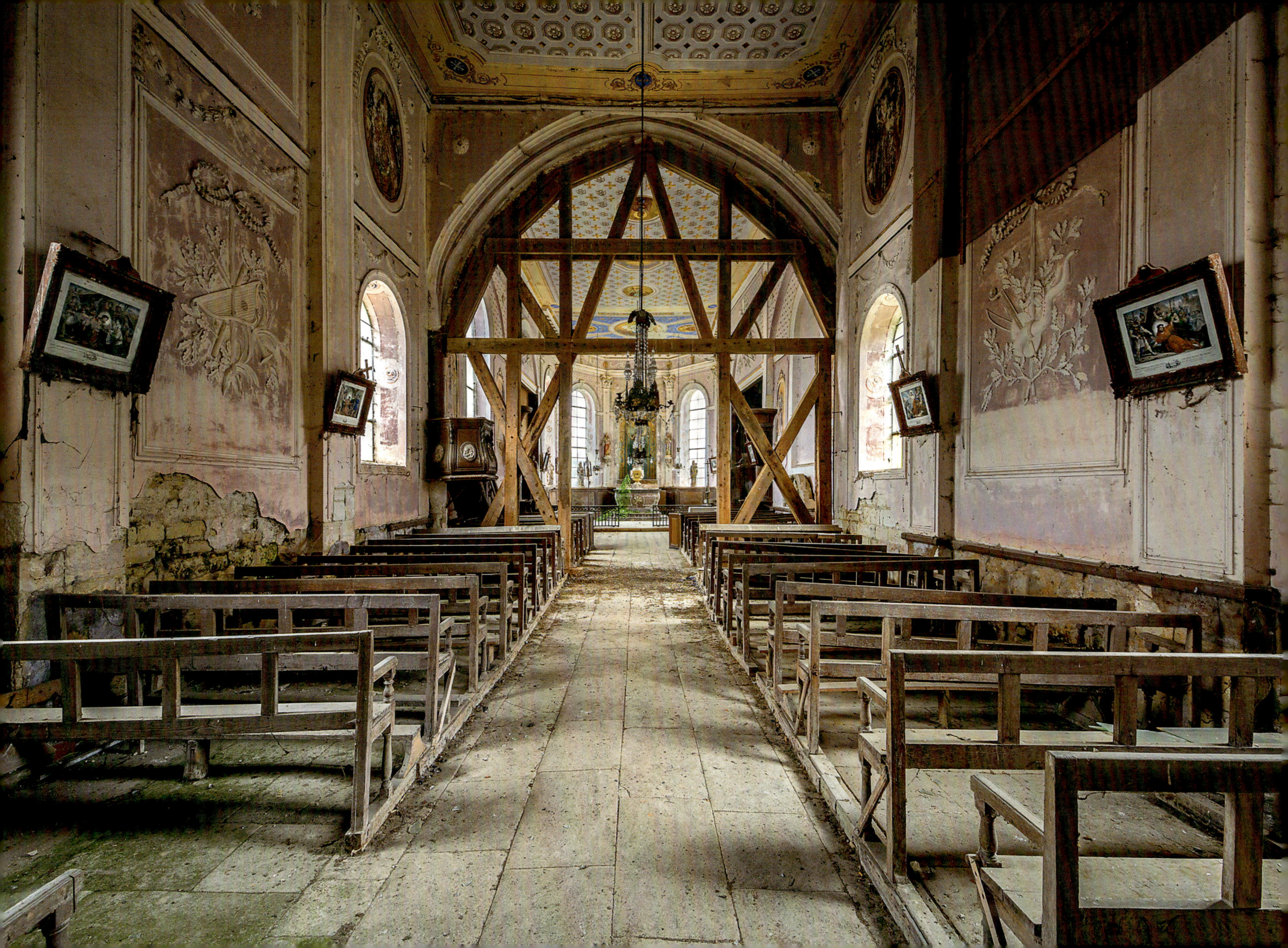

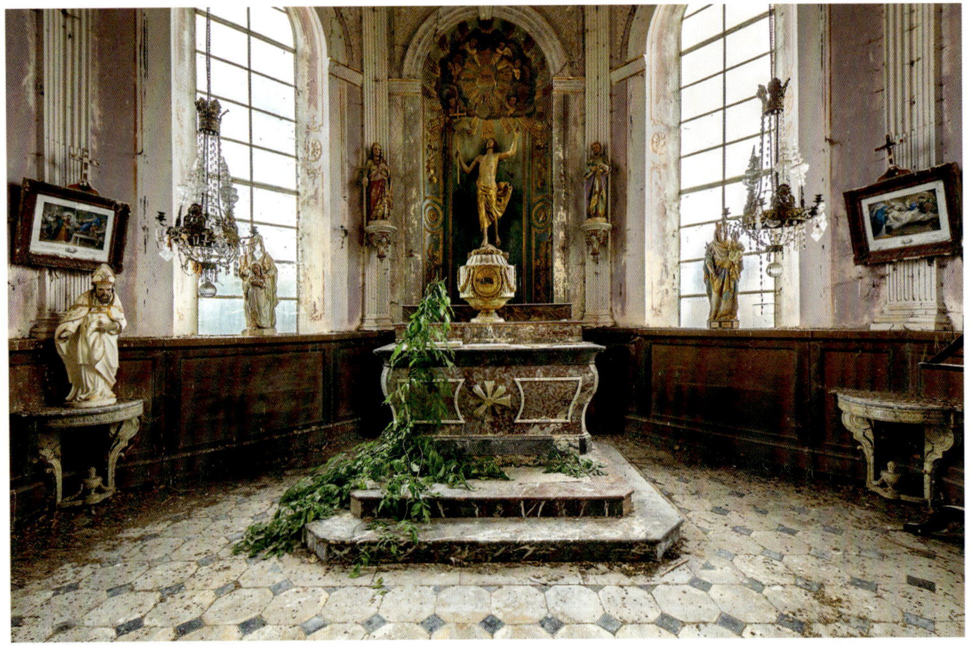

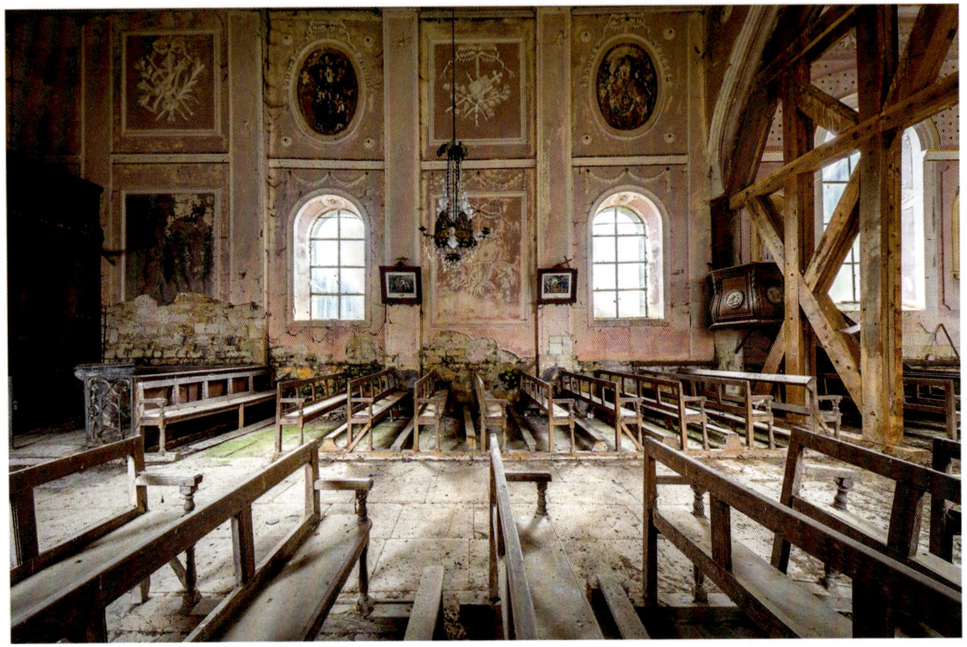

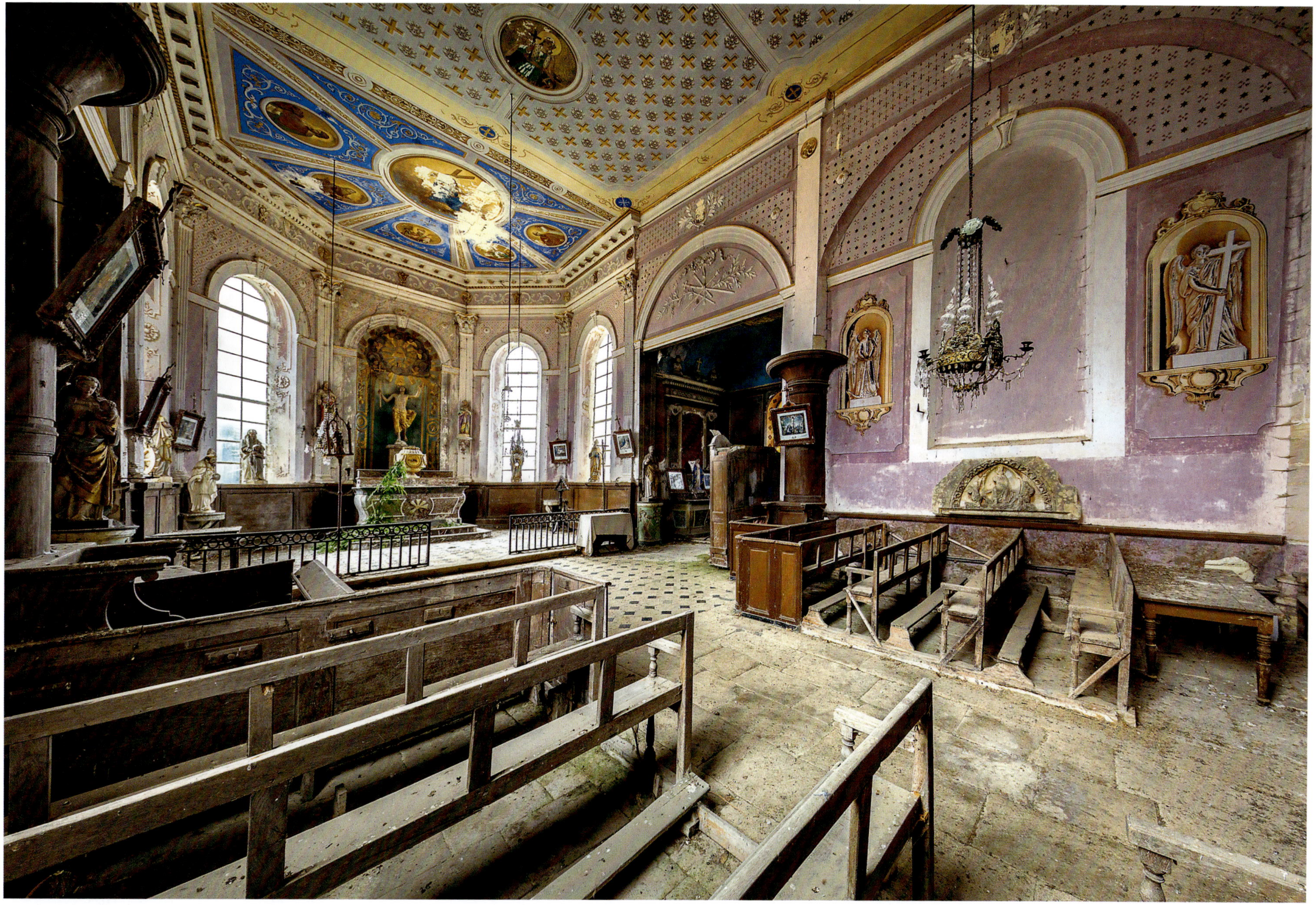

A sock factory • *Grand-Est*

The golden age of French manufacturing! This old factory, from 1819 and topped by a beautiful metal structure covered with glass, used to make Merino wool stockings and socks in Scottish, silk and cotton yarns for the biggest brands. Its owner, guided every day by his passion, offered his customers refined, innovative and contemporary products, and taught his traditional and authentic craft skills. At the time, employers were required to hire local people, and this company employed a considerable number, which contributed to its notoriety. As I met local people, I could feel their nostalgia. In all likelihood, the closure of the factory was a shock for the region and surrounding villages. None of the many sewing machines are still in operation, as the jobs have long since been relocated to Eastern Europe. Now the wooden crates are slowly decaying, and the old machines are fading and rusting in the weather as the spools of thread sway gently in the wind.

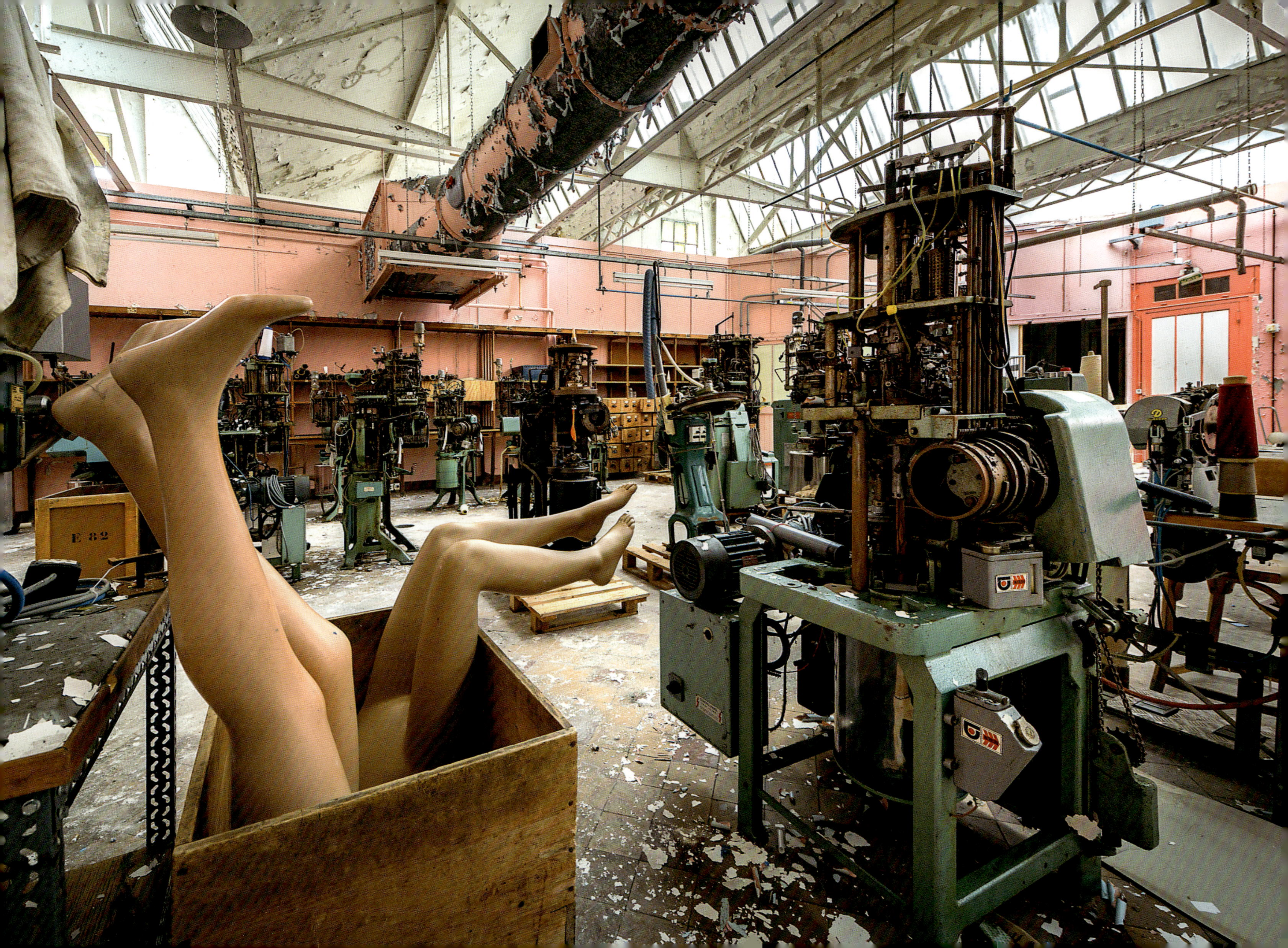
E 82

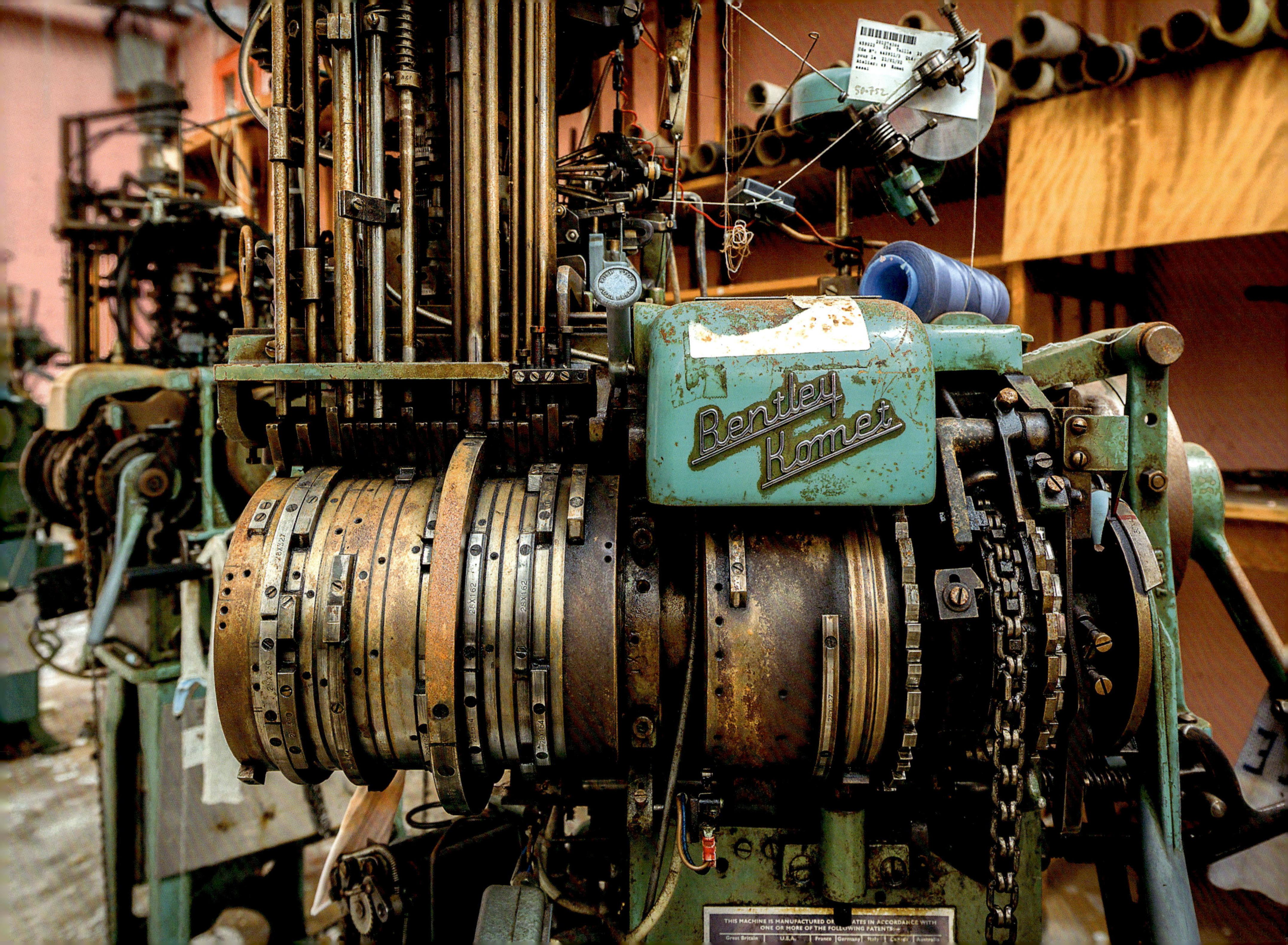
Bentley
Komet

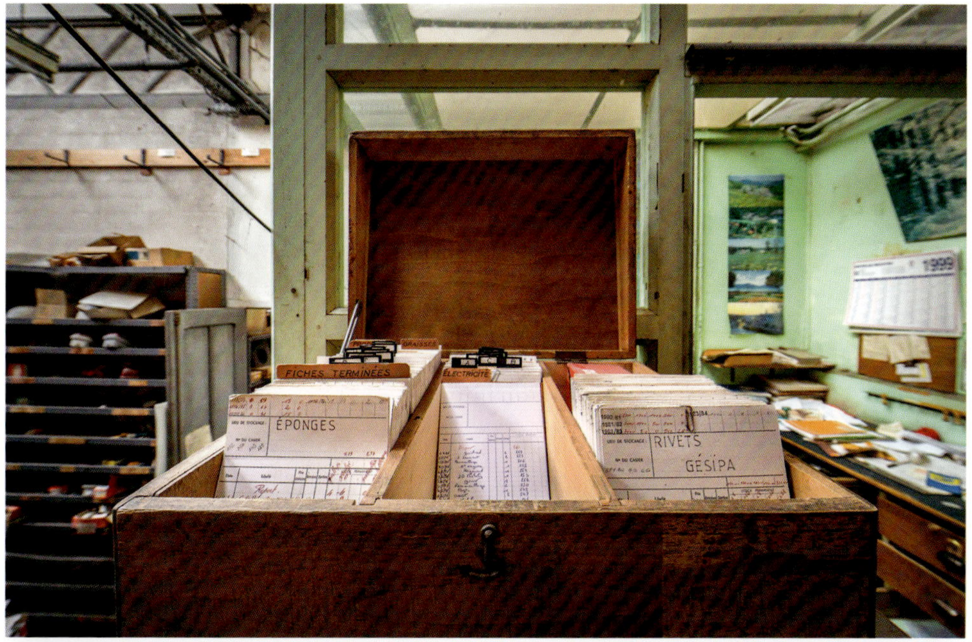
FICHES TERMINÉES
ÉPONGES
RIVETS
GESIPA
1999

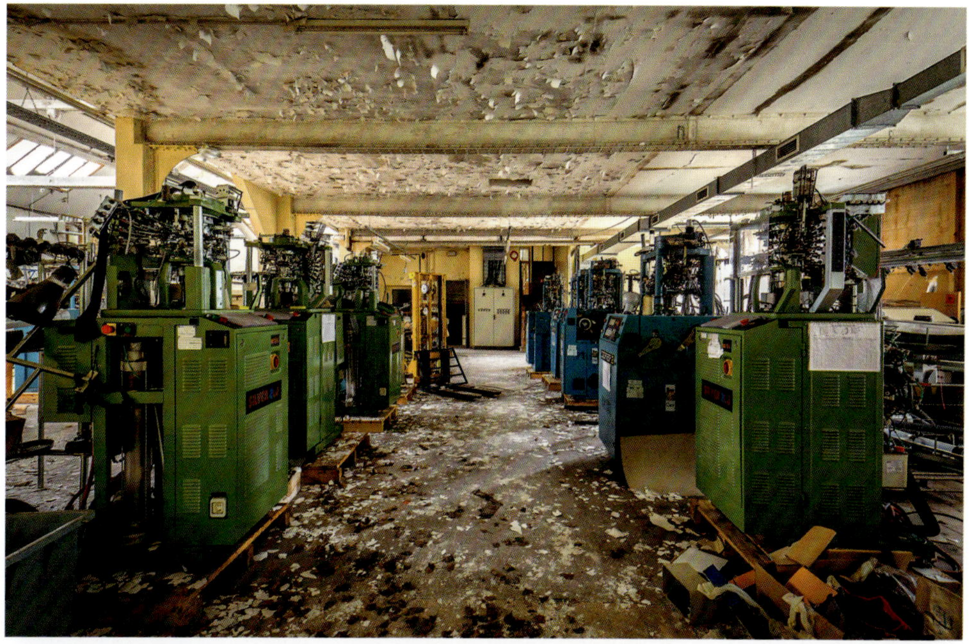

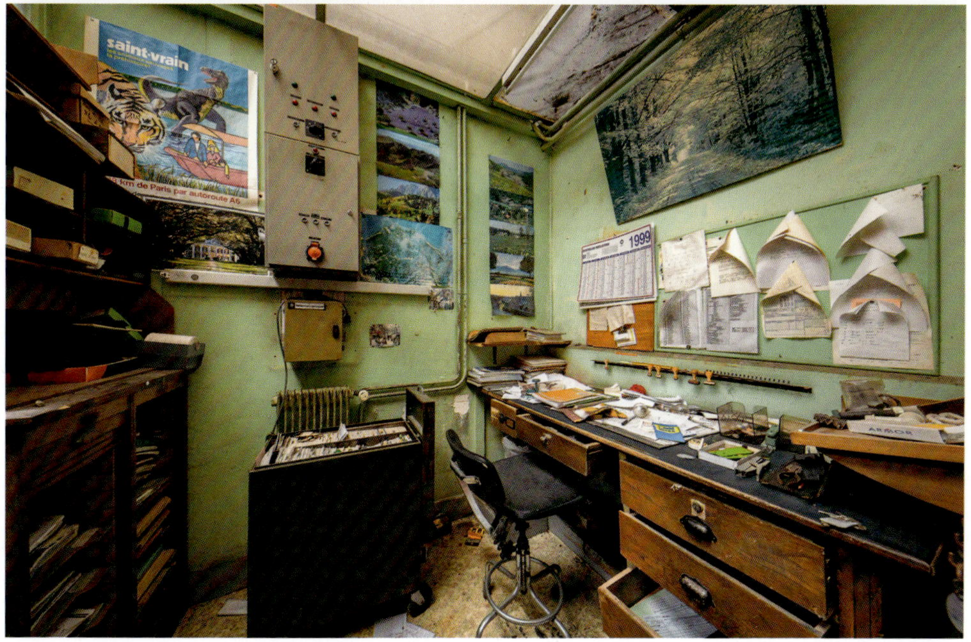
saint-vrain
1999
ARMOR

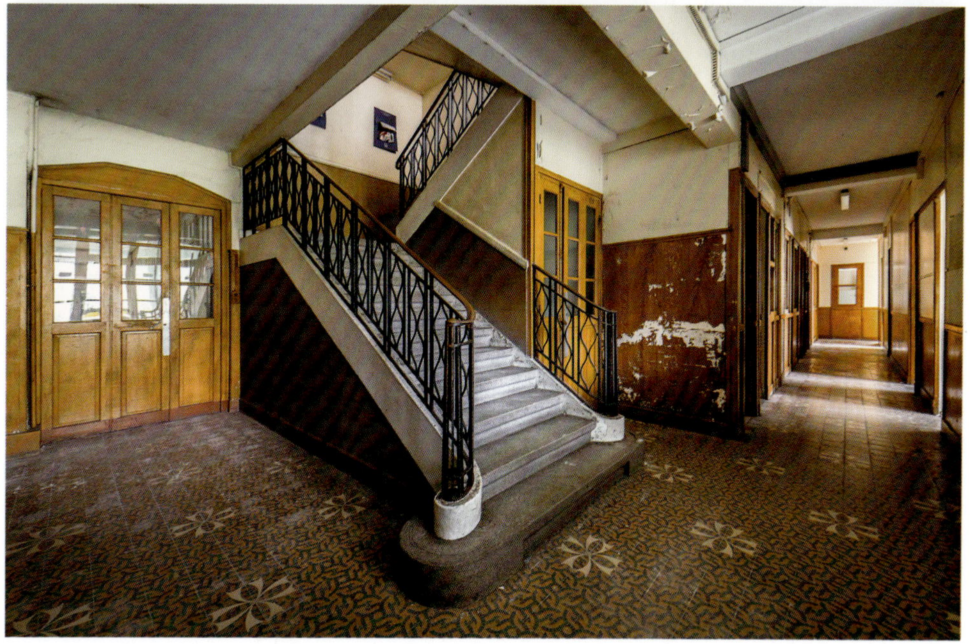

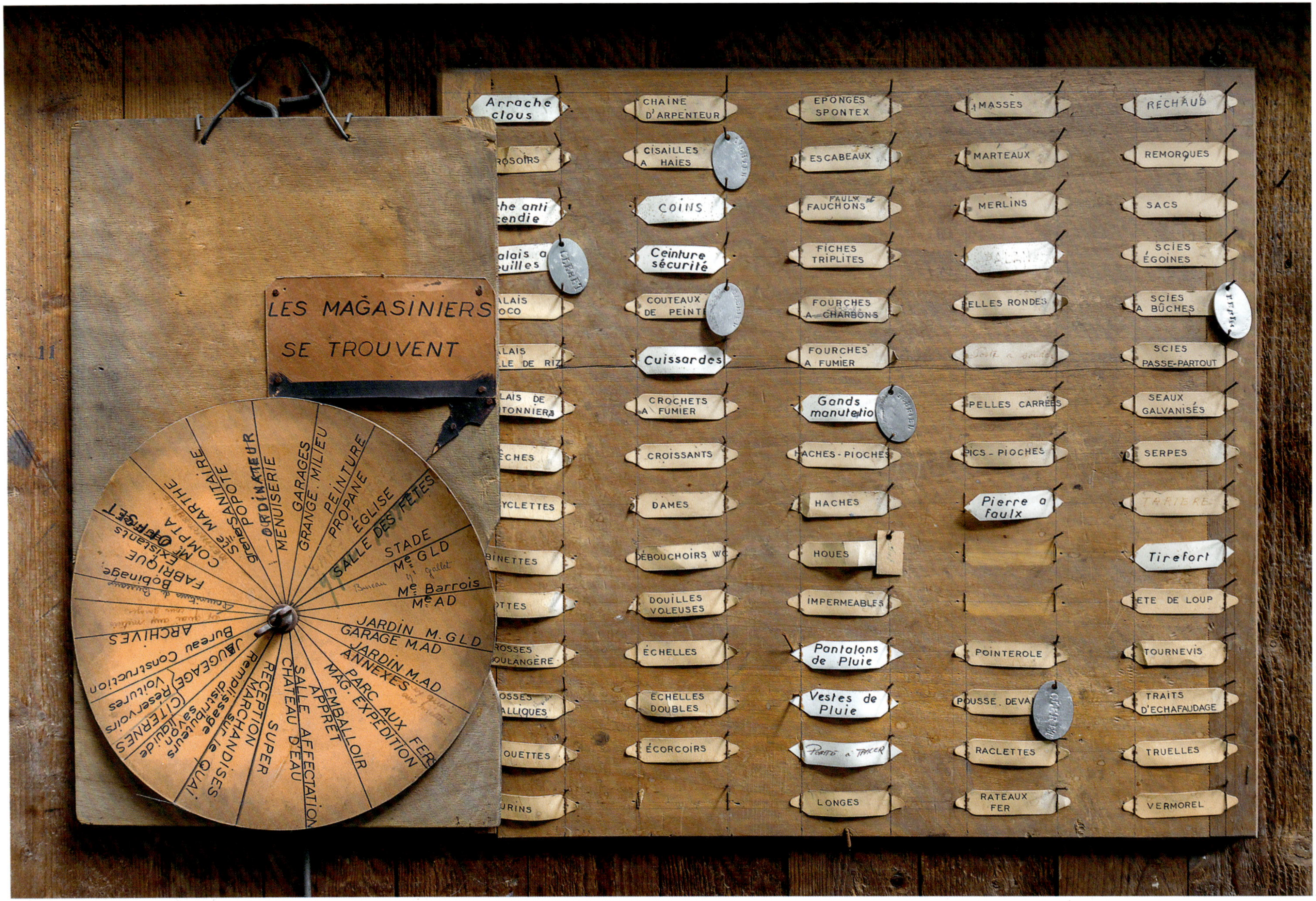

LES MAGASINIERS
SE TROUVENT
Arrache clous
CHAINE D'ARPENTEUR
EPONGES SPONTEX
MASSES
RECHAUD
CISAILLES A HAIES
ESCABEAUX
MARTEAUX
REMORQUES
COINS
FAUCHONS
MERLINS
SACS
FICHES TRIPLITES
SCIES EGOINES
Ceinture sécurité
FOURCHES A CHARBONS
SCIES A BÛCHES
FOURCHES A FUMIER
SCIES PASSE-PARTOUT
Cuissardes
CROCHETS A FUMIER
Gands manutentio
PELLES CARRÉES
SEAUX GALVANISÉS
CROISSANTS
HACHES-PIOCHES
PICS - PIOCHES
SERPES
DAMES
HACHES
Pierre a faulx
DÉBOUCHOIRS WC
HOUES
Tirefort
DOUILLES VOLEUSES
IMPERMEABLES
ECHELLES
Pantalons de Pluie
POINTEROLE
TOURNEVIS
ECHELLES DOUBLES
Vestes de Pluie
TRAITS D'ECHAFAUDAGE
ECORCOIRS
RACLETTES
TRUELLES
LONGES
RATEAUX FER
VERMOREL
GARAGES
GRANGE MILIEU
PEINTURE
PROPANE
EGLISE
SALLE DES FETES
STADE
MENUISERIE
ARCHIVES
JARDIN M.GLD
GARAGE M.AD
JARDIN M.AD
ANNEXES
PARC AUX FER
MAG. EXPEDITION
EMBALLOIR
APPRET
SALLE AFFECTATION
CHATEAU D'EAU
SUPER
RECEPTION
MARCHANDISES

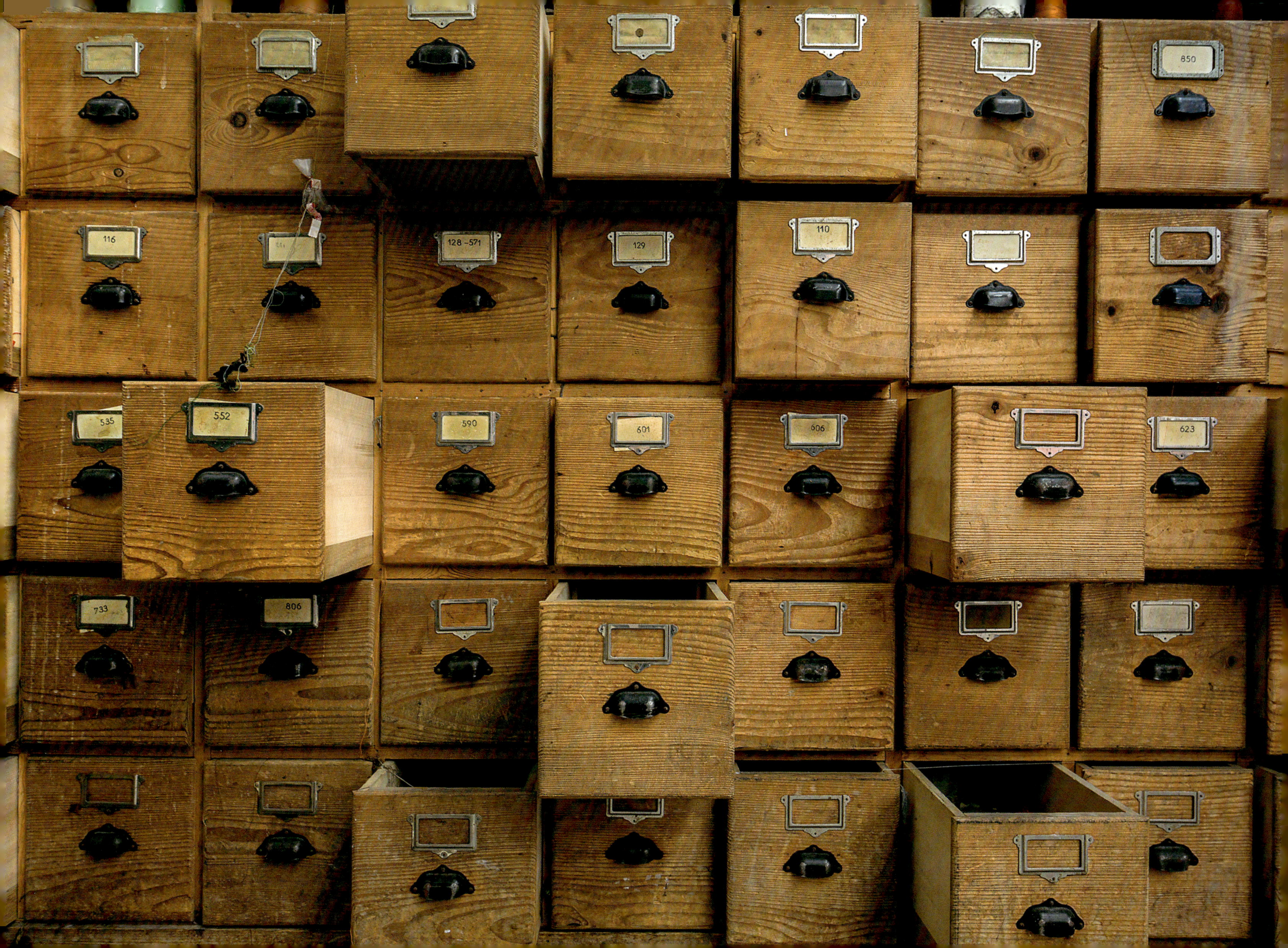
850
116
128-571
129
110
535
552
590
601
606
623
733
806

Pottery S • *Grand-Est*

Old buildings covered with a series of saw-tooth roofs caught my attention. The roofs, with dual pitches of different slopes, are typical of industrial workshops. The steeper surface was usually glazed to bring enough light into the heart of the building. These special roofs have become so much a part of our collective imagination that even today, although they have largely disappeared, the silhouette of a saw-toothed building with a steam chimney is the typical image of a factory.

For years, this earthenware factory produced quality tableware. It is now completely empty of everything that once made it a bustling factory. The place is covered in a white dust that sticks to my clothes at the slightest contact. Inside one of the outbuildings, wooden shelves laden with moulds are crumbling under their weight. A maze of rail tracks once used to have trolleys, that were continuously loaded and unloaded, circulating along it. All the hollow moulds catch my eye: they are negative moulds used to reproduce pieces in series. Fine earthenware – mainly of white clay, flint or quartz, and often with highly coloured glazes – used to be produced here. The faience factory produced decorated vases, candelabras and numerous plates with histories that conveyed patriotic and religious values or reflected on current events. At the end of the 19th century, architectural ceramic frescoes even covered breweries, shops and spas.

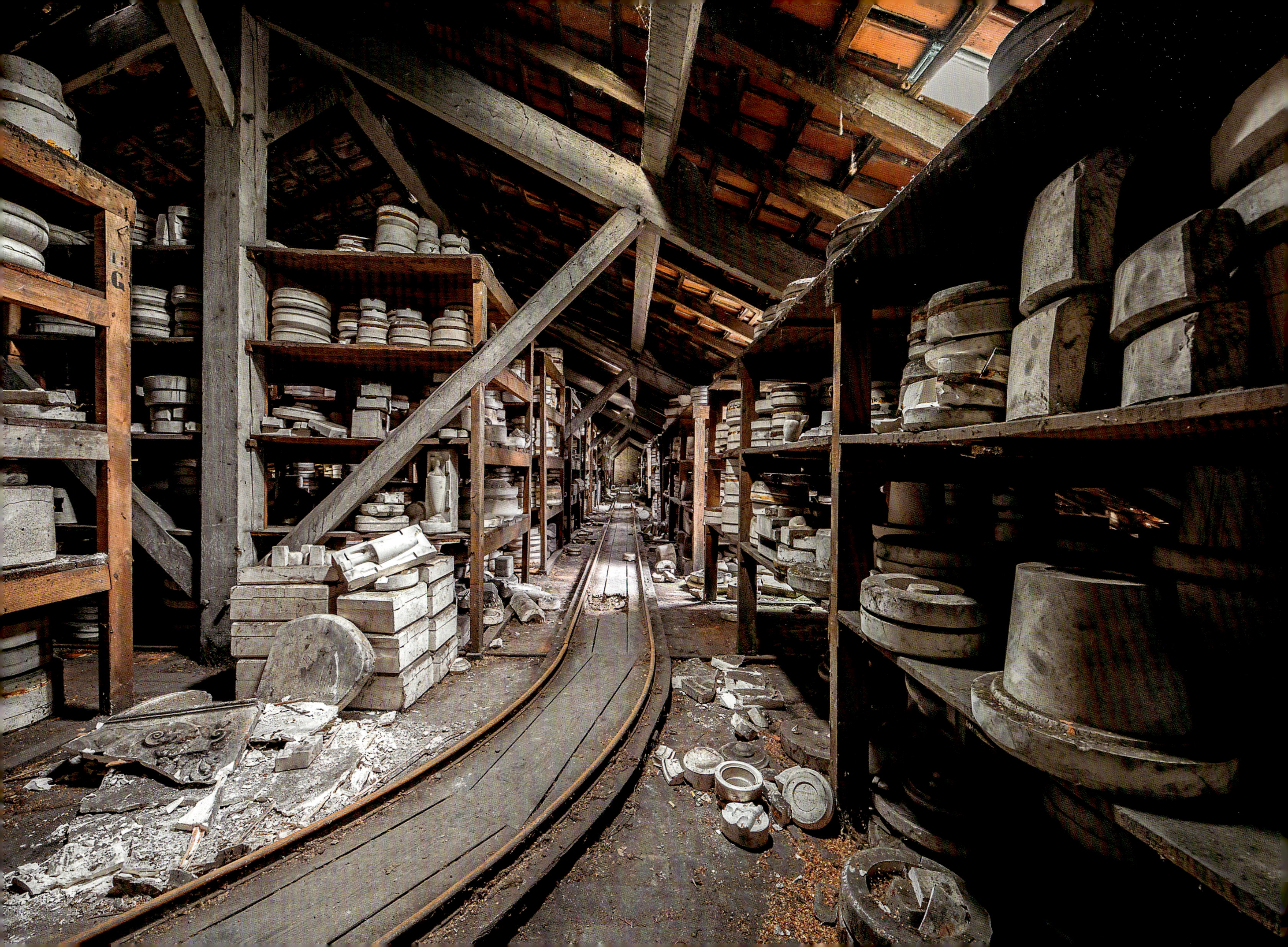

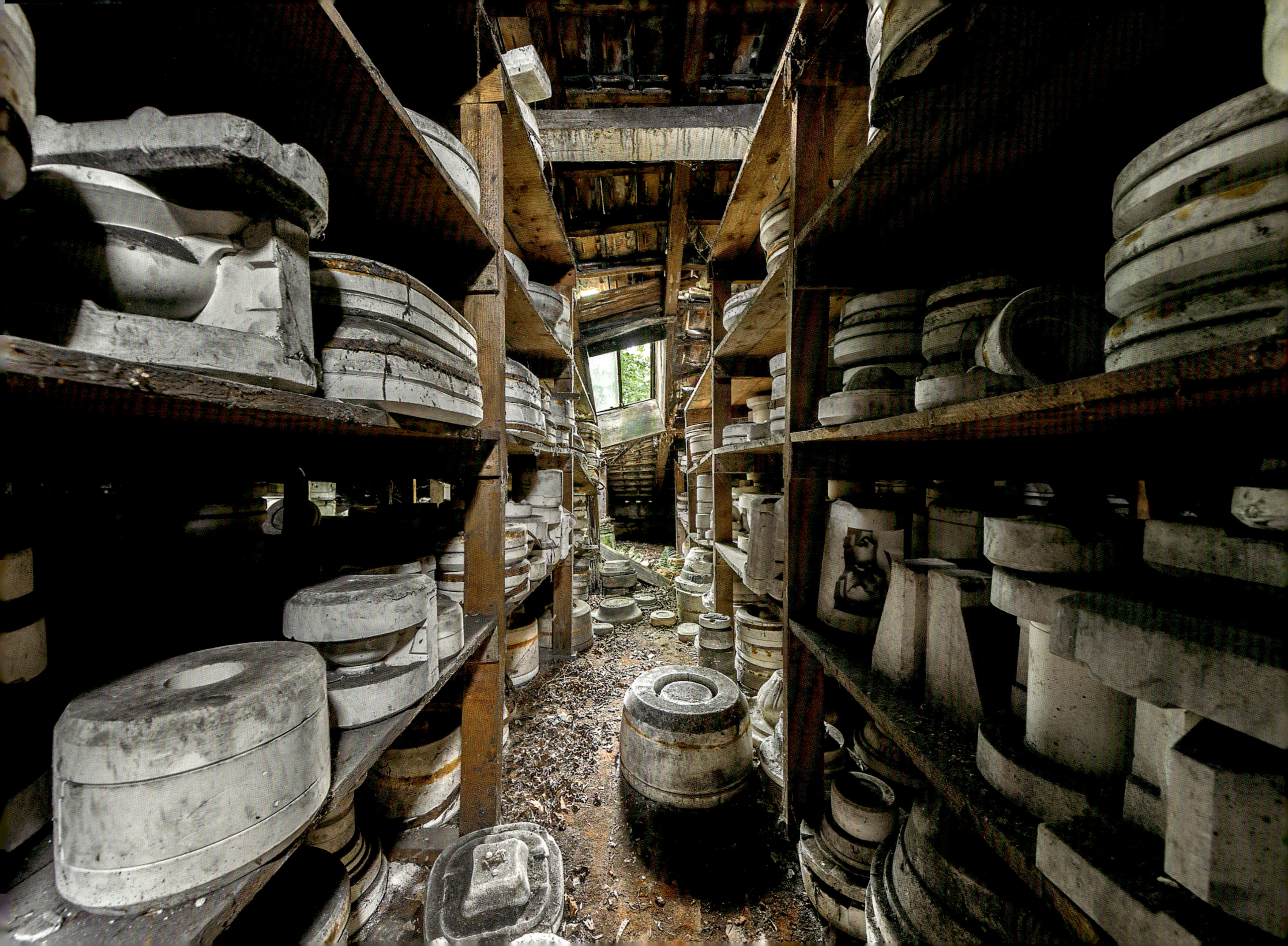

At that time, the factory was one of the largest ceramic manufacturers in Europe, employing around three thousand people. But the Industrial Revolution was in full swing, with increased competition, fierce social demands and international tensions. The factory was finally bought out in 1979 and the new management abandoned the concept of tableware that had made its reputation, including the famous Obernai service decorated by Henri Loux, to focus on the manufacture of tiles, walls and floors. This was a turning point in the history of earthenware in this town. In 2002, there were only 130 workers still in the business, fighting to maintain their production facilities after a takeover plan by 19 employees and managers who had become shareholders. Unfortunately, the factory was again in difficulty and was put into compulsory liquidation. The court ordered the end of the activity in 2007, and the site has been abandoned since.

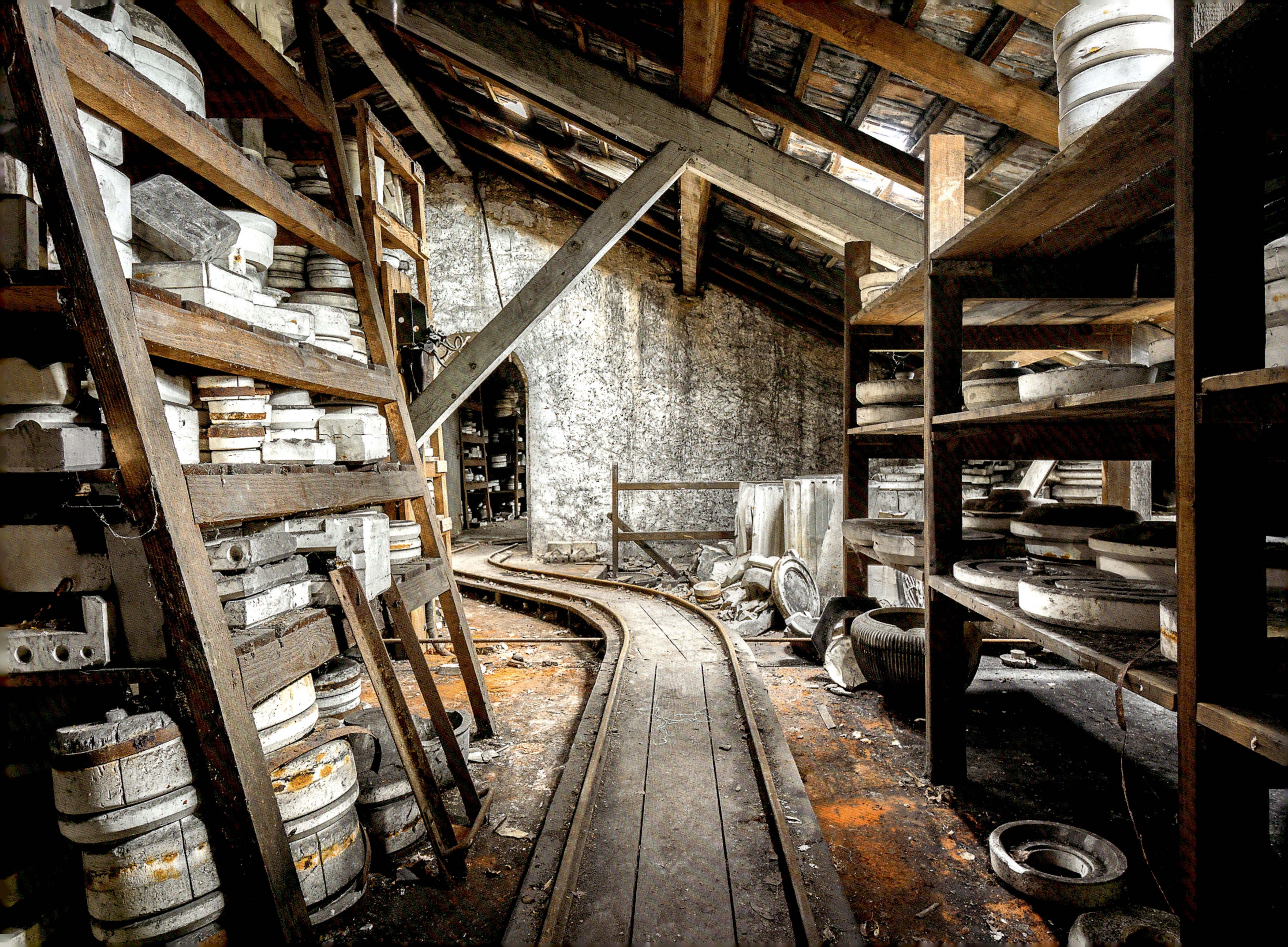

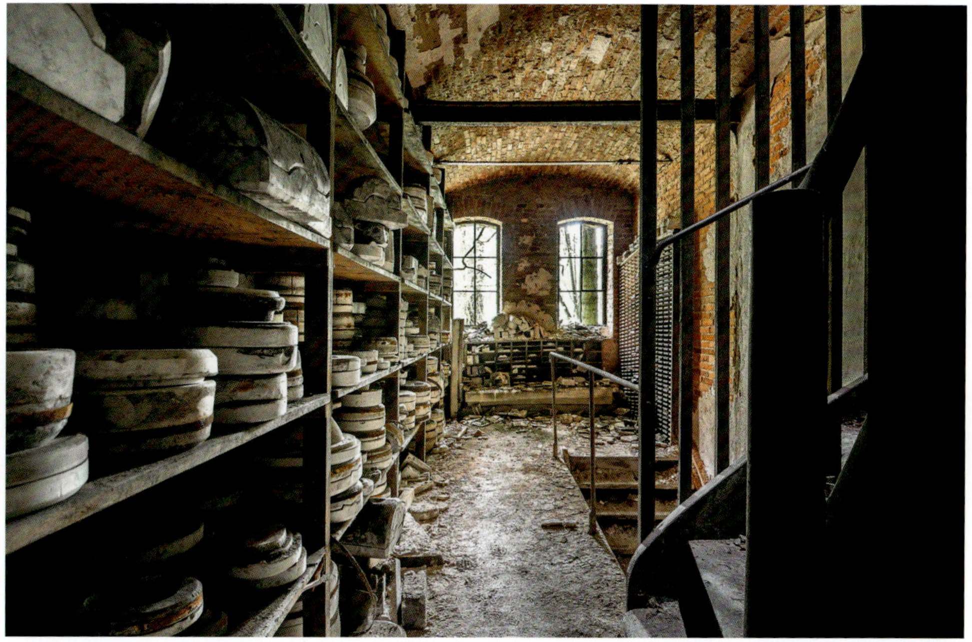

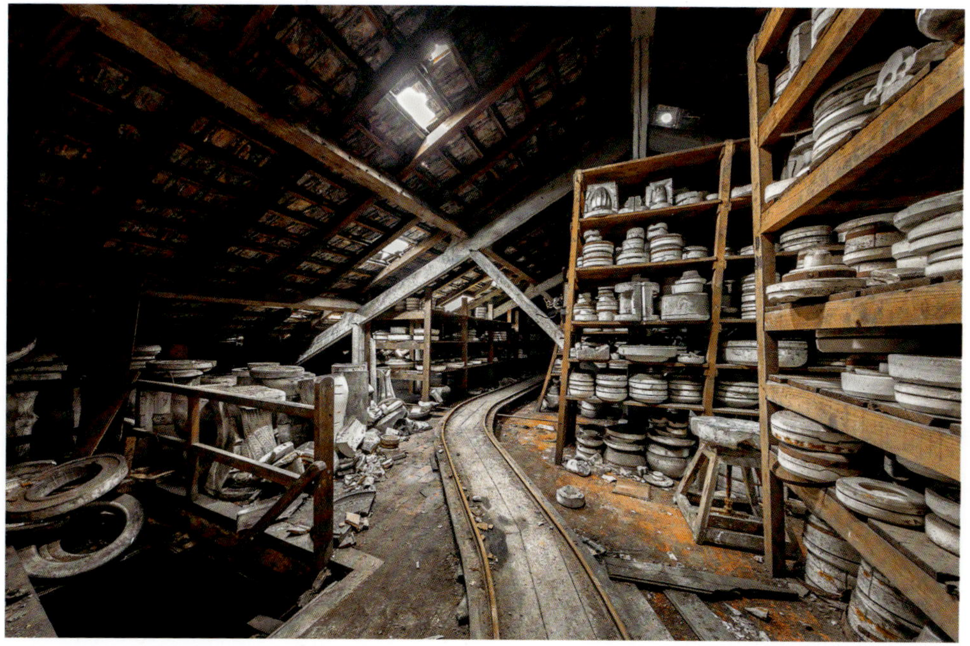

War treasures • *Grand-Est*

This is an incredible graveyard of pre-war cars. Tightly packed together and covered with a veil of rust, these vehicles from another time languish in the tunnel of an old quarry in the pitch-black. Some cars of this private collection that has fallen into oblivion are devoid of paint because rust has completely eaten away the metal. Their tyres are cracked, their leather seats dry and dust has crept into the interior.

Why are they here? Is it to protect them? Were they hidden to avoid being requisitioned during the Second World War? This surprising discovery still holds many mysteries.

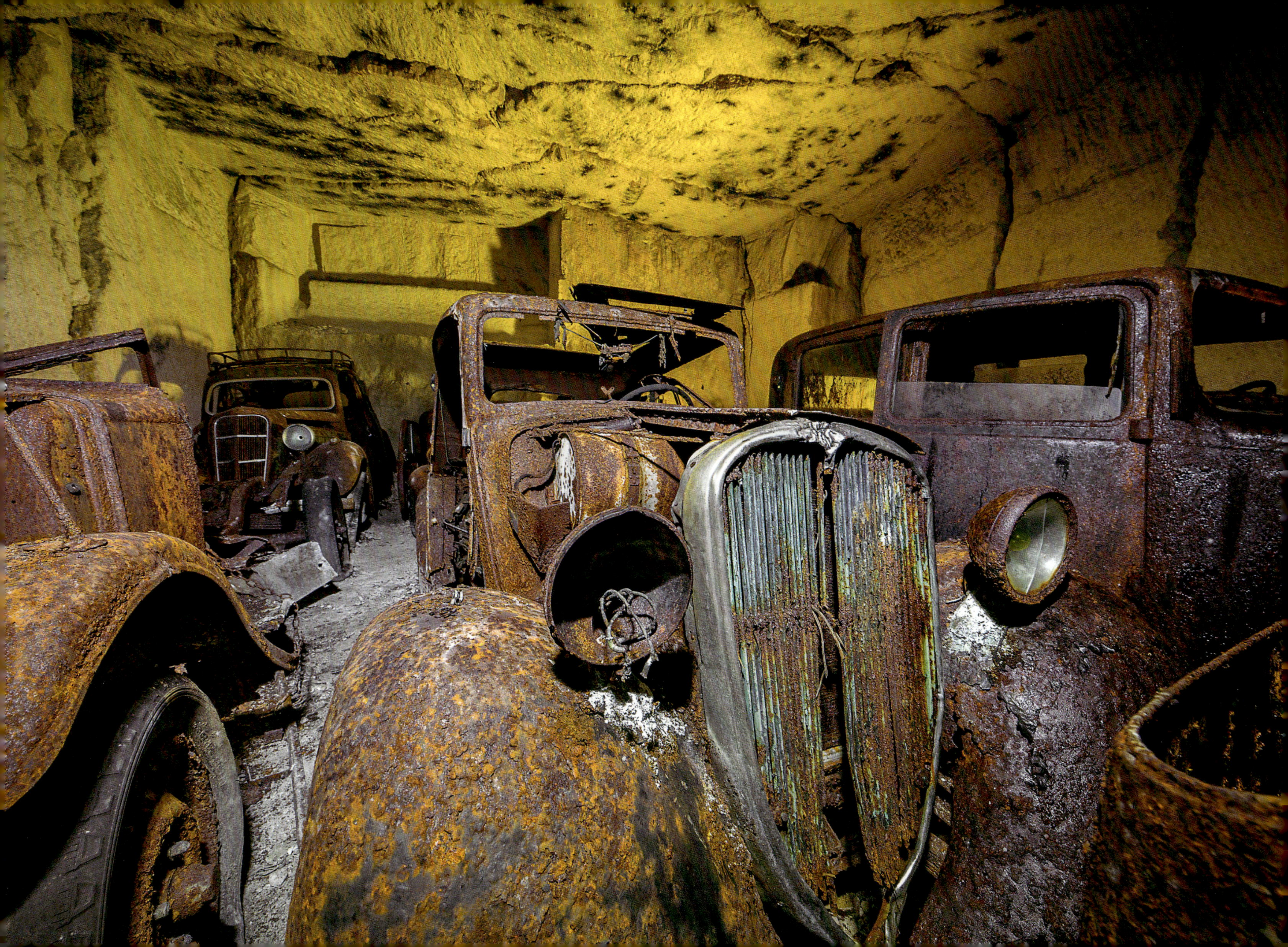

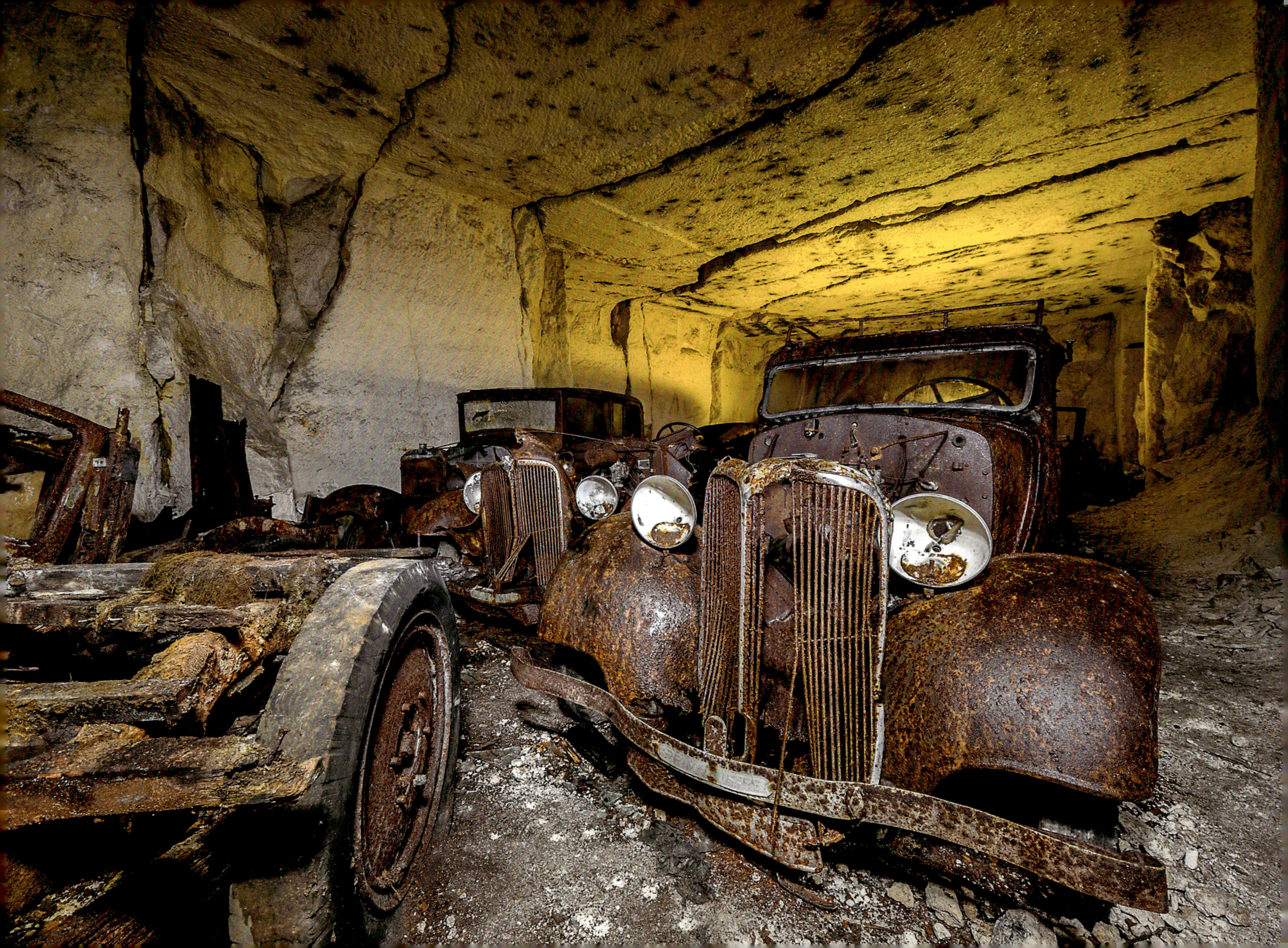

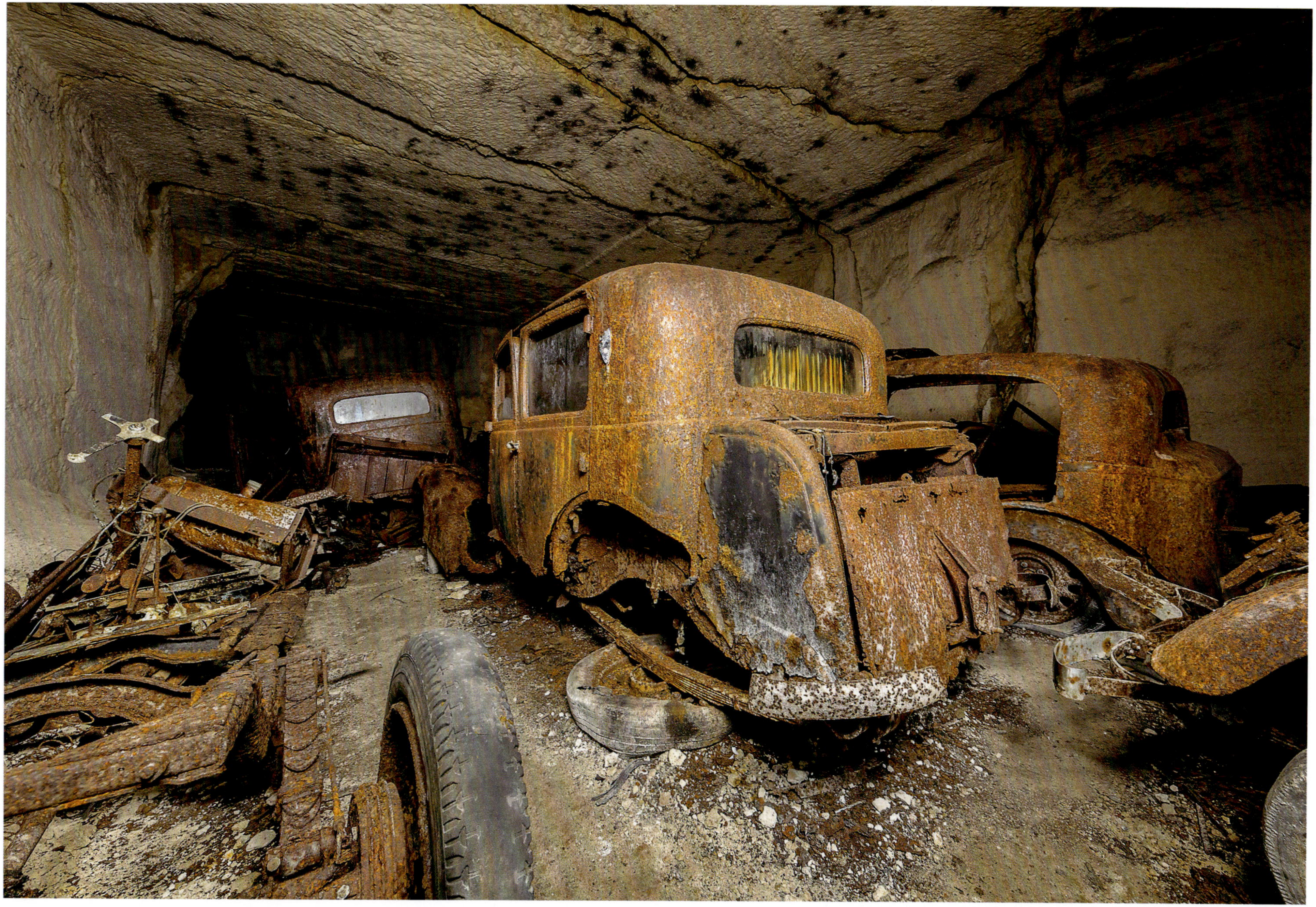

The Étoile garage • *Grand-Est*

This forgotten shed, which is falling into ruin, houses old cars piled up on top of each other or jammed together with others in an incredible mishmash. I discreetly sneaked around every corner and could only notice the indescribable jumble the place was in.

The cars are mostly Mercedes covered in dust, moss and even shrubs, but there are also a few old Volvos to be found.

This incredible warehouse, where no one dares to venture any more, will soon collapse.

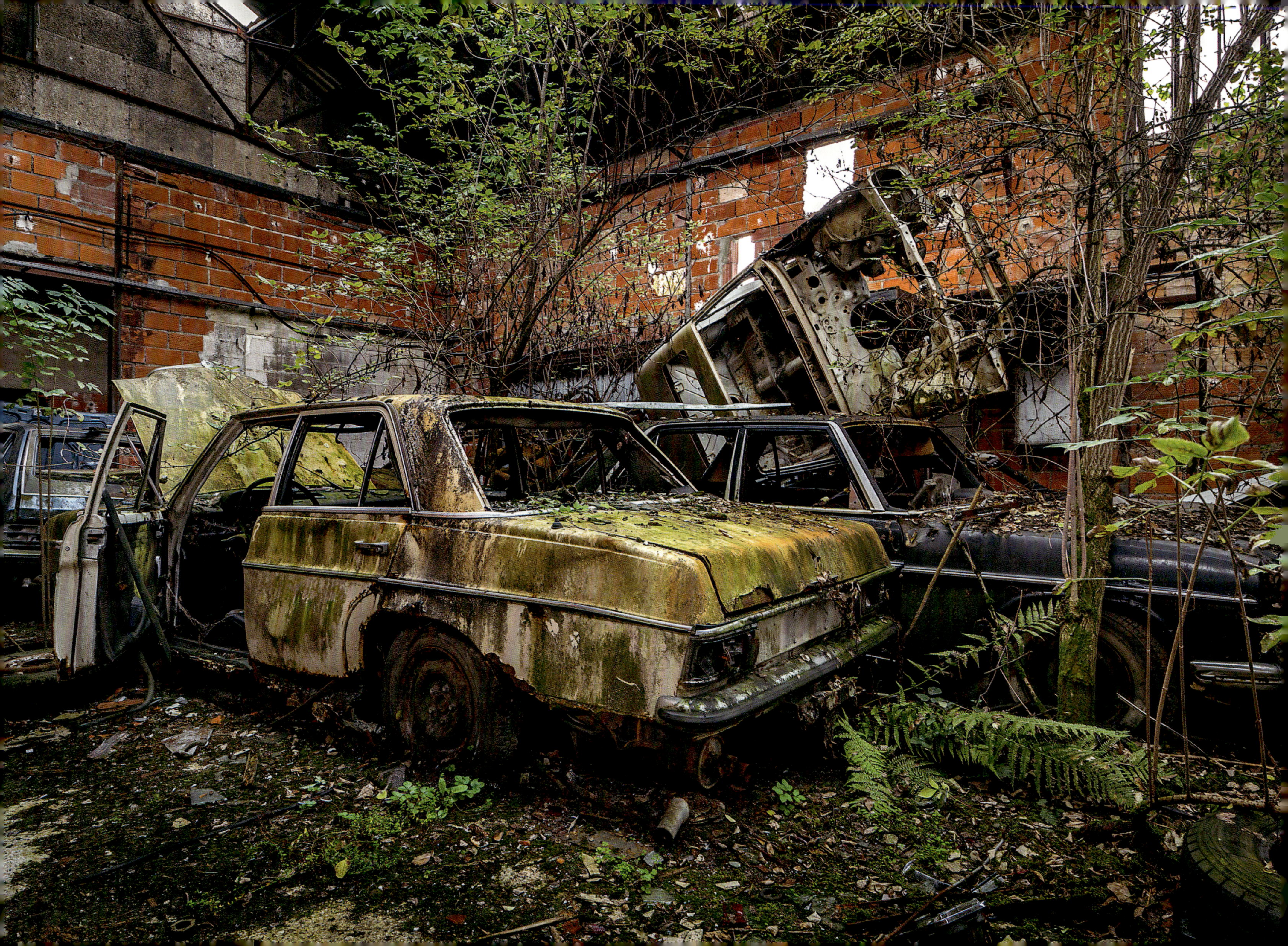

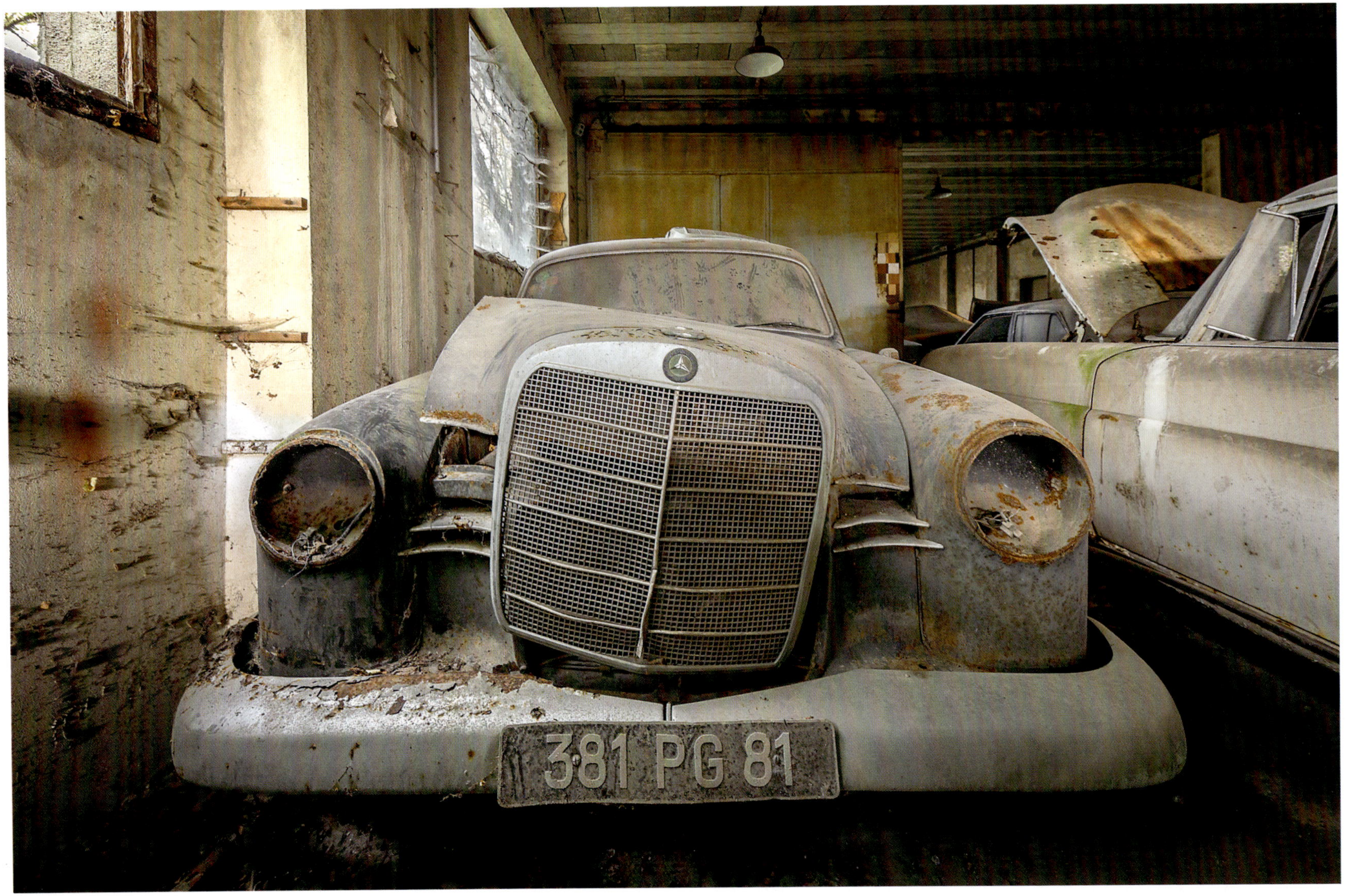
381 PG 81

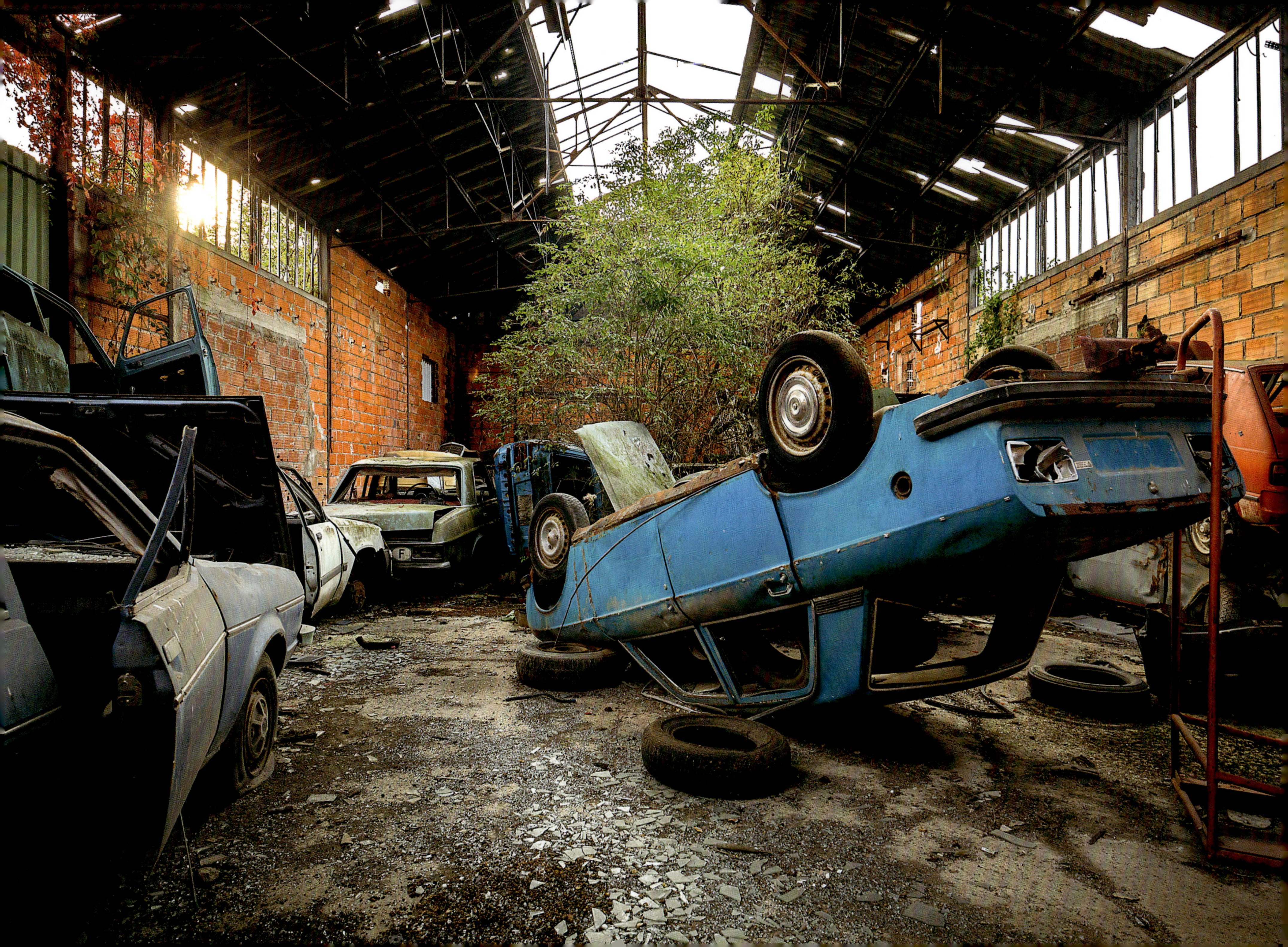

Lost Queens • *Grand-Est*

There are so many forgotten treasures in this old orangery of an 18th-century castle! Classic cars covered in dust and lined up one after the other have been stored here for years.

Surprisingly, I hardly paid any attention to the Citroën DS, Jaguar, Mercedes and Dodge Stealth, those old jewels of the car industry. I was too busy admiring the sublime Lamborghini Espada, which steals the show. Despite its four real seats, the sporty car stands out with its design and was intended for a wealthy clientele sensitive to pure performance. This rare model was designed by the Italian Marcello Gandini – the design engineer of the Lamborghini Miura, Marzal, Diablo, De Tomaso and the sublime Alfa Romeo Montreal. The Espada, powered by a six-barrel V12 engine with 325 horsepower, had a top speed of 250 km/h. From 1968 to 1978, 1,227 examples of this Italian beauty were sold.

This one is registered in Bergamo, Italy. What is it doing so far from its homeland?

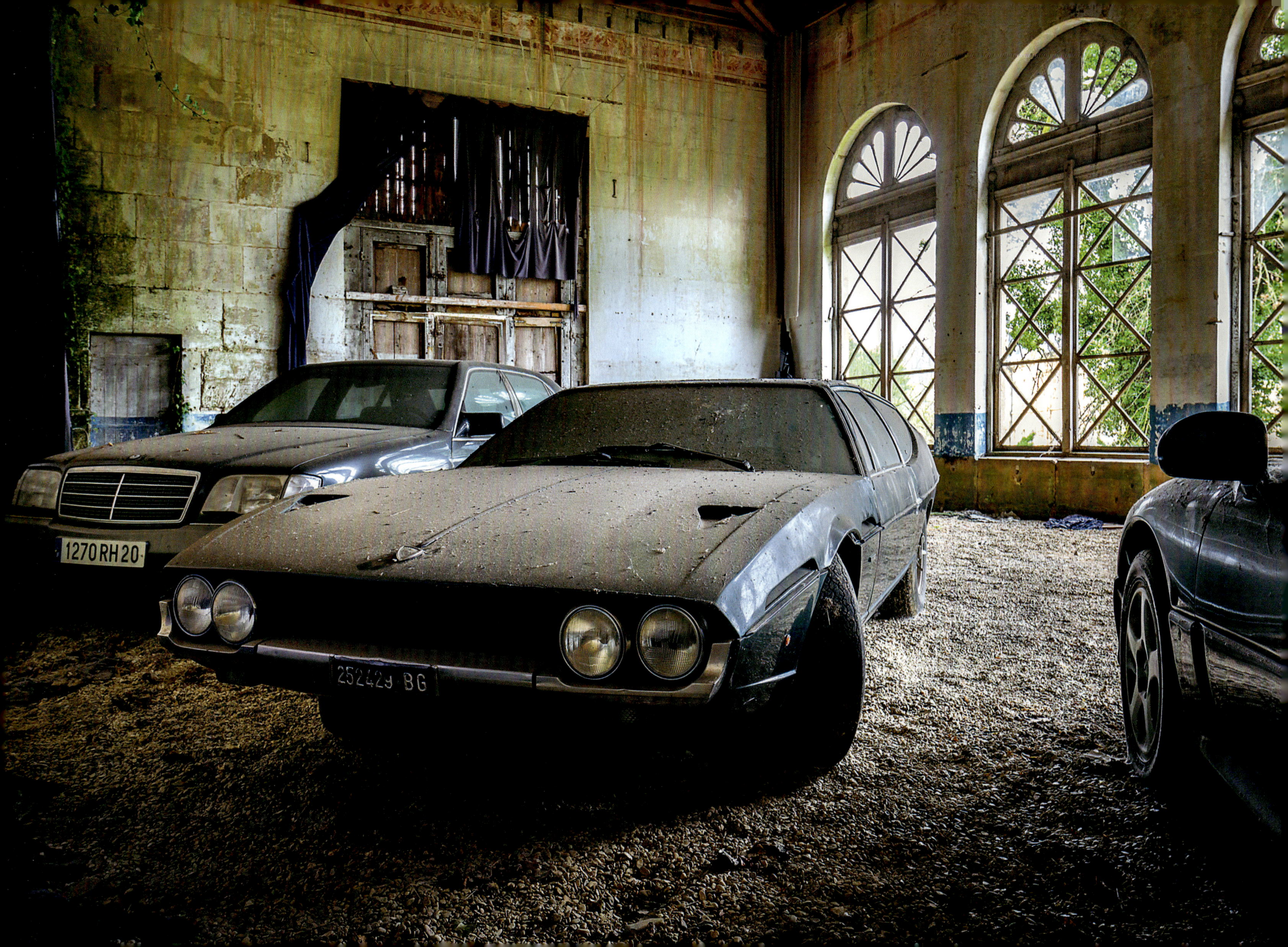
1270RH20

Oldtimers • *Grand-Est*

Sometimes, it's impossible to imagine what lies dormant in a shed. Here, it's two metal lovers.

The humidity of the place accounts for the dilapidated state of these two moss-covered cars. A few years ago, their owner, a Citroën dealer, used to store his favourite vehicles in the neighbouring woods. Photos of a vast area of land littered with wrecks parked like soldiers in a row are still circulating on the web. It was a real car cemetery in the woods! Citroën DS and ID, Simca, Renault 8, Peugeot 403, 2CV and other French models of the past were overgrown with brambles, ivy and moss, and surrounded by dandelions. Rust and the passing seasons have taken their toll on these vehicles, which were not sufficiently popular to entice the classic car market at the time. Eventually, the owner was ordered by the municipality to clean up the site.

Today, there is not much left of the row of 80 Citroën tractions that made the place so attractive. All that remains are these two jalopies, languishing under a skeletal shed.

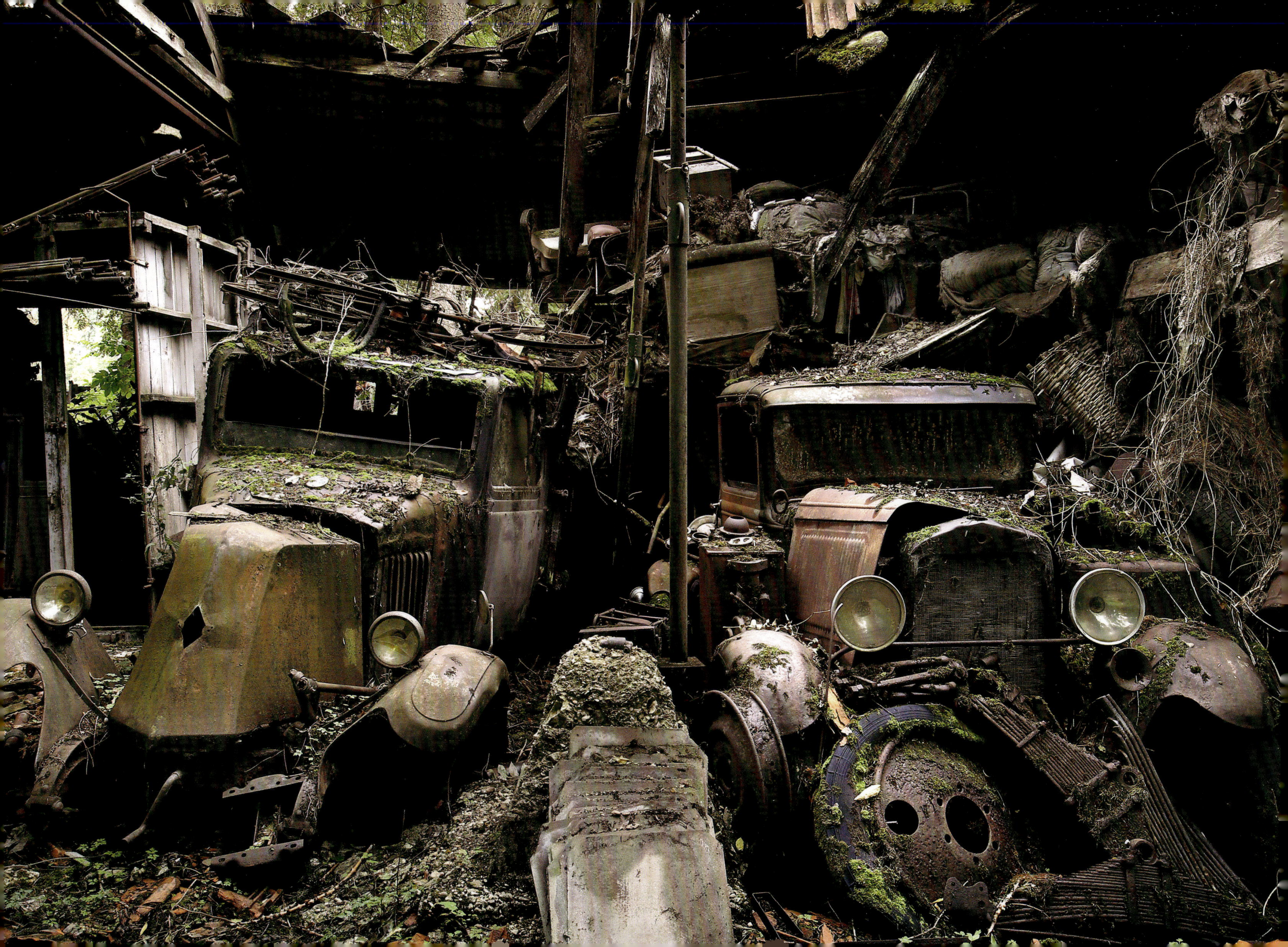

Top Gun • *Grand-Est*

An airfield open to public air traffic was inaugurated in July 1913 in the Grand-Est region. From 1953 to 1965, it served as an operational airbase and dispersal base for NATO and could accommodate 50 fighter aircraft. Three dispersals, three large aircraft hangars and a gunnery mound for setting and aligning aircraft guns were built in 1956, when the platform was used by the US Air Force to maintain its liaison aircraft. Three fantastic aircraft from the 1940s and 50s, all outstanding in their design and performance, are still parked here.

First, there is the Fouga Magister, the world's first jet trainer. This is a two-seater, subsonic jet aircraft designed in France in the early 1950s. It is recognisable by its V-shaped tailplane, sometimes called a 'butterfly' tail. This model was selected by NATO in 1954 because it was considered the most suitable aircraft for training and improvement due to its aerobatic capabilities. It was also adopted by several aerobatic patrols, including the Patrouille de France (the precision aerobatics demonstration unit of the French Air and Space Force), which used it for 16 years, from 1964 to 1980.

There is also a twin-engine French Noratlas. With a twin-beam configuration allowing easy access to the rear cargo doors, it was designed for troop transport and used from 1949 until the 1990s.

The last aircraft is an American anti-submarine warfare maritime patrol Neptune, used by the US Navy between 1947 and 1978. Submarines existed during the First World War, but it was during the Second World War that they best demonstrated their ability to cause harm to enemy war fleets.

Who owns these three models? A collector with a passion for exceptional aircraft? No one knows.

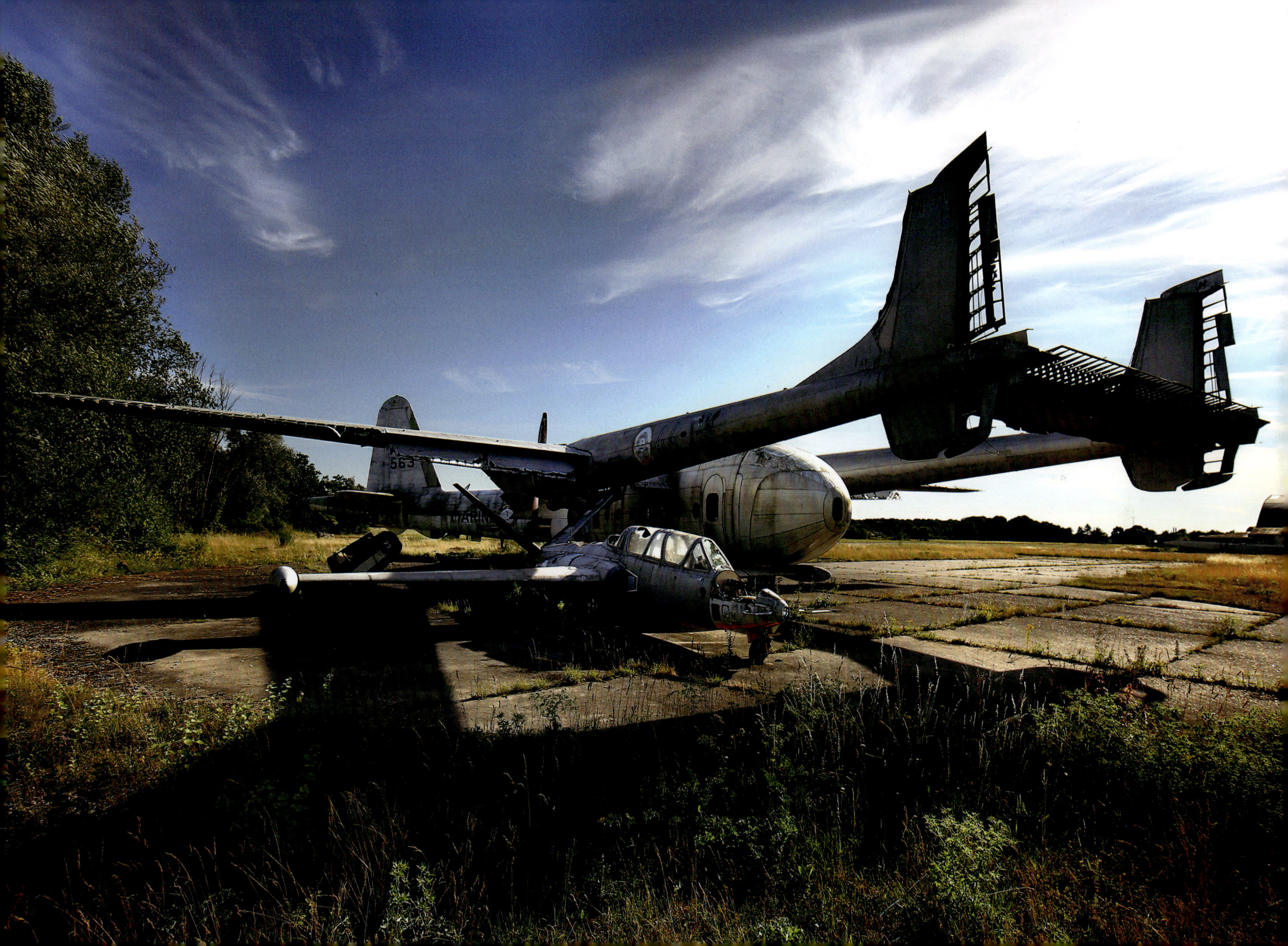
563

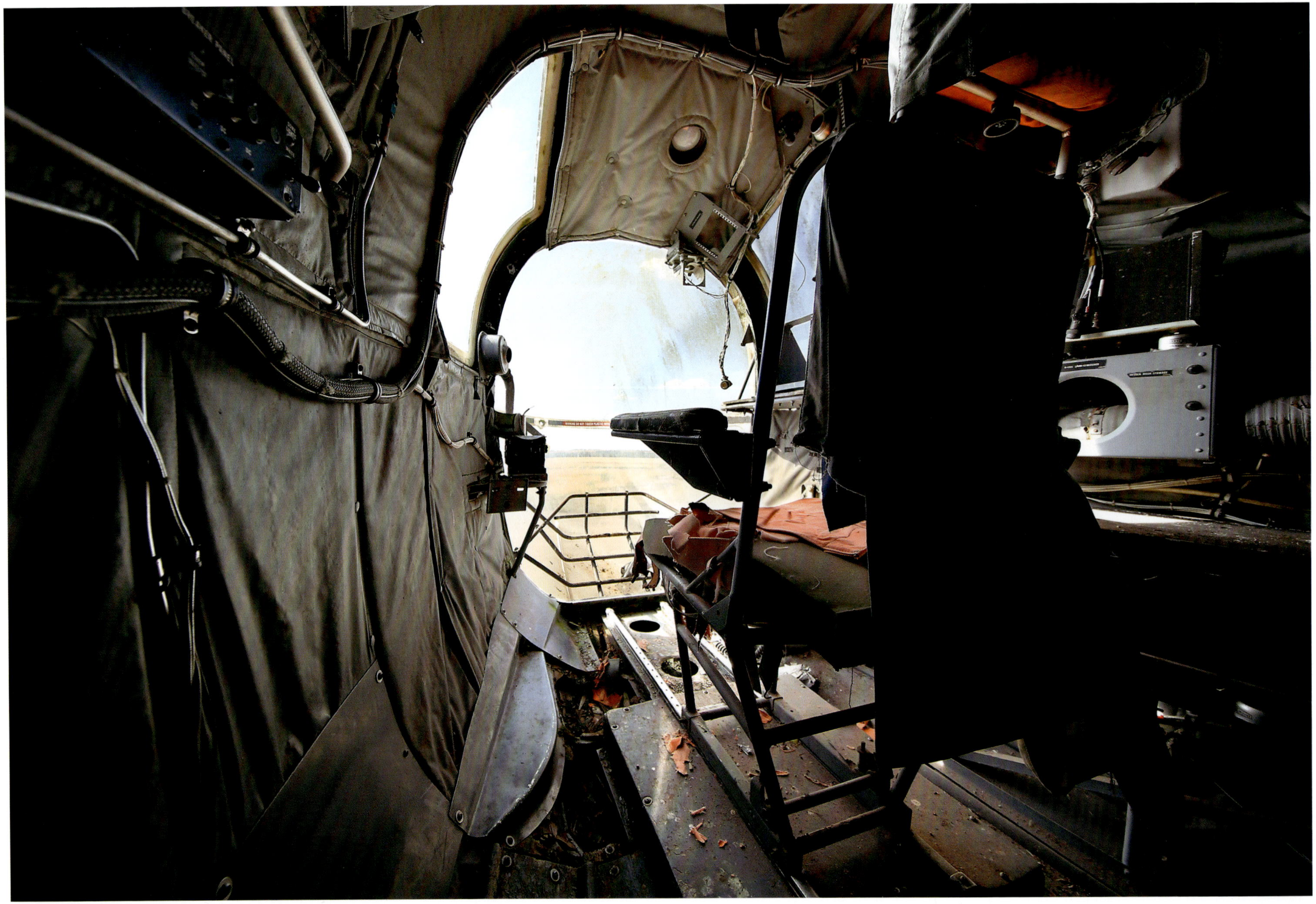

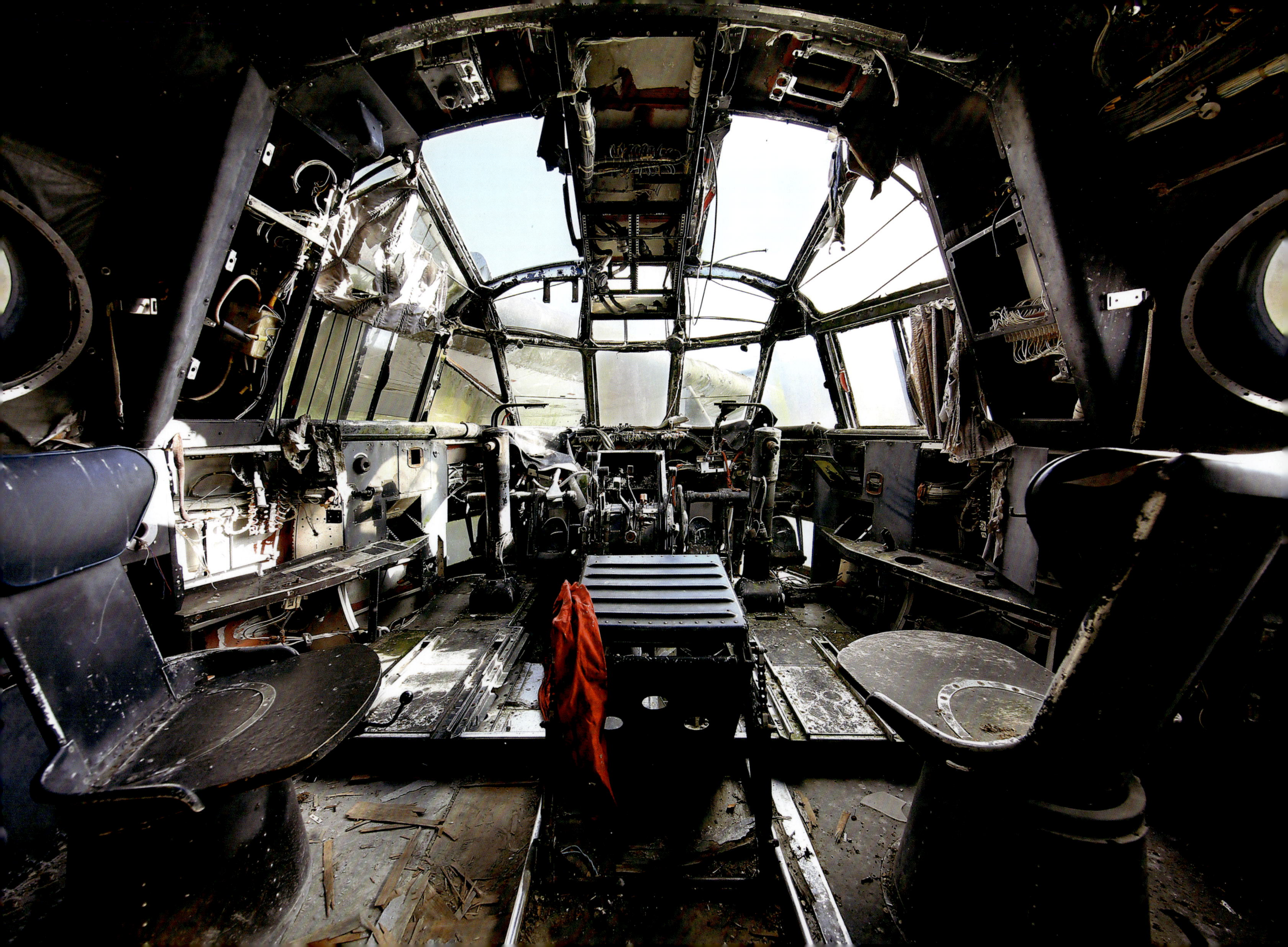

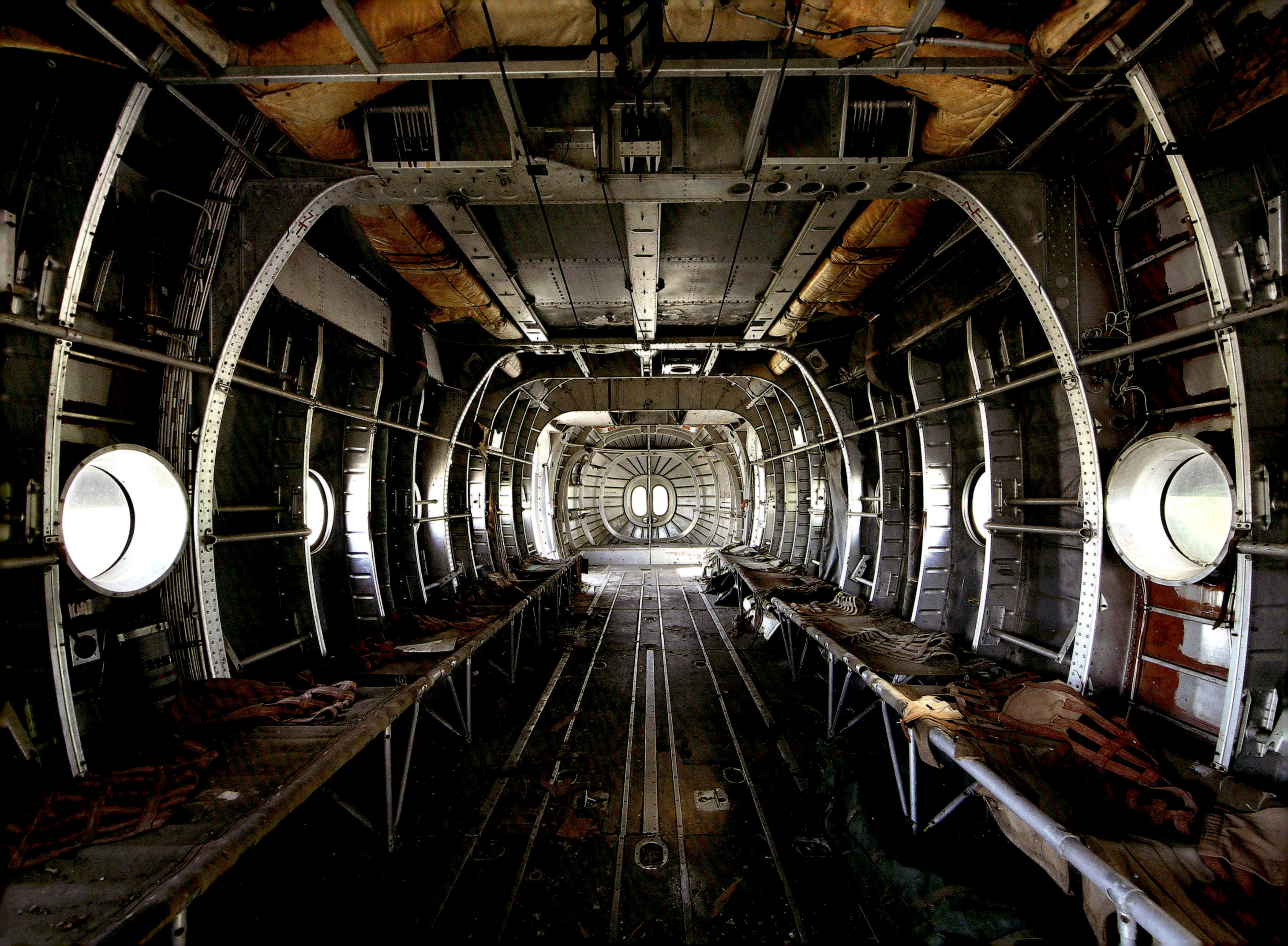

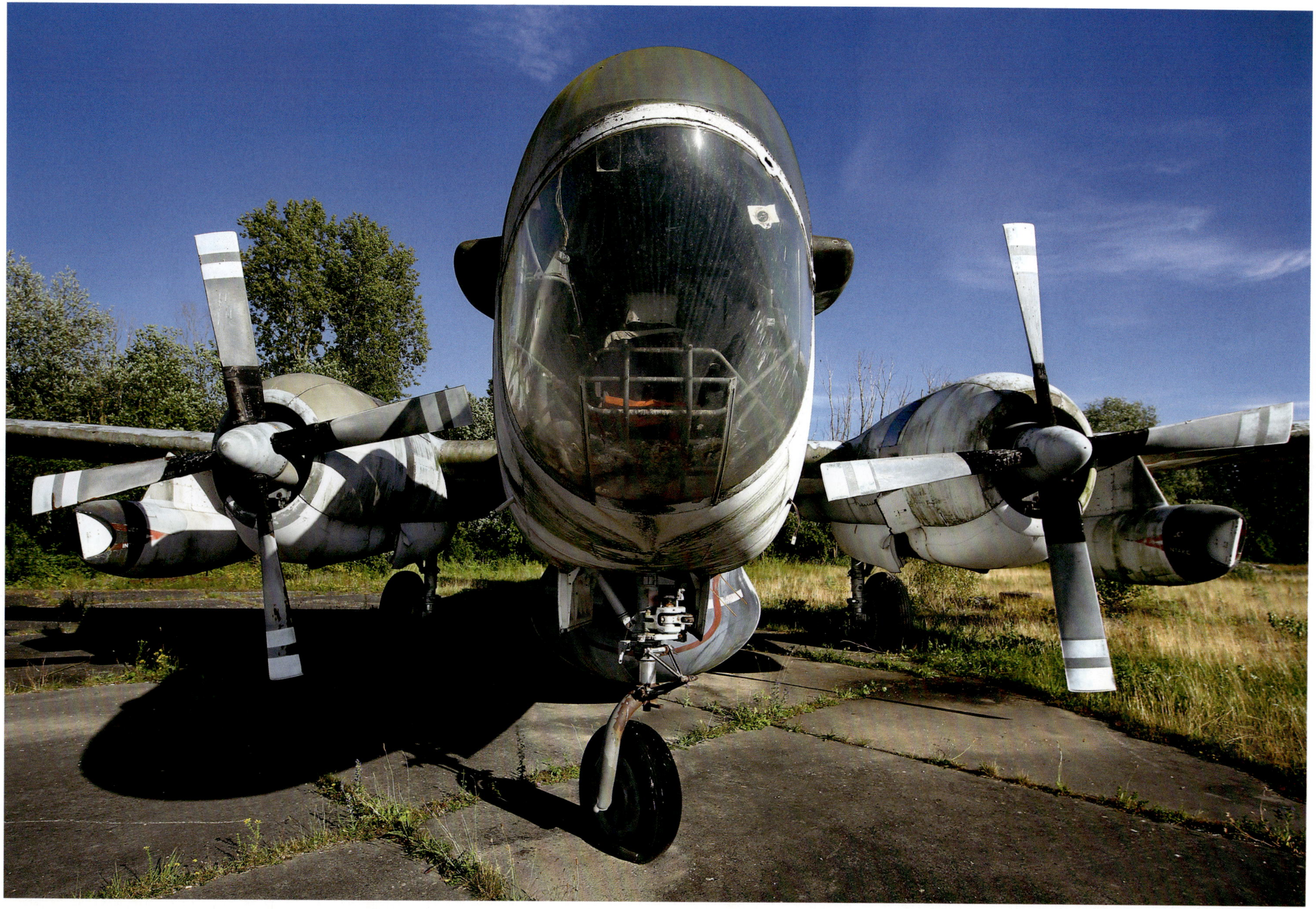

Samourai castle • *Nouvelle-Aquitaine*

Over five eras, successive owners of this feudal castle were keen to embellish it and mark the history of the place, redesigning it many times and adding new buildings to form a particularly colourful and heterogeneous ensemble.
Its impressive square tower with battlements, clearly visible from a distance, and the round tower, seem to date from the end of the 13th century. On the lintel of the door of the square tower is a coat of arms that is yet to be identified. It features azure and three bezants, on top of which is a knight's helmet. A distinguished dovecote and a pretty corner turret were added in the 16th century. However, it was not until the 19th century that a main building was added to connect the two towers. Finally, in the last century, a Merovingian necropolis was discovered in the woods to the north of the castle.
Inside, large rooms with walls decorated with fleur-de-lys, coats of arms, helmets and knick-knacks are a surprisingly harmonious mix of ornaments. Particular attention was devoted to a fireplace flanked by two carefree boys.
A new owner has acquired this charming castle in the hope of opening a gîte (holiday rental) and giving these beautiful spaces a new lease of life. We wish him a bright future.

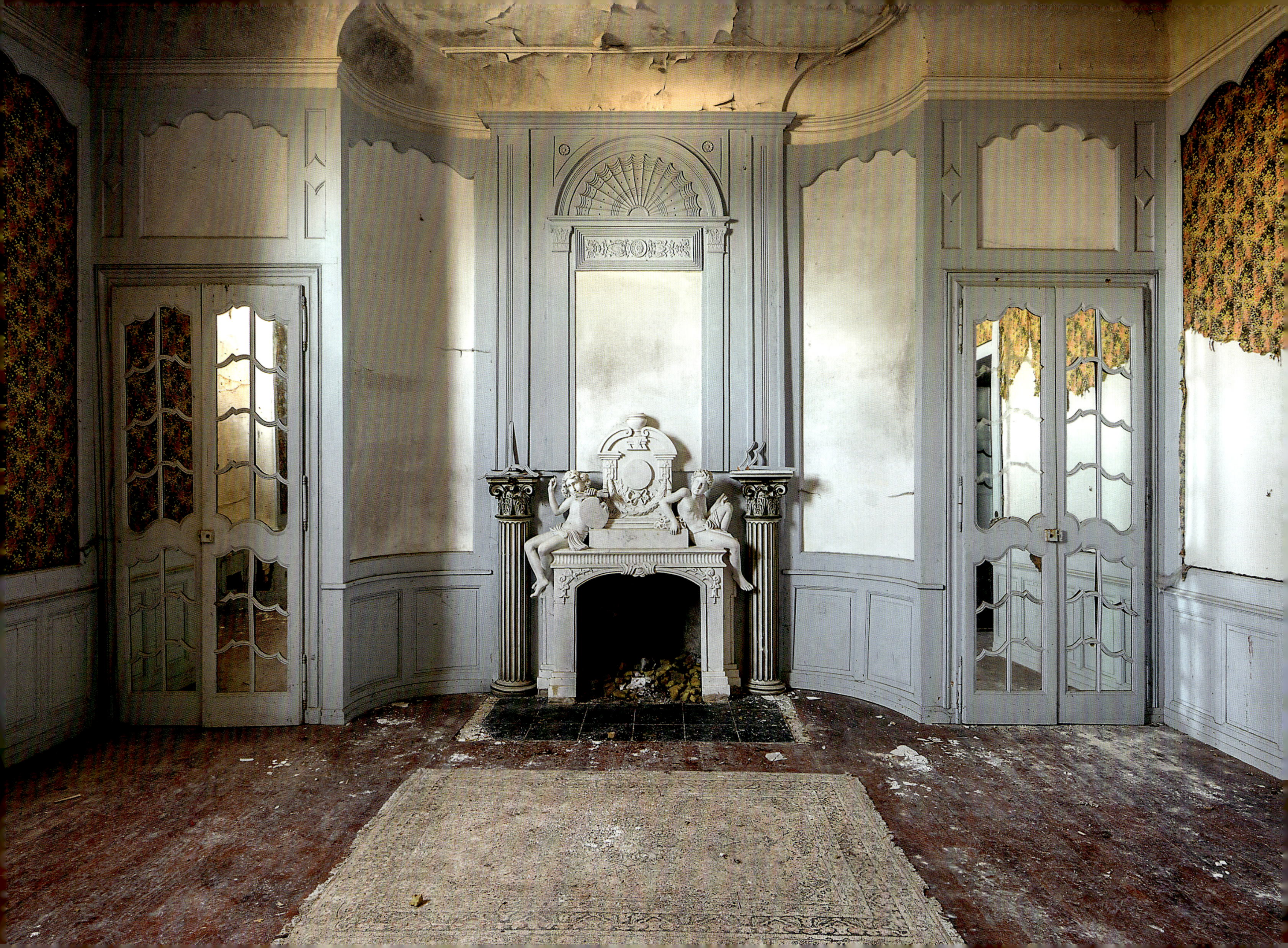

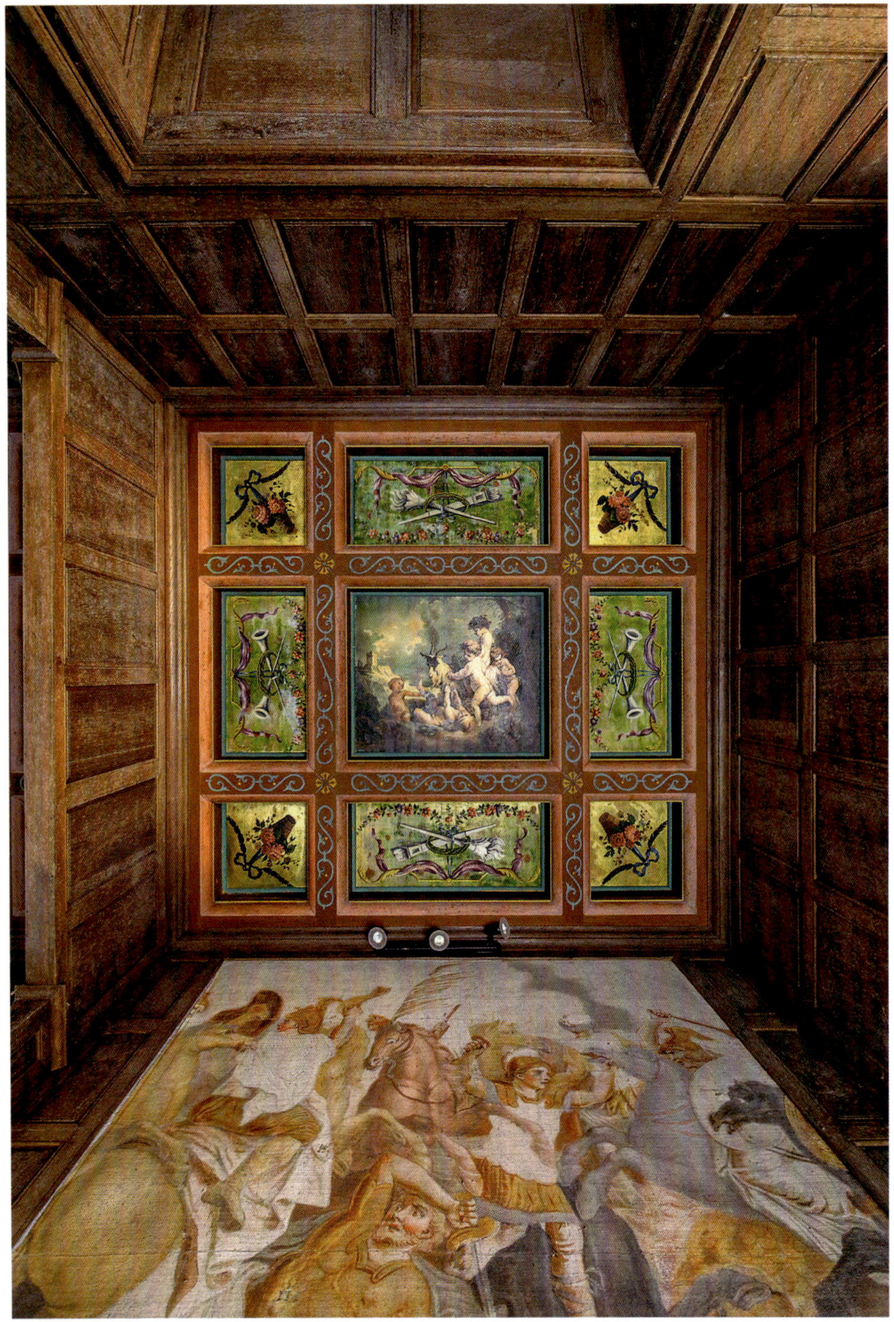

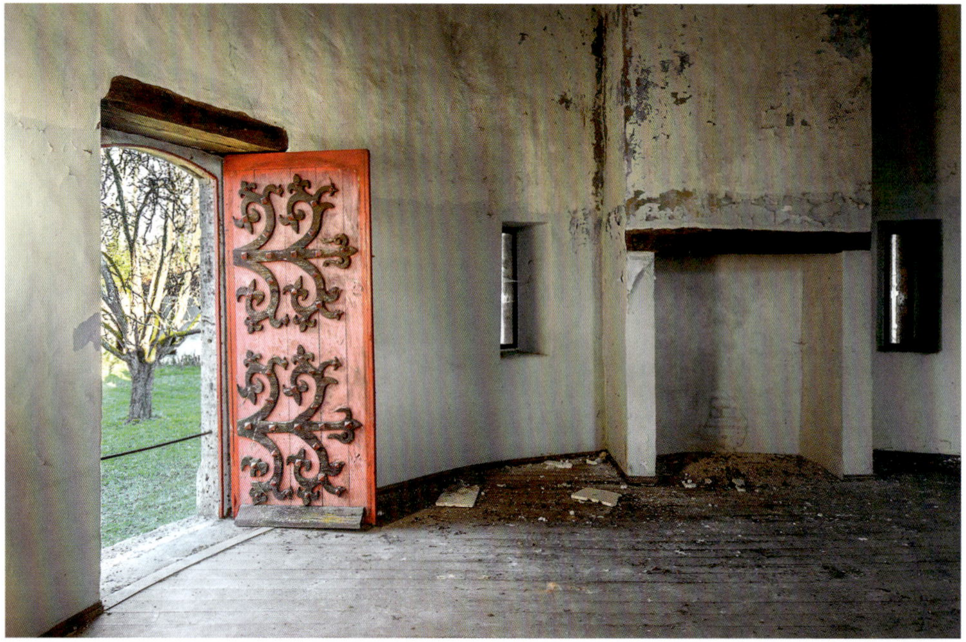

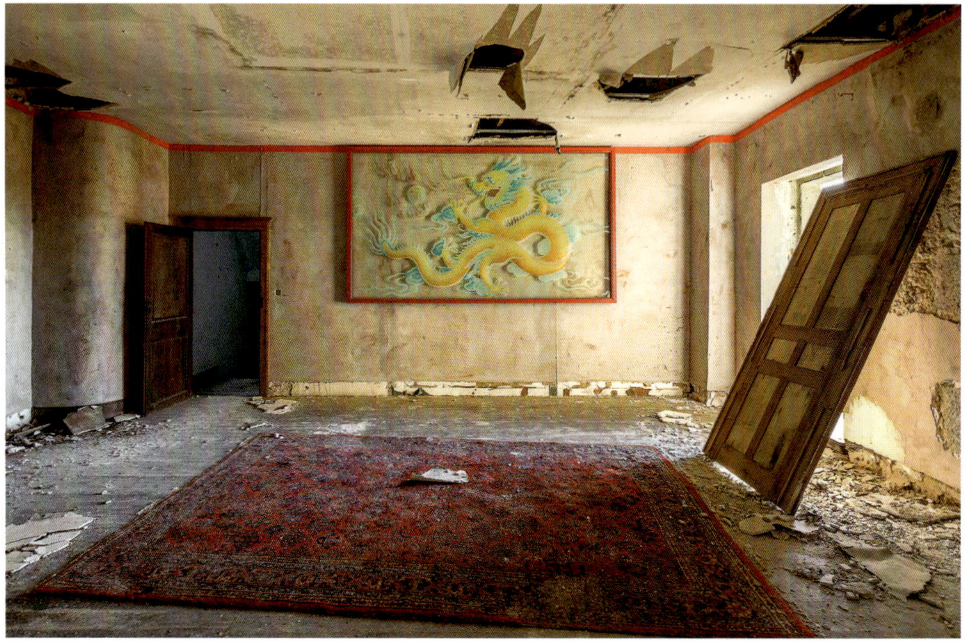

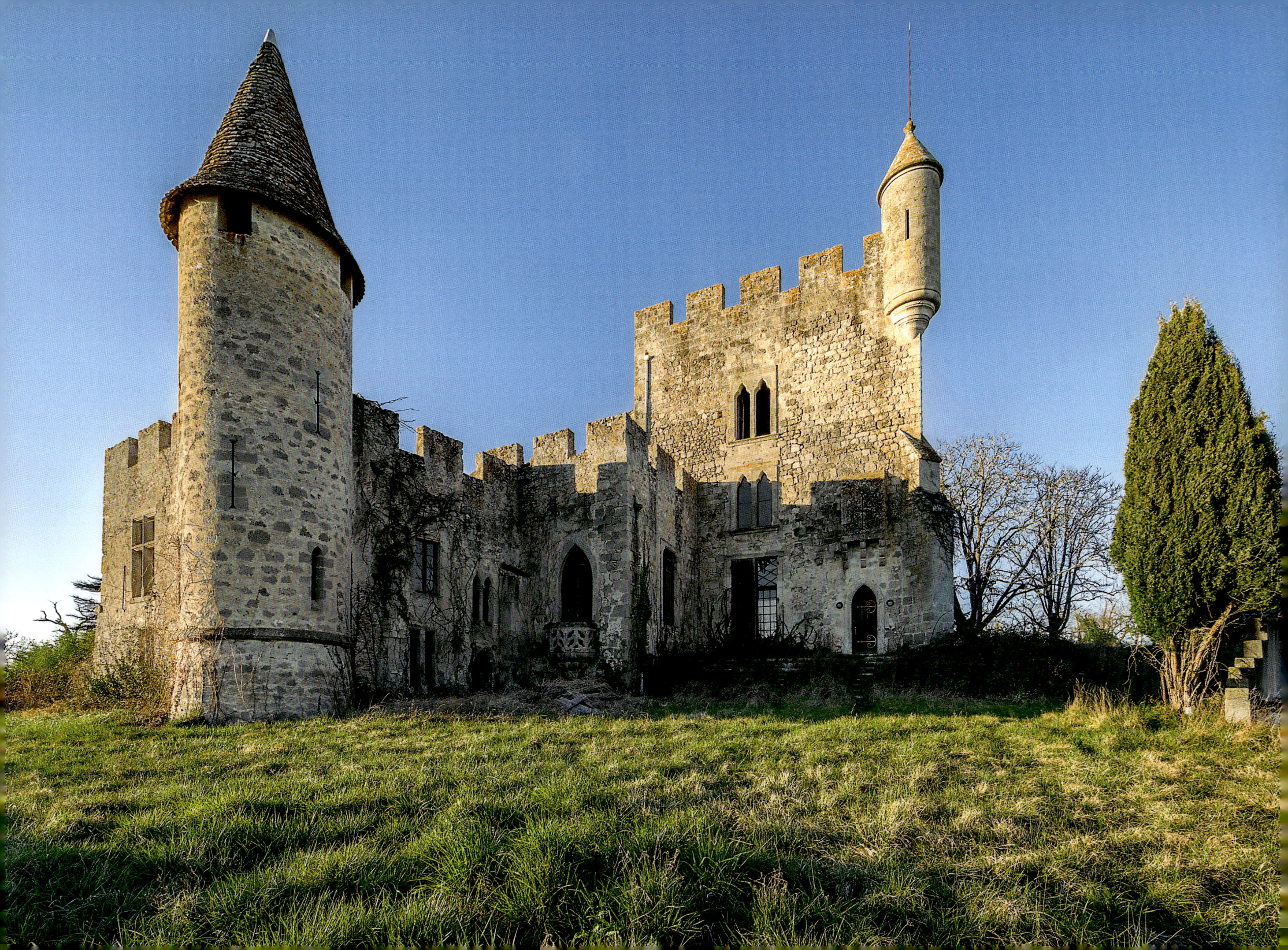

Castle of Dukes • *Bourgogne-Franche-Comté*

The castle the Dukes of Burgundy owned on the hill overlooking a village was a real gem. It is easy to understand why it and its outbuildings are classified as historic monuments.

Built between 1655 and 1700, this manor house consists of a main building built on foundations and square towers flanking each end of its facade. In one of these towers is a stone staircase, unique in France. There are still traces of a drawbridge in the forecourt, where a carriage gate is fitted. The main courtyard is superbly brought to light by a long wall supporting a balustraded terrace. As for the interior, it has been stripped of furniture, but visitors will be surprised to discover exceptional wooden staircases, a neo-Gothic style dining room, a Moorish bathroom, remarkable stained-glass windows in a gallery and a reception room, and lounges with views opening onto the valley. The whole castle is decorated with tapestries featuring fleur-de-lys and a floor tiled with coloured mosaics using the 'tesserae' method. The residence was refurbished in the 19th century and is a pure marvel. Taking a walk in the 15-hectare French-style park will let you admire the three-niche dovecote, the former chapel, both covered with lava cladding, and a 17th-century pavilion.

The castle was bought by a local resident who fell in love with it. There is a hope that it will regain its former glory.

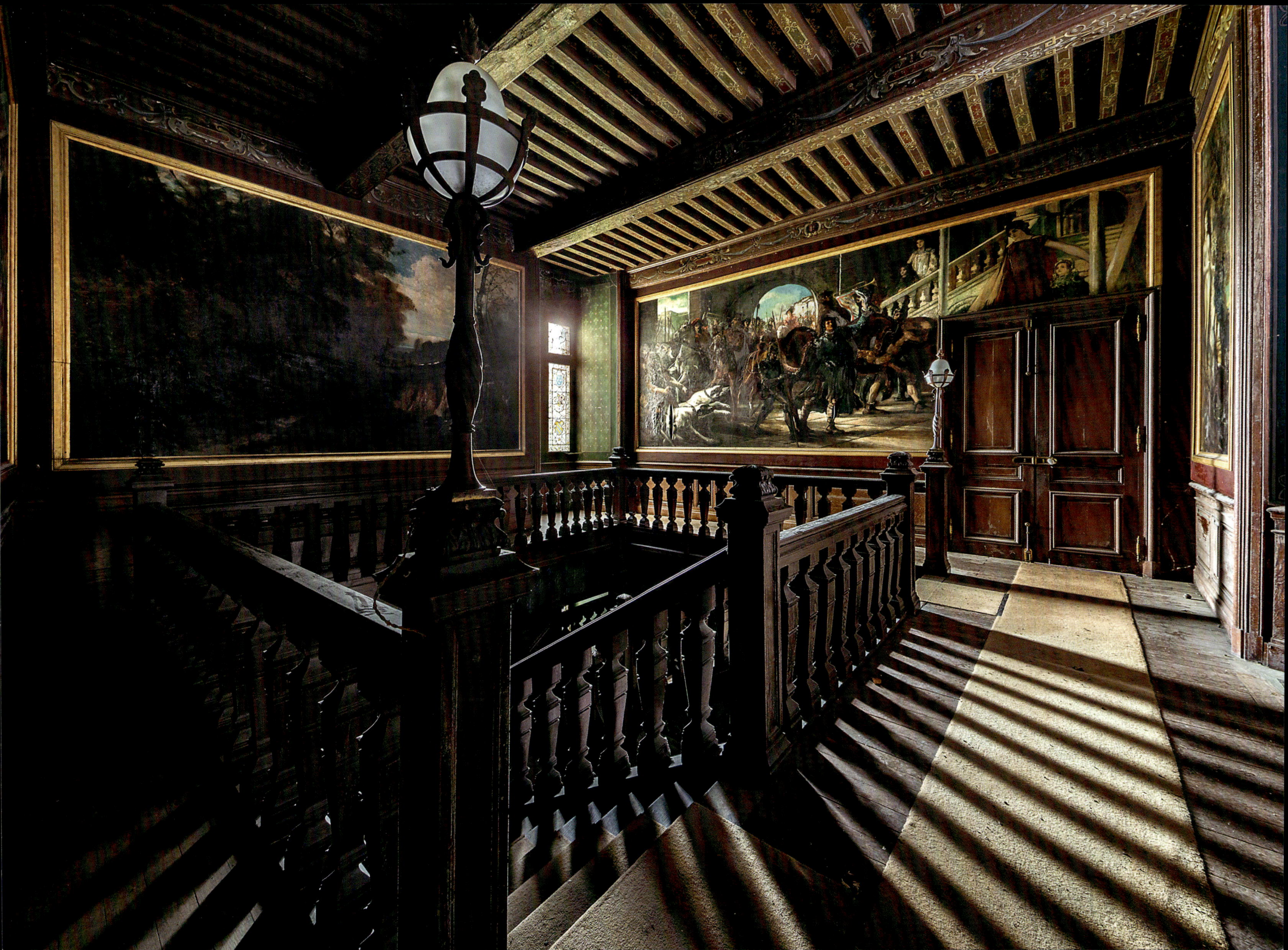

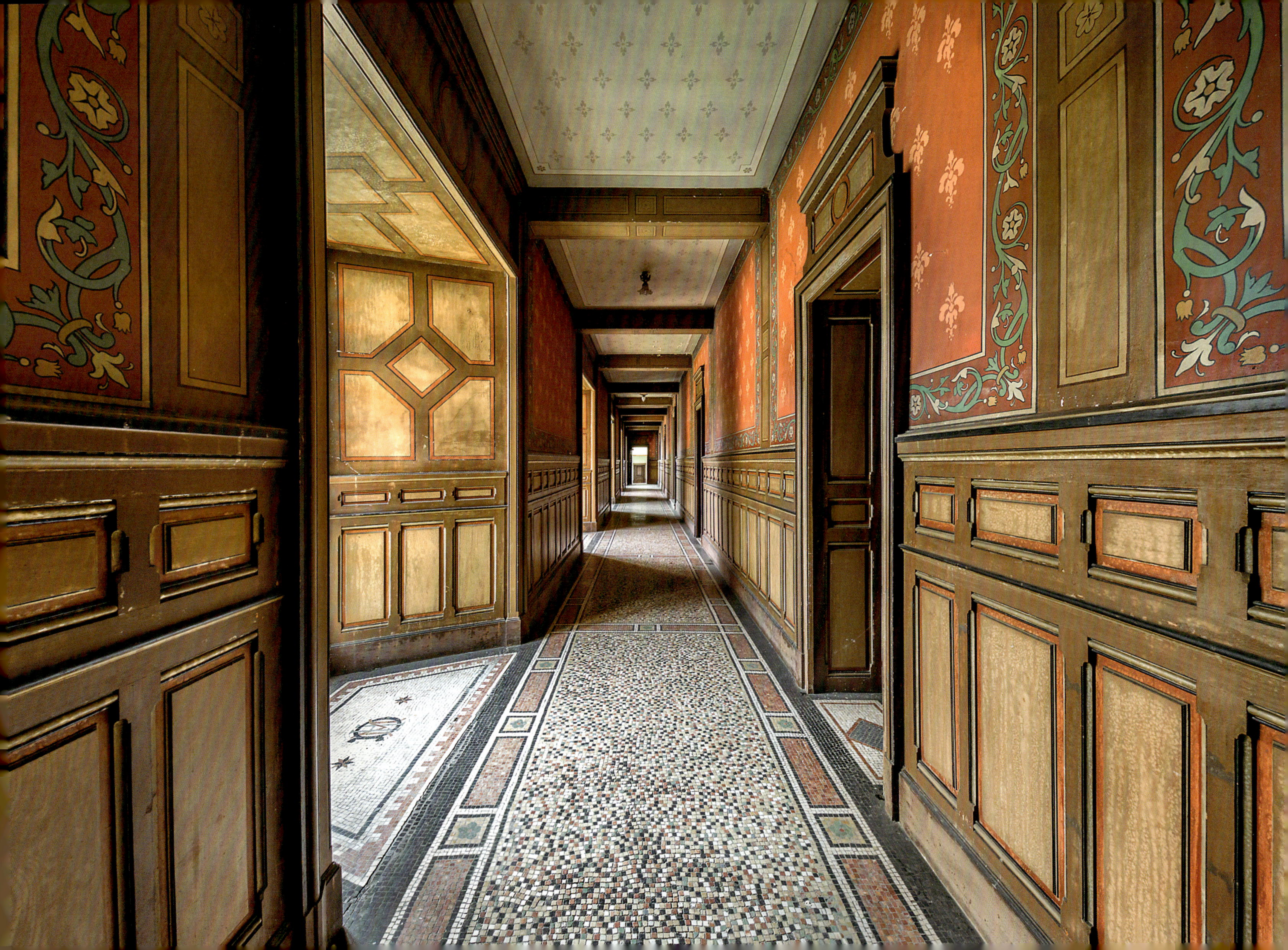

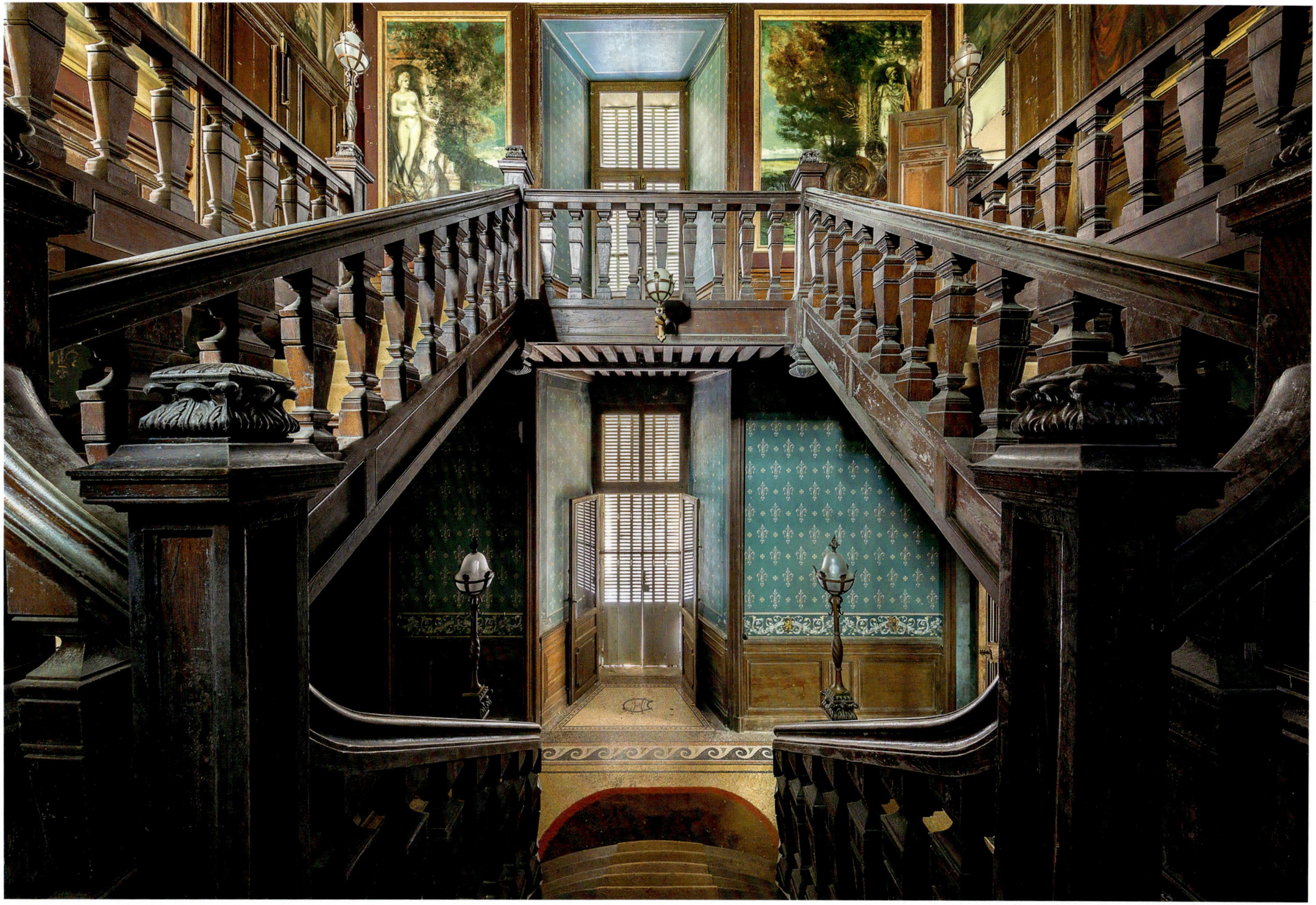

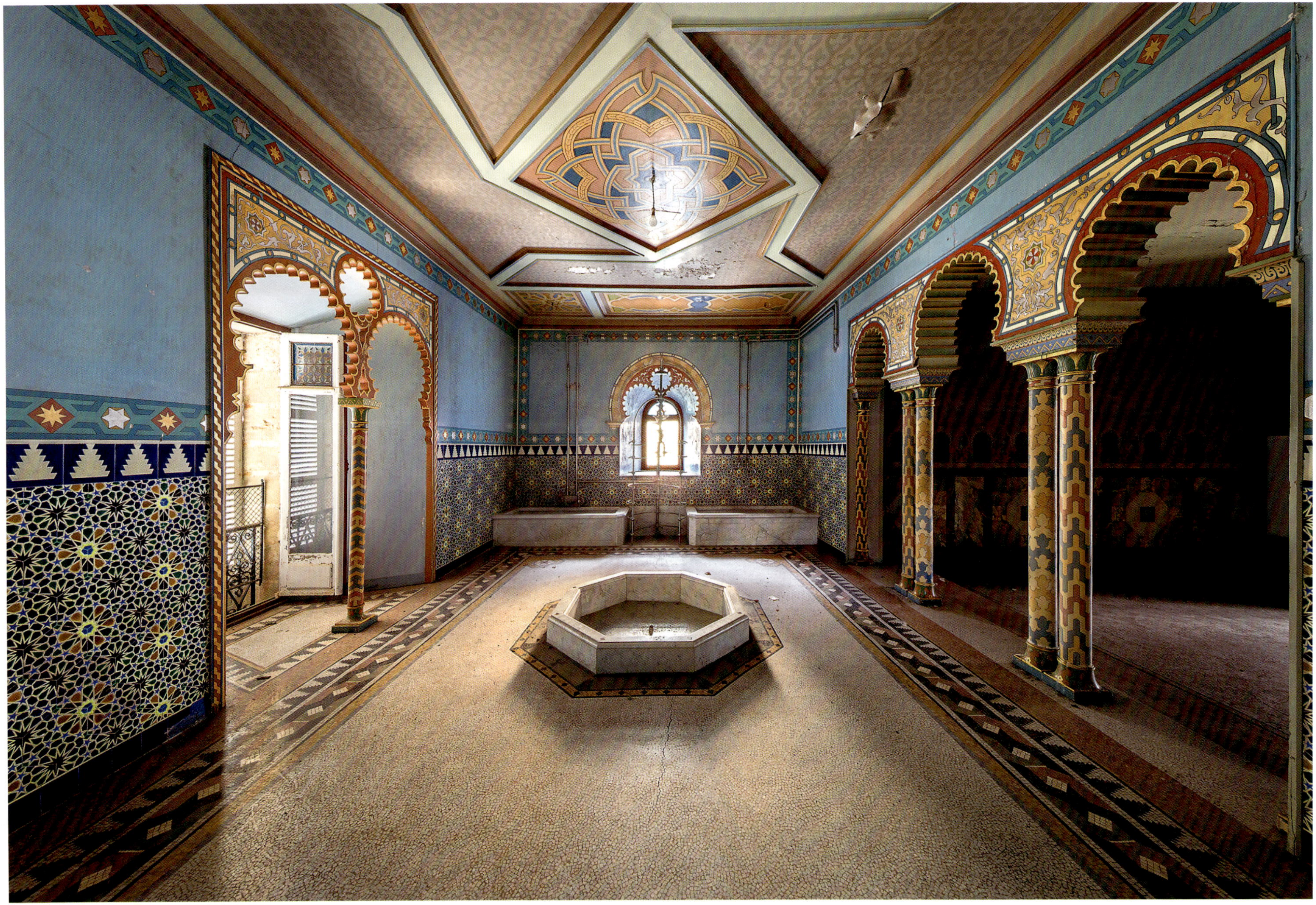

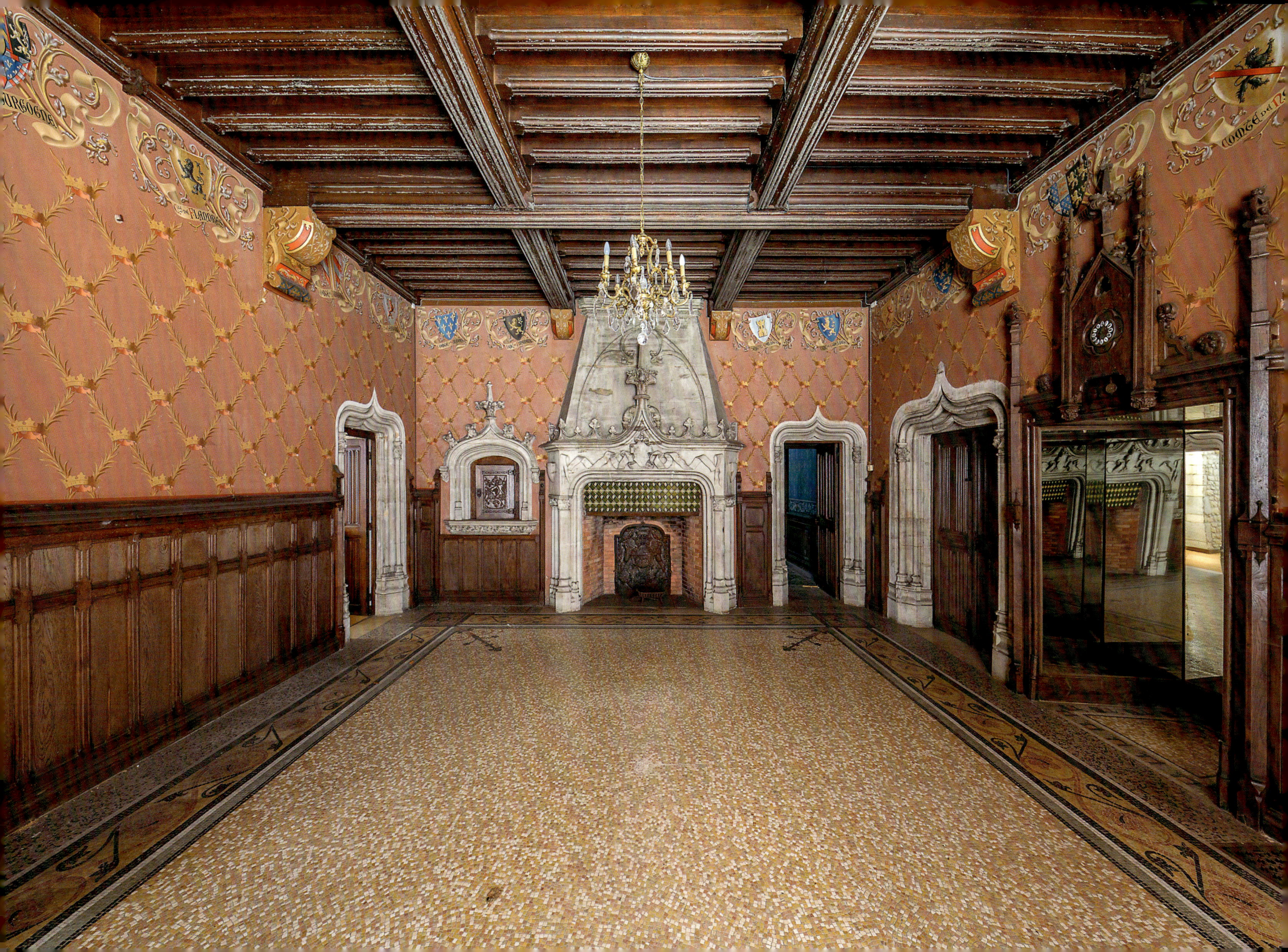

A secret chateau • *Bourgogne-Franche-Comté*

Several alterations have taken place during the long history of this 16th-century manor house that is protected by moats and fortified enclosures. Only the porch and two towers have survived the centuries. In 1868, Count Armand de Montrichard, owner of the site, had a modern, Renaissance-style castle built and linked it to the existing complex with a gallery. The effect is quite harmonious.

The castle cuts a fine figure. It is big and beautiful. But it has been deserted for a long time. Full of old things, it is a maze of split-levels where I enjoy getting lost. The owner has integrated a chapel into the main body of the building, which is illuminated by the glow of its stained-glass windows. The huge, dusty kitchen is teeming with a thousand and one utensils. It is easy to imagine the hustle and bustle that once took place here. The living room, on the other hand, seems to be waiting for someone to wake it from its slumber to host receptions and family parties. A large, bright room is lined with bookcases filled with books that have accumulated over the years. Sewing machines have also been placed here. I can easily imagine a gentleman reading here as he puffs away on a cigar while the lady of the house sews pretty dresses for the summer. An imposing wooden staircase flanked by a pretty balustrade takes me to a landing from which an orangey beam of light emerges. Corridors on either side of this landing lead to the bedrooms. There is still a multitude of other rooms on the upper floors and in the attic, each one more crowded than the last with objects that have been stored for ages.

In 2020, an association was created with the aim of saving this beautiful building, which remains neglected to this day due to a lack of funds to maintain it. The sale of the property could help move things forward.

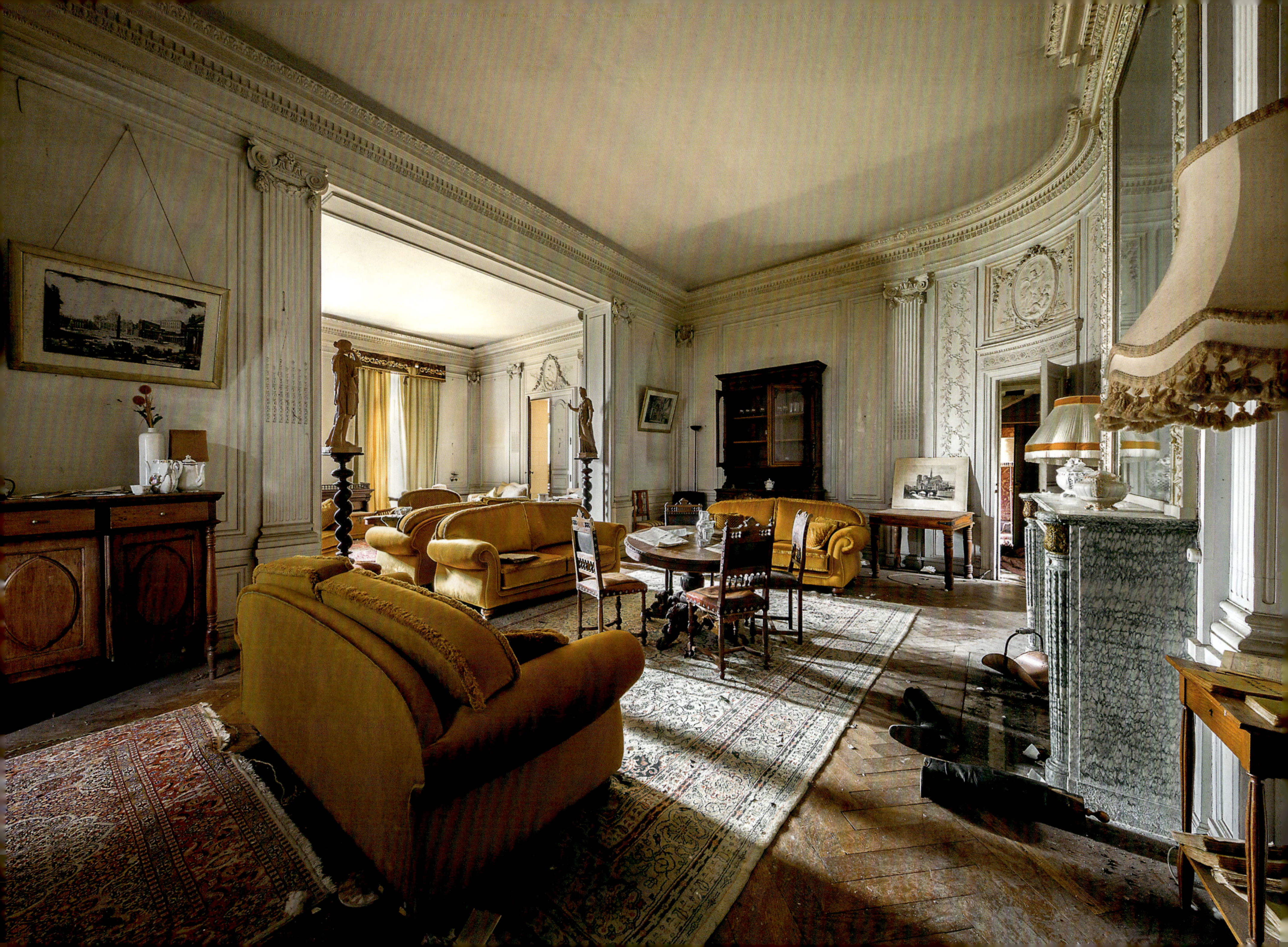

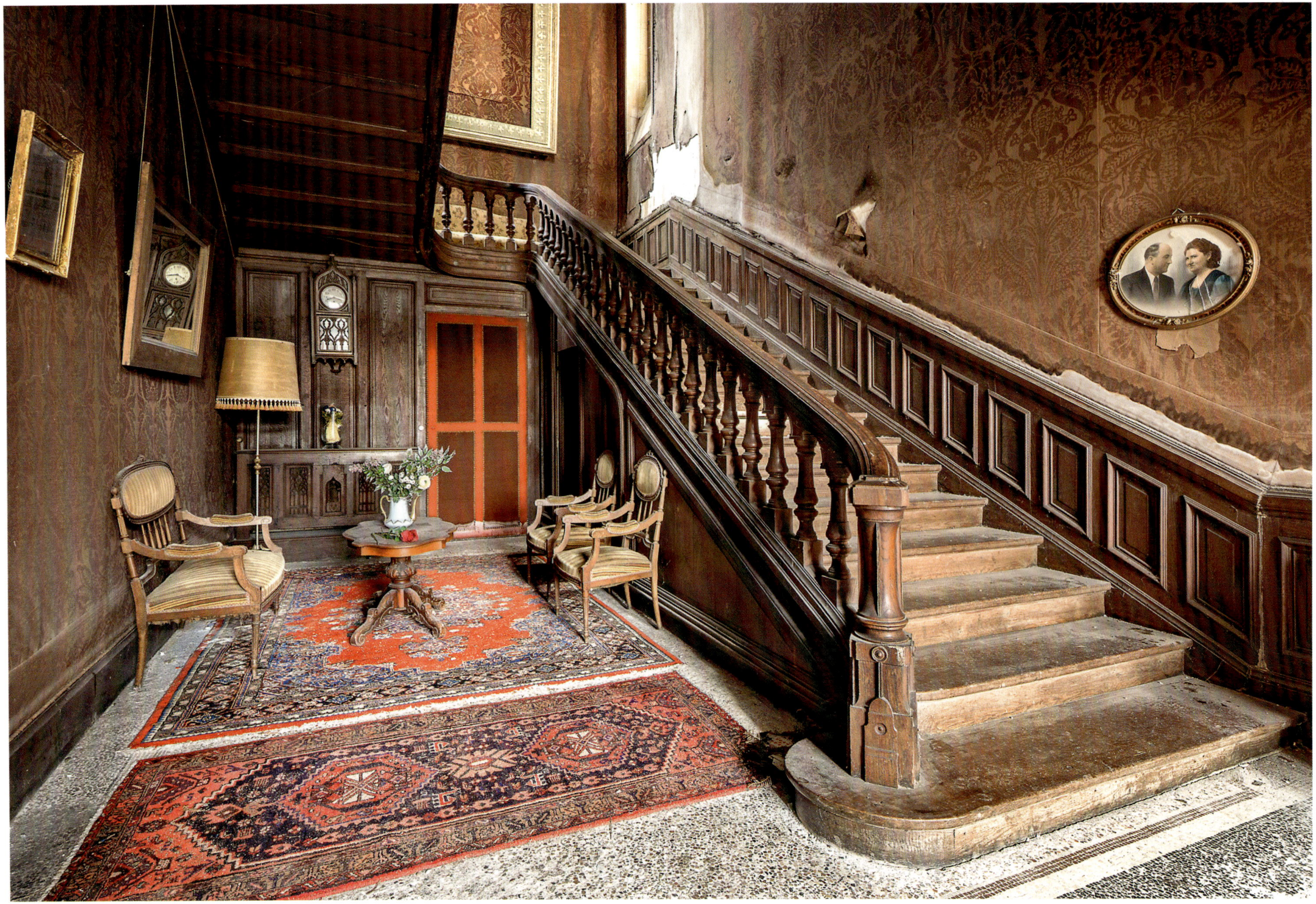

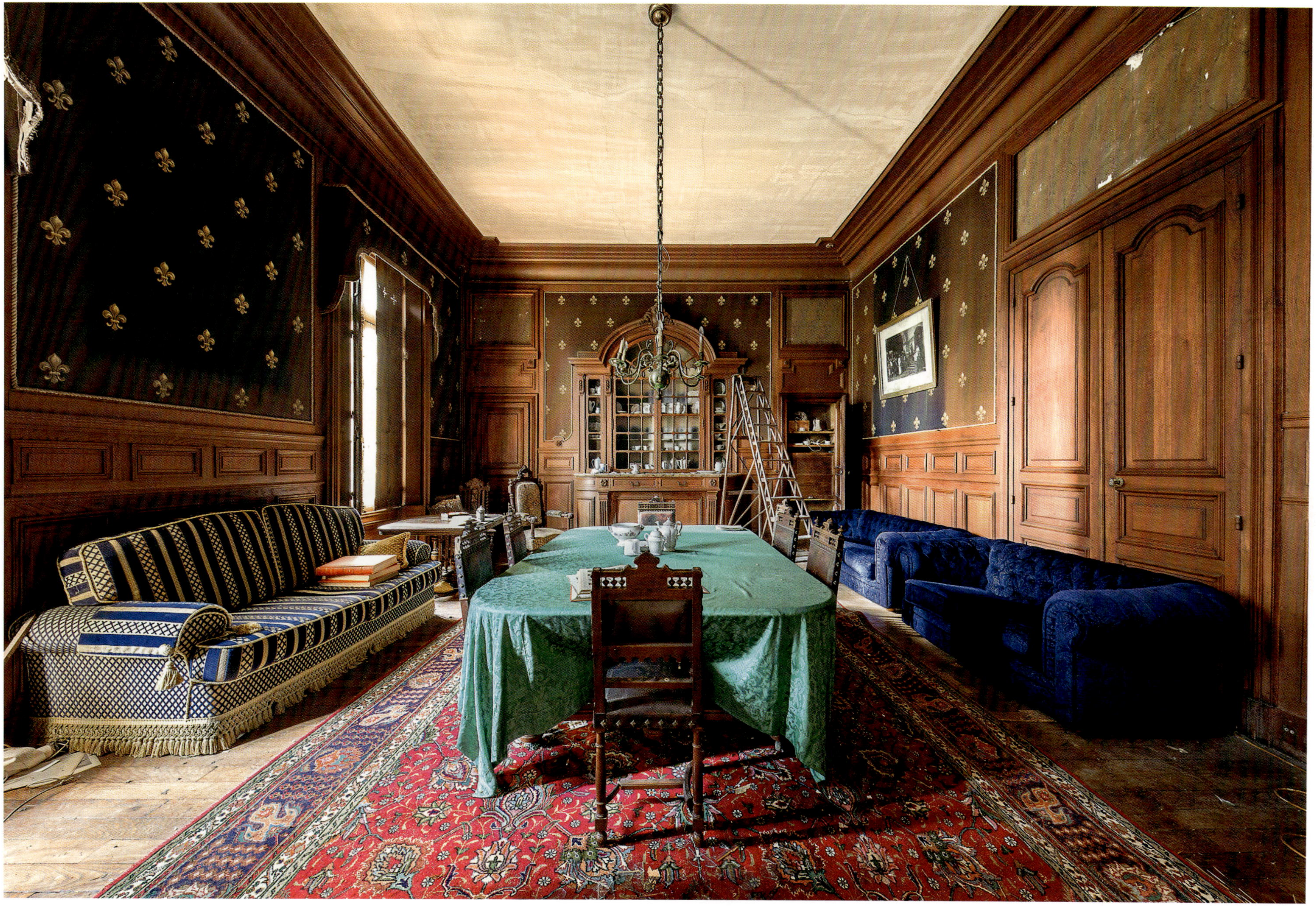

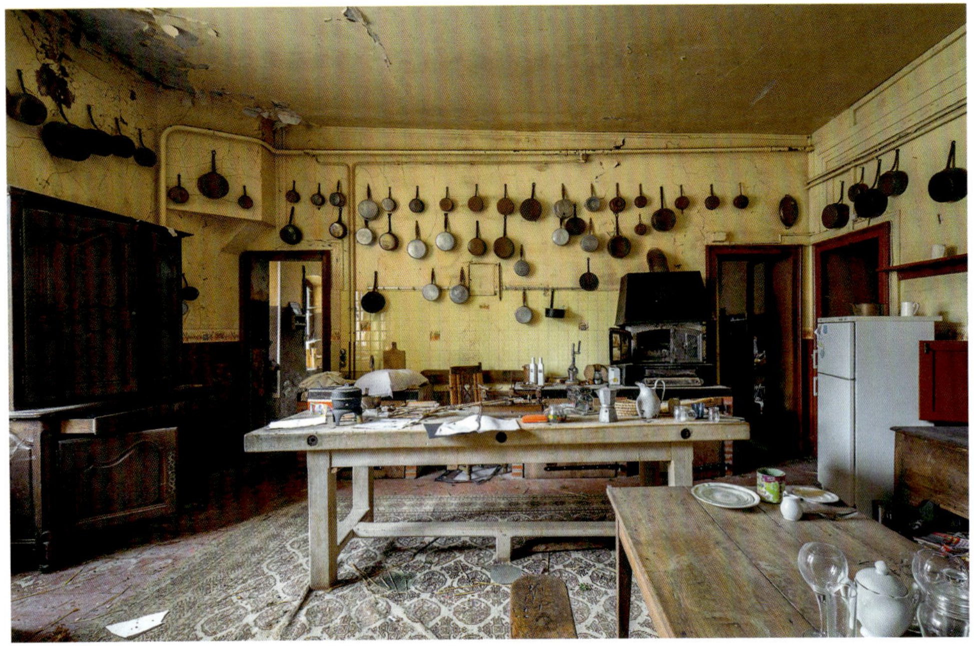

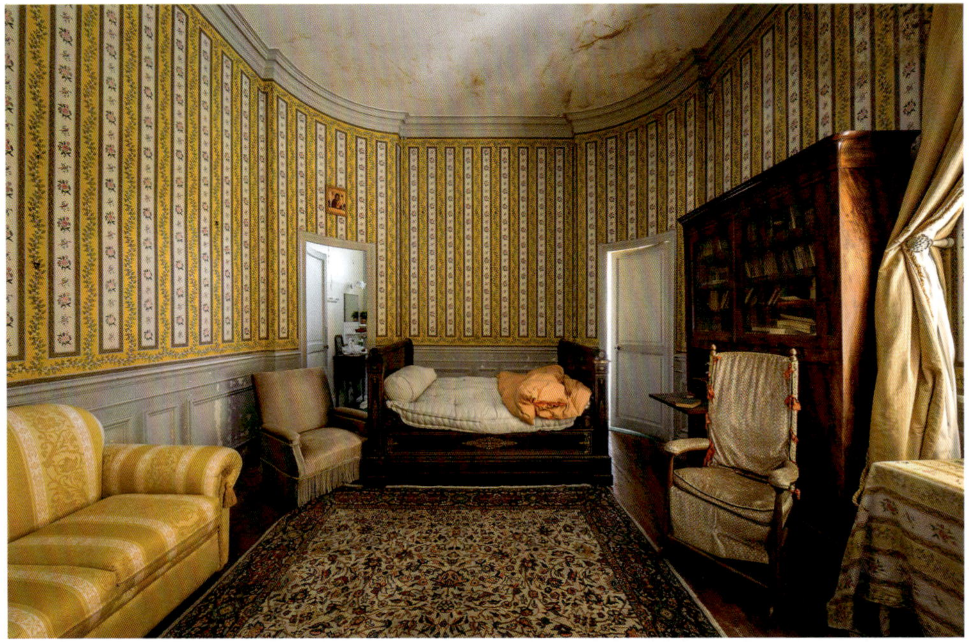

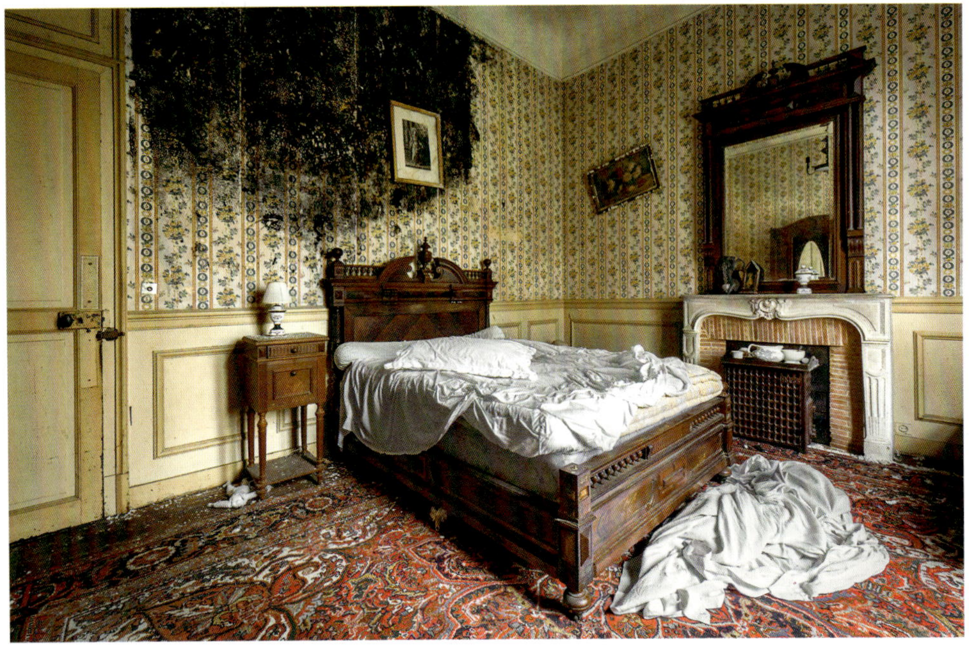

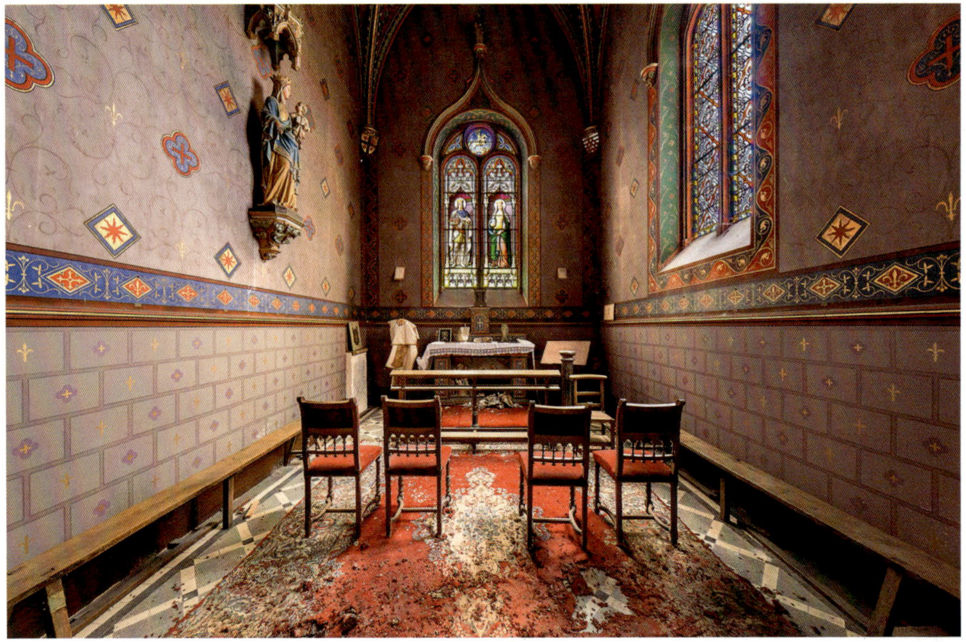

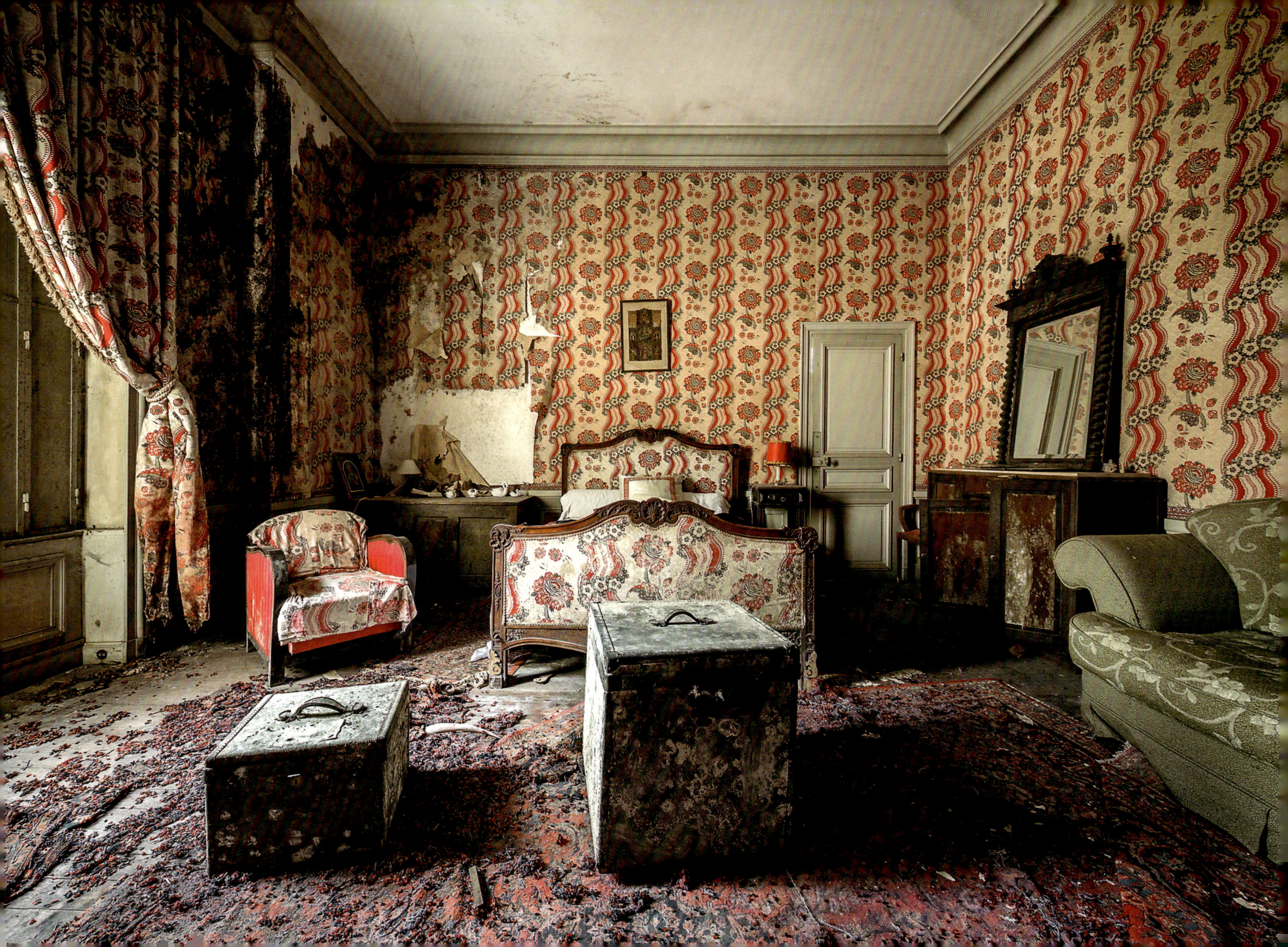

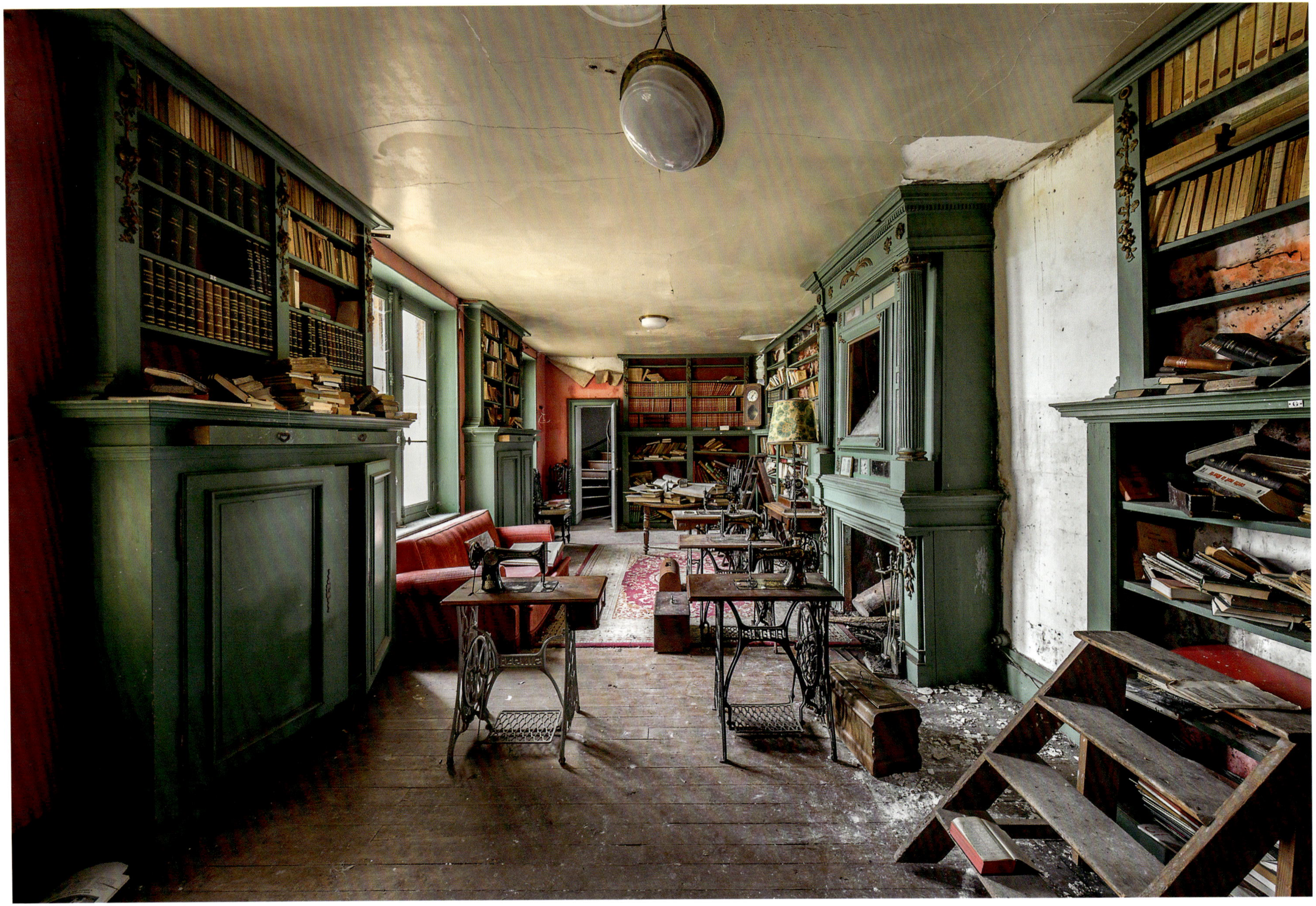

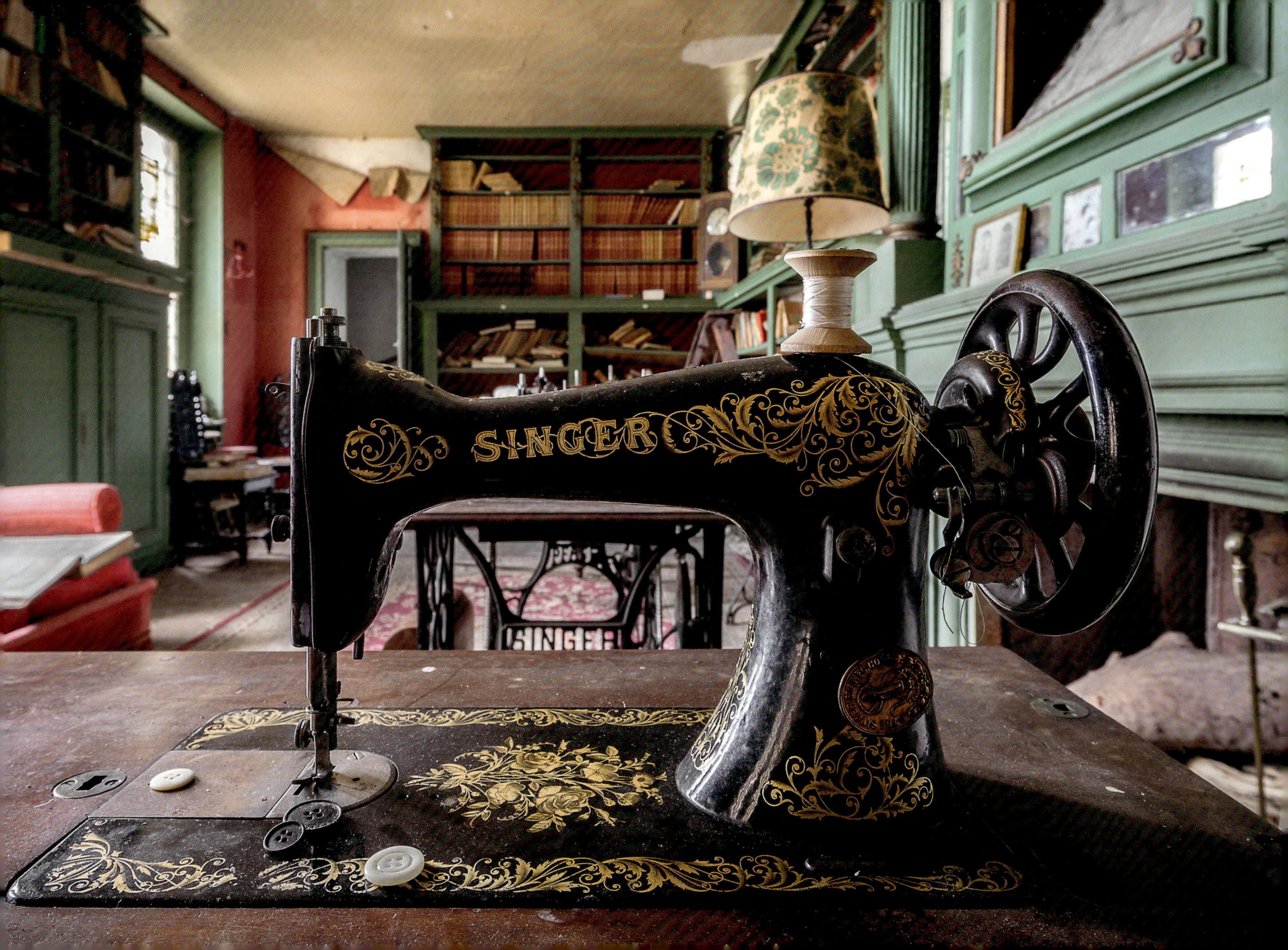
SINGER

The theatre of Dole • *Bourgogne-Franche-Comté*

The city's first permanent theatre was built in 1754 in a military building adjacent to the stables. After the stables collapsed, the idea emerged to build a new performance venue that would contribute to the development of musical art in the region. The ambitious project was carried out in the upper part of the city, where there were many private mansions and the more distinguished citizens lived. The construction work lasted from 1840 to 1844, according to the plans of the engineer-architect Jean-Baptiste Martin. The aristocracy of the whole region came to the inauguration.

Classified as a historic monument since 1996, the theatre is remarkable. Although it has endured through the ages, it remains practically intact with its superb neoclassical facade featuring a central forecourt supported by columns. The theatre is an Italian-style hall, shaped like a horseshoe to magnify the space between the stage and the large foyer. Six hundred seats are spread over five levels in boxes and balconies originally in duck blue with gold features. The decor, painted on wood and marouflaged canvas by the decorators Och and Chenillon, still glistens.

In 2015, the building was closed to the public for a complete renovation. That was the perfect moment for me to set up my camera and capture this marvellous, flamboyant room. The building reopened in 2021 in a welcoming and impressive setting. By adopting a soft and tempered approach to the renovation and restoring its original colours, it was possible to work around the constraints of the existing Italian-style building to adapt it without disturbing its very special atmosphere. This new, modern venue regularly hosts concerts, plays and dance performances.

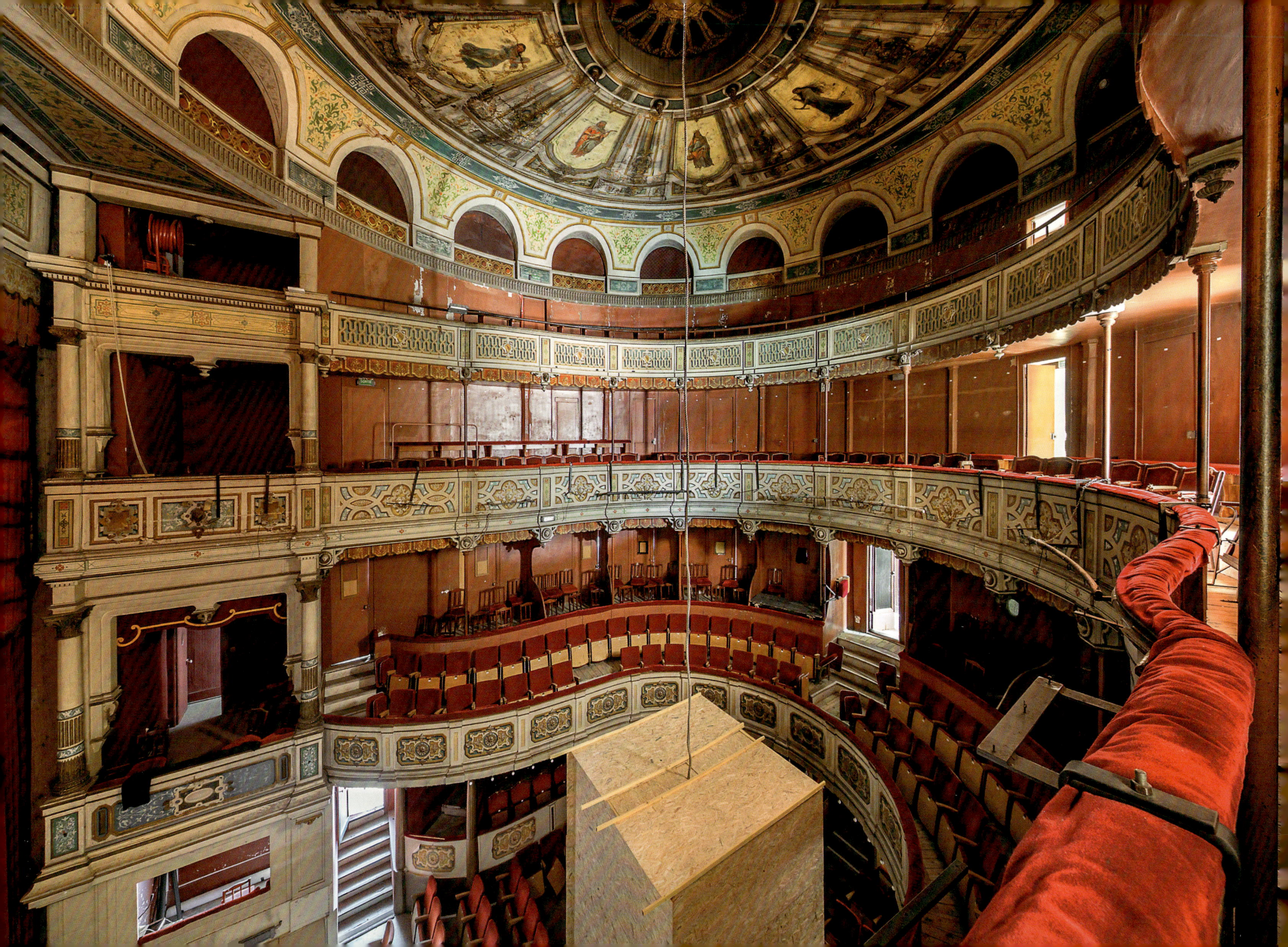

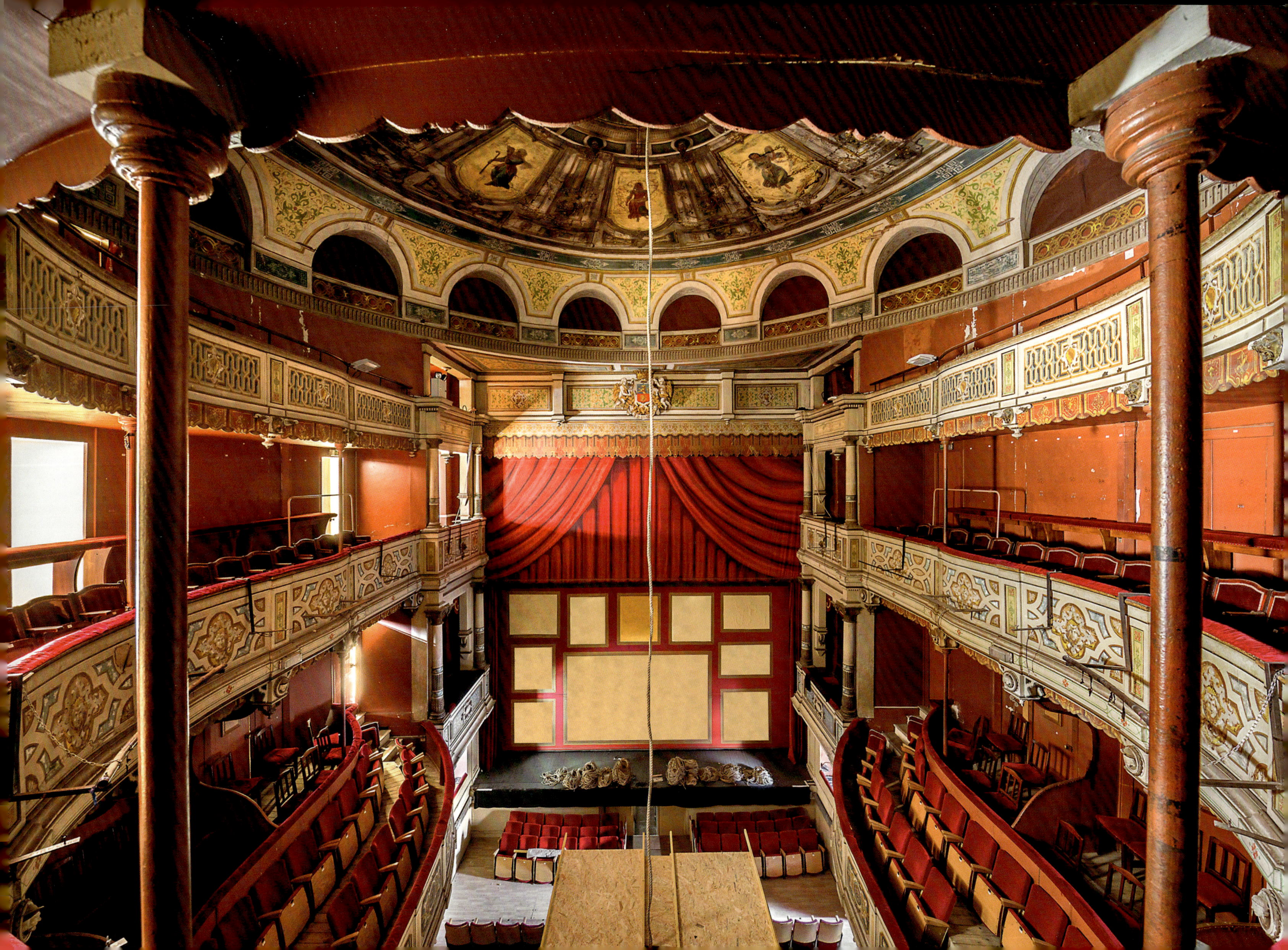

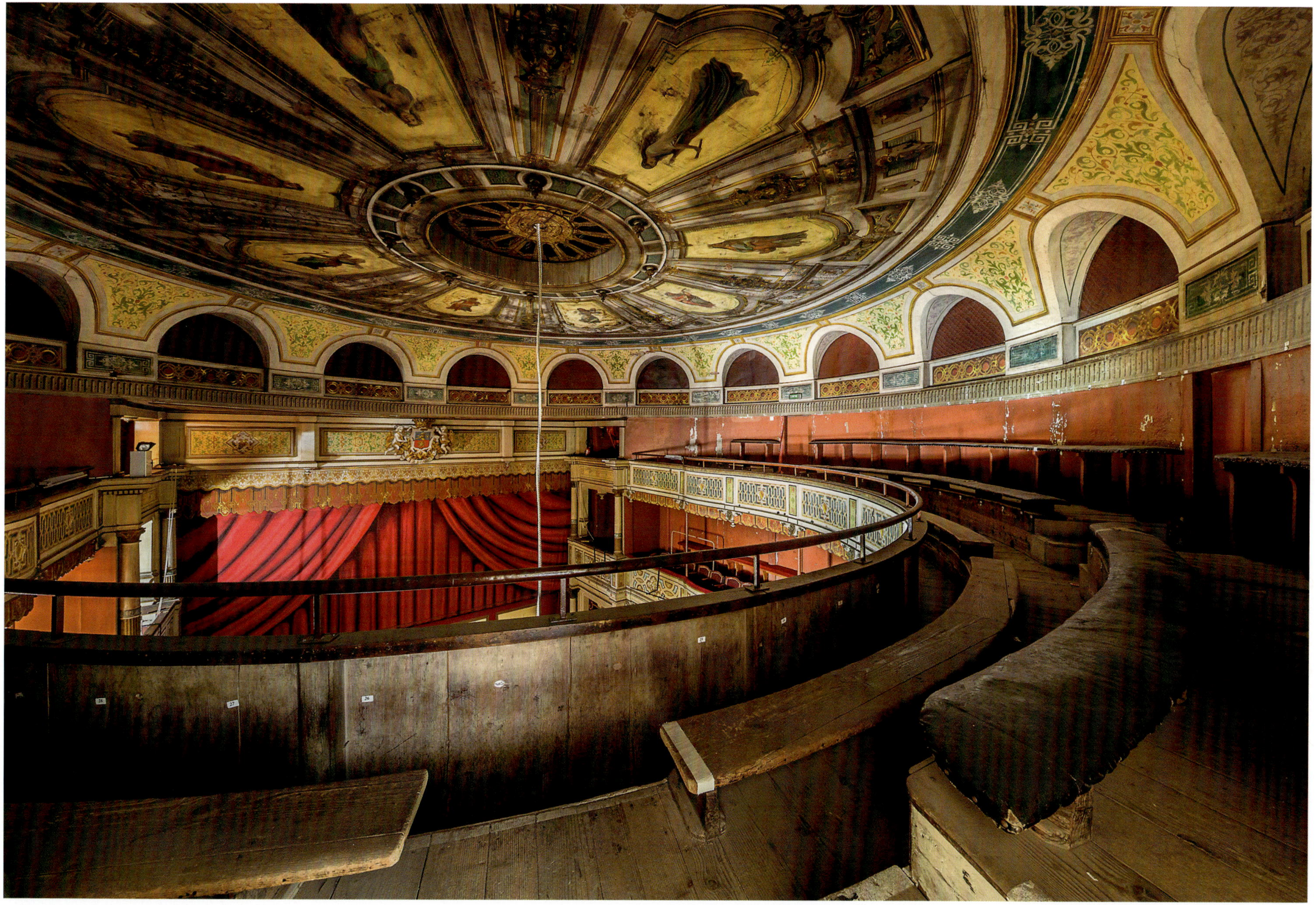

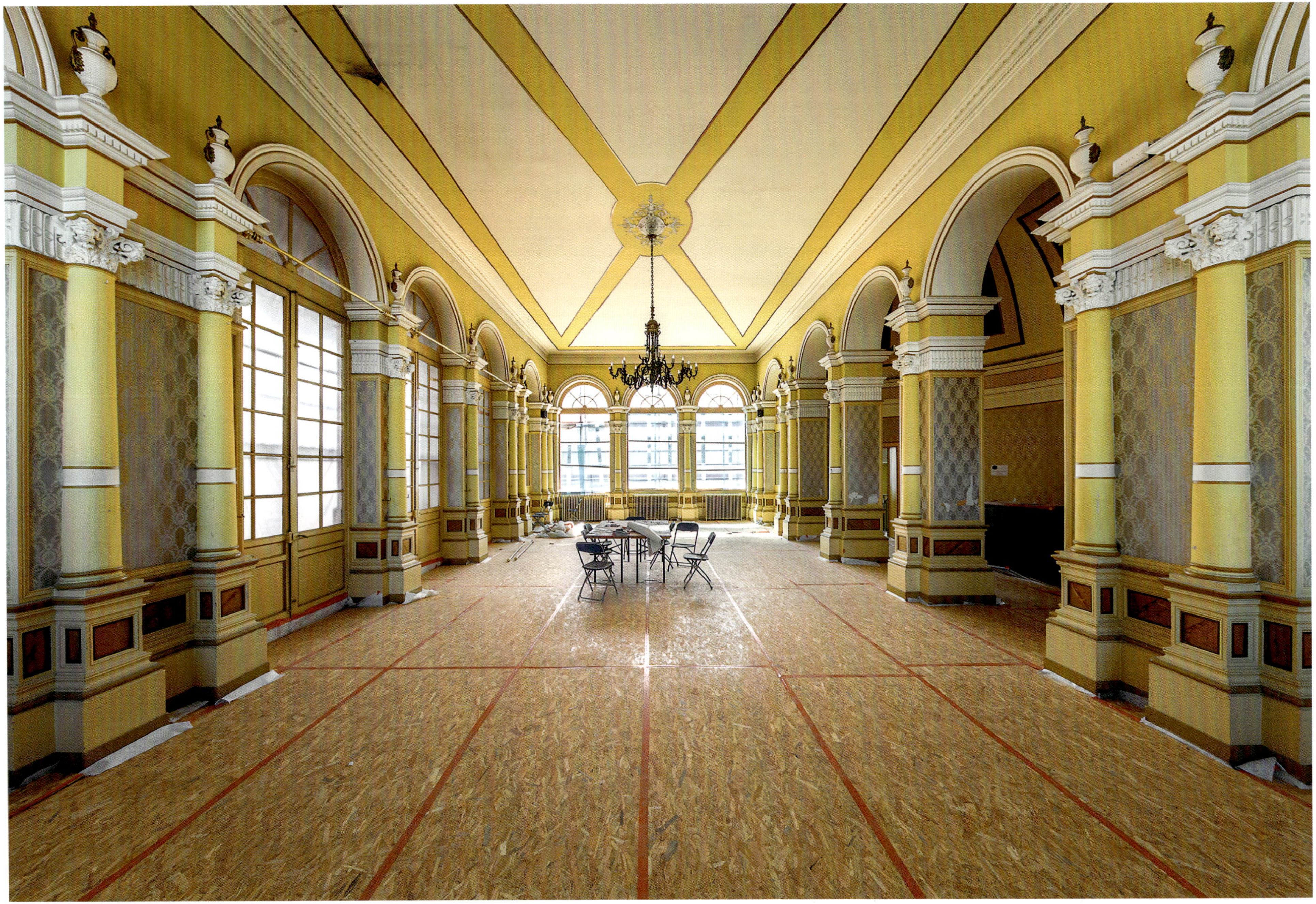

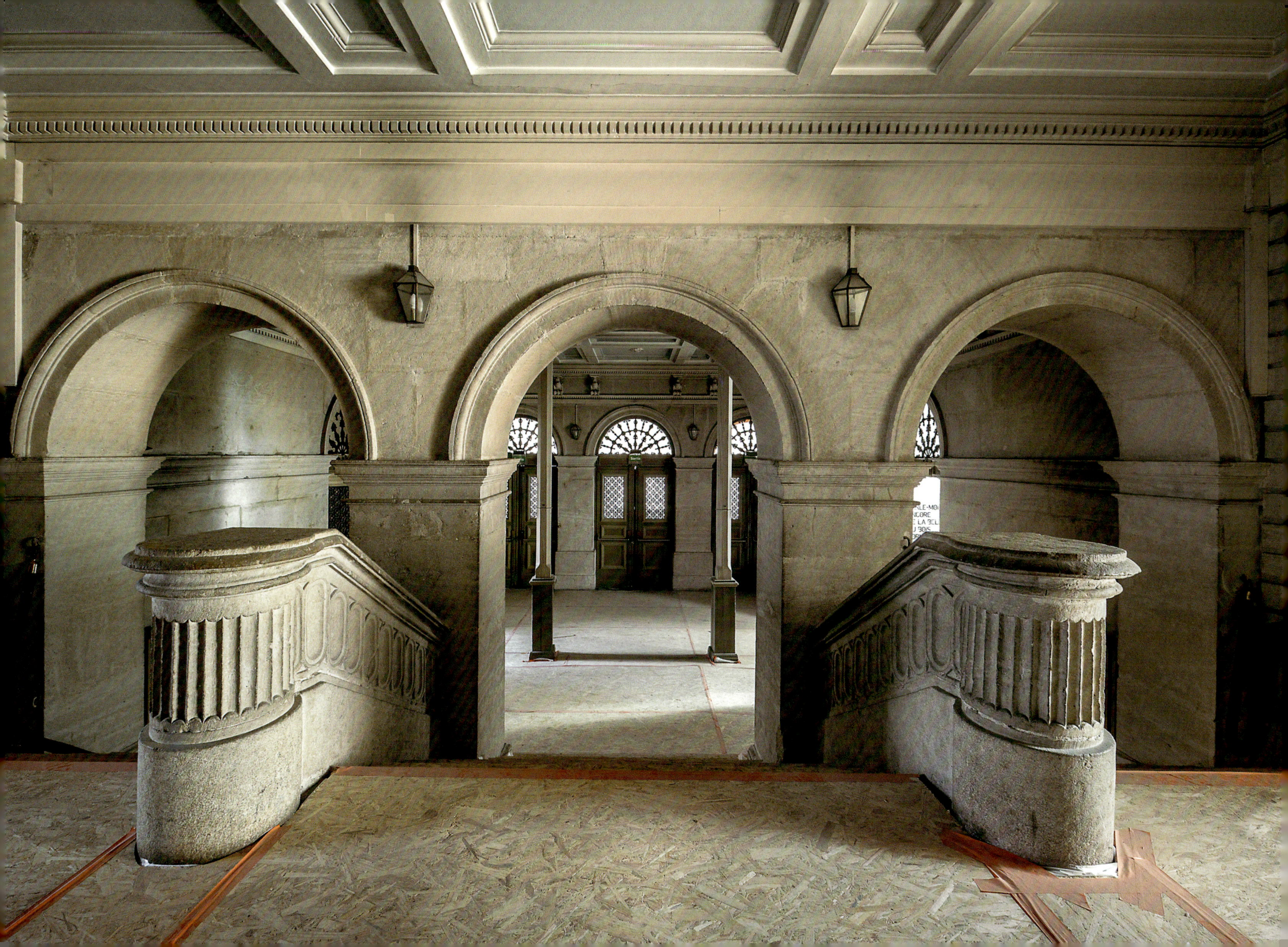

The pram garage • *Bourgogne-Franche-Comté*

In the middle of a village, not far from the church, is a discreet property enclosed by hedges that does not seem to be out of the ordinary. But if you make your way through the grass, an incredible discovery awaits!

Covered with brambles and nettles, old vehicles, mainly French and English, are scattered around the property. From deeply cold winters to intensely hot summers, the seasons take their toll. Autumn with its dead leaves and spring with its moss also have no mercy for these cars. Among others, the Triumph Spitfire, with its 'broken face', would have made any enthusiast happy.

Left to their sad fate, other cars are majestically piled up and squeezed together in a shiny shed. There are several Renault Dauphines, a Citroën Type H and an Acadiane, Mercedes-Benzes, two Panhard PL17s, a Peugeot 202 (a model that was produced between 1938 and 1949), a Simca 5 and many more. Three red vans from a former construction company still have a shine to them, as if they are living their best life.

In one of the adjoining halls is an old blue pram dating back to the Second World War. It gave its name to the place. Over time, cars were gathered around it, until the owner could no longer keep up. The pram has now disappeared. The atmosphere of this private collection turned car graveyard is striking.

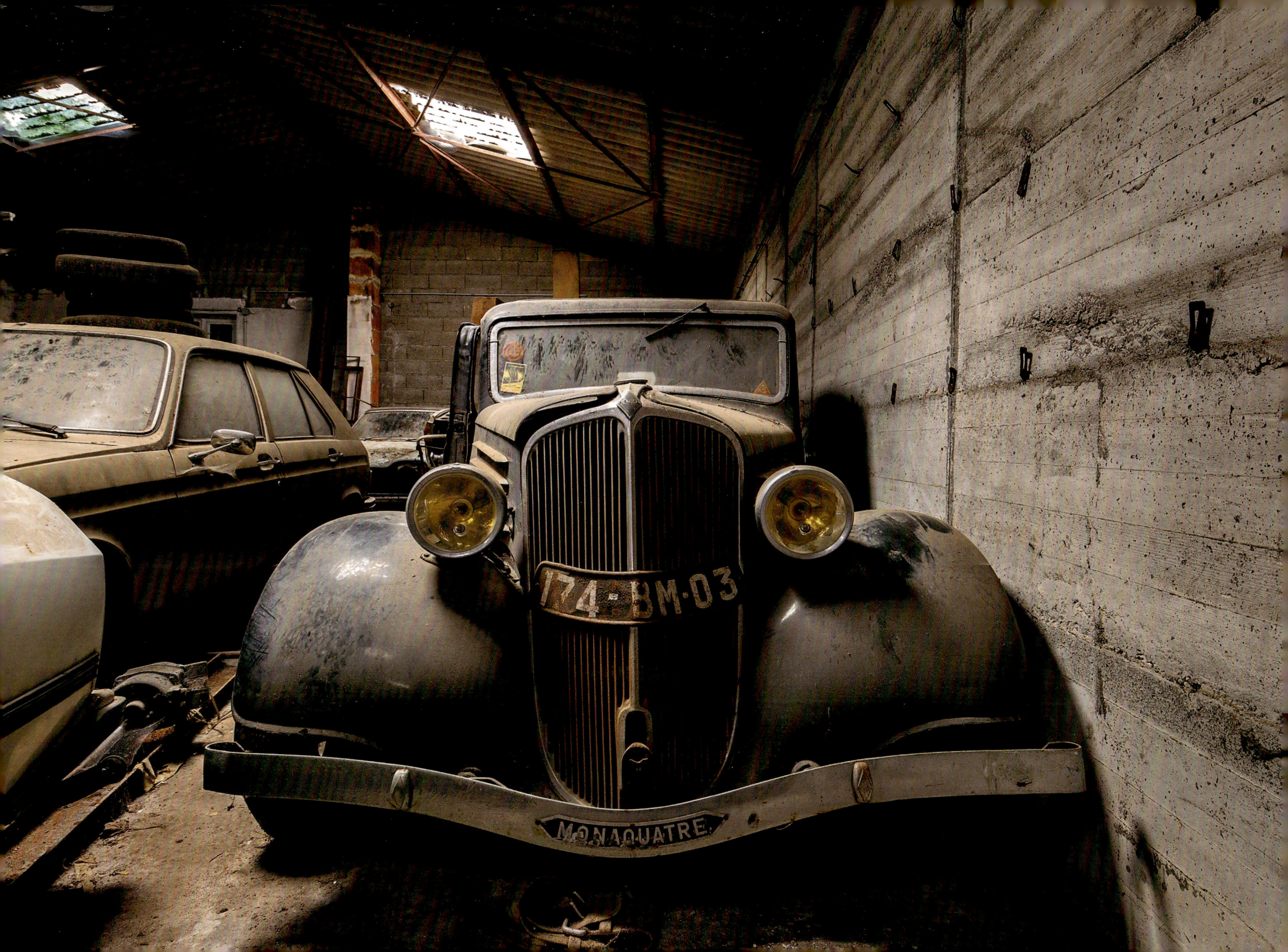
174-BM-03
MONAQUATRE

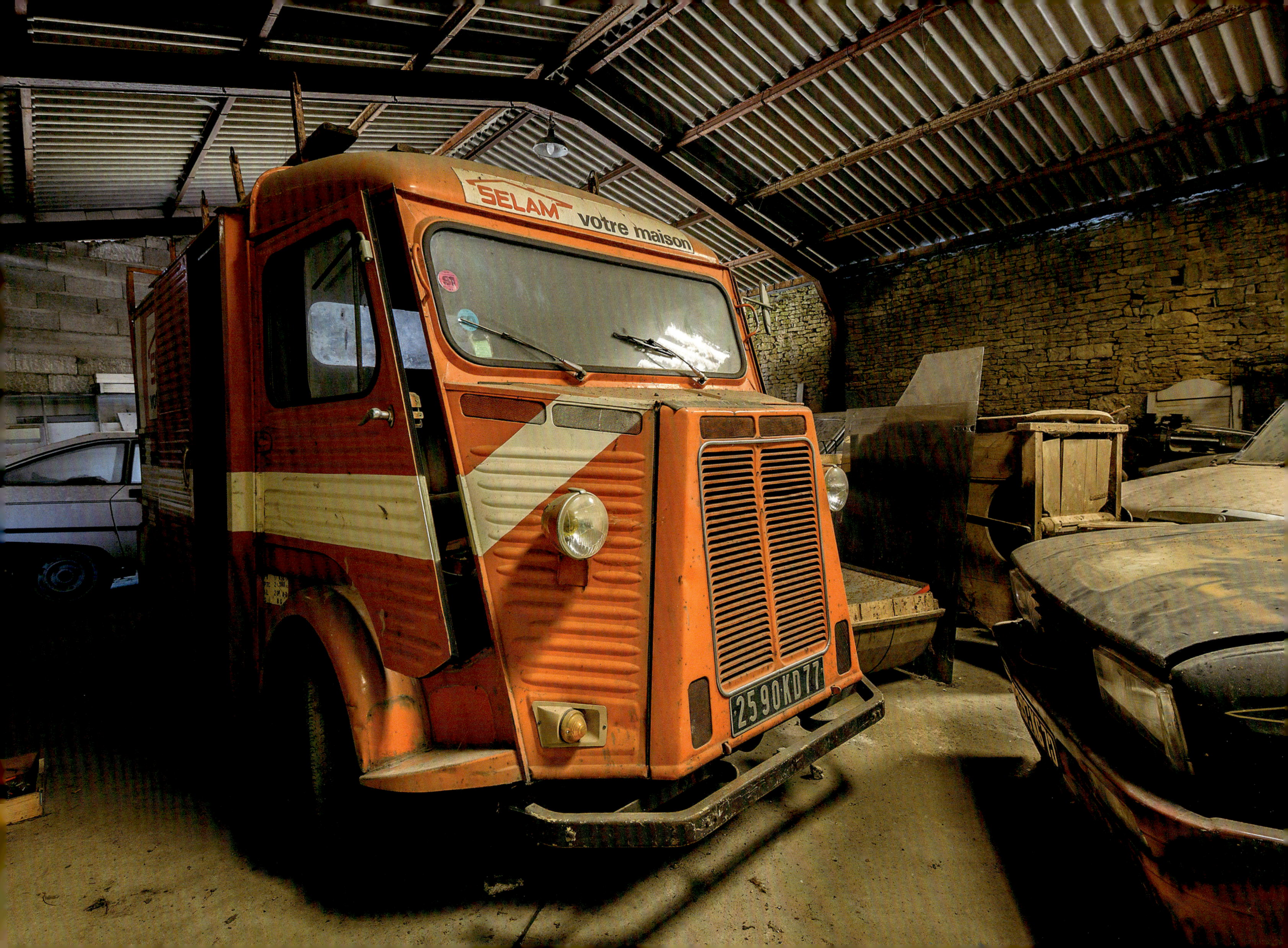
SELAM
votre maison
2590KD77

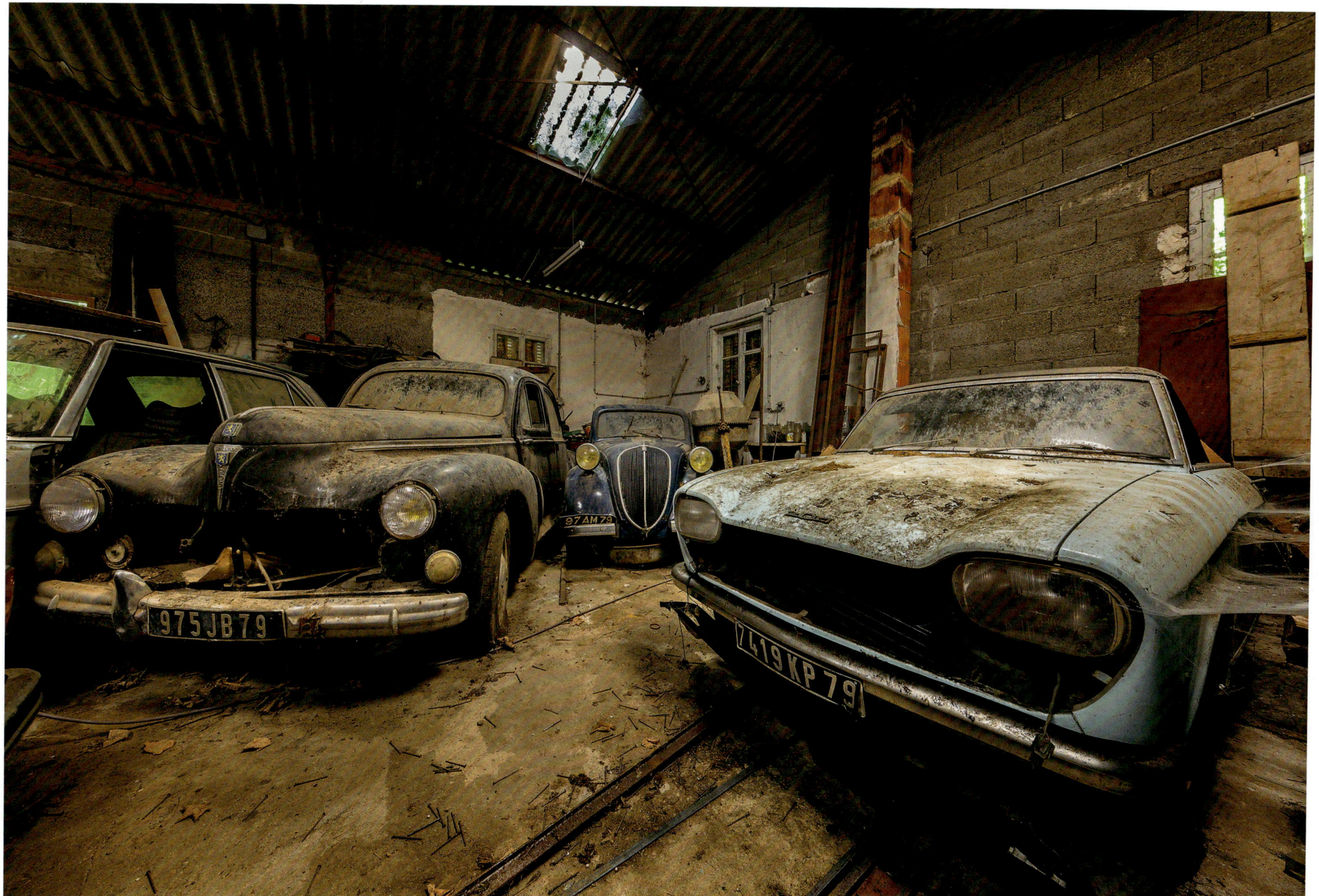
975JB79
97AM79
7419KP79

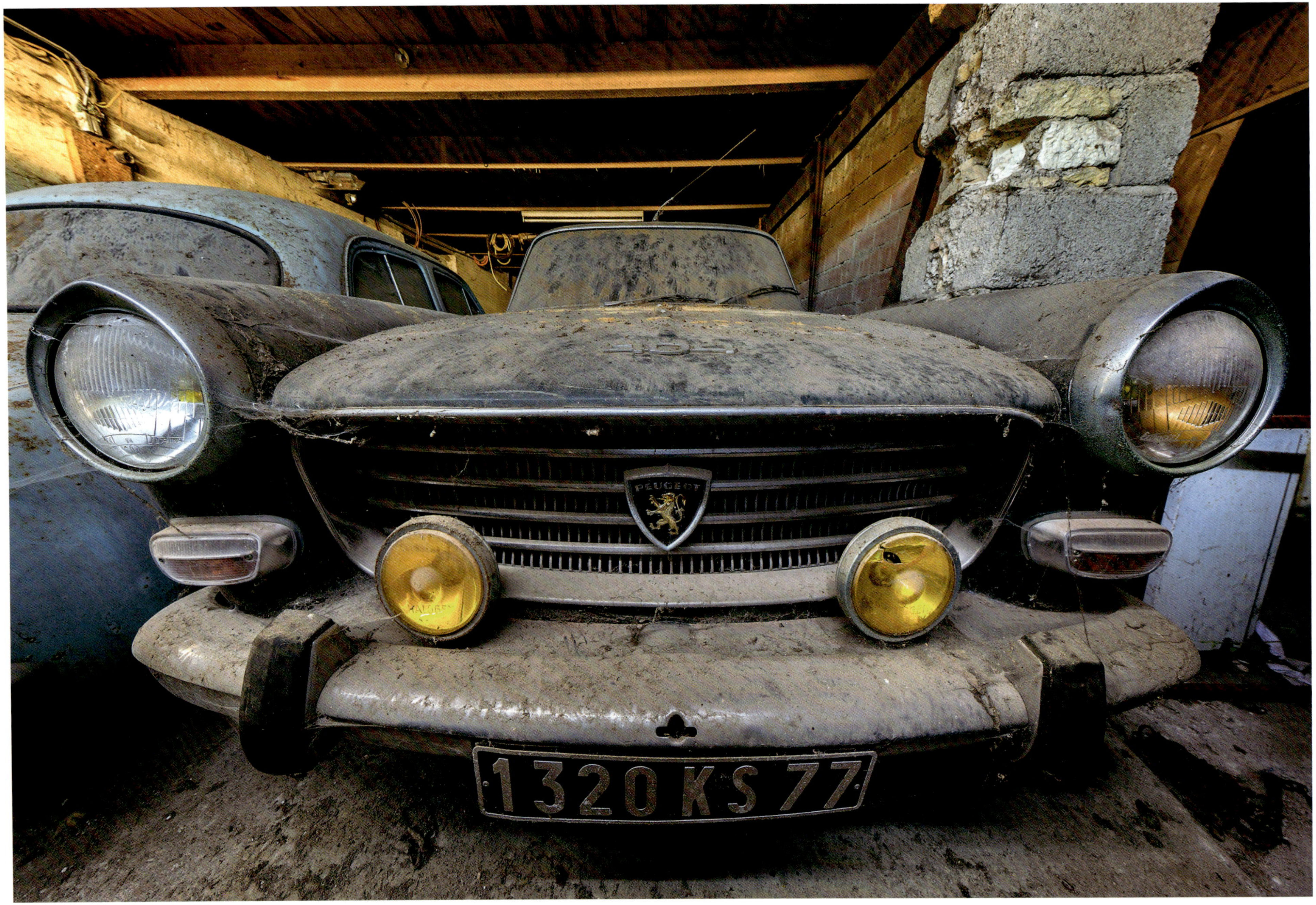
PEUGEOT
1320 KS 77

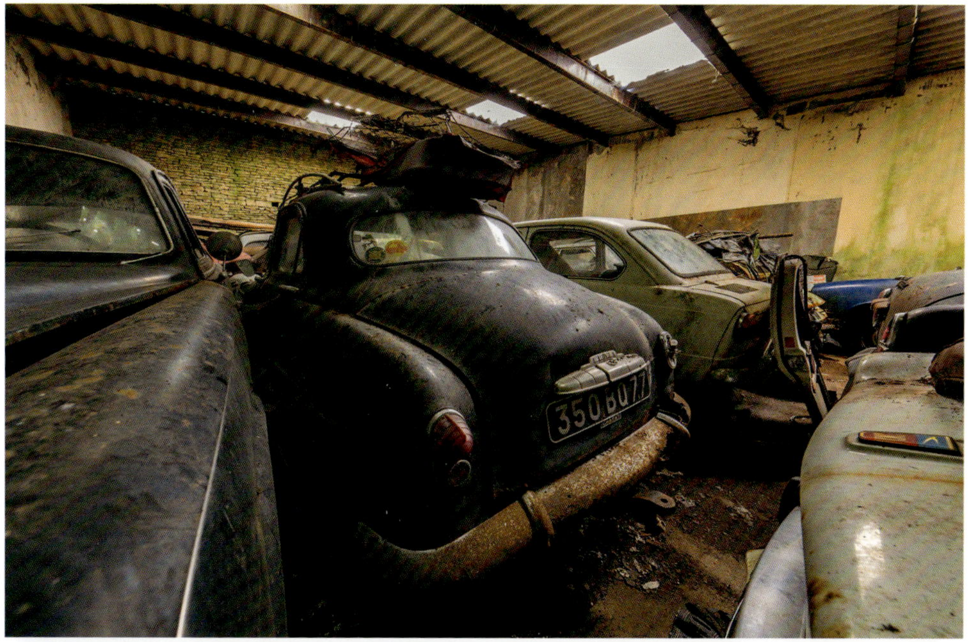
350 BU 77

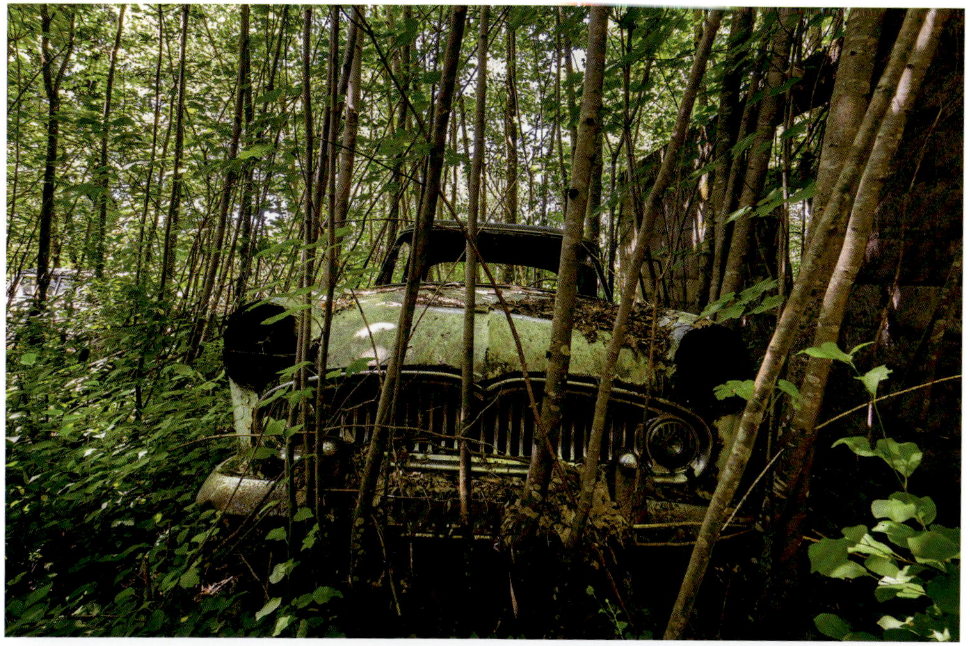

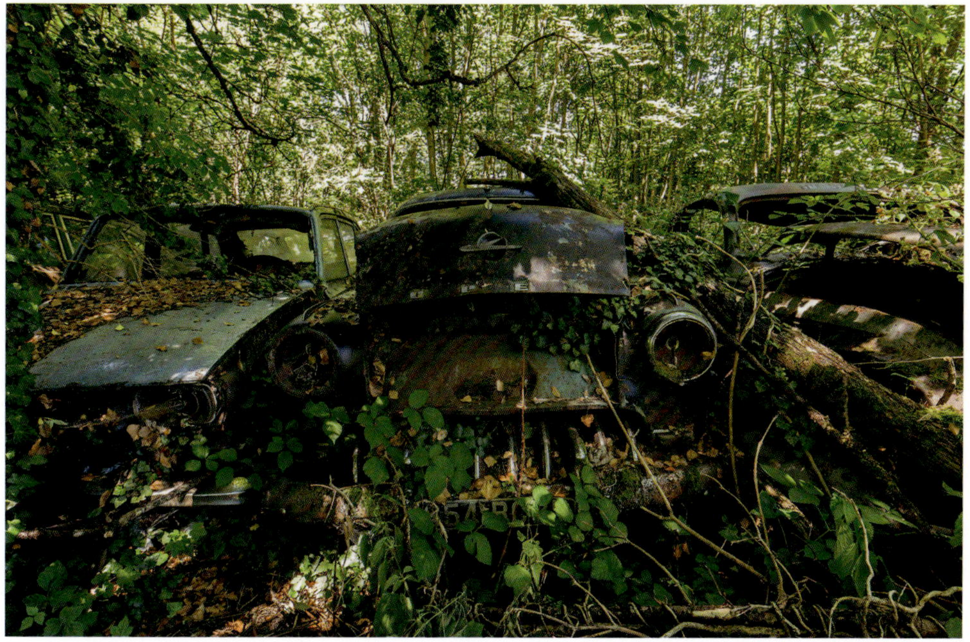

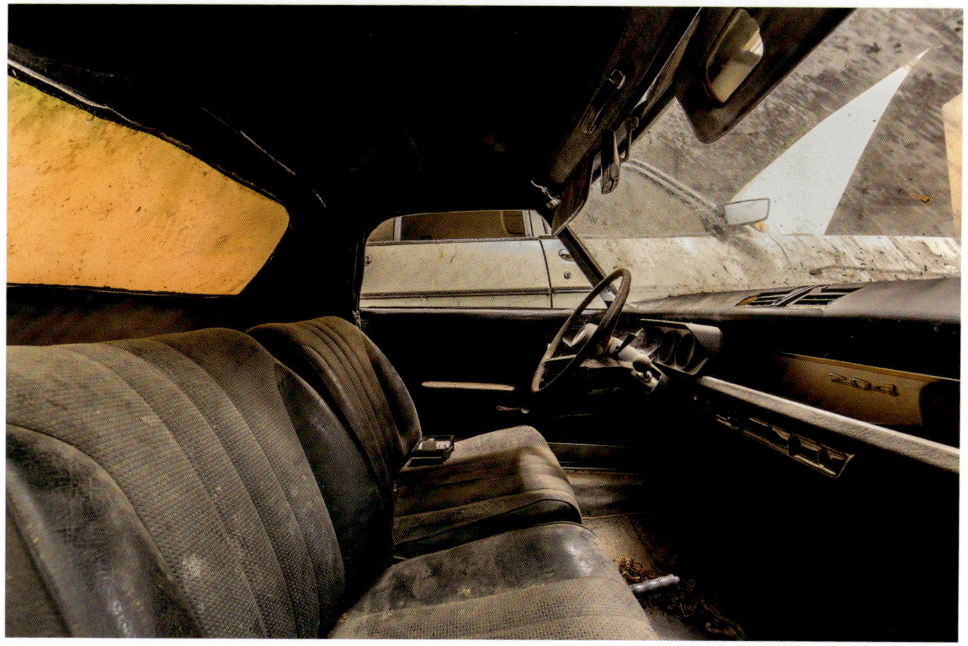

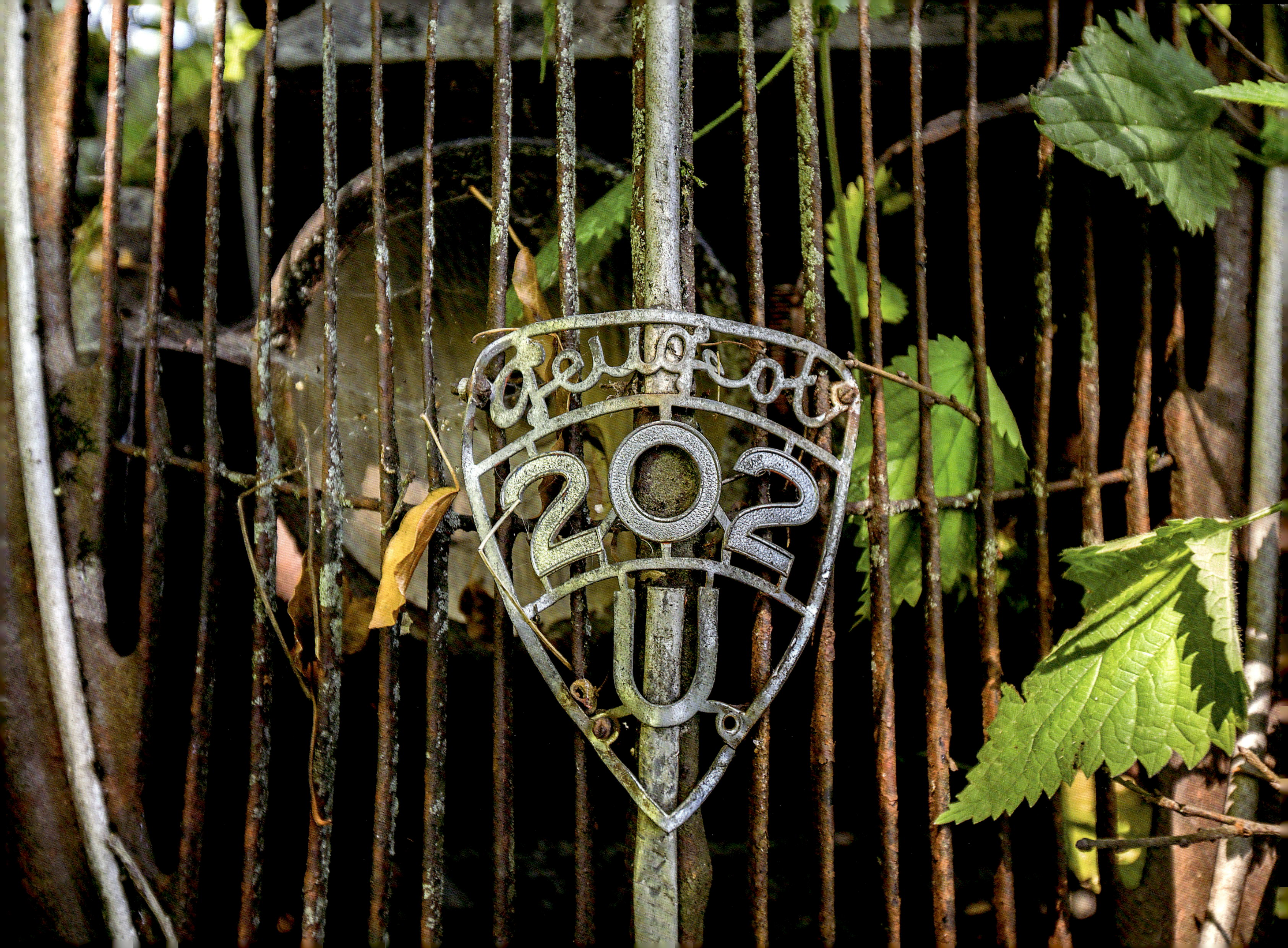
Peugeot
202
U

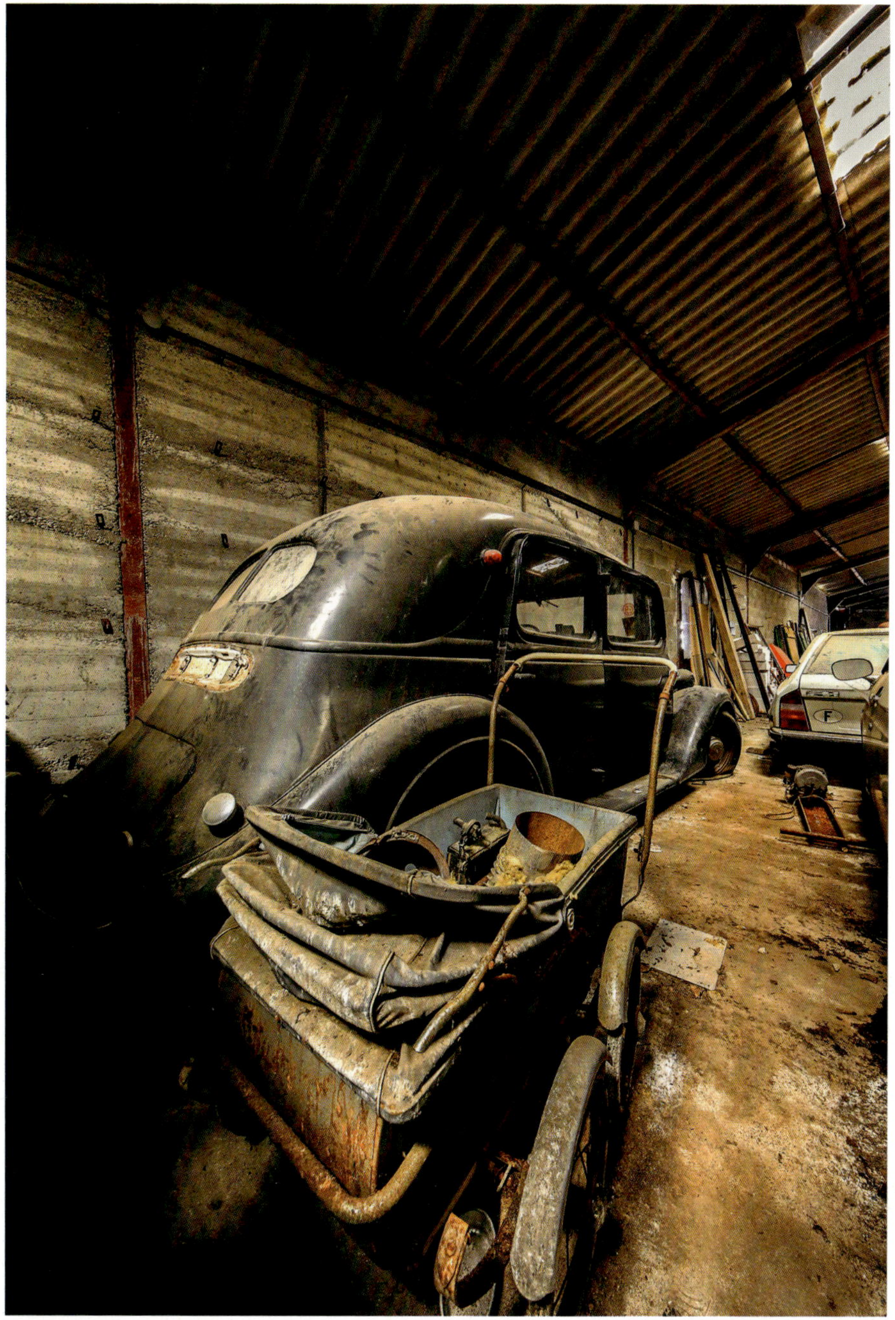

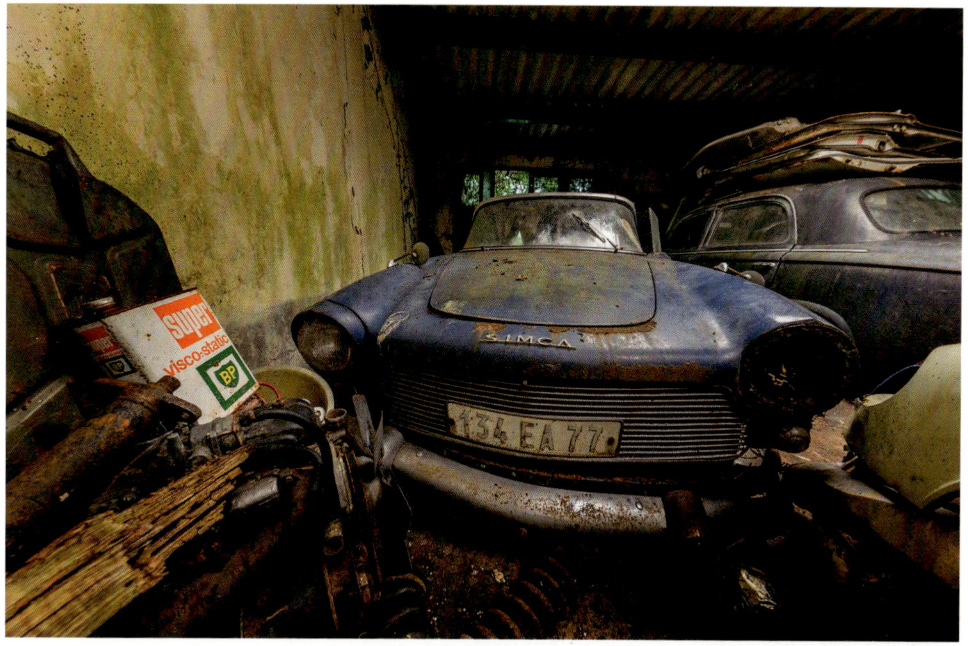
super
visco-static
BP
SIMCA
134 EA 77

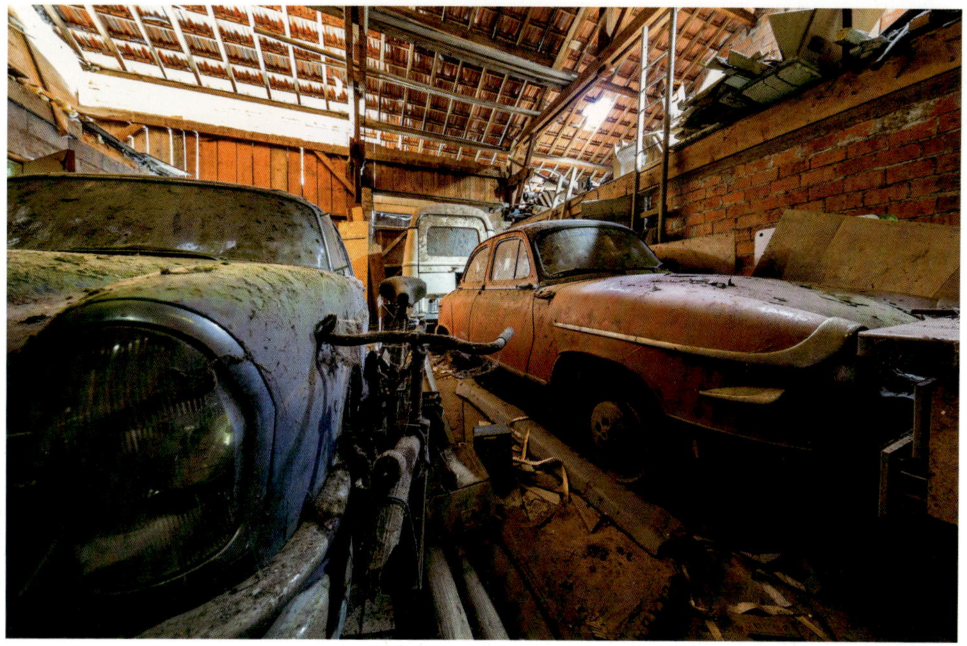

The manor house with the pram • *Occitania*

There is a charming, abandoned manor house in the city centre waiting for life to return within its walls.

Cement tiles were invented in France in the mid-19th century, when the idea of coloured tiles with inlaid patterns was in vogue. For more than a century, this enabled the working classes in the countryside and the more affluent classes in the city to enjoy a decorated and colourful floor with the most beautiful effect. As a result, large catalogues of tiles with a wide range of patterns, colours and formats were produced.

The typical patterned cement tiles of this manor house have been placed not only on the ground floor but also on the stairs and even on the upper floor. It's a real beauty.

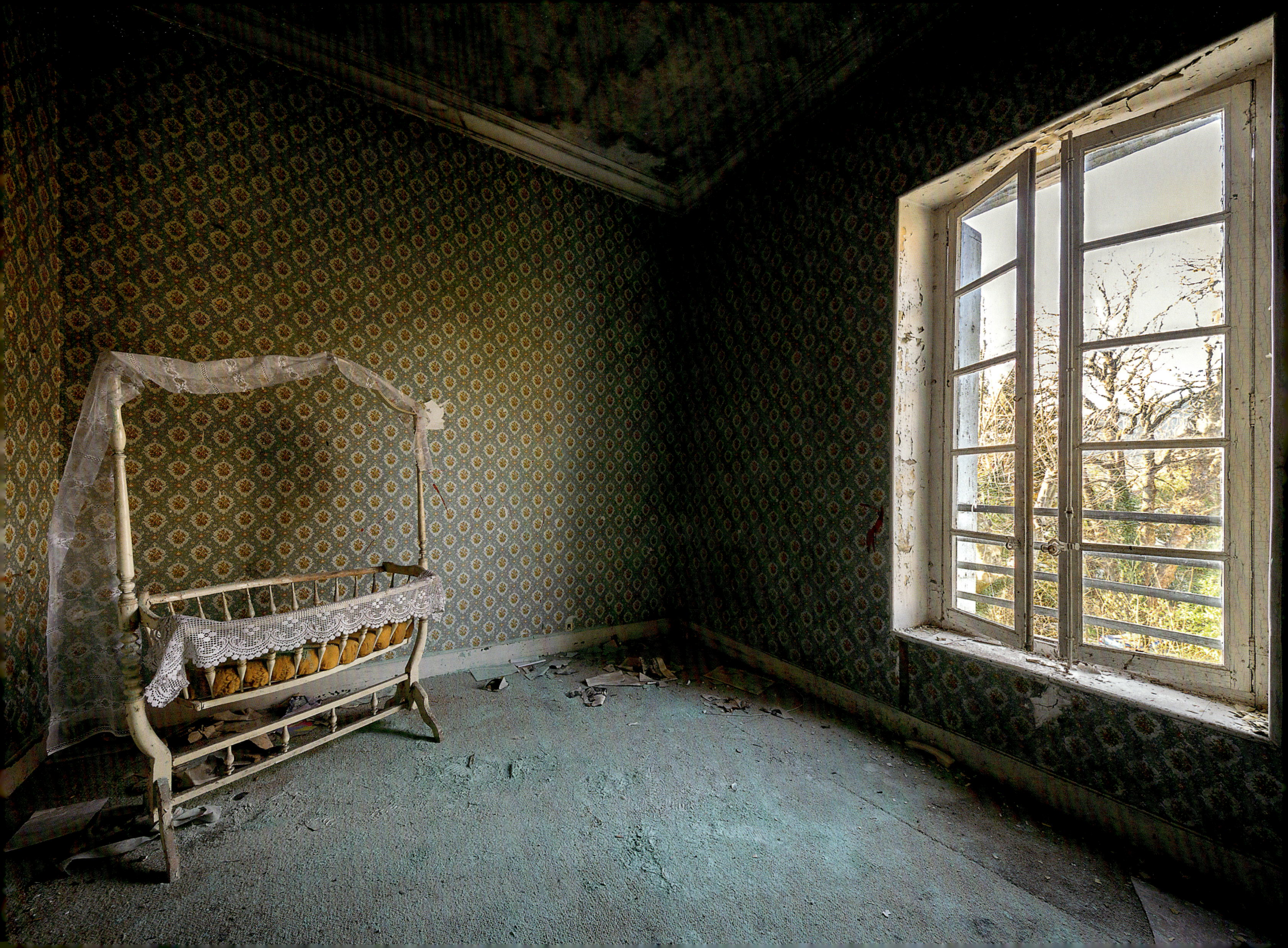

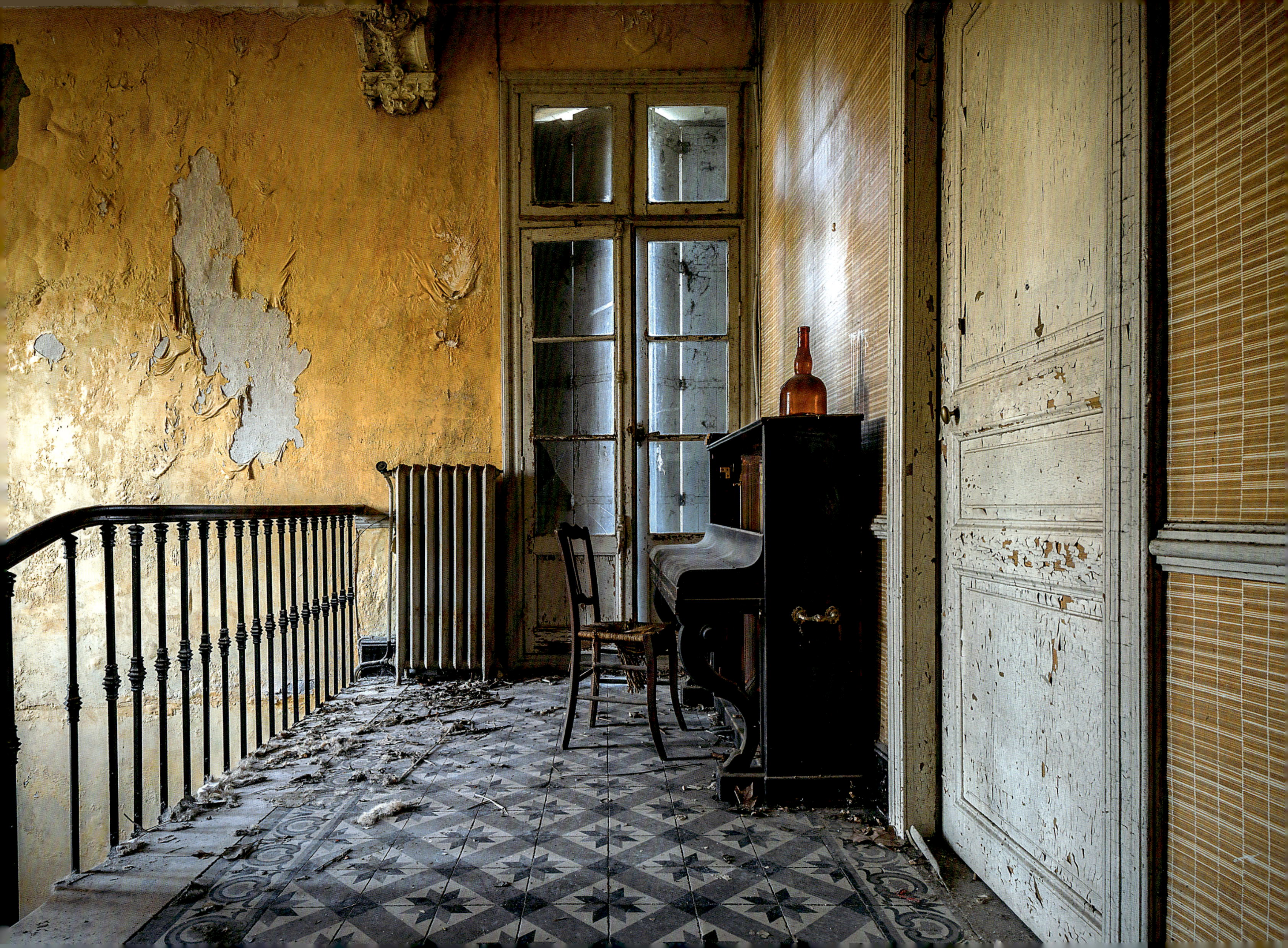

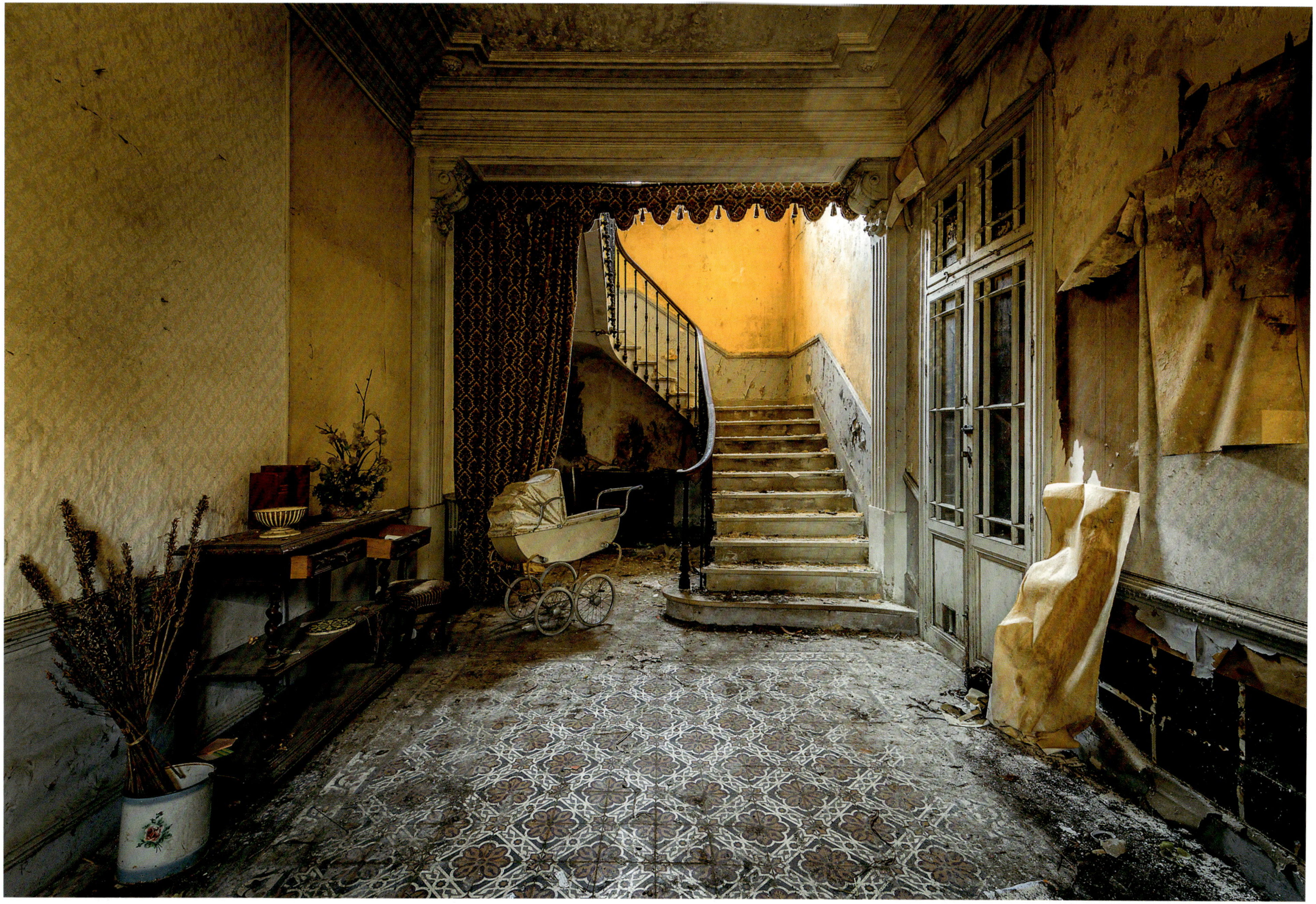

The Pope's castle • *Occitania*

Although all the furniture is still here, no one lives in this small castle on clay-limestone terraces in the heart of the vineyards, an environment that must have been pleasant to live in. Only one part has been restored and is used to produce noble grape varieties.

Facing south, century-old vines rub shoulders with younger plots of Syrah and Grenache – deep, aromatic varieties that produce fine, balanced grapes. The twins who have taken over the family estate are guided by a philosophy of combining heritage, winemaking know-how, agronomic expertise and oenological knowledge. The result was almost instantaneous, and medals came pouring in, including the AOC certification of authenticity. It is an exceptional association, revealing a collection of authentic and refined wines, and an adventure that is first and foremost a human one.

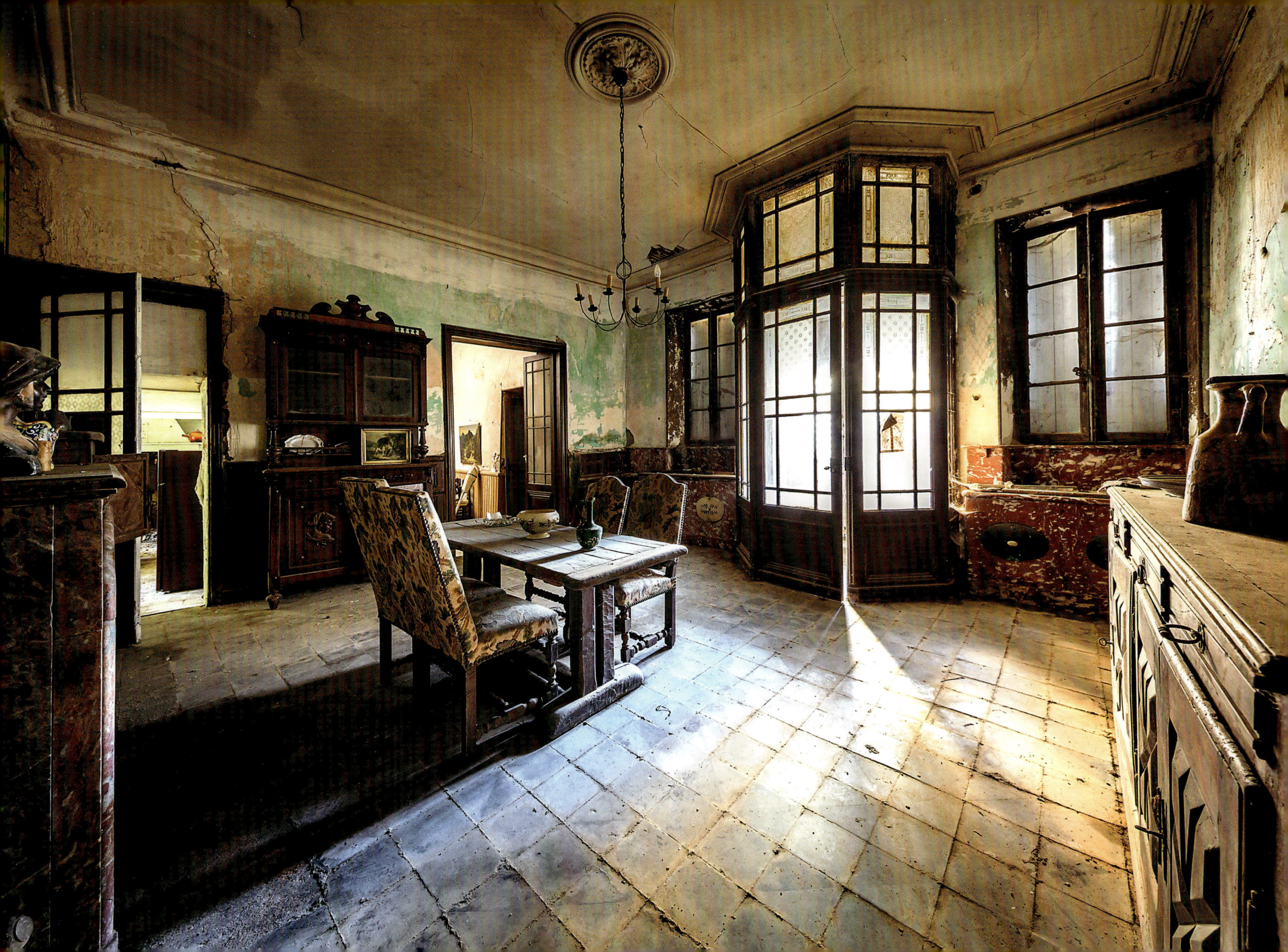

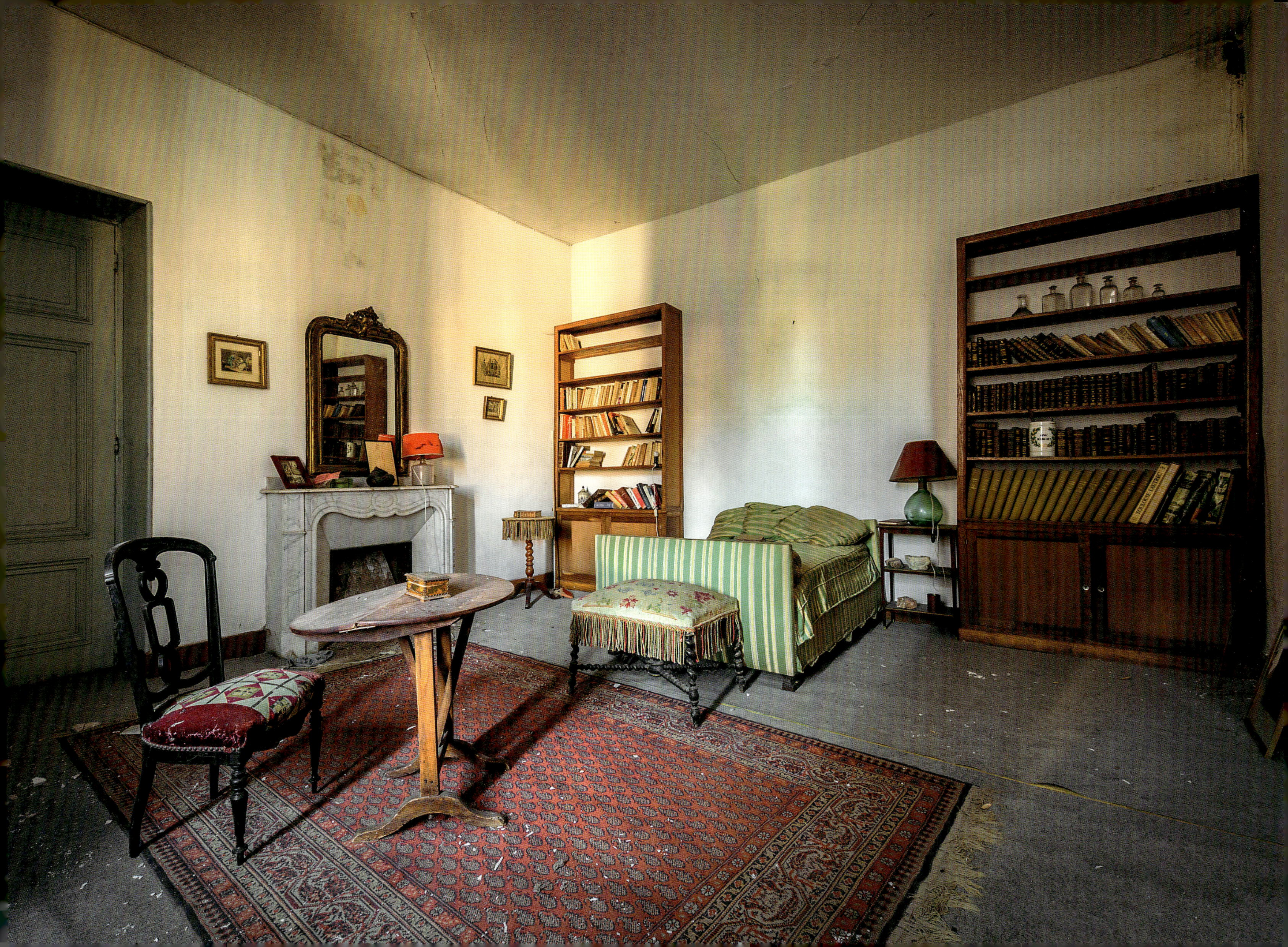

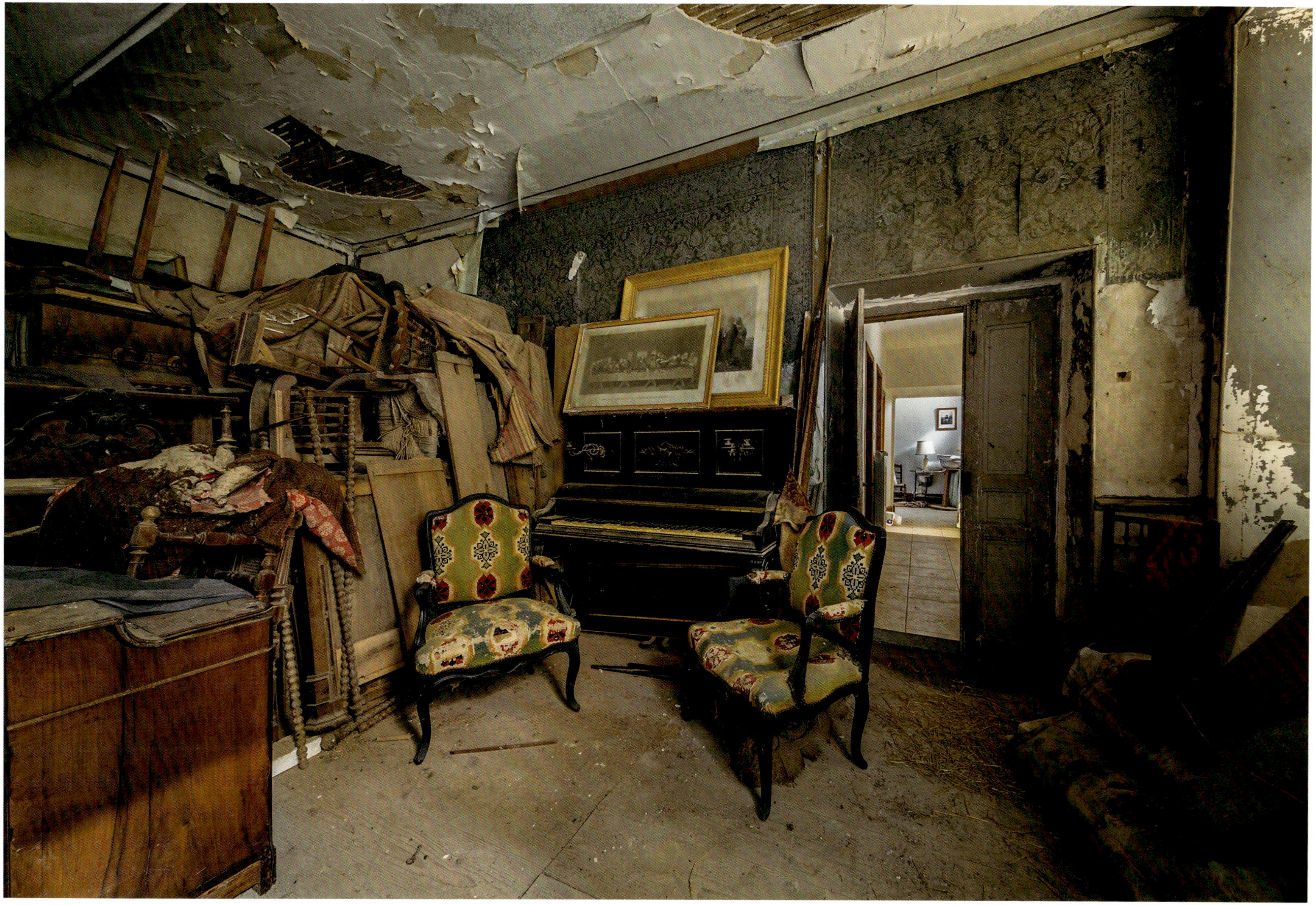

The knight's castle • *Occitania*

Sleeping Beauty could have lived here ...

The construction of this medieval castle by the lord and marshal-duke of Gontaut-Biron dates back to the beginning of the 14th century, and more specifically to 1303, if we are to believe the inscriptions on the walls. Ravaged by fire in 1888, it was rebuilt as an exact replica in the 19th century and enjoys a beautiful view of the Pyrenees.

It became a military hospital for 22 months during the First World War and operated continuously until its closure in the spring of 1916. During the Second World War, the chateau again provided a service to France: while her husband was taken prisoner, Anne de la Rochefoucault made their home available to the Louvre Museum, which was looking for safe havens in the south-west. That is how the castle came to house the collections of Egyptian antiquities, under the guidance of a young employee of the Louvre Museum who was to become one of the most famous Egyptologists in the world: Christiane Desroches Noblecourt. Abandoned for many years, it was finally bought by an Englishman in the 1990s.

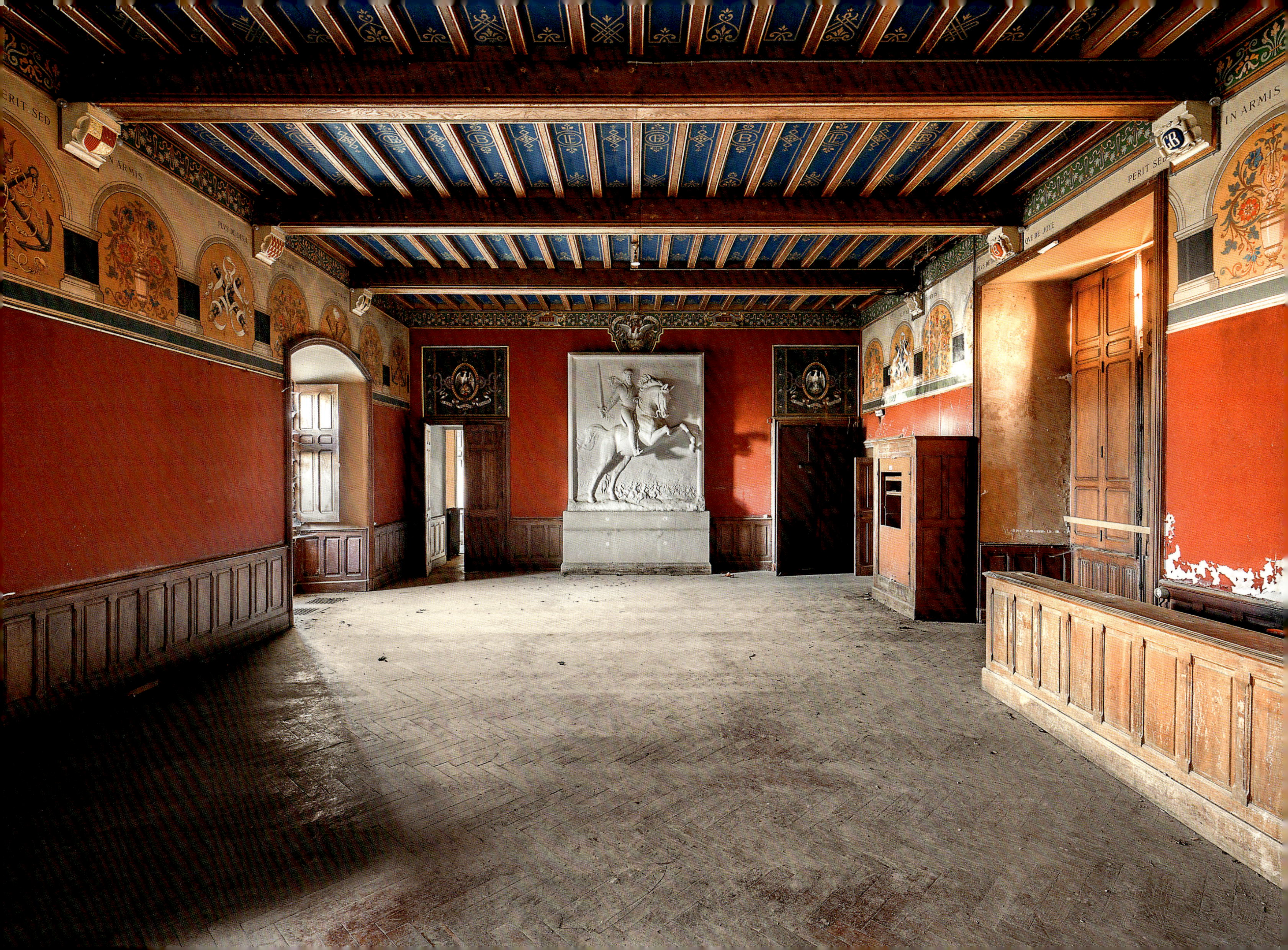
IN ARMIS
PERIT SED

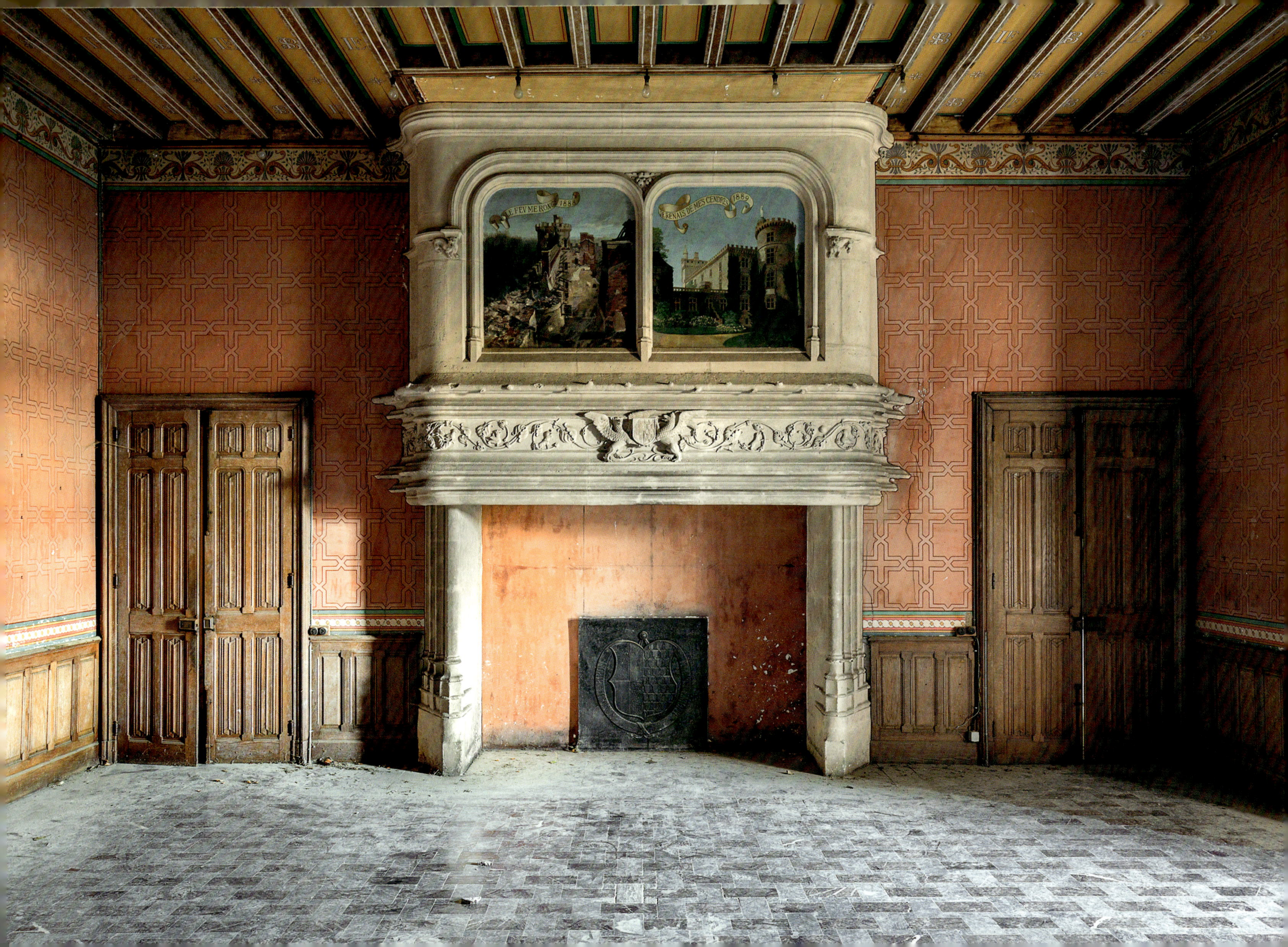
LE FEV ME RONG 1888
RENAIS DE MES CENDRES 1889

The owner visited regularly at the start, but there are no signs of him now and he cannot be reached, according to the mayor. Although the castle with its feudal mound, facades and roofs, courtyard and ditches to the south and east, surrounding wall, outbuildings, and greenhouse have been fully protected since 2005, only diplomatic pressure could help ensure its restoration now.

The castle is a marvel, on the outside and inside. On the ground floor, the great hall, Marguerite de Navarre's bedroom, the dining room, the rooms of the keep with their decorative fireplaces and the neo-Gothic wooden staircase are fabulous. There is also a sculpture of a knight carved in white stone and a family tree of the family coats of arms as well as paintings, including those above a hearth which show the castle before and after its reconstruction: '1888 - I rise from my ashes - 1889'.

Unfortunately, a dangerous building order was placed on part of the castle after some of the battlements fell off. Above all, the deplorable state of the roof demands urgent renovation.

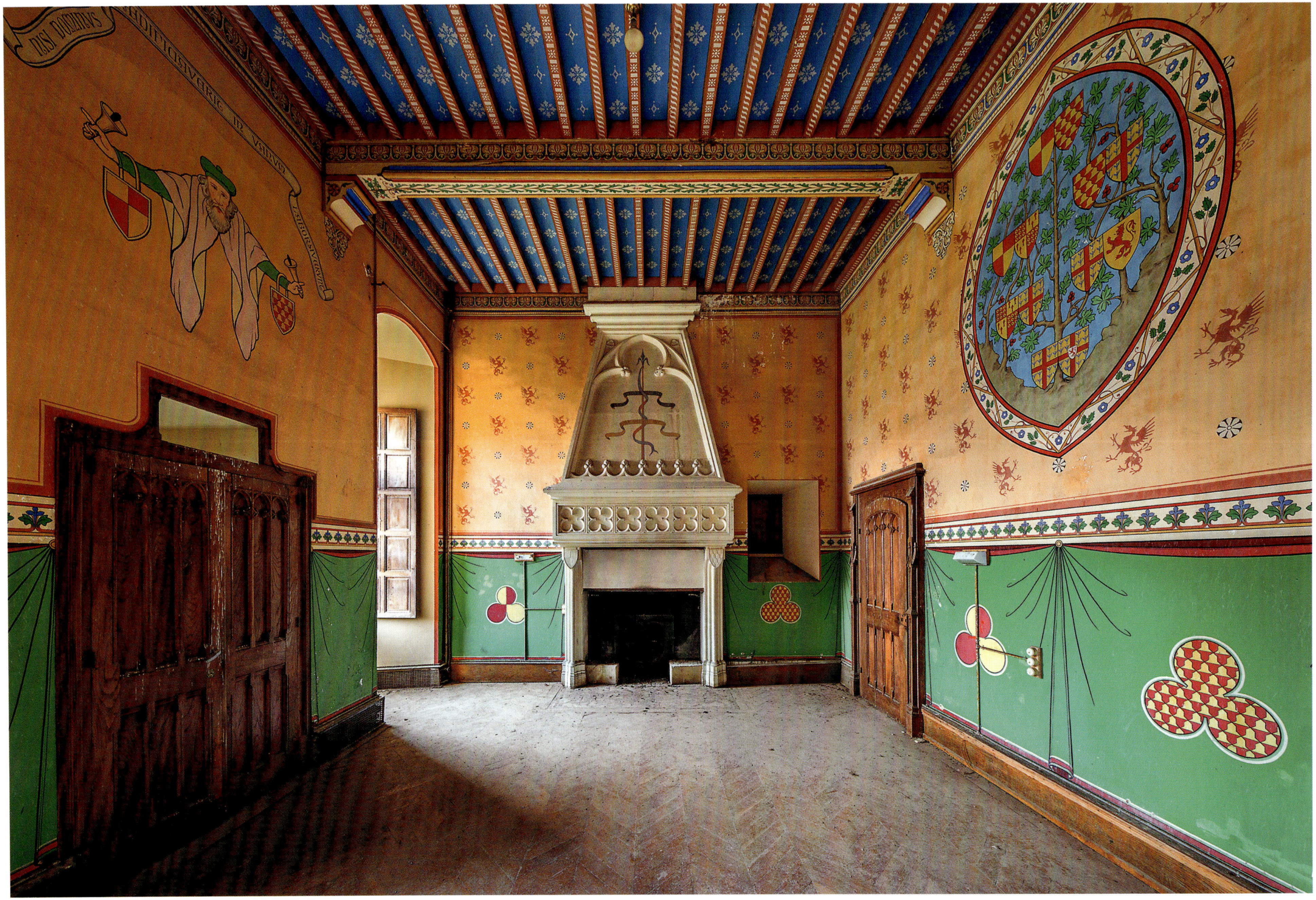

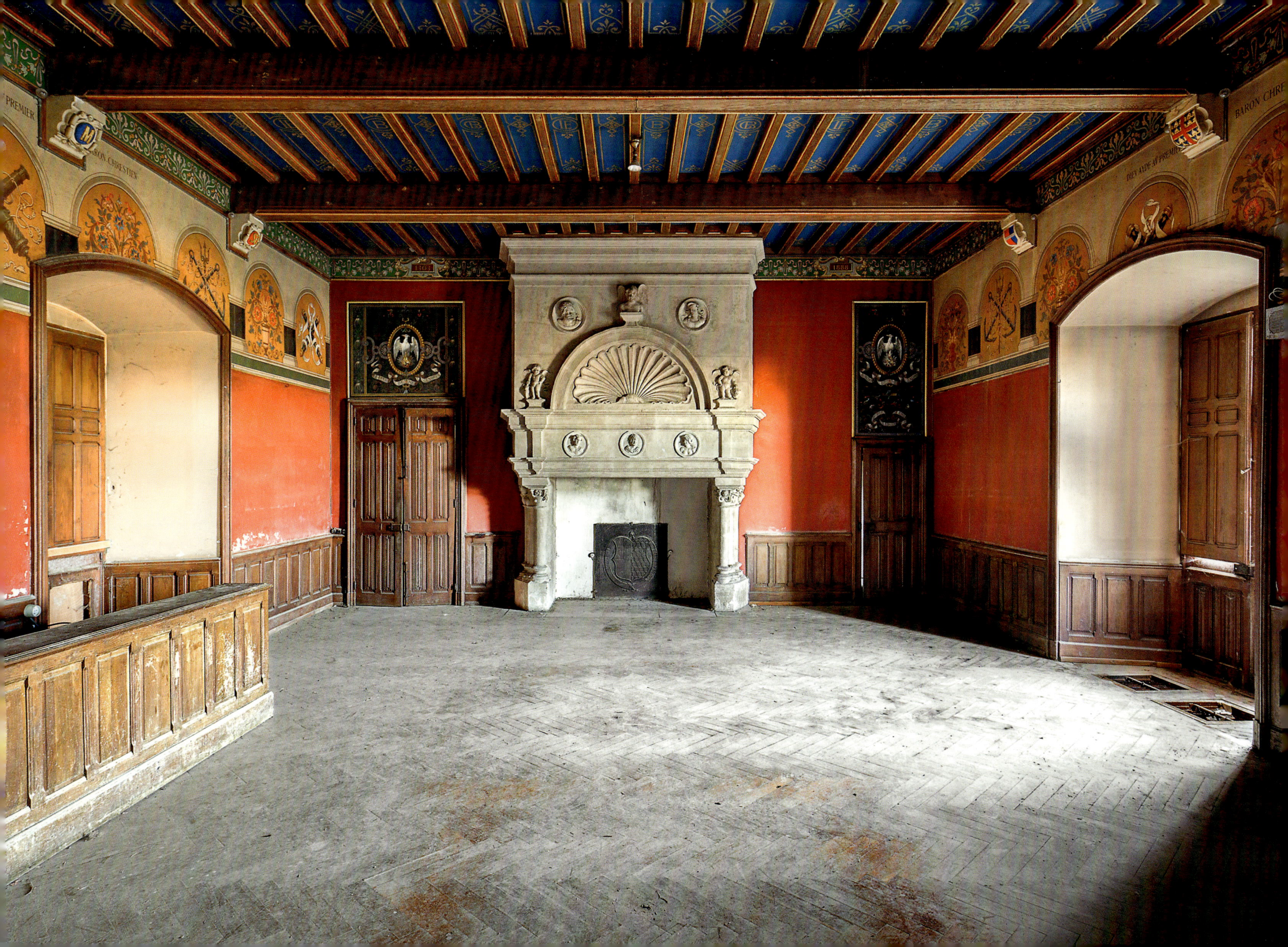
PREMIER
BARON CHRESTIEN

The castle of the Marquis • *Occitania*

A medieval castle surrounded by dense woods and undergrowth still stands on the hillside of a tiny hamlet that was once part of a marquisate.

The classical facades and the towers of the building still stand on the eastern and western corners of the courtyard. Inside is an Ionic-ordered hall originally intended to be covered by a voussoir. The light reflected by this ceremonial hall of graded white stone is dazzling. Curiously, four holy water stoups, used for aspersions and blessings, are built into each wall. In the dining room, a superb Louis XV marble fireplace topped by a finely carved and moulded plaster overmantel is adorned with an eagle representing the family's influence. It is in the adjoining barn that the height of wonder awaits: horse-drawn carriages. For generations, this seigneury belonged to the family of the Marquis de Timbrune, General of Valence, whose son decided in 1763 to build a sumptuous castle on the foundations of the old, dilapidated family home. Marquises, counts and army generals then succeeded one another until it was sold in 1834. Due to a lack of care and no doubt a lack of money – as wealth did not always last in those days – this 15th-century castle, although listed as a historic monument, is in a very advanced state of decay and a danger to those who enter it.

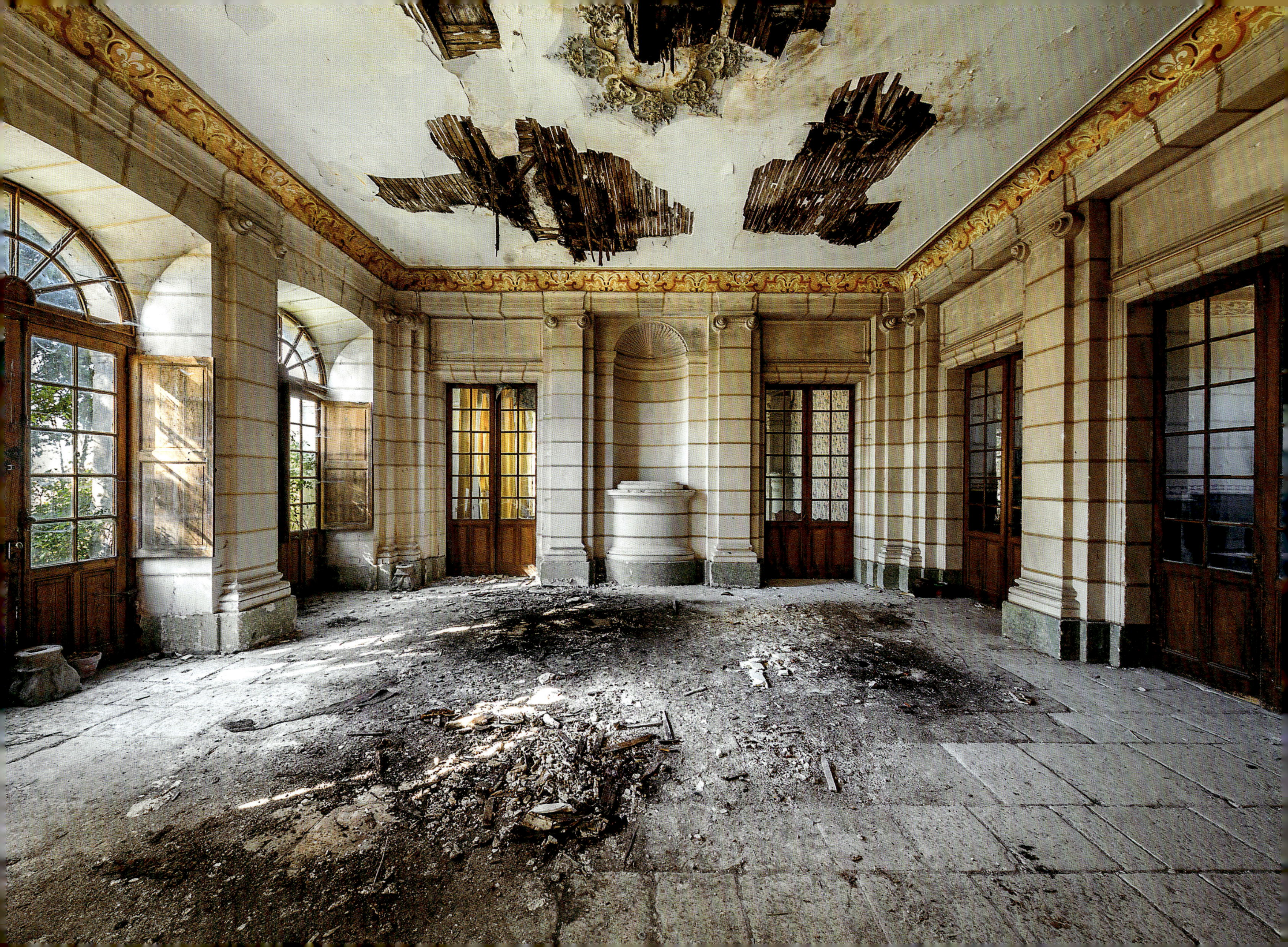

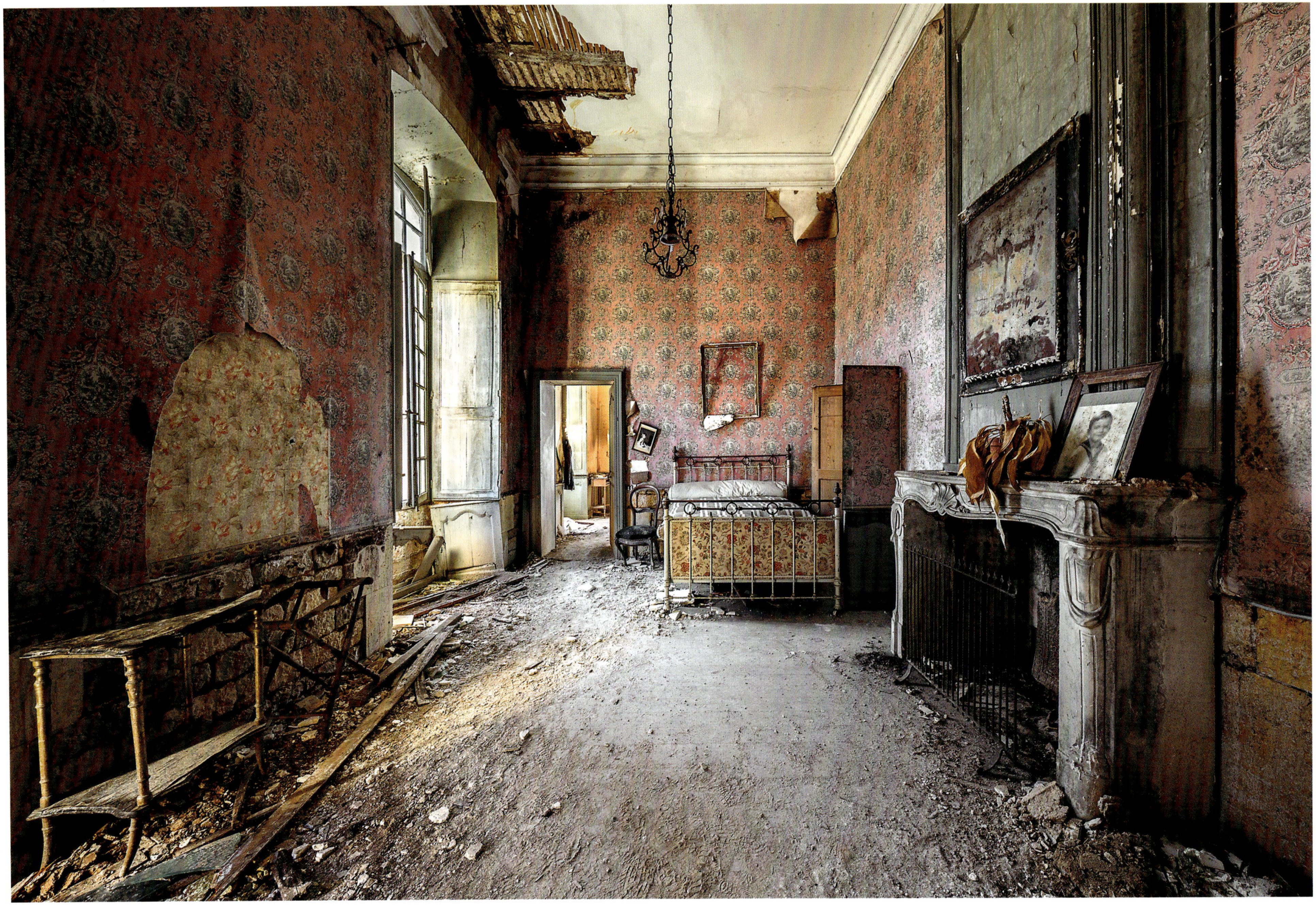

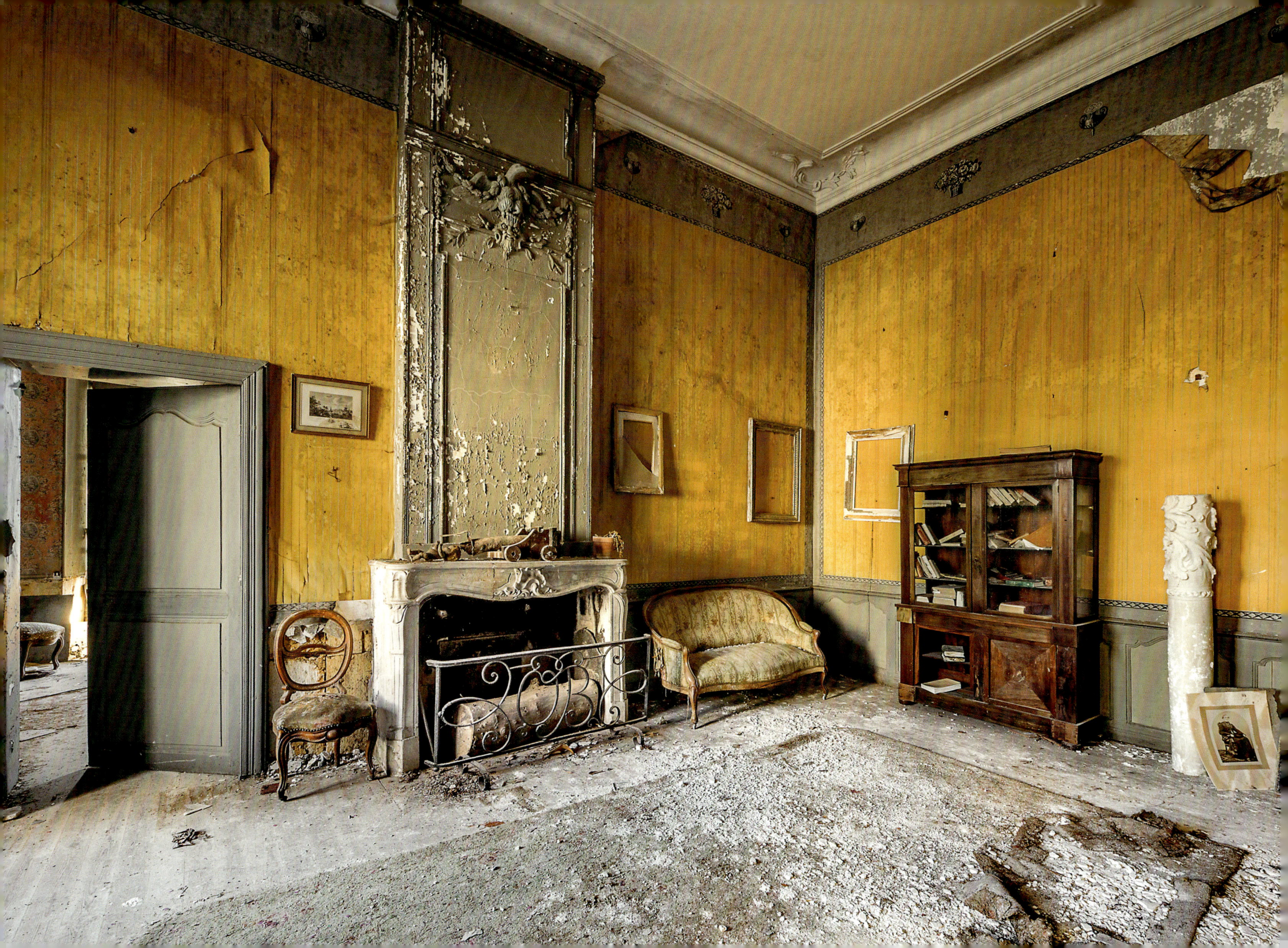

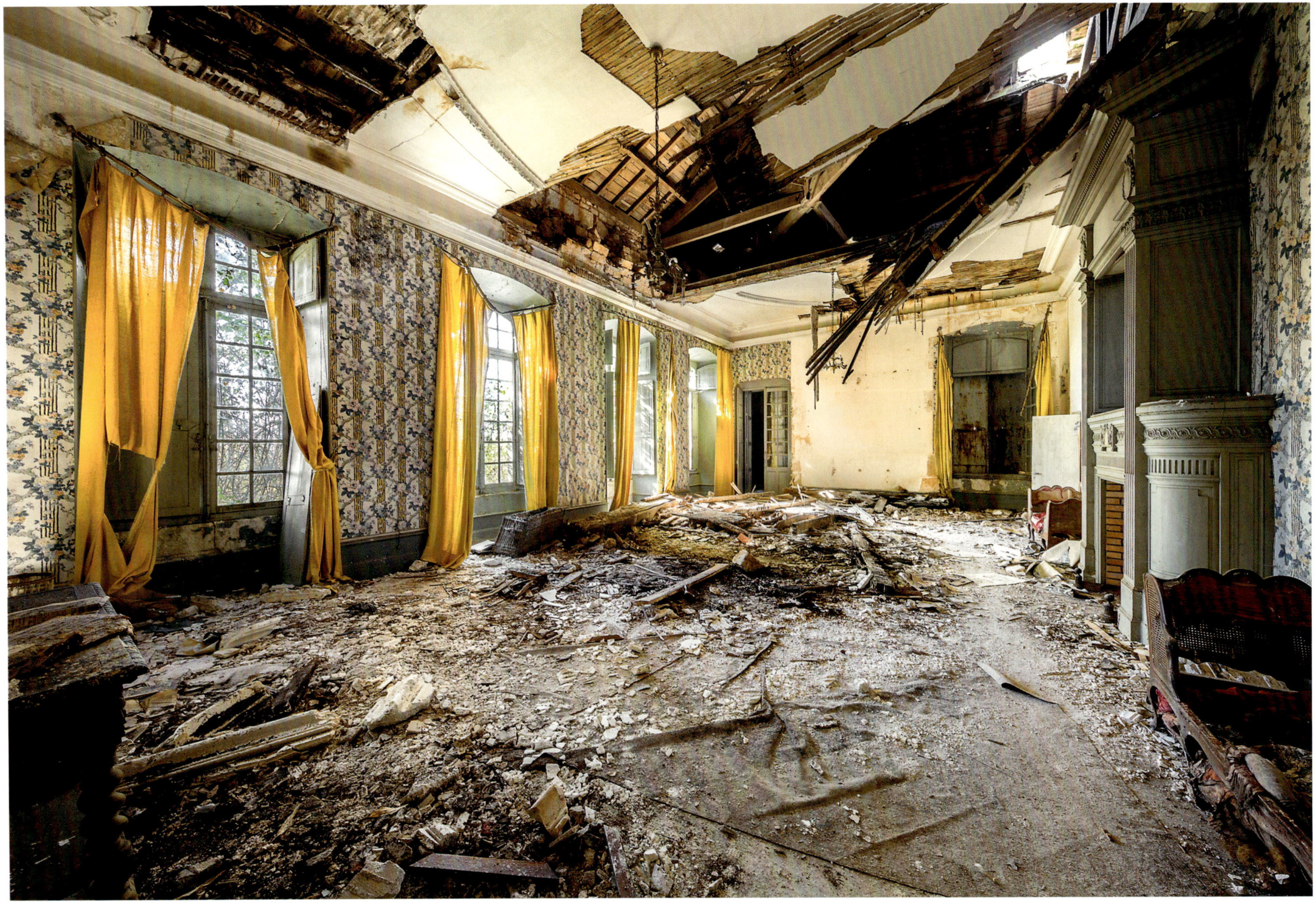

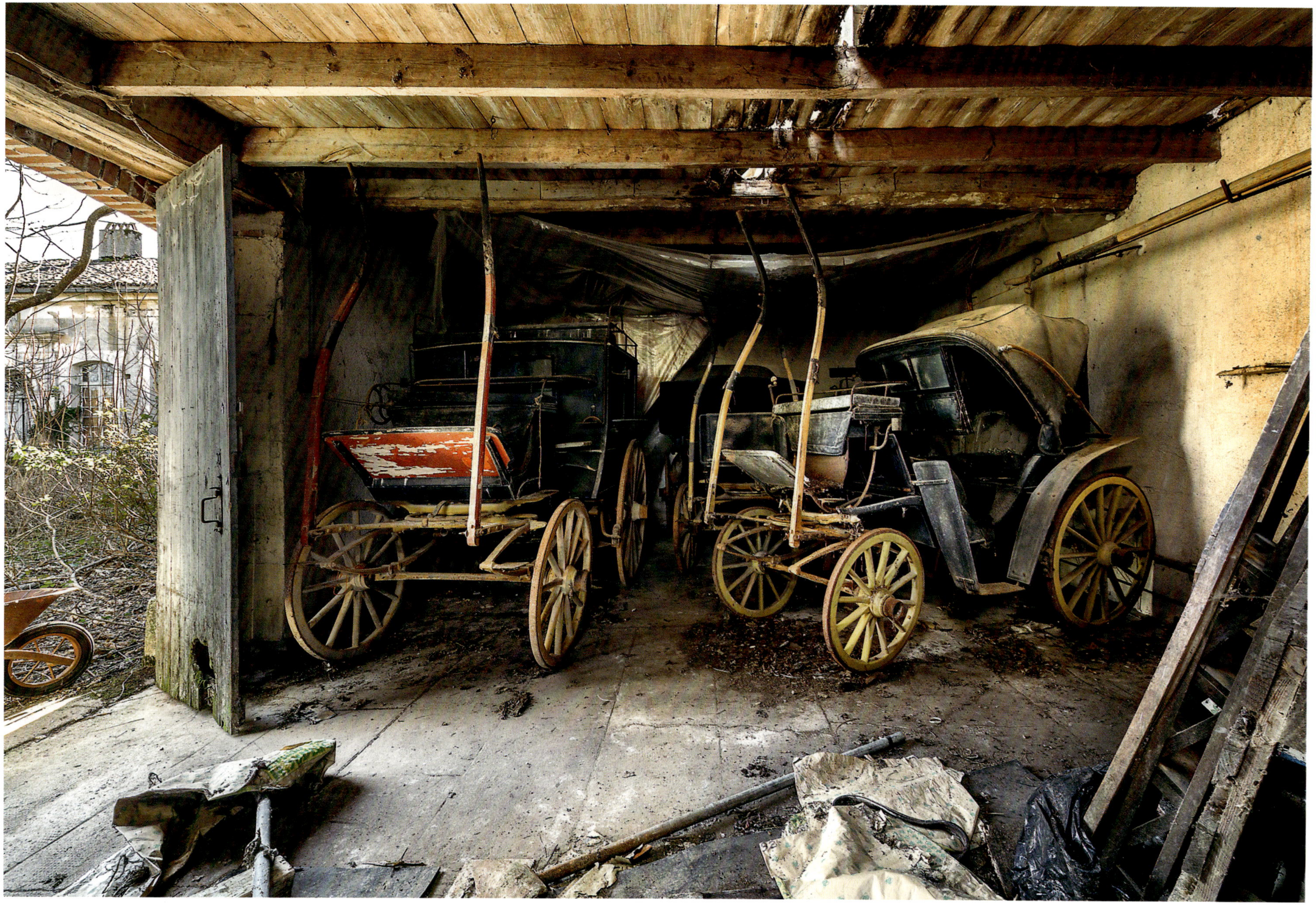

The amphitheatre of the purgatory • *Occitania*

This morgue, once called an amphitheatre, was part of a very large French hospital complex.

Although the mortuary is a marginal activity, sidelined by the hospital world, it is no less important than the other care services. Its priorities are to welcome and inform families, but above all to have specialised and dedicated staff care for the deceased.

Abandoned in favour of a new building, this blood-red examination room is chilling.

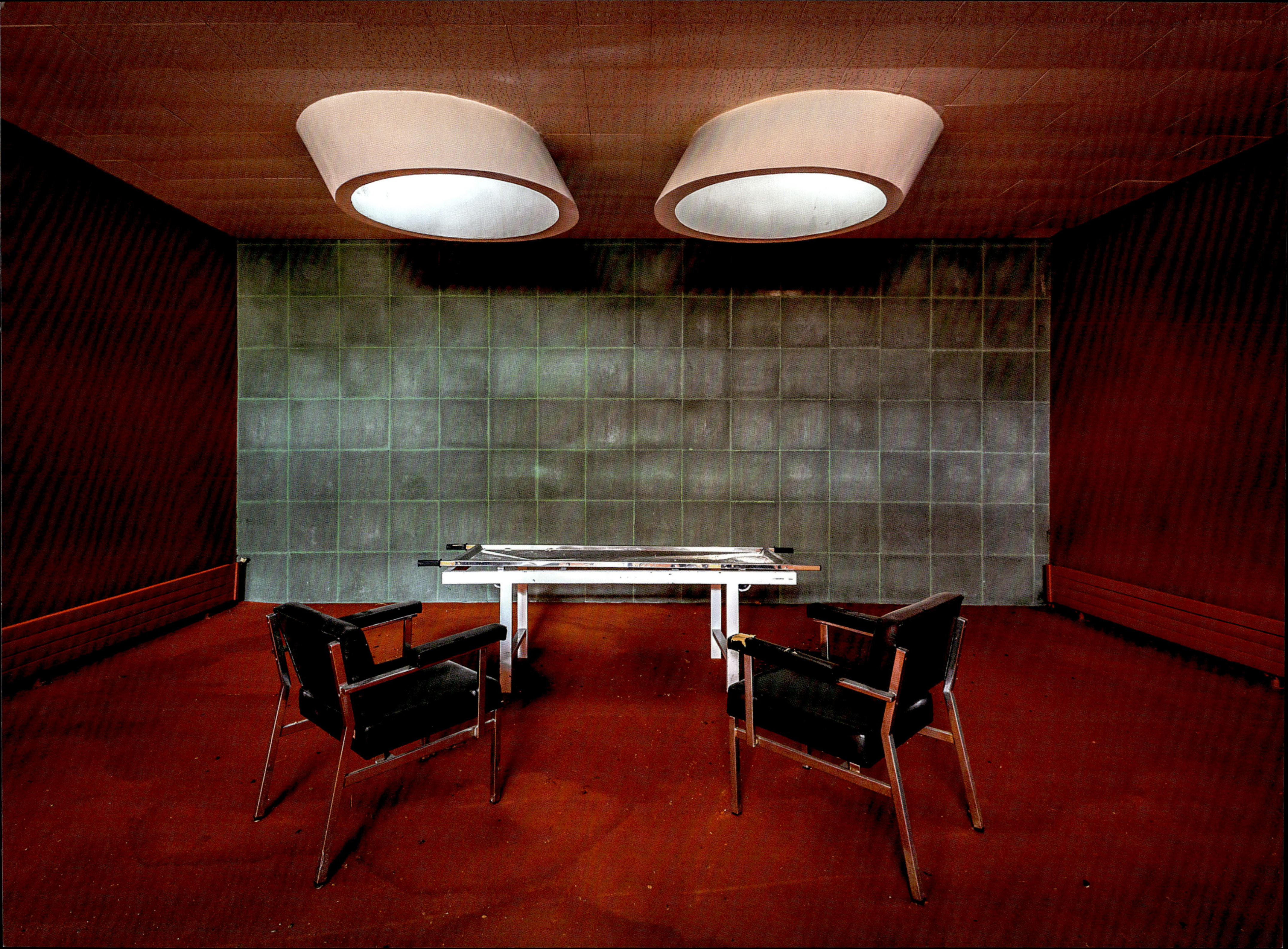

The divine oratory • *Occitania*

Set in the middle of fields, this small, private chapel with shimmering colours has stood the test of time. Above the load-bearing support are frightening human figures with an apotropaic function: to ward off evil influences from entering the building.

The chapel is an outbuilding of a castle that is still occupied. Its vaulting has been damaged by the weather, to the point of collapsing to the ground. Like many buildings of the past, it too will probably end up in ruins.

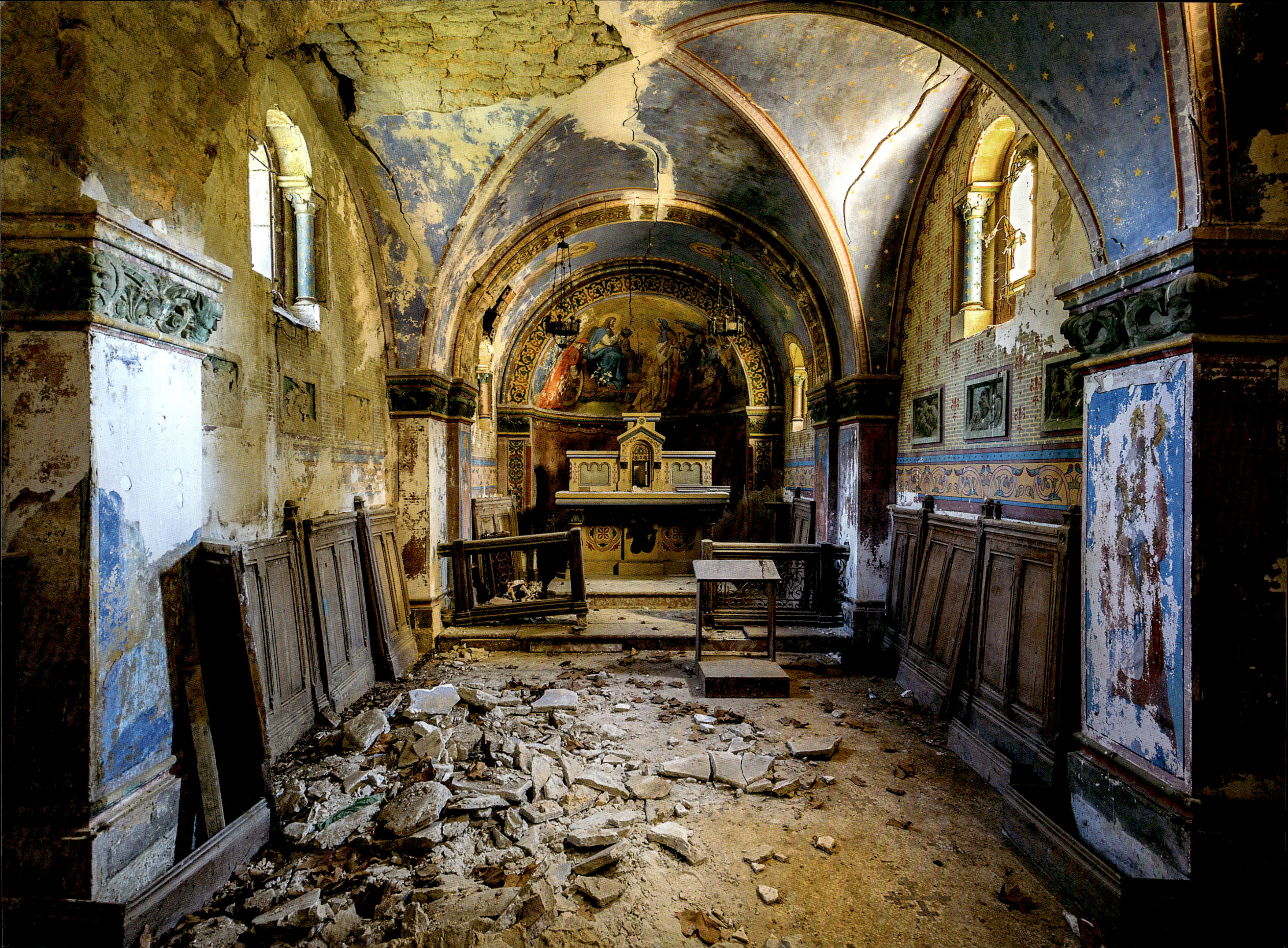

Saint-Bernard barracks • *Occitania*

This old storage space called Caserne Saint-Bernard is far from being an eye-catcher, yet it houses an impressive collection of dusty fire trucks abandoned for several years. Fortunately, this huge red brick building, open to the elements, has managed to protect them.

Among the vehicles are many Berliets, including a remarkable 30-metre hydraulic EPA with an automatic swinging ladder, assembled in the 1960s. It is disheartening to see these vehicles with probably not a drop of water, oil or petrol left. When you know how much care the fearless firefighters take of their prized equipment, seeing them in this state is such a shame.

It is inconceivable these fire trucks will ever be scrapped; it is better to leave them in this safe haven, out of respect and in memory of the lives saved, perhaps for eternity.

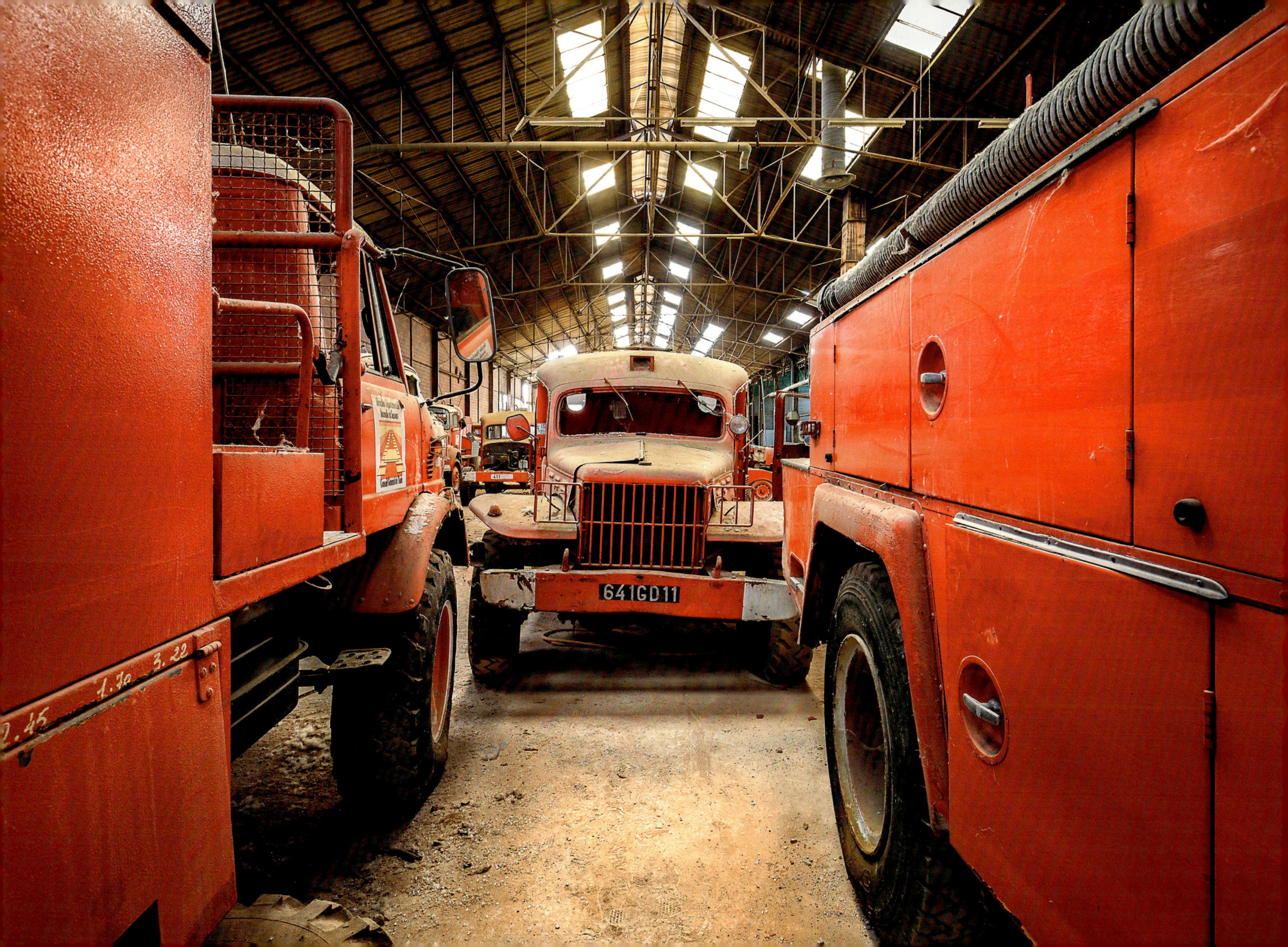
641GD11

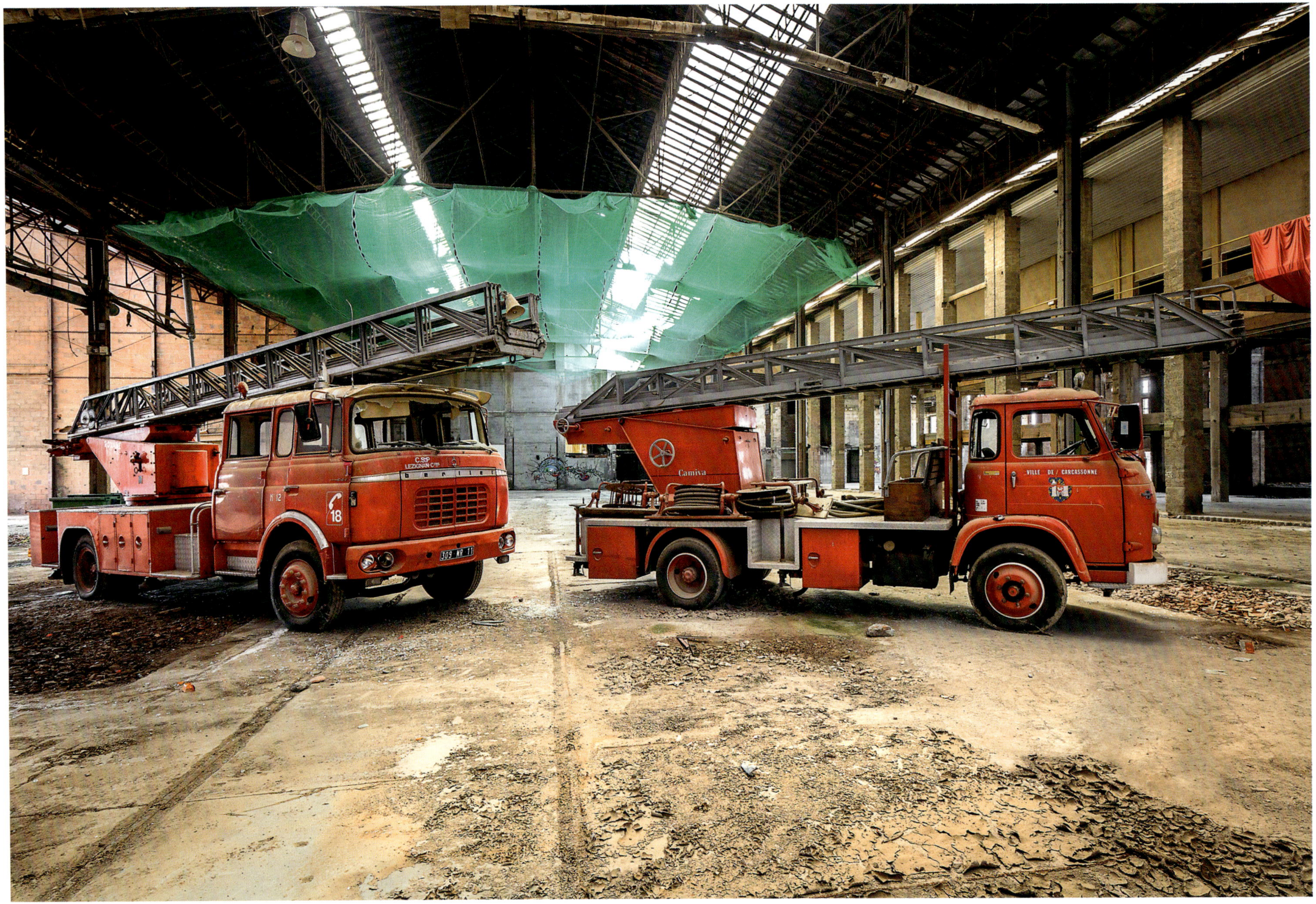
18
Camiva
VILLE DE CARCASSONNE

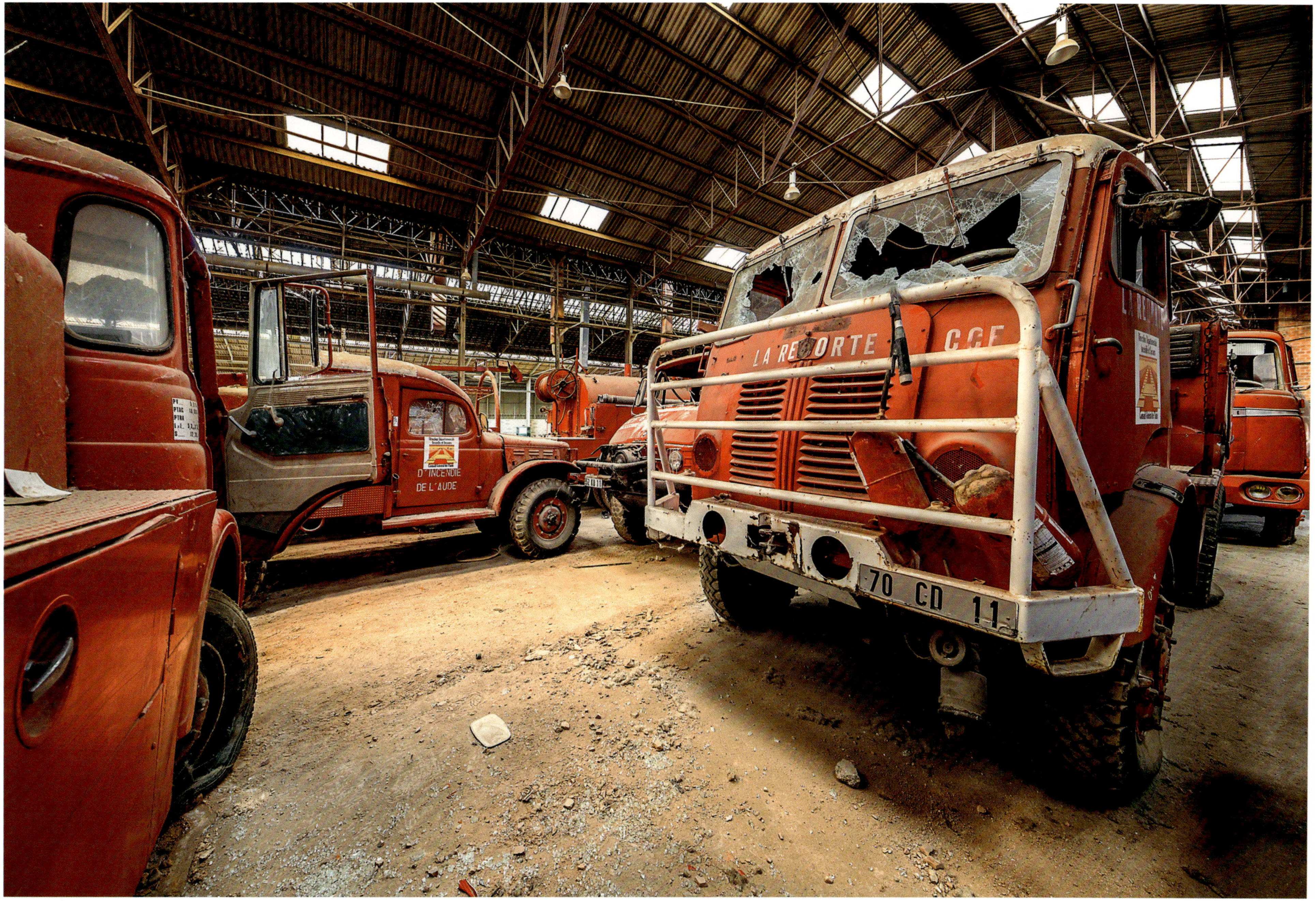

D'INCENDIE
DE L'AUDE
70 CD 11

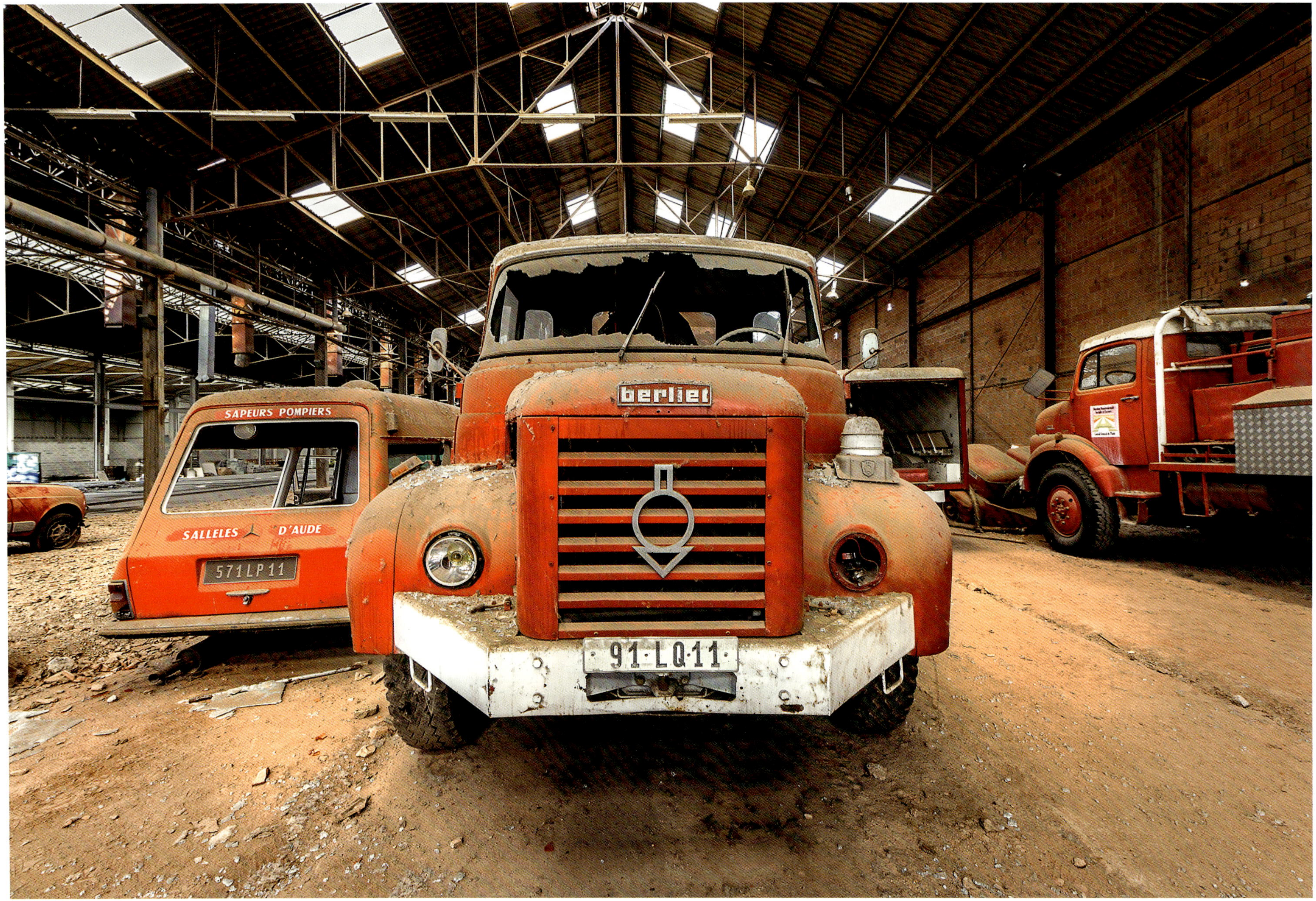
SAPEURS POMPIERS
SALLELES
D'AUDE
571LP11
berliet
91·LQ11

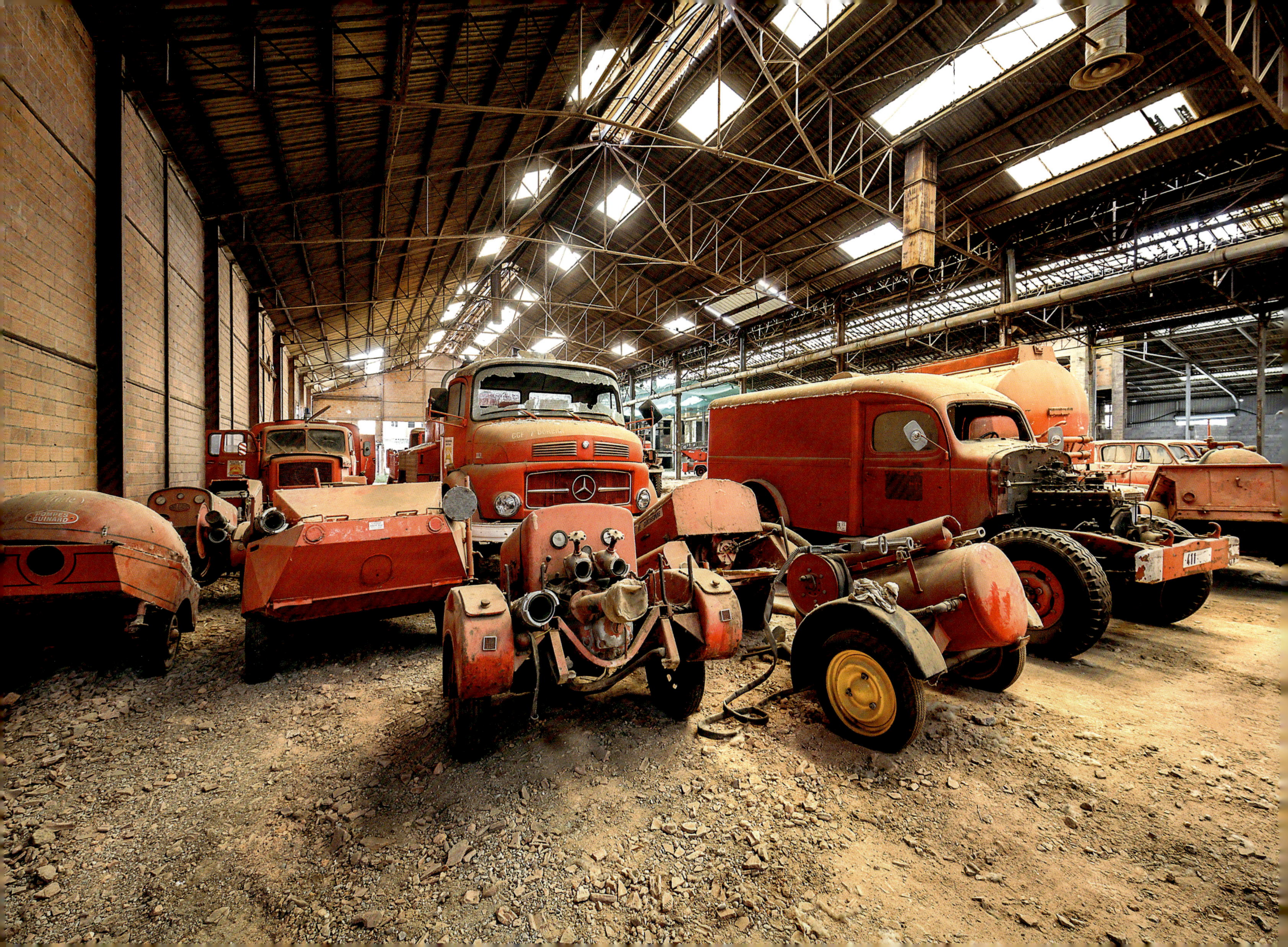

The La Verrière orphanage • *Occitania*

Who would believe that this village of 521 inhabitants, which no one can trace any more, was at the heart of a barony until the Revolution?

Set in green surroundings, this building, which has been abandoned for years, is a former orphanage. The setting, which feels like a good environment to live in and must once have been lively and bustling, still offers a sense of security. The beautiful woodwork in the entrance hall is still in good condition, and the doorways and glass roof are remarkable, even if the ivy is starting to invade this bright space. On the other hand, the roof is leaking, and the ceilings are rotting and collapsing on the parquet floor upstairs.

No one cares any more about a place that was once a refuge for children. How much longer will it hold up?

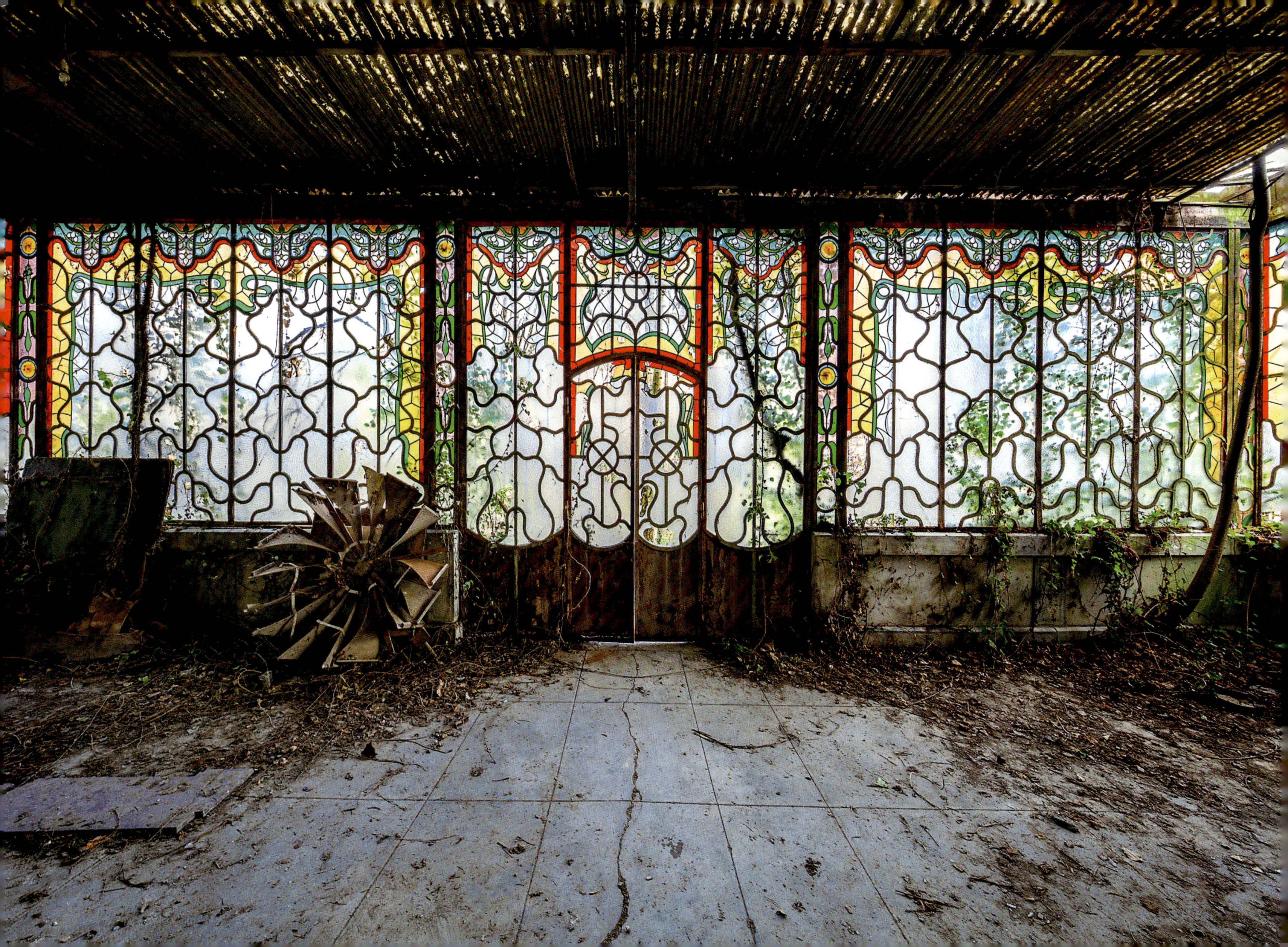

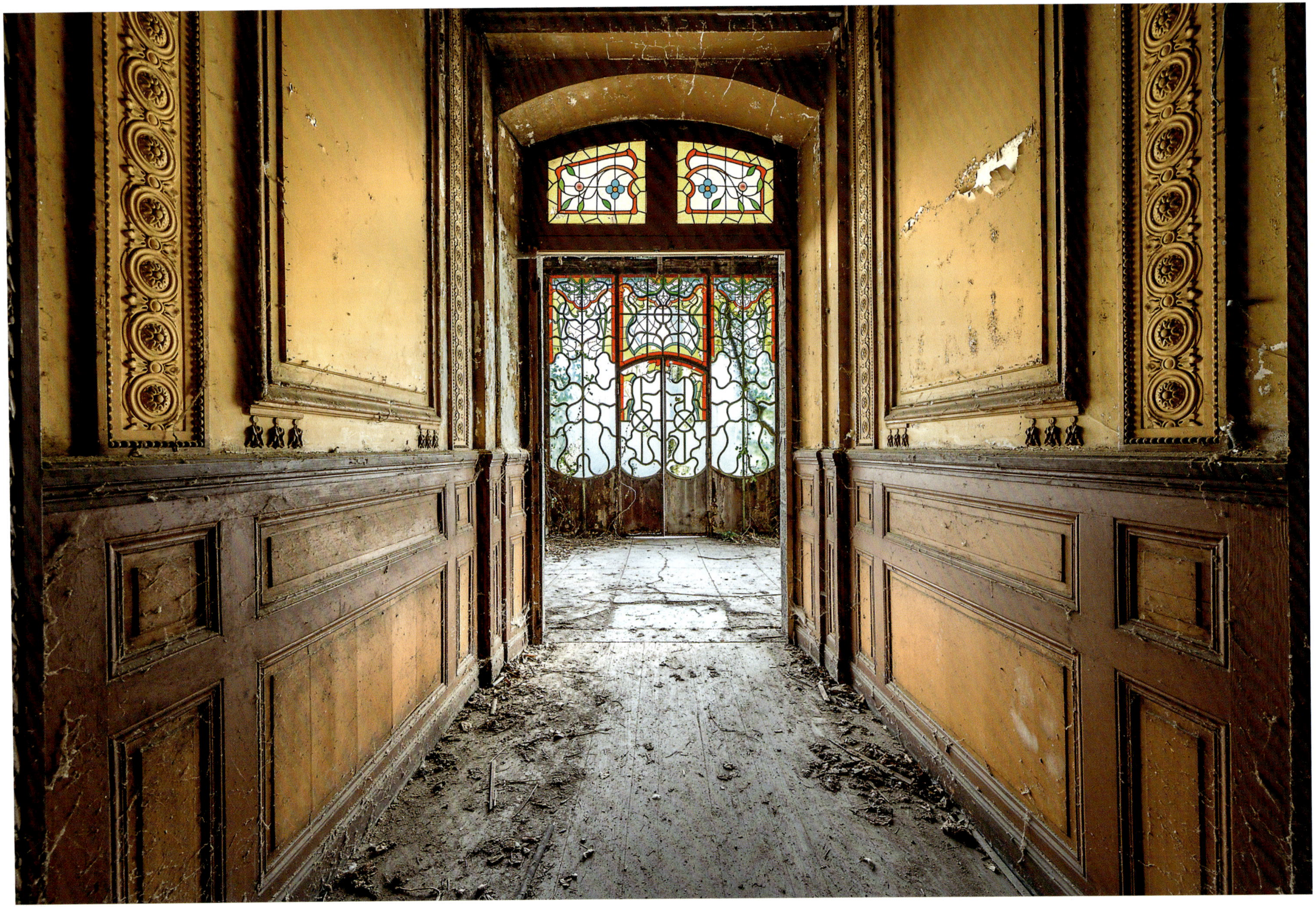

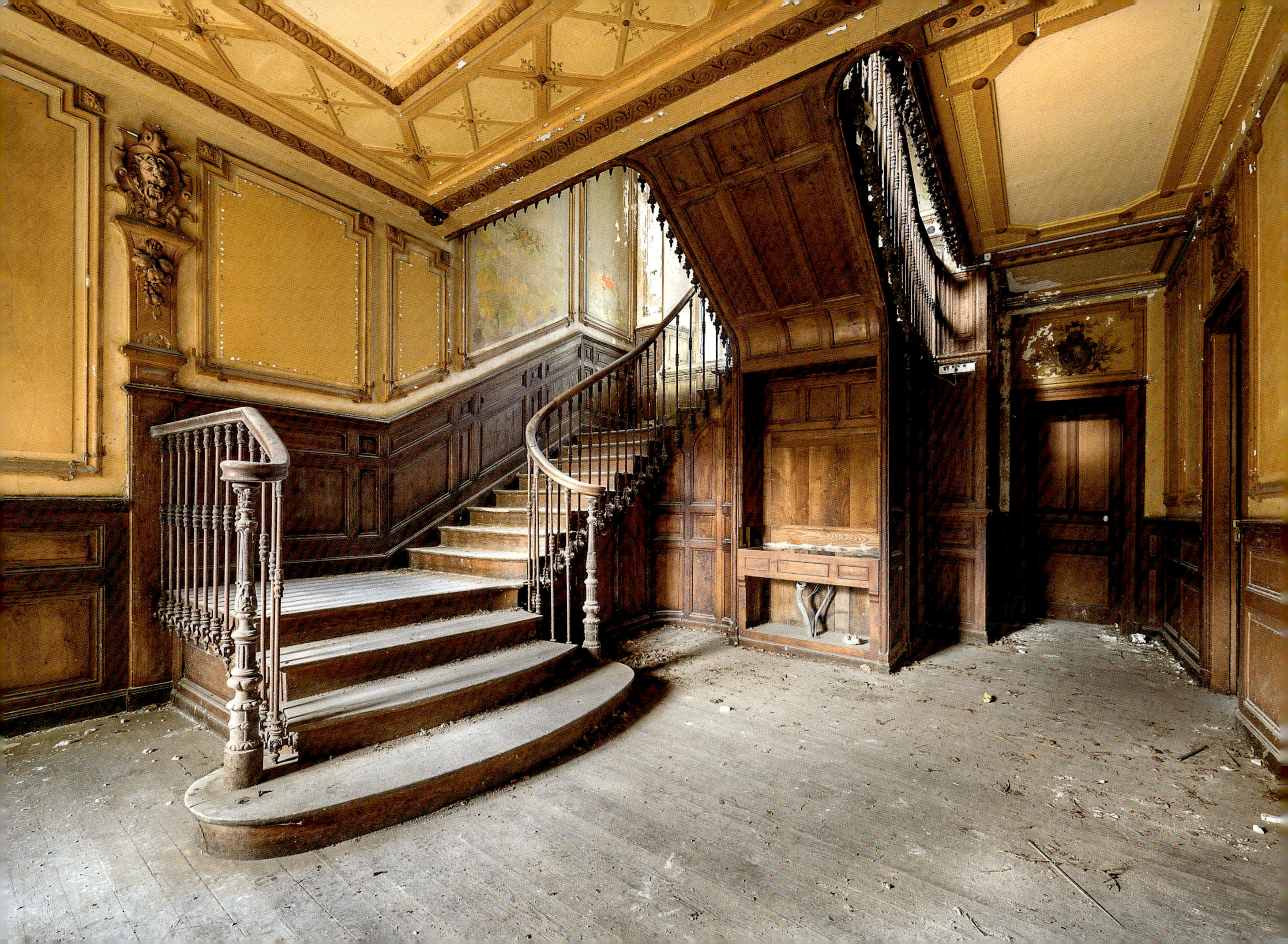

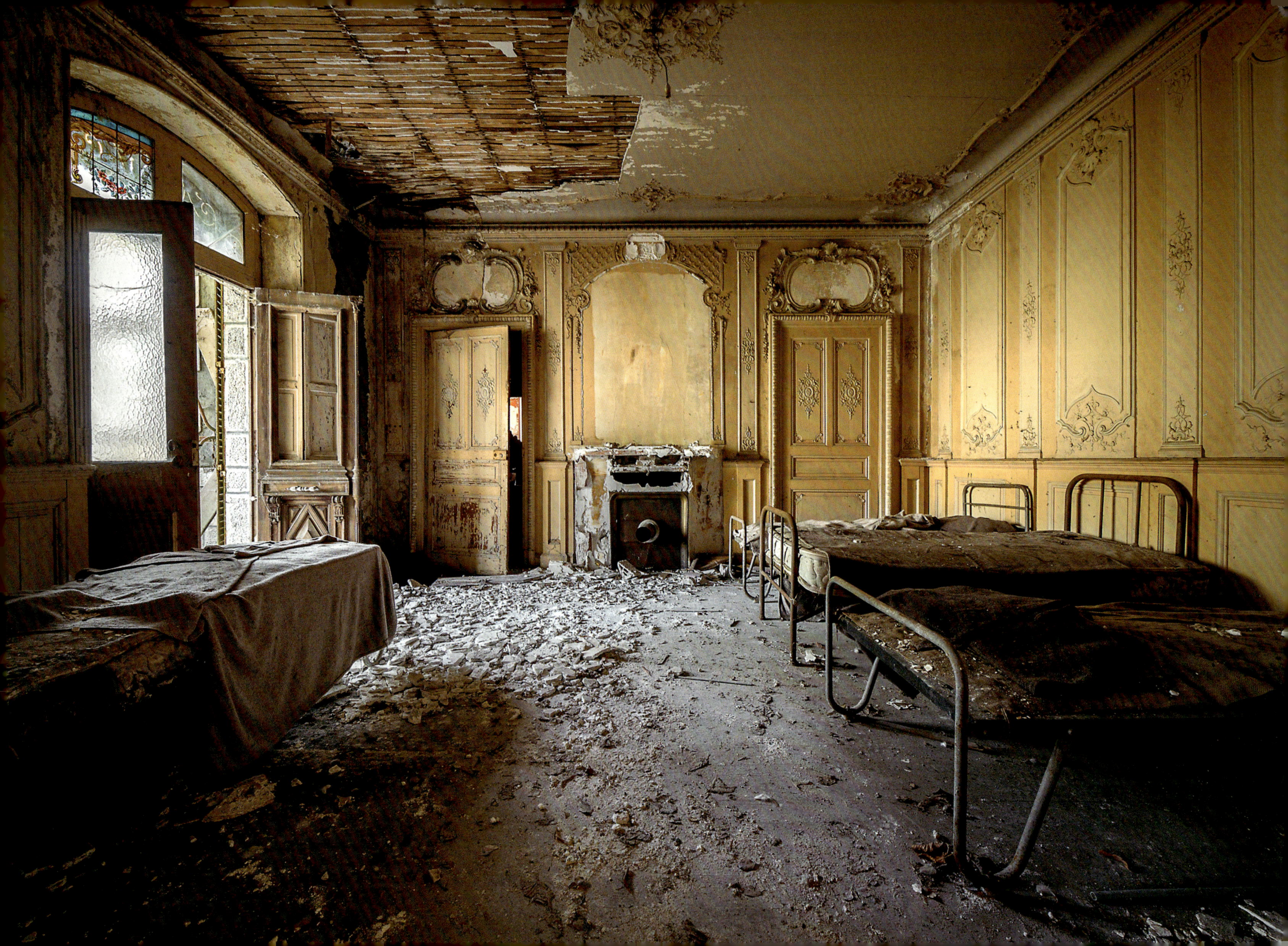

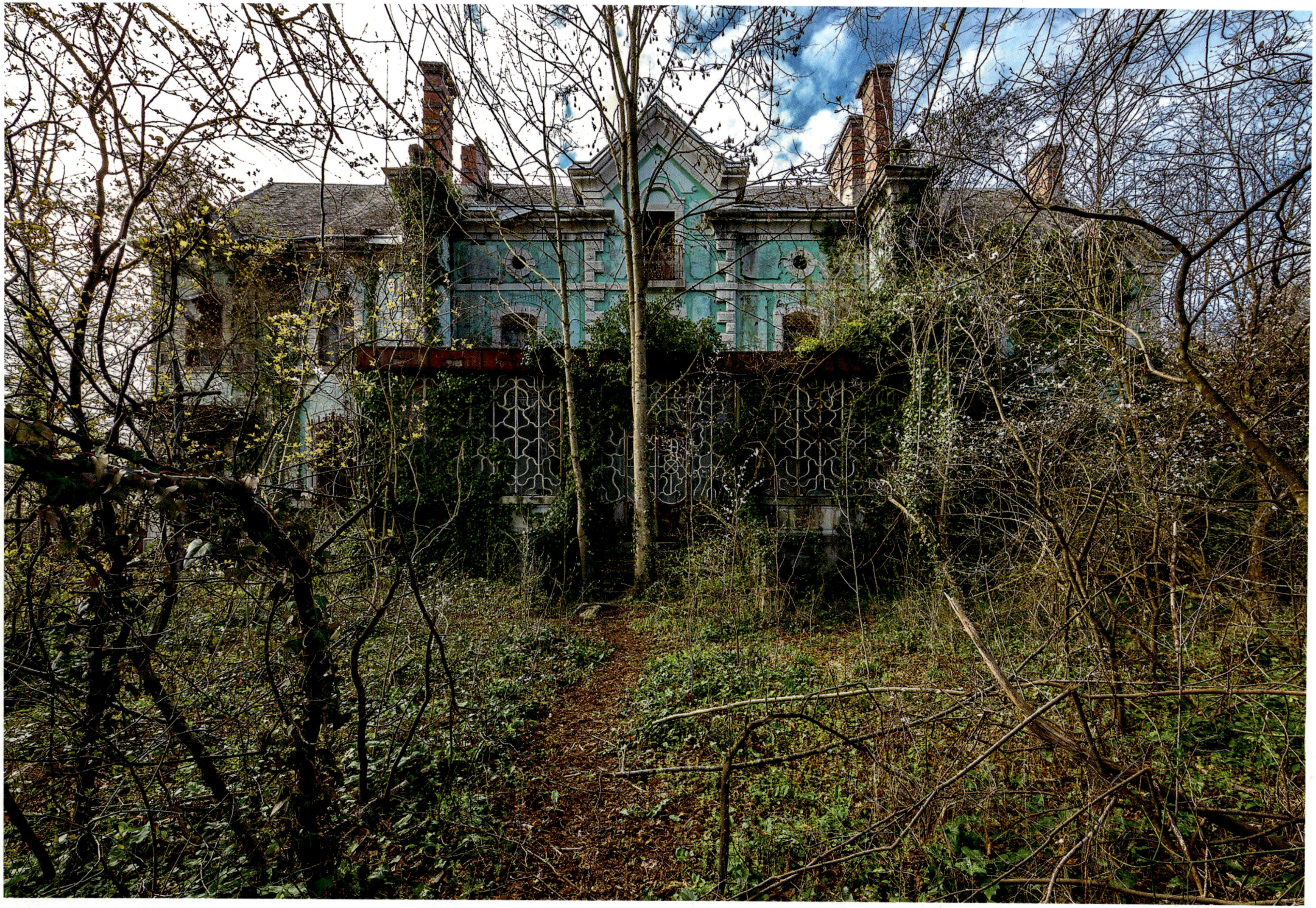

The Salmson garage • *Occitania*

It was through a broken window that this exceptional car caught my eye. Based in Billancourt, the Société des Moteurs Salmson, commonly known as Salmson, was one of the major French aeronautical and automobile manufacturers from 1913 to 1962. Its founder, Emile Salmson, was an engineer who had been designing aircraft engines since 1908 and whose company was a pioneer in the field. The engine manufacturer also became an aircraft manufacturer after the First World War, and that is how Salmson took off, manufacturing 3,200 A2A biplanes for aerial reconnaissance. With a range of action that was unrivalled at the time, these were the first aircraft of the future Aéropostale aviation company, equipped with high-performance engines and holding historical and world records.

The company, which already employed more than 6,000 people, decided to focus on speed and venture beyond aviation, into car manufacturing. From 1919 on, the company started to produce beautiful cars and then, in the post-war period, more comfortable cars. The Randonnée model (1950–1954) was produced in this context under the references E72, G72, G72bis, G72ter and G80. Salmson, whose slogan at the time was 'Quality through precision', promoted its model with the message, 'The tireless rival of the most powerful cars'. With its pontoon body, the Randonnée was truly elegant. It was a luxurious car, but production was limited.

At the height of the 'Trente Glorieuses' (France's 30-year period of economic growth), the large road cars of the Salmson factories were unable to compete with subsidised mass car production, so Salmson sold their five hectares to a property developer. Salmson went bankrupt on 26 February 1962, but the brand had time to become a legend among French car makers.

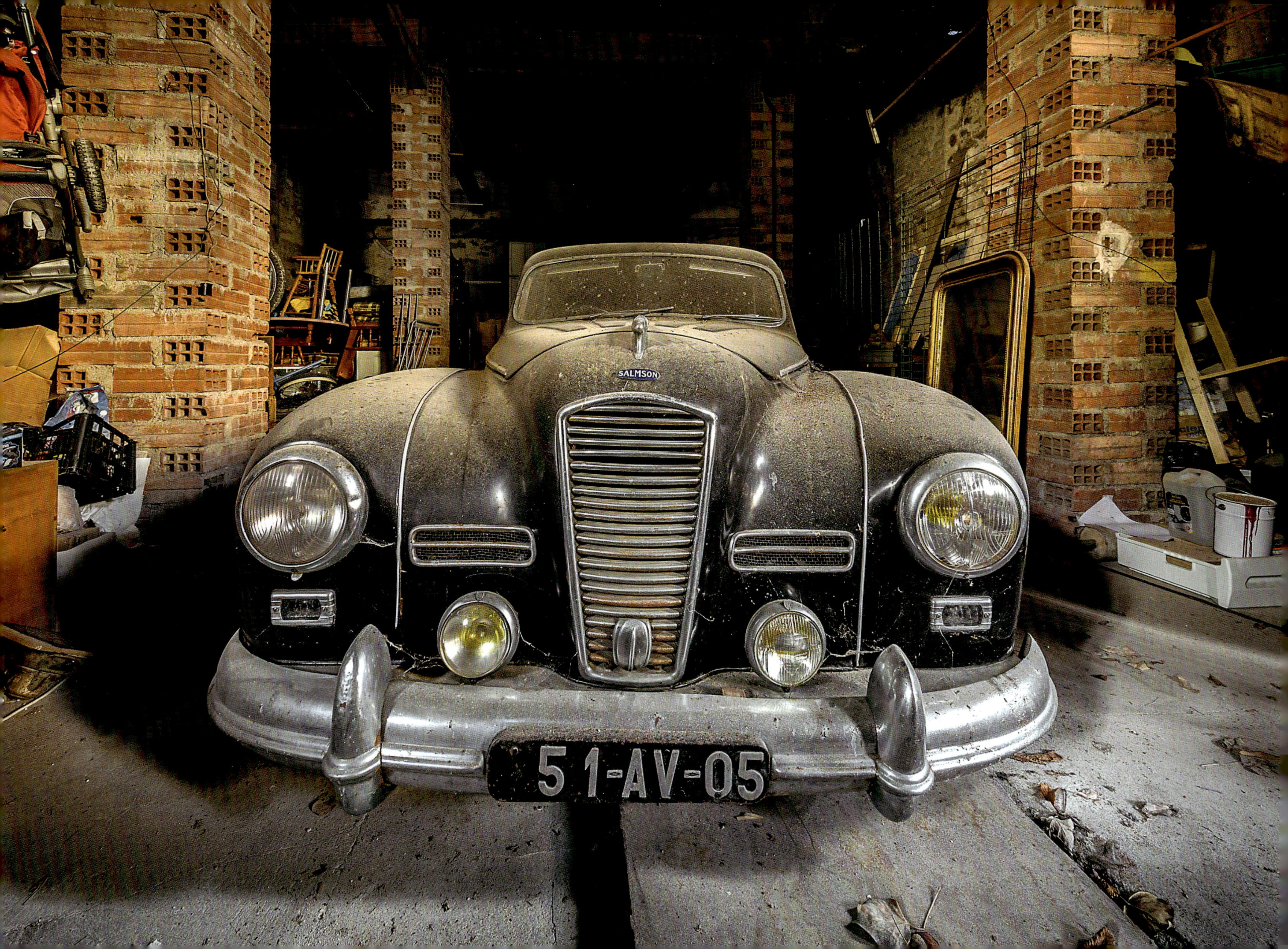
SALMSON
51-AV-05

About the author

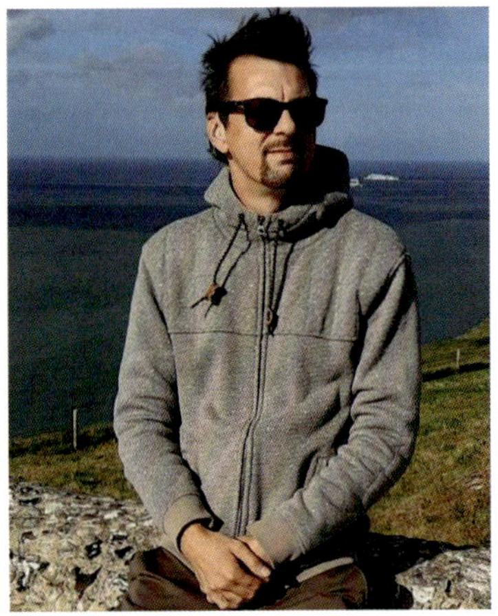

Born in 1988, Robin Brinaert lives in the Hainaut province of Belgium.

A recognised specialist in urbex ('urban exploration'), Robin has been photographing abandoned places in Europe for more than 10 years.

Robin is also the author of the magnificent book *Abandoned Italy*, published by the same publisher.

Acknowledgements

It is customary to say thank you, which is why I would like to warmly thank my faithful travel companion and partner Jérôme Michez, my friend Alyssia Roelandt, my friend Jérôme Blondiau and my father for his contribution to some of my escapes, my mother for her administrative work, her research and the writing of the texts that will enlighten you on the places I visited. It was a long job, I must admit.

Please note that not all the places listed in this book can be visited freely. It is essential to enquire about the accessibility conditions of each location.

Also available

Atlas

Atlas of extreme weather
Atlas of geographical curiosities
Atlas of unusual wines

Photo books

Abandoned America
Abandoned Asylums
Abandoned Australia
Abandoned churches – Unclaimed places of worship
Abandoned cinemas of the world
Abandoned France
Abandoned Italy
Abandoned Japan
Abandoned Lebanon
Abandoned Spain
Abandoned USSR
After the Final Curtain – The Fall of the American Movie Theater
After the Final Curtain – America's Abandoned Theaters
Baikonur – Vestiges of the Soviet Space Programme
Forbidden Places
Forbidden Places - Vol.2
Forbidden Places - Vol.3
Forgotten Heritage
Oblivion
Venice deserted
Venice from the skies

'Soul of' guides

Soul of Amsterdam – A guide to the 30 best experiences
Soul of Athens – A guide to 30 exceptional experiences
Soul of Barcelona – A guide to 30 exceptional experiences
Soul of Berlin – A guide to the 30 best experiences
Soul of Kyoto – A guide to 30 exceptional experiences
Soul of Lisbon – A guide to 30 exceptional experiences
Soul of Los Angeles – A guide to 30 exceptional experiences
Soul of Marrakesh – A guide to 30 exceptional experiences
Soul of New York – A guide to 30 exceptional experiencess
Soul of Rome – A guide to 30 exceptional experiencess
Soul of Tokyo – A guide to 30 exceptional experiences
Soul of Venice – A guide to 30 exceptional experiences

'Secret' guides

Secret Amsterdam
Secret Bali
Secret Bangkok
Secret Barcelona
Secret Belfast
Secret Berlin
Secret Brighton – An unusual guide
Secret Brooklyn
Secret Brussels
Secret Buenos Aires
Secret Campania
Secret Cape Town
Secret Copenhagen
Secret Dublin – An unusual guide
Secret Edinburgh – An unusual guide
Secret Florence
Secret French Riviera
Secret Geneva
Secret Glasgow
Secret Granada
Secret Helsinki
Secret Istanbul
Secret Johannesburg
Secret Lisbon
Secret Liverpool – An unusual guide
Secret London – An unusual guide
Secret London – Unusual bars & restaurants
Secret Los Angeles
Secret Madrid
Secret Mexico City
Secret Milan
Secret Montreal – An unusual guide
Secret Naples
Secret New Orleans
Secret New York – An unusual guide
Secret New York – Curious activities
Secret New York – Hidden bars & restaurants
Secret Paris
Secret Prague
Secret Provence
Secret Rio
Secret Rome
Secret Seville
Secret Singapore
Secret Sussex – An unusual guide
Secret Tokyo
Secret Tuscany
Secret Venice
Secret Vienna
Secret Washington D.C.
Secret York – An unusual guide

Photographs and text: Robin Brinaert

Design: Emmanuelle Willard Toulemonde – **Translation:** Olivia Fuller – **Copy-editing:** Lee Dickinson – **Proofreading:** Kimberly Bess – **Publishing:** Clémence Mathé

Registration of copyright: October 2023 – Edition: 01
ISBN: 978-2-36195-608-0
Printed in Slovakia by Polygraf